Sweet Thunder
Music and Libretti in 1960s Italy

LEGENDA

LEGENDA, founded in 1995 by the European Humanities Research Centre of the University of Oxford, is now a joint imprint of the Modern Humanities Research Association and Maney Publishing. Titles range from medieval texts to contemporary cinema and form a widely comparative view of the modern humanities, including works on Arabic, Catalan, English, French, German, Greek, Italian, Portuguese, Russian, Spanish, and Yiddish literature. An Editorial Board of distinguished academic specialists works in collaboration with leading scholarly bodies such as the Society for French Studies and the British Comparative Literature Association.

MHRA

The Modern Humanities Research Association (MHRA) encourages and promotes advanced study and research in the field of the modern humanities, especially modern European languages and literature, including English, and also cinema. It also aims to break down the barriers between scholars working in different disciplines and to maintain the unity of humanistic scholarship in the face of increasing specialization. The Association fulfils this purpose primarily through the publication of journals, bibliographies, monographs and other aids to research.

Maney Publishing is one of the few remaining independent British academic publishers. Founded in 1900 the company has offices both in the UK, in Leeds and London, and in North America, in Boston. Since 1945 Maney Publishing has worked closely with learned societies, their editors, authors, and members, in publishing academic books and journals to the highest traditional standards of materials and production.

ITALIAN PERSPECTIVES

Series Editors
Professor Zygmunt Barański, University of Cambridge
Professor Anna Laura Lepschy, University College London

In the light of growing academic interest in Italy and the reorganization of many university courses in Italian along interdisciplinary lines, this book series, founded by Maney Publishing under the imprint of the Northern Universities Press and now continuing under the Legenda imprint, aims to bring together different scholarly perspectives on Italy and its culture.

Italian Perspectives publishes books and collections of essays on any period of Italian literature, language, history, culture, politics, art, and media, as well as studies which taken an interdisciplinary approach and are methodologically innovative.

Managing Editor
Dr Graham Nelson, 41 Wellington Square, Oxford OX1 2JF, UK
www.maney.co.uk/series/italianperspectives
www.legenda.mhra.org.uk

Sweet Thunder

Music and Libretti in 1960s Italy

Vivienne Suvini-Hand

LEGENDA

Modern Humanities Research Association and Maney Publishing
Italian Perspectives 16
2006

Published by the
Modern Humanities Research Association and Maney Publishing
1 Carlton House Terrace
London SW1Y 5DB
United Kingdom

LEGENDA is an imprint of the
Modern Humanities Research Association and Maney Publishing

Maney Publishing is the trading name of W. S. Maney & Son Ltd,
whose registered office is at Suite 1C, Joseph's Well, Hanover Walk, Leeds LS3 1AB

ISBN 1 904350 60 7 / 978-1-904350-60-6

First published 2006

Printed in Great Britain

Cover: 875 Design

Copy-Editor: Dr Avery T. Willis

CONTENTS

For Luigi
and my parents
Margaret and Seán

ACKNOWLEDGEMENTS

I would like to thank the following individuals for their help and support in writing this book: Professors Zygmunt Barański, Laura Lepschy, Paul Diffley, Brian Moloney, Michael Caesar; and Dr Nicola Verzina of the 'Fondo Maderna' in Bologna. I would also like to thank Dr Graham Nelson, the Managing Editor of Legenda for his guidance and advice; the Arts and Humanities Research Board for their award of a Research Leave Scheme grant which enabled me to bring this work to a conclusion, and the British Academy for awarding me a personal grant. Parts of this work have appeared in *Italian Studies* and *The Italianist*. I am grateful to the editors for their kind permission to allow me to reprint this material. Finally, for their tolerance and moral support, most thanks are due to my husband, Luigi, and to my children Violetta, Rosanna, and Gabriele.

Vivienne Suvini-Hand
April 2006

LIST OF ILLUSTRATIONS

INTRODUCTION

This study offers a detailed examination of the literary influences behind the experimental music of five twentieth-century Italian composers: Luigi Dallapiccola (1904–75), Bruno Maderna (1920–73), Luciano Berio (1925–2003), Giacomo Manzoni (1932-), and Armando Gentilucci (1939–89). It will concentrate on one composition by each of the five composers: Dallapiccola's *Ulisse*, Maderna's *Ausstrahlung,* Berio's *Laborintus II,* Manzoni's *Parole da Beckett*, and Gentilucci's *Strofe di Ungaretti*. The chosen compositions cover just over a decade of Italian musical history (from 1960 to 1971), and each is of a different musical form: *Ulisse* (1960–68) is a large-scale opera; *Laborintus II* (1963), a piece of musical theatre in which music, text, and gesture are integrated; *Strofe di Ungaretti* (1967), a sextet for mixed voices; *Parole da Beckett* (1970), a composition for two choirs, three groups of instruments, and a tape; and *Ausstrahlung* (1971), a piece for female voice, solo flute and oboe, orchestra and tape recording. The different musical form of each work allows for an investigation into the diverse methods of composition employed by experimental composers across the eleven years in question. What the works have in common is their heavy reliance on literary influences, for the precise focus of this study is collage libretti comprised of or inspired by exclusively literary texts. It is for this reason that the time-frame of the study is limited to 1960–71, for it was in this particular period that the phenomenon of the libretto as a form of literary collage prevailed. [1]

The intention of this study is to analyse closely the literary extracts that have been used to compile each of the five libretti; to examine the personal and/or political reasons behind the composers' choice of writers and texts; to comment upon the relationship between the texts and the music; and, above all, to examine the fine network of subtle relationships that exist between the different literary extracts, and (in the case of Dallapiccola, Berio, and Maderna) the many and different writers that have been juxtaposed in the libretti. To date there has been no such comprehensive survey of the five works in question, nor of the phenomenon of collage libretti as a characteristic feature of 1960s Italy.

The first chapter, in its tracing of the development of Italian music from *Verismo* to the Seventies, aims to locate the five composers to whom this study is dedicated within the context of experimentalism in Italian music, and to explicate the latter in the light of contemporary European and American influences.

Chapters Two to Six are devoted to the five selected works, in chronological order. In Chapter Two, it is shown how *Ulisse* draws not only on Homer's *Odyssey* and Dante's presentation of Ulysses in *The Divine Comedy*, but also on a multitude of other writers of varied nationality and ranging from the classical to the modern age: Aeschylus, Hölderlin, Tennyson, Cavafy, Pascoli, Machado, Joyce, and Mann. The chapter focuses on how and why quotations from these writers are torn from their original contexts and skilfully woven into the Ulysses story to underscore Dallapiccola's personal and Christian interpretation of the myth of Ulysses, who, in the opera, posits only communion with God as an answer to the existential problems of modern living.

The libretto of Berio's *Laborintus II* was put together by Sanguineti — a leading exponent of the Neo-Avant-garde movement — and consists of a montage of lyrics from the bible, as well as from early medieval (Isidore of Seville), late medieval (Dante), and modern authors (Pound, Eliot, Sanguineti). The chapter on *Laborintus II* emphasizes how the focal point of the libretto is Dante and his critique of usury, but shows how, around that theme, Sanguineti weaves a labyrinthian network of other motifs, all of which broadly concentrate on the cycle of evil which has endured from the earliest time (the original Fall, the pre-diluvial and post-diluvial era) through to, literally, the 'middle' ages, and the contemporary neo-capitalist sixties.

Gentilucci's sextet, *Strofe di Ungaretti*, takes its lyrics from three poems belonging to two famous collections by Ungaretti: *Sentimento del tempo* (1919–35), and *Il Dolore* (1937–46). Together the poems set a family tragedy and private bereavement against the universal tragedy of World War II, and the grief of the Italian people and the world at large. The chapter on the *Strofe* demonstrates how the strong, communicative thrust of the libretto, where the speaker encourages himself and others to leave behind tragic thoughts and embrace a new beginning goes hand in hand with Gentilucci's rejection of the aesthetics of negativism in twentieth-century music, and his preference for morally 'engaged' works which emphasize the need for action and communication. It also shows how the main stylistic and thematic features of the texts — the alternation of excessive emotionalism and muted grief, and a preoccupation with the Bergsonian concepts of time and memory, respectively — are imitated and reinforced on a musical level. On the level of religious credence, however, the composer and writer are shown to be at variance: from the 'dissonance' caused by domestic and national tragedy, 'consonance' for Ungaretti is posited as a Godly state of being; the 'dissonance' of Gentilucci's music is associated with the loss of a centripetal and harmonious vision of the universe with God at its centre, and the consonance that it reaches in the last two bars of the piece is firmly associated with man.

The libretto of Manzoni's *Parole da Beckett* consists of a compilation of twenty-three fragments of lyrics taken from Samuel Beckett's *How it is, Happy Days, Waiting for Godot, All that Fall* , and *Poems in English*. The chapter on the *Parole* highlights how Manzoni's relationship with Beckett's lyrics is complex and multi-faceted. On the one hand, the music assumes a certain autonomy over the Beckett texts, evinced, for example, by Manzoni's chosen title — *Parole da Beckett* (*Words from Beckett*), and not *Parole di Beckett* (Beckett-Words) — which shifts the emphasis from 'Beckett' to 'words', words which the composer treats as raw, elementary sound. On the other hand, certain features in the nature of the music and the structuring of the libretto demonstrate Manzoni's desire to reinforce Beckett's idiosyncratic style and vision. Since the text cited most often (*How it is*) has been clearly chosen for the allusions it makes to Dante, the chapter also explores the similarities and differences in Manzoni's and Beckett's relationship with the medieval poet, and in their respective moral visions of man and the universe: whereas both reject Dante's view of a divinely coherent universe ruled by an inexorable, yet just, God, it is suggested that Manzoni's humanist and philanthropic attitude finds itself at odds with Beckett's reinforced cynicism and the absence of communication which characterizes the protagonists of his literary universe.

Maderna's *Ausstrahlung* was commissioned for the celebrations in Persepolis in 1971 to commemorate the birth of Cyrus, the Great, considered to be the founder of the Persian Empire. The libretto consists of lyrics taken from ancient Indian and Persian texts. The Indian sources consist of quotations from Dandin's (A.D. c665–710) *Kavydarsa*; Book 4 — the *Bhagavadgita* — of the Indian epic, the *Mahabharata*, composed in the first or second century A.D.; and the *Atharvaveda*, or sacred text of the Indo-Aryans, the majority of which was completed by 1500 B.C. These texts are united with verses from famous Persian poets: Rudaki (A.D. c858–941), Khayyam (A.D. c1050–1125), and Sadi (A.D. c1184–1291), and a passage from the *Avesta* which contains the sacred writings of Zoroastrianism, the religion founded in the sixth century BC by the Iranian prophet, Zoroaster. *Ausstrahlung* is, first and foremost, a celebration of the spiritual and of God, and the chapter on the work demonstrates both how Maderna has carefully chosen and arranged the Indian and Persian texts so as to highlight the similarities and differences in the visions of the divine presented in them, and how he successfully makes his music simulate and mirror these diverse images of divinity, which are linked to an investigation into the origins of language, literature, and musical sound itself.

As demonstrated by the summaries above, all of the compositions dealt with here display a preoccupation with religious issues, and three of them — Dallapiccola's *Ulisse*, Berio's *Laborintus II*, and Manzoni's *Parole da Beckett* — are heavily influenced by Dante. Given that the composers under discussion (apart from Dallapiccola) were of Marxist orientation, this emphasis upon religion is a surprising phenomenon, but is to be understood in the context of the 'boom' period of the early sixties when Italy enjoyed an 'economic miracle', which transformed it from a poor and largely agrarian country into one of the world's biggest industrial powers, with Italian brand names such as FIAT, Zanussi, Olivetti and Pirelli dominating foreign markets. [2] Whereas for many Italians this new consumer society led to an improvement in the *material* quality of life, it also brought with it a waning in *spiritual* values, and gave rise to a culture where even works of art were reduced to the level of competing commodities. The 'difficult' and unconventional methods of composition employed by the artists dealt with in this study — their use of dodecaphony (Dallapiccola), total serialism (Berio, Maderna), Webernian minimalist techniques (Gentilucci), and the creation of dense bands of sound combined with electronic music (Manzoni) — displayed a refusal to compete with market-place values and the new capitalist society. As well as the private reasons these composers may have had for using religious texts, the emphasis upon religion in the libretti examined was also aimed at reasserting a spiritual and/or humanitarian, if not strictly religious perspective within the new industrial society, with man, not money, at its centre.

Equally registering its disaffection with new capitalist values was the main literary movement of the times — the Neo-Avant-garde (1956–69). [3] The Neo-Avant-garde, also known as the Gruppo '63, clearly influenced the libretti of the five composers under discussion. In tune with the general climate of dissent demonstrated by the students' and workers' protests of 1968–69, and seeking to promote the very concepts of conflict and alienation which capitalism gave rise to and sought to repress by way of consensus, the Neo-Avant-garde revolutionalized traditional notions of literary language and structure. The rationality and coherency of conventional language was jettisoned in favour of the alogical and the incoherent, and conventional structure was replaced by, what Umberto Eco called, 'organized disorder', sometimes represented in the form of a collage where phrases and sentences from other texts were literally pasted together, and sometimes in the form of an *opera aperta* (open work) aesthetics where the reader himself was made to be involved in the creation of the work of art. At the same time, this 'organized disorder' was claimed to be an effective method for increasing a work's capacity for generating information. Sanguineti's *Laborintus* (1956) — a long prose poem, considered by many to be the very first Neo-Avant-garde text, and parts of which are actually used in the libretto of Berio's *Laborintus II* — provides an example *par excellence* of the Neo-Avant-garde rejection of conventional literary practice: it is characterized by syntactical dislocation, the use of *plurilinguismo* (many languages — in this case French, Greek. Latin and English, as well as Italian), a mixture of lexical registers (specialized terminology from the fields of psychoanalysis, music, philosophy, science and medicine), and a general reliance on eclecticism: the text avails itself of Jungian thought, Joycean internal monologue, ideas belonging to the French *École du regard*, semiotics and Ferdinand de Saussure's theory of the sign, and Russian Formalism, to name just a few of its many sources.

This element of eclecticism is most pronounced in three of the libretti under consideration: as explained, Dallapiccola draws on Italian, Greek, German, English, Spanish, and Irish authors spanning the middle ages and the twentieth century; Berio's literary borrowings range from the biblical to the Neo-Avant-garde; and Maderna's Indian and Persian influences travel in time from the sixteenth century BC to the thirteenth century AD. The diverse sources on all three occasions are juxtaposed without any respect for chronological time, and the coherency of conventional discourse is further disrupted by Berio and Maderna's heavy reliance on *plurilinguismo*. Maderna, in his use of aleatory, also employs on a musical level the *opera aperta* aesthetics of Eco; while the replacing of a logical and developed coherency of thought with the apparently alogical and fragmentary is most pronounced in Manzoni's *Parole da Beckett*, and to a lesser extent in Gentilucci's *Strofe di Ungaretti*. All of the libretti employ a Neo-Avant-garde collage technique, and as Chapters Two to Six aim to demonstrate, they are testament to Eco's theory that greater information does indeed result from a disturbance in the coherency and predictability of the message. The libretti's 'disorderly' juxtapositions of quotations and references to diverse authors, or to the diverse works of an individual author, have been very carefully 'organized' to generate similarities and differences in viewpoints, and intricate labyrinthine connections of thought. The result is that the libretti are highly crafted and richly suggestive works of art, resonant with the ideas and concepts of far-reaching cultures which have been extrapolated from their original contexts and made relevant to contemporary Italian living.

Unless otherwise stated, all translations in this study are mine.

Notes to the Introduction

1. In spite of the prominence assumed by the music of Luigi Nono in 1960s Italy, there is no complete chapter dedicated to this composer in the present study (but see discussions of Nono on pp. 16, 22, 102–103, 128). This is because none of Nono's works written in the time-frame of this study (1960–71) fits the category of the compositions the study aims to examine — collage libretti, made up of literary texts. The two most important works composed by Nono in the period in question are *Intolleranza* (1960) and *A floresta é jovem e cheja de vida* [The forest is young and full of life] (1965–66). The libretti of both of these works are comprised of non-literary texts. For a study of Nono's works, see *La nuova ricerca sull'opera di Luigi Nono*, ed. by G. Borio, G. Morelli, V. Rizzardi (Florence: Leo S. Olschi, 1999), and *Le musiche degli anni Cinquanta*, ed. by G. Borio, G. Morelli, V. Rizzardi (Florence: Leo S. Olschi, 2004).

2. For further information on the 'economic miracle' see G. Bocca, *Miracolo all'italiano* (Milan: Feltrinelli, 1980); M. Caesar and P. Hainsworth, 'The Transformation of Post-war Italy', in *Writers and Society in Contemporary Italy*, ed. by M. Caesar and P. Hainsworth (Leamington Spa: Berg, 1984), pp. 4–15; M. Clark, 'The economy and society under the Republic', in *Modern Italy 1871–1982* (London: Longman, 1984), pp. 348–73; S. M. Di Scala, 'The Economic Miracle and its effects', in *Italy. From Revolution to Republic. 1700 to the Present* (Boulder: Westview Press, 1995), pp. 306–25; C. Duggan, 'From Economic Miracle to Social Protest: Italy in the 1960s', in *A Concise History of Italy* (Cambridge: Cambridge University Press, 1994), pp. 261–69; D. Sassoon, 'From "Miracle" to Crisis, 1963–69', in *Contemporary Italy. Economy, Society and Politics since 1945* (New York: Addison Wesley Longman Limited, 1997), pp. 42–58.

3. For further information on the Neo-Avant-garde, see R. Barilli, *La neoavanguardia italiana: dalla nascita del 'Verri' alla fine di 'Quindici'* (Bologna: Il Mulino, 1995); *Gruppo 63. Critica e teoria, ed. by* R. Barilli and A. Guglielmi (Turin: Testo & Immagine, 2003); R. Esposito, *Le ideologie della neo-avanguardia* (Naples: Liguori, 1976); F. Gambaro, *Invito a conoscere la neoavanguardia* (Milan: Mursia, 1993); *I novissimi. Poesie per gli anni '60*, ed. by A. Giuliani (Turin: Einaudi, 1965); F. Muzzioli, *Teoria e critica della letteratura nelle avanguardie italiane degli anni sessanta* (Rome: Istituto della Enciclopedia Italiana, 1982); W. Siti, *Il realismo dell'avanguardia* (Turin: Einaudi, 1973); S. Suleiman, *Subversive Intent: Gender, Politics and the Avant-Garde* (Cambridge: Harvard University Press, 1990); C. Wagstaff, 'The Neo-Avant-garde', in *Writers and Society*, pp. 35–61.

CHAPTER 1

Twentieth-Century Italian Music in the Context of European and American Experimentalism from *Verismo* to the Seventies

Italian *Verismo*

In 1888 the publisher and director Edoardo Sonzogno advertised a competition for a one-act opera to mark the occasion of the opening of his new opera house, the Teatro Costanzi, in Rome. The competition was won by Pietro Mascagni's *Cavalleria rusticana* (1890), based on a play of the same name by the Sicilian writer, Giovanni Verga (1840–1922). Together with Luigi Capuana (1839–1915), Verga was the main exponent of a school of literature known as *Verismo* (Realism). Closely related to French Naturalism, *Verismo* displayed an interest in regionalism, employed a narrative style which was objective and impersonal, and attempted, in its mixing of dialect with standard Italian, to convey the down-to-earth language of the lower social classes. The success of Mascagni's opera gave rise to a new musical genre — *Verismo* — a term that eventually became synonymous with a focussing upon the gritty lives of the under-classes, sensational tales of adulterous passions and brutality, bursts of tuneful and emotional melodies, and, often, the use of popular song and dance. *Cavalleria* was followed by a host of imitations, notably Ruggero Leoncavallo's *I pagliacci* (1892), and Umberto Giordano's *Mala vita* (1892). The former combines the Veristic 'slice of life' approach with more complex elements. A version of the Shakespearian proverb 'All the world's a stage', it is a tragicomic play within a play, with *commedia dell'arte* characters and masks. Giordano's *Mala vita* is a blunt portrayal of the 'wretched life' of a Neapolitan prostitute.

Continuing in the vein of high drama and memorable melodies, Giacomo Puccini (1858–1924), in 1893, produced his first successful opera, *Manon Lescaut*. However, although his name is generally attached to Veristic opera, Puccini's material was far more wide-ranging than that of his *Verismo* contemporaries (he touches on subjects as diverse as bohemianism, love and politics during the Napoleonic wars, orientalism, colonialism, and the Wild West); and his success lay largely in altering the *Verismo* genre by dispensing with its shock tactics and making echoes to the *bel canto* tradition. Puccini went on to dominate the musical scene with *La bohème*, premiered in 1896, *Tosca* (1900), *Madama Butterfly* (1904), *La fanciulla del West* (1910), *Il Trittico: Il Tabarro, Suor Angelica, Gianni Schicchi* (1918), and *Turandot* (1926).

Twentieth-century Classicism

The turn of the century appeal of *Verismo* completely overshadowed the great Italian instrumental tradition. In recognition of this, three musicians — Giuseppe Martucci (1856–1909), Giovanni Sgambati (1841–1914), and Leone Sinisgaglia (1868–1944) — set about composing exclusively for instruments and organizing concerts in an effort to pioneer instrumental music. But their efforts failed, largely because they lacked a thorough knowledge of the Italian tradition, and tended to imitate German symphonic music, particularly that of Brahms. It was left up to the *generazione dell'ottanta* — a number of composers born in the 1880s — to bring about a major musical revival. These composers included Ferruccio Busoni (1866–1924), Ottorino Respighi (1879–1936), Ildebrando Pizzetti (1880–1968), Gian Francesco Malipiero (1882–1973), Alfredo Casella (1883–1947), and Giorgio Federico Ghedini (1892–1965), and their names became associated with a movement known as 'Classicism' or 'Neo-Classicism'.

The terms 'Classicism' and 'Neo-Classicism' are frequently used interchangeably by musicologists (the latter term is preferred here).[1] What is being denoted is an attempt, on the part of a number of composers writing particularly between the two wars, to return to the original Classical style, which incorporated anything ranging from the early seventeenth century (Monteverdi and Gesualdo) to the late Baroque (Bach, Handel, Vivaldi, Scarlatti) and to the classical era proper of the late eighteenth century (Haydn and Mozart). In short, Neo-Classicism emulated the eras that had preceded nineteenth-century Romanticism, whose exaggerated gestures and formless indulgences the 'new' Classicists were rejecting. The Classical principles of order, discipline, balance, and structure — considered to be universal properties of music which had been swept aside during Romanticism — were favoured over the concept of music as expressing emotion and arousing emotion. Musically, Neo-Classicism brought with it a resurrection of traditional forms such as the symphony, sonata, and concerto. Small orchestras or chamber music groups were generally preferred over the huge orchestras that had been associated with Strauss or Mahler. Equally significant was Neo-Classicism's preference for pre-nineteenth-century forms such as the suite, gigue, divertimento, toccata, fugue, passacaglia, and chaconne. In place of the rich chordal textures of Romantic and Impressionist music, the Classicists used a horizontal or linear style, with clear, sharp lines, and precise, regular rhythms. But it was not that the 'new' Classicists were blindly imitating the 'old' Classicists. One could, for example, never mistake the music of Stravinsky with that of Haydn or Mozart. Rather, the 'new' Classicists blended the basic tenets of the Classical tradition with their own personal styles, and with elements of experimentalism in the form of extended tonality, modality, or even atonality. For this reason, 'Neo-Classicism' could not be regarded as nostalgic or backward-looking; on the contrary, it was decidedly progressive and modern, making it 'difficult and even artificial to regard Neo-Classicism and postmodernism as separate except in historical sequence'.[2]

The three most renowned names in the field of twentieth-century Classicism are Busoni, Casella, and Malipiero. The last two will be important to the discussion of Luigi Dallapiccola (see p. 14). Before deciding to reside in Italy at the age of thirty-two, Alfredo Casella had lived abroad for nearly twenty years, studying in Paris (with Ravel under Fauré), and travelling as a harpsichordist to Russia and Germany where he met and worked with Rimsky-Korsakov, Mahler, and the young Stravinsky. His 'cosmopolitan' experiences are reflected in the music of his first 'phase' (generally posited as the period lasting up to 1913) which bear the influences of Fauré (in *Barcarola e scherzo*, 1903), the Russian nationalists, and Mahler (in his first two symphonies). When he returned to Italy in 1915, he took up the post of Professor of piano at the Liceo di S. Cecilia in Rome, and devoted himself to leading the Italian public away from the provincialism of *Verismo* opera, and introducing Italy to all that was new in European music in the early 1900s. Accordingly, he founded, along with a small group of composers (including Malipiero, Pizzetti and Respighi) the 'Società Italiana di Musica Moderna' (SIMM) which gave controversial concerts of both Italian and foreign music. Casella was, at this point in time, in the second phase of his career — the avant-garde phase, postulated as lasting from 1913 to 1920 — and completely under the spell of Schoenberg. His music of this period (notably the orchestral piece, *Pagine di guerra*, 1918, and the piano works, *Pupazzetti*, 1920, and *Piano Sonatina*, 1916) bears the influences not only of Schoenberg, but also of Stravinsky and Bartók. These three composers also featured largely in performances given by Casella's new musical society — the 'Corporazione delle Nuove Musiche' (CDNM), created in 1923 (the SIMM having come to a demise in 1919). The CDNM, supported by D'Annunzio, aimed to bring to Italy 'the latest expressions and the most recent researches of contemporary musical art' (Waterhouse, *The New Grove*, p. 233), and the group toured throughout Italy mostly performing Stravinsky's *Les noces* (1923) and Schoenberg's *Pierrot lunaire*, conducted by Schoenberg himself. *Pierrot lunaire* — a piece for a female speaker and wind and string instruments, premiered in Vienna in 1912 — was Schoenberg's first important and highly influential atonal composition (see pp. 15–17). It was through the activities of the CDNM that the young Dallapiccola had his first contact with the Viennese avant-garde. In terms of Casella's own personal creativity, he had, at this point in time, in a drastic change of tack, reached his third and final stage — the Neo-Classical period which lasted roughly from 1920 to 1944. His models were the Baroque masters, Vivaldi, and in particular, Scarlatti. Following the example of Stravinsky's *Pulcinella* (1919), based on music by Pergolesi,[3] Casella's *Scarlattiana* (1926) for piano and thirty-two instruments takes its themes from Scarlatti's sonatas. The composer claims this leap from the avant-garde to the Neo-Classical occurred because the Italians needed a new music which was more consonant with a 'Mediterranean' sensibility, and specifically to fulfil this need he wrote his *Concerto* for string quartet (1923–24) which he viewed as a type of Italian complement to Schoenberg's *Pierrot lunaire*:

> Desideravo [...] che il *Pierrot lunaire* venisse accompagnato da un lavoro italiano che valesse a dimostrare quanto la nostra sensibilità, la nostra tradizione fossero indipendenti dall'arte del maestro viennese.[4]

> [I wanted *Pierrot lunaire* to be accompanied by an Italian work whose worth lay
> in demonstrating how much our sensibility and our tradition were independent
> from the art of the Viennese master.]

As intimated in the quotation, Casella's Classicism was also bound up with feelings
of intense nationalism which in the 1930s led him to identify with Fascism: his 1937
opera, *Il deserto tentato*, was written in praise of Mussolini's invasion of Abyssinia.
But his frenzy for 'romanità' (evident as far back as 1926 in his 'Neo-Classical'
Concerto romano) did not, however, prevent him from supporting performances
of foreign music, as evinced by the 1937 programme for the Festival di musica
contemporanea della Biennale di Venezia, directed by Casella himself, which
features a performance of Schoenberg's dodecaphonic *Suite,* 1921–23 (See *New Grove,*
p. 234). Malipiero's name is nearly always linked to that of Casella for the manner
in which, during the twenties, he assisted him in modernizing Italian music, and
weaning the Italian public off what he considered to be the shallow sentimentality
of Puccini and late nineteenth-century opera. He collaborated with Casella on the
activities of both the SIMM and the CDNM. If he is often referred to as a Neo-
Classicist, it is because of his abiding interest in seventeenth and eighteenth century
music — particularly that of Monteverdi and Vivaldi. From 1926 to 1942 he edited
Monteverdi's entire works in sixteen volumes,[5] and after his retirement from the
Liceo Musicale di Venezia where he was a professor of composition, he proceeded
to edit the complete instrumental works of Vivaldi.[6] In addition, he wrote book-
length studies and essays on both Monteverdi and Vivaldi, and on a plethora of
other composers and musical subjects.[7] The influence of the Baroque is strongly
felt in his musical compositions, especially those operas composed between the
two wars. In *San Francesco d'Assisi* (1920–21) the Monteverdian arioso combined
with Gregorian chant endows the work with what Waterhouse calls a 'Giottoesque
calm' (*New Grove,* p. 699); while the use of baroque counterpoint, together with
archaic modes (forms of scales prevalent in the middle ages) in *Filomena e l'infatuato*
(1925) and *Merlino mastro d'organi* (1926–27) lends both operas a distinctly archaic
flavour. But the archaic in all of these compositions is also fused with a pronounced
experimentalism. The experimentalism of Malipiero's music lies in the manner in
which it assimilates various musical tendencies and movements — Impressionism,
Expressionism, atonalism, and occasionally in the later works, dodecaphony — but
identifies with none of them. Thematically too, Malipiero's operas are innovative
and distinctly avant-garde, making often cryptic, symbolic statements about music
itself. For example, in *Merlino mastro d'organi* (a sequel to *Filomena e l'infatuato*, where
'the infatuated one' literally cannot live without the sound of Filomena's singing),
'l'infatuato' has become Merlino who is possessed by Filomena's soul which proceeds
to take vengeance on all men in whom music inspires love. Merlino attracts such men
by his organ playing, and then kills them with his 'orge sonore' ('sonorous orgies').
He himself, however, is eventually killed by a deaf and dumb traveller, but the soul of
Filomena survives, and a new singer is born. Malipiero's most important compositions
after 1930 are the seven ('anti-') symphonies written between 1930 and 1950 which
rejected all German principles of thematic development and recapitulation, replacing
these with a more deliberately open, fluent, and improvisatory style.

Schoenberg and Atonal Music

Although the ultra-modern operas of Malipiero were composed, in part, as a reaction against Puccini's operas and their lowbrow popularism, Malipiero's criticism of Puccini is not entirely justified, for even the *Verismo* composer, in his later works, shows signs of having been affected by the musical avant-garde. Puccini's *Turandot*, composed between 1920 and 1924, has in fact little in common with tonal 'Realism'. A psychological piece, concerned (like Malipiero's *La morte delle maschere*, 1922) with masks and identities, *Turandot* is also often tonally ambiguous, with dissonant sounding chords (ninths and elevenths played in parallel sequences), and an advanced use of harmony. Such musical innovations were clearly influenced by the gradual erosions in tonality which first became pronounced at the end of the nineteenth century, and which eventually culminated in the radical innovations brought about by Arnold Schoenberg (1874–1951), an Austrian composer who worked in Germany, and then, from 1933, in the USA (having been driven out from Germany by the Nazis for being a Jew and a composer of 'decadent' music). Tonality in European music was based on the principle that in the twelve tones that make up a scale, seven belong to the key, while five lie outside it. Gradually the distinction between these seven diatonic tones and the five chromatic ones began to disappear, and major and minor tonalities fused and combined into a single chromatic scale. While still remaining within the boundaries of the key, Wagner (1813–83) stretched chromaticism as far as possible, and questioned the necessity of returning to the key-note or tonic. Schoenberg took the process one step further. In his three pieces for piano, entitled *Drei Klavierstücke nos 1–2*, written in 1909, he completely jettisoned traditional methods of composition — dispensing with tonal centres, key signatures, and the traditional application of harmony — in favour of one where all the twelve notes in the chromatic scale were given equal importance, and regarded as being related freely to each other, rather than to a central key-note. Atonal music was born, although the term did not meet with approval by Schoenberg who considered 'atonal' as an irrational label, signifying something that did not relate to the nature of tone, and who preferred to define his music as 'pantonal', thereby suggesting his synthesis of all tonalities. Within this rupture of the traditional syntax of Western music, dissonance became the norm. Most of Schoenberg's early work, including the now celebrated *Pierrot lunaire*, met with hostility and/or derision, but that did not prevent him from returning to Vienna after his service in the First World War, and re-emerging in 1924 with the creation of the twelve-tone method by which he brought logic and structure to the potential chaos of atonality.

The Twelve-Tone Method

The difference between atonal and twelve-tone music — also called 'dodecaphony' and 'serialism' — is that in the former the composer is able to choose notes at will from the entire chromatic scale, whereas in the latter the twelve notes of the scale are arranged for each piece in a particular order or series (hence the term 'serialism'). The series chosen is called the 'tone row', and it acts as the unifying idea at the basis of the piece in question. Each piece of dodecaphonic music has, therefore, a unique arrangement of the twelve tones, not to be found in any other composition. Since all twelve tones in the chromatic scale are considered to have equal value, no one tone in the row is allowed to appear more than once, for to do so would suggest its heightened importance, and lend it the semblance of a tonic. The tone row may be used in its original form, but also in three other versions: retrograde (written backward from the end to the beginning); inverted (turned upside down, so that an upward leap becomes a downward leap and vice-versa); and retrograde-inverted (upside down and backward) (for an example of all four versions in Dallapiccola's *Ulisse*, see p. 60). A row may begin on any one of the twelve tones of the scale, allowing for forty-eight possibilities, and an inexhaustible system, for all the possible combinations of twelve tones in forty-eight positions have been posited as adding up to roughly half a billion. In fact, the principle of variation — creating the maximum variation of musical forms from the minimum of material (the twelve notes of the tone row) — was one of Schoenberg's most guiding principles. The notes of the series may not only be sounded in the form of a horizontal melody, but also in the harmonies and counterpoints of the whole composition, so that the tone row, to some extent, gives shape and form to the general sound of the piece. But only to some extent, because although the original tone row is generally audible at the very beginning of the piece, it does not take on the nature of a 'theme' as in traditional tonal music, for when played in its inverted and retrograde forms, it is no longer distinguishable to the ear. This failure to detect themes, and the need for a very concentrated response on the part of the listener account in large part for the unpopularity of dodecaphonic music (see Venuti's comments on Dallapiccola's *Ulisse,* p. 68). Another factor which makes a variation of the original tone row difficult to discern is the interchangeable nature of octaves in the dodecaphonic system. Each of the seven 'C''s, for example, on the piano keyboard are regarded not as individual tones, but as interchangeable representatives of, what is called, the 'pitch class C'. This gives rise to the huge 'jumps' in register and, consequently, the jagged zigzagging effect of dodecaphonic notation. It also partly accounts for why twelve-tone music is notoriously difficult to play, and especially, to sing, since vocal parts generally require that the singer possess a huge register. Schoenberg himself described his *Concerto* for violin and orchestra, 1934–36, as 'unplayable'; and he doubted whether his (unfinished) opera, *Moses und Aron*, first performed posthumously in Zurich in 1957, would ever be performed at all. His other most important twelve-tone compositions include the *Serenata* (1920–23), *Quarto quartetto* (1936), the *Trio* for strings (1946), *A Survivor from Warsaw* for speaker and orchestra (his personal testament, written in 1947, to the sufferings inflicted by Nazism on the Jewish people), and the *Fantasia* for violin and piano (1949).

The 'Second Viennese School'

Schoenberg's two major disciples were Alban Berg (1885–1935) and Anton Webern (1883-1945). They, along with other less well-known composers and musicians such as Roberto Gerhard, Karl Rankl, Josef Rufer, Nikos Skalkottas, Erwin Stein, and Egon Wellesz, followed up Schoenberg's discoveries in their own work, and although of different nationalities, they are referred to collectively as constituting the 'Second Viennese School'.

Berg amalgamated the twelve-tone method with a more traditional style. His music preserved the foundations of diatonic melody, and relied heavily on Classical notions of structure, keeping the traditional thematic movements, although the themes were now derived from the tone row series. Whereas perfect intervals were largely eschewed in dodecaphonic music, being considered too pregnant with tonal implications, Berg arranged his series around as many perfect intervals as possible, thereby maintaining a strong sense of tonality. As a result he managed to create a musical language that was both original and communicative. In his two famous operas — *Wozzeck* (composed from 1914–21, and first performed in 1925) and *Lulu* (composed from 1928–35, but left incomplete, and first completed and performed by Friedrich Cerha in 1937) — he uses traditional musical forms, such as sonatas, fugues, and rondos, which the listener recognizes at least on a subliminal level, to give unity to individual scenes, as well as easily identifiable leitmotifs which help steer the audience through the labyrinth of counterpoints and tone rows.

Webern's influence on subsequent composers was so vast that there exists a 'post-Webernian' style. Whereas Berg chose to combine the serial technique with traditional methods of composition, Webern, by the time he reached his third twelve-tone period of composition, beginning in 1924, completely rejected the tonal system, and pursued pure serialism without any tonal nostalgia. What characterizes the music of this final stage is a sense of minimalism: he composed miniature works, simple in vocal and instrumental sound, in spite of their complex musical conceptions. Anything superfluous was rejected — such as two instruments where one was enough — in an effort to condense and pare the music down to its bare essentials. Vertical combinations were thinned out, and even silences were 'composed', with rests forming an integral part of the structure of pieces. With Webern the huge Wagnerian orchestra was reduced to a few instruments whose colour effects he exploited to the full. Strings (as, for example, in his *String Quartet*, 1905) often play in a multitude of different ways and combinations: muted, *col legno*, with tremolo effects or harmonics, or pizzicato. Importantly, he put his own mark on serial technique in the manner in which he broke the twelve notes of the tone row up into units of two or three notes each, creating 'melodies' or motifs around these miniature particles of sound. These fragmented or atomized motifs gave the impression of discontinuous points of light or colour, so that the term *pointillism*, after the pointillist school of painting, emerged in relation to Webern's style. He was concerned with what is sometimes called the 'parameters' of music: pitch, duration, tempo, dynamics, and method of attack, all of which he subjected to the Schoenbergian principle of variation. Hence, very high pitches can rest beside very low pitches, long notes beside short notes, quick tempos beside slow tempos, double forte's beside double pianos (he tended to use the latter more than the former, and is sometimes referred to as the composer of the 'pianissimo espressivo'), and methods of attack such as sforzato, tenuto, staccato, legato, crescendo and diminuendo can all occur in the same piece. These techniques are apparent in works such as *Symphony* (1927–28), and *Variations* (1940) for orchestra, and many of them — especially the use of *pointillism* and varied dynamics, together with a general sense of Webernian minimalism — played a large part in influencing the music of Armando Gentilucci (see Chapter 4). Hence, Webern took the principle of variation which was originally the very essence of serial composition, and applied it to all the other parameters of music, thereby leading inevitably to the 'total serialization' of music that was to be developed by Boulez, Stockhausen (both pupils of Messiaen),[8] and others belonging to the Darmstadt School of the early 1950s, to be considered shortly.

Dodecaphonic Music in Italy: Luigi Dallapiccola (1904–75)

Born in the Austrian province of Pisino, Istria, Dallapiccola was uniquely placed to become the intermediary between Austro-German experimentations and the Italian tradition. Although he shared, from the very beginning, the Neo-Classical interest in early music, especially that of Gesualdo and Monteverdi (in 1942 he revised the latter's *Il ritorno di Ulisse in patria*, and adapted it for the modern stage), Dallapiccola preferred to distance himself from the Neo-Classical composers proper, and his overriding preference for vocal compositions clearly sets him apart from them and their predilection for instrumental music. But in spite of that, Kämper has convincingly detected allusions in the third and fourth of the *Sei cori di Michelangelo Buonarroti il Giovane* (1933–36) to Malipiero's *Sette canzoni* and *Torneo notturno*;[9] and the first piece in which Dallapiccola displays any dodecaphonic tendencies — *Divertimento* (1934) for voice and five instruments — is dedicated to Casella who, in fact, conducted the work at the Prague Festival organized by the SIMM in 1935. Kämper (p. 36) sees this dedication as probably owing to the presence of two of Casella's *loci classici* in the *Divertimento*: the 'Bourrée' and the 'Siciliana'. But it could well be functioning as a token of 'thanks' to Casella who was not only instrumental in getting Dallapiccola's *Partita* (1932) and *Divertimento* published by the Milan publishers, Carisch, but who also 'introduced' Dallapiccola to Schoenberg's music, for it was following the performance of Schoenberg's *Pierrot lunaire* in Florence in 1924, organized by Casella's CDNM, that Dallapiccola became enthused by the twelve-tone method. His enthusiasm for it was not shared by his rather conservative Florentine colleagues and by Fascist Italy as a whole where anything 'atonal' was associated with anti-Fascism and, hence, communism. As Reginald Smith Brindle puts it in his autobiography, when it became known that Dallapiccola's technique involved the use of Schoenberg's serialism, everyone in Florence 'regarded him as a kind of devil sprouting horns'.[10] Performances of twelve-tone music were very rare, and literature on the subject was almost impossible to obtain. Dallapiccola, therefore, learned the technique alone, through a process of trial and error.

It is in the finale of the *Divertimento* that the attraction for the twelve-tone method is first felt: here the theme becomes unexpectedly chromatic, and ranges over nine semitones. The next step along the twelve-tone road occurs in the fifth and sixth choruses of the *Sei Cori*, written, importantly, after Mussolini's Ethiopian campaign, an event which Dallapiccola claimed to have radically altered his vision of the world and his method of composing, making him more anti-Fascist and more musically radical. As well as employing *Sprechgesang* ('Speech-song'), a type of vocal utterance midway between speech and song that had been invented by Schoenberg and used in the *Pierrot lunaire*, chromaticism, as in the *Divertimento*, creeps in unexpectedly, with a formation of rising fourths (alternatively perfect and augmented) repeatedly permeating the tonal key of C minor until the whole chromatic scale has been sounded. Dallapiccola's next piece, *Tre laudi* (1936–37) — settings of medieval texts in honour of the Virgin by Jacopone da Todi, and, according to Dallapiccola, a protest against Fascism in the form of religious faith[11] — experiments further with the twelve-tone method in its deliberate use of a single series in its original and retrograde forms.

The success of all of Dallapiccola's major works from the late 30s to the late 40s — notably, his one-act opera, *Volo di notte* (1937–38), the choral work, *Canti di prigionia* (1938–41), and the opera *Il prigioniero* (1944–48) — lies in their skilful combination of twelve-tone procedures with more traditional methods of composition. In fact, *Il Prigioniero*'s insertion of diatonic elements within the dodecaphonic series gives rise to a lyricism which has been described as almost 'romantic' in character (A. Sellors, *New Grove*, p. 1051). Dallapiccola once wrote that the twelve-note method should not be so tyrannical as to exclude a priori both expression and humanity (see Machlis, p. 415). However, his characteristic tempering of the severity of the dodecaphonic thinking with tonal and modal elements came to an end in 1952 when he moved, with the *Quaderno Musicale di Annalibera*, resolutely into the realm of pure dodecaphony. Only a year before he had composed the completely tonal work, *Tartiniana,* a violin concerto based on themes by Tartini — not an exercise in nostalgia, but a work aimed at testing tonality, and accruing further evidence of its limitations. As Dallapiccola himself put it, 'Dopo ogni episodio tonale la mia tecnica dodecafonia ha acquistato maggior rigore' [After every tonal episode, my dodecaphonic technique acquired greater rigour].[12] The *Quaderno* (eleven short piano pieces dedicated to his daughter) is based on a single tone row, and could be considered as an experiment in all of the technical, compositional, and expressive possibilities of the tone row for a larger work-in-progress. In the *Canti di liberazione* (written from 1951–55 as a counterpart to the *Canti di prigionia*) Dallapiccola uses the same tone row series as in the *Quaderno*, but, for the first time, in all of its four variations: original, inverted, retrograde, and retrograde-inverted. His compositions from the late 50s on are completely dodecaphonic: *Requiescant* (1957–58), for mixed choir and orchestra, comes close to 'total serialism' (see 'The Darmstadt School', below) in the manner in which not only pitch, but also time-values are treated serially; and in *Ulisse* (1960–68) each character or group of characters are ascribed their own symbolic twelve-tone row (see pp. 100–01).

The Darmstadt School and Total Serialism

After World War Two, there was a revival of interest in serial music which was largely owing to the desire on the part of artists to make a *tabula rasa* of all traditional forms of music, and start creating again with something new. A European movement arose aimed at developing further Schoenberg's original serial technique so as to make it apply not only to pitch, but also to rhythm, dynamics, attack, and timbre. In practice this meant establishing twelve gradations (in line with the twelve notes of the chromatic scale) for each of these categories, and serializing them. In terms of rhythm, therefore, a series could range from one demisemiquaver to twelve (a dotted crochet). A single composition could have twelve different dynamic markings (say, for example, six gradations of softness, ranging from mp to ppppp, and six gradations of loudness, ranging from mf to fffff); twelve indications of attack (sforzato, tenuto, legato, staccato etc); and twelve timbres or colours, created by twelve different instruments, not necessarily from different families.[13] The gradations for each of these categories were worked out prior to composition. Total serialism was, therefore, a method of composition which was rigorously mathematical. As Griffiths points out, its composers saw themselves as concerned primarily with structure and organization, as 'architects or engineers in sound'.[14]

The movement had its headquarters from the early 1950s onwards at the Kranichstein Institute in Darmstadt, where composers and students would meet during the summer months to discuss the state of the art. The most important of these composers whose named became synonymous with the Darmstadt School were Pierre Boulez (b. 1925), Karlheinz Stockhausen (b. 1928), Luigi Nono (1924–91), and Bruno Maderna (1920–73) (for Nono and Maderna see pp. 5, 21–22, 102–03, 128, and p. 3 and Chapter 6, respectively). Although acknowledging direct lineage from the Second Viennese School in general, these composers posited the works of Webern in particular as inspiring the transition from serialism to total serialism. Webern's concern with the parameters of music, as well as his attention to minutiae and structure (see pp. 13–14), all pointed the way forward toward the scientific and technical preoccupations of total serialism.

Boulez's most famous pieces to be composed according to the principles of total serialism were *Structures* (1951) for two pianos, *Le Marteau sans maître* (1953–54), and *Pli selon pli* (1957–62). Of these, *Le Marteau* is his best-known work. Based on three short, surreal poems by René Char, it is music of the bell-and-percussion variety and evokes the gamelan of Bali where Boulez had a period of residence. Written for contralto and a group of six instruments (the 'sixth' to be played by a single player, but comprising nine types of percussion instruments), the piece is characterized by a series of contrasts: sound with dramatic silences; steady, regular rhythm with free rhythm; and traditional instruments capable of sustaining sound (e.g. the voice, flute, and viola) with more exotic, percussive ones, including bongos, maracas, claves, a bell, tam-tams, and a gong. Startling contrasts of this kind were to become a feature of *musique concrète* (see below, pp. 32–34), as were new uses of acoustic space that were brought into play by Stockhausen's *Gesang der Jünglinge* (1956) and *Gruppen* (1955–57).

Gruppen was the development of an idea begun with *Gesang der Jünglinge*. Whereas in the latter, several groups of loudspeakers were placed around the auditorium (a technique imitated in Manzoni's *Parole da Beckett*, see p. 137), in *Gruppen*, 109 orchestral players, divided into three separate orchestras, each with their own conductor, are positioned in different parts of the auditorium, and surround the audience, in an attempt to involve a greater audience participation. In *Gruppen*, tempo is serialized, and each orchestra plays simultaneously with the others and in a different tempo. At the climax of the work, and in an attempt to underline the experiment with music and space, a huge brass string is swung from one orchestra to another.

It was at the end of the 1940s that Maderna first attended the Darmstadt summer courses, and his experiences there put him in contact with the musical intelligentsia of Milan, notably Luigi Pestalozza, Cathy Berberian, Luciano Berio, and Giacomo Manzoni. Together, in 1955, they helped set up the Studio di Fonologia Musicale della RAI, inaugurated a musical peridiodical, *Incontri Musicali*, and founded an ensemble, directed by Maderna, which they used as a platform for the performance of their own music.

The seriousness with which Maderna regarded serial composition is demonstrated alone by the vast quantities of preparatory work — pages of diagrams, drawings, and tables plotting pitch, rhythm, metre, colour, attack, dynamics, and other musical parameters — for nearly every composition written up until the 70s. His interest in numbers, structure, and organization is made evident in his description of *Quadrivium* (1969):

> Il titolo [...] è forse un po' letterario. Pensavo alle quattro arti liberali: aritmetica, algebra, musica e astronomia [...] Inoltre il numero quattro è magico. Quattro elementi ... quattro volti della terra ... Quattro percussionisti solisti ed una grande orchestra divisa in quattro gruppi ... [...]. L'organizzazione, la struttura è quella di un cubo. Talvolta le facce diventano un blocco unico, talvolta si separano e rinfrangono [15].

> [The title is perhaps a bit literary. I was thinking of the four liberal arts: arithmetic, algebra, music and astronomy. Moreover, the number 'four' is magic. Four elements [...] four faces of the earth [...]. Four percussion soloists and a big orchestra divided into four groups. The organization and structure is that of a cube. Sometimes its faces become a single block, sometimes they separate and break up again.]

Yet, in blatant and, often, intentional contradiction with such regimental procedures, many of Maderna's works, including *Quadrivium* itself, also employ aleatory. Aleatory, although antithetical in nature to serial music, occurred at precisely the same time as the latter. From the Latin *alea*, meaning dice, aleatory is a term rather loosely used to describe music or other art forms where elements of chance, random choice, and indeterminacy are involved in the composition or performance of the piece. (For its provenance in America, and its association with the name of John Cage, see below, pp. 18–19). *Serenata per un satellite* (1969) is the finest example of Maderna's aleatoric techniques. Composed for the launching of the satellite 'Boreas' on 1 October, 1969 from the American base of Vandemberg, directed by the European Space Operation Centre (ESOC) of Darmstadt, the piece is, in the words of Berio, a 'gioco musicale' [musical game] (*Dialogo*, pp. 128–29). The choice, nature, and distribution of the instruments is left entirely up to the conductor, and can vary from performance to performance. The actual score is composed of musical fragments, laid out so as to evoke, graphically, the trajectory of a satellite in orbit. The instrumentalists can choose which of the score's 'fragments' to play, either individually, all together, or in groups, and they can improvise freely, but only with the notes written. The conductor has the awesome task of controlling the performance, and of giving it musical form and development. The work was first performed in Darmstadt, a few minutes before the actual launch of 'Boreas' (for the use of aleatory in *Ausstrahlung*, see pp. 151–52).

Maderna also widely employed an *opera aperta* ('open work') aesthetic, composing works with many sections which could all exist and be performed independently of each other, or be combined with other completely different pieces. In fact, in the first performance of *Serenata per un satellite*, the instrumentalists, who were familiar with Maderna's work, took it upon themselves to employ an 'open work' aesthetics, for they inserted into *Serenata* sections of other of Maderna's compositions — sequences from *Musica su due dimensioni* (1958), the *Concerto per oboe n. 2* (1967), and *Widmung* (1967). In writing aleatoric and 'open' works Maderna was contesting the notion of a work of art as something rigidly structured with a unique and predetermined content, and proposing in its stead the concept of a composition as something endlessly alive and always in a state of being born.

The American Influence: John Cage

Aleatory was basically an American 'invention', which became associated with the name of John Cage whose radical musical inventions found their inspiration in his teacher and mentor, the Californian-based composer, Henry Cowell. Cowell, in his *Mosaic* — a string quartet written in 1934 — had proposed the idea of 'elastic' form: the performer was asked to collaborate creatively with the composer in deciding the order in which the fragments of the 'mosaic' should be played. John Cage took this concept of 'elasticity' and developed it into the world-wide musical phenomenon of aleatory.

Born in California in 1912, Cage studied non-western, folk, and contemporary music with Cowell in New York, and serial technique with Schoenberg in California. He first came to public attention in a concert held in February, 1943, at the Museum of Modern Art, New York. The pieces by Cage selected for performance demonstrated an interest in untreated, percussive, and gamelan sounds with Oriental associations. They included the *Bacchanale* (1940) for the subsequently notorious 'prepared piano', where the piano, by the insertion and attachment of a myriad objects such as bolts, screwdrivers, pieces of wood, rubber, metal and glass, between and onto the strings, thereby altering their timbre and pitch, was transformed into a sort of one-man-band percussive instrument [16].

His interest in 'chance' procedures in music, derived from his fascination with Oriental philosophy. Cage's *Music of Changes* (1951) was directly inspired by the *Oriental I Ching*, a work on random number productions obtained by the throwing of coins or yarrow stalks. In *Music of Changes*, each note was chosen by a process of tossing three coins six times to arrive at one specific number in *I Ching*, a number which then led the composer to a position on one of his twenty-six numbered charts which would determine the pitch of the note in question. The same procedure was repeated for each of the other musical parameters: duration, timbre, attack etc. The forty-three minute piece supposedly, therefore, necessitated an incalculable number of coin tosses. In *Imaginary Landscapes no. 4* (1951) for twelve radios and twenty-four players and conductor, the element of chance is provided by what is 'on the radio' at the time of the performance (at its première on 2 May, 1951, there was, unfortunately, very little 'on the radio', since there was a lengthy delay, and most radio stations had gone off the air before the piece had even started!); and in *Piano Concerto* (1957–58), indeterminacy is taken one step further, since each player is instructed to play all, some, or none of his parts, in any order at all. Theoretically, therefore, *Piano Concerto* could result in absolute silence, like a previous composition — the famous *4' 33"* (1952) written for 'any instrument or instruments', and consisting of four minutes, thirty-three seconds of silence. In its first performance, the pianist, David Tudor placed a score on the piano, sat completely still on the piano stool, and then closed the lid of the piano after the allotted time. Cage has spoken about *4' 33"*, and other similar pieces, as ways of isolating and highlighting, within the time span specified, the 'natural', random sounds of the real, contingent world, thereby mirroring the aesthetics of *musique concrète* (see below, pp. 32–34). The 'real life' element of *4' 33"* was developed further by Cage in his 'gesture' pieces. These involved unorthodox activities such as scratching mike heads, rubbing record needles, and amplifying electronic distortions to the extent that, aurally, they border on the thresholds of pain. Some of these techniques are to be found in *Theater Piece* (1960): a hotchpotch of action and gesture fitted indiscriminately and illogically into a specified time span.

Clearly, a strong subversive element underlay Cage's experimentalism. As Salzman has put it:

> Instead of being conceived as sound, performances may be based on visual definitions, programs of activity, ideas of non-sound or silence. Instead of defining time, the compositions are themselves defined by the random passage of time, extending to indeterminate or theoretically infinite length. Instead of a music of definable identity, we have conceptions whose essence is lack of identity.[17]

They were techniques which many eminent composers of the time took offence at — notably Stockhausen, who once defined Cage's work as 'an anarchistic protest against the European tradition [...] in a musical no-man's land'.[18] In spite of such criticism, the importance and impact of Cage's pioneering experiments which encouraged new ways of thinking about and listening to music can be felt not only in the influence it exerted upon leading members of the Darmstadt School — notably Maderna and Boulez[19] — but also upon a whole variety of subsequent cultural phenomena, including pop art, 'happenings', musical theatre, and even the widespread 'mixing' and 'scratching' of contemporary pop music.

Electronic Music

The introduction of the tape recorder in the 1940s launched the new medium of

progressing to the role of teacher in 1957. There most of his music was first performed, and together with Boulez and Stockhausen, he became a major figure in the European avant-garde. His theatrical compositions of the 60s tackle engagé issues. In fact, it was Nono's belief that all artistic activity should be motivated by moral and ethical issues arising from social and political circumstances. He was also of the view that if a piece was to make an impact on a contemporary audience, it must avail itself of all the latest advancements and experiments in musical technique and technology. For this reason, electronic and aleatoric methods are consistently used in Nono's works, his music theatre included. The latter consists of two major pieces: *Intolleranza* (1960), and *A Floresta é jovem e cheja de vida* (1966). At its Venice première in 1961, *Intolleranza* provoked an uproar. Dealing explicitly with the victimization of immigrants, racialism, the exploitation of the working classes, and Fascist violence, the neo-Fascists accused Nono of writing a work that was anti-Italian, and like the composer's name, was composed of 'negatives'. *A Floresta* continues in the same vein of political radicalism. The libretto comprises a collage of non-literary texts — newspaper articles, law court depositions, and documents relating to capitalism, the working class struggle, and the fight for freedom in 'third world' countries — and they alternate to provide a kaleidoscopic picture of contemporary human, social, and political injustices. A phrase from Fidel Castro is juxtaposed with that of an anonymous worker from Detroit, or of an Italian partisan, or a military specialist from the department of USA defence — all within a highly experimental musical structure, where singers are chosen for the timbre of their voices and their acting, rather than their singing ability; where pre-recorded voices on tape alternate with 'live' voices; and spatial experiments are explored to the full with sound being diffused in a variety of volumes from different places in the auditorium. However, more than for his music theatre, Nono is best known for his early masterpiece, *Il canto sospeso* (1956), a composition for soloists, choir, and orchestra, whose libretto is composed of excerpts of letters written by nine resistance fighters (among whom a Bulgarian teacher, a Russian girl, an Italian printer, a Greek student, and a Polish peasant) just before their executions. His most ambitious work is the opera *Al gran sole carico d'amore* (1972–74) where revolutionary and socialist documents are fused with literary texts under the general theme of men and women's struggle for liberation. The colourful libretto that emerges cites from Fidel Castro, Che Guevara, Karl Marx, Rosa Luxembourg, Malcolm X, Bertolt Brecht, Lenin, Tania Bunke, Celia Sanchez, Cesare Pavese, and Arthur Rimbaud, from whom the title of the work is taken. For the manner in which the work 'forsakes the trappings of the opera house', *Al gran sole* is sometimes tentatively placed in the category of 'music theatre' (see *The New Grove*, p. 535), but the proportions of the opera are generally considered too vast to justify inclusion within the smaller-scale genre.

Like Nono's, Berio's music theatre takes the form of social commentary, but with slightly less strident political orientations. Materialist society is one of the main targets of his criticism (a supermarket, Berio once said, could obliterate the human personality as much as a concentration camp[21]). *Laborintus II* is his most forceful comment on the neo-capitalist system (see Chapter 3), and he returns much later to the topic in *Outis* (1996), and also to a certain extent in *La vera storia* (1977–81). The latter is based around the image of the Italian 'festa' (popular holiday or 'feast-day') which Calvino, who provided the lyrics to much of the pre-composed music, described as 'a temporal discontinuity, where transgression takes the place of the norm, where the squandering of energies and goods takes the place of economic logic'.[22] Other social themes embraced in Berio's musical theatre include contemporary society's neglectful treatment of the dying, and modern man's misplaced trust in technological and manufacturing science, emphasized, respectively, in O*pera* (1970) — an 'azione scenica' which gravitates around the theme of death — by references to a current New York production of a play called *Terminal* by Jo Chaskin's Open Theatre, and allusions to the sinking of the Titanic. Like O*pera*, *Un re in ascolto* (1979–84) is also very much a metapoetic work, containing allusions to theatre, and commenting upon the genre itself: in its Shakespearean text written by Calvino and re-worked by Berio, the King Prospero is striving to realise his vision of 'another theatre' before he dies, and he dies alone on an empty stage at the end of the work. For Berio, however, music theatre was a natural development of his own musical style, rather than an adopted *genre*. Pieces like *Circles* (1960) and indeed even some of the *Sequenzas* for solo instruments composed in the 60s, have a strong theatrical element. In *Circles*, a setting for voice and percussion of poems by e. e. cummings, the mezzo-soprano moves in a circle around the stage as she sings a circularly structured piece of music where three poems are broken down into phonetic parts, and then reconstructed. The work blurs the boundary lines between concert performance and musical theatre. Similarly, in the *Sequenza* solos the attention is less focussed on the music than it is on the dramatic intensity of the solo, virtuoso performer: *Sequenza III* (1965–66) demands a series of extravagant vocal fireworks; in *Sequenza IV* (1965–66) the pianist is required to play arduously difficult music with his feet, as well as his hands; and *Sequenza VI* (1967) for viola, involves some spectacular and unorthodox bowing techniques. The emphasis in each is clearly on the solo performance as a 'spectacle' with highly charged dramatic possibilities.

This blurring of the boundary lines between solo and concert performances, and musical theatre was also sometimes symptomatic of other European compositions, like Hans Werner Henze's *H. M. Enzensberger: Hommage à Gödel* of 1971 for bass baritone, violin, thirty-three instruments, and a tape, and György Ligeti's *Aventures* (1962) and *Nouvelles aventures* (1962–65) for voice and chamber ensemble. The latter two existed as concert works before their composer glimpsed their theatrical potential and added scenarios in 1966. A much clearer definition of music theatre as, quite simply, small-scale dramatic works comprising music, text, and gesture, emerged in Britain under Peter Maxwell Davies (b. 1934) and Harrison Birtwistle (b. 1934), who, for the purposes of promoting the genre and performing their own repertory, together formed the Pierrot players. Maxwell Davies' *Eight Songs for a Mad King* (1969) drew on Schoenberg's original *Pierrot lunaire* in its presentation of madness — in the British composition, the mad King George III is hounded by the musicians in his own ensemble. Birtwistle's *Down by the Greenwood Side* (1969), a 'dramatic pastoral' about the passing of the seasons, with strong folk and ballad elements, is more in the vein of Stravinsky's ritual theatre works.

By the mid-70s music theatre had almost entirely died out, and those 'azioni sceniche' that were still been written (such as Nono's aforementioned *Al gran sole*, 1972–74, and Maderna's *Satyricon*, 1974) tended to be larger in scale than the norm, and bordering on the definitions of 'opera', thereby suggesting that music theatre had only existed as a temporary measure, as a means of tentatively approaching once again the operatic genre.

Notes to Chapter 1

1. Machlis is one of the few musicologists who insists upon a distinction between the two terms. According to Machlis, 'Classicism' embraces 'artists of diverse temperaments all over Europe', whereas 'Neo-Classicism' 'is a narrower term which came to be applied to the music written by Stravinsky, Hindemith, and other composers during the 1920s and 30s' (by whom he means, Bartók, Milhaud, Honegger, Prokofiev, Copland, and Roger Sessions). The distinction, in some respects, causes even further confusion, for as Machlis himself notes, Stravinsky considered the label 'Neo-Classicist' as inaccurate one, since he and other so-called 'Neo-Classicists' were influenced by the late Baroque, and not the Classical era proper. J. Machlis, *Introduction to Contemporary Music* (London: J. M. Dent & Son, 1961), p. 160.

2. *The New Grove Dictionary of Music*, ed. by S. Sadie (London: Macmillan, 2001), p. 753.

3. Stravinsky's *Pulcinella* is based on music by Pergolesi, with the exception of the aria 'Se tu m'ami', composed by Alessandro Parisotti in the nineteenth century, but which for many years was believed to be a Pergolesi original.

4. A. Casella, *I segreti della giara* (Florence: Sansoni, 1941), p. 219.

5. F. Malipiero, *Tutte le opere di Monteverdi* (Nel Vittoriale degli Italiani, 1926–42).

6. F. Malipiero, *Antonio Vivaldi: Opere* (Milan: Ricordi, 1947).

7. See *L'opera di Gian Francesco Malipiero*, con una introduzione di Guido M. Gatti (Edizioni di Treviso, 1952), pp. 277–81.

8. Boulez's 'total serialization' was heavily influenced by the second of Messiaen's *Four Studies of Rhythms*, entitled 'Mode de valeurs et d'intensités' (1949), a piano work which applies serial organization to duration and loudness as well as to pitch.

9. D. Kämper, *Luigi Dallapiccola* (Florence: Sansoni, 1985), p. 36.

10. R. Smith Brindle, *Autobiography*, chapter 25. Quoted in <http://www.musicweb.uk.net/brindle/autobio25.htm>, pp. 1–8 (p.1).

11. A comment recorded in E. Helm, 'Luigi Dallapiccola in einem unveröffentlichten Gespräch', *Melos NZ*, II, 6 (Nov-Dec, 1976), 469.

12. See H. Nathan, 'Luigi Dallapiccola: Fragments from Conversations', *The Music Review*, XXVII, 4 November (1966), 294–312 (p. 296).

13. A piece could be written for twelve wind instruments, divided, for example, into three groups of four clarinets (a B flat, A, bass B flat, and high E flat clarinet),or four different flutes (standard concert, piccolo, alto, and 'drum and fife' band flute), or four different oboes (standard, oboe d'amore, oboe da caccia, and French baritone oboe).

14. P. Griffiths, *Modern Music* (London: Thames and Hudson, 1978), p. 144

15. See M. Romito, 'Quadrivium', in *Dialogo con Maderna*, ed. by M. Raimondo (Milan: Rai, 1989), pp. 128–32 (pp. 128–29).

16. Cage's pieces for prepared piano could have been influenced by Cowell's 'piano-tone-clusters', played by striking the keys with the flat of the hand, the forearm, or with wood blocks, and /or by the technique also used by Cowell of plucking and playing the piano strings as one would play a harp.

17. E. Salzman, *Twentieth-Century Music* (New Jersey: Prentice-Hall, 1967), p. 163.

18. Quoted in G. Abraham, *The Concise Oxford History of Music* (Oxford: Oxford University Press, 1990), p. 853.

19. The influence exists in Boulez's *Third Sonata* (1957), whose individual sections Boulez assembled, in performance, in different combinations. In *Domaines* (1961–68) for clarinet and

orchestra, the concept of mobility is taken even further, for not only is the order of the musical sections moved around from performance to performance, but the clarinettist also *physically* moves among six groups of players placed at different points on the stage. Watkins points out that this technique of spatialization was also one previously advocated by Cage, who once said: 'There is the possibility when people are crowded together that they will act like sheep rather than nobly. That is why separation in space is spoken of as facilitating independent action on the part of each performer'. G. Watkins, *Soundings. Music in the Twentieth Century* (New York: Schirmer Books, Glenn Watkins, 1988), p. 563.

20. Quoted in F. Routh, *Contemporary Music* (London: The English Universities Press, 1968), p. 119.
21. Quoted in 'Luciano Berio', *The Times*, 28 May 2003, p. 30 (anonymous obituary).
22. Quoted in D. Osmond-Smith, *Berio* (Oxford: Oxford University Press, 1992), p. 99.

FIG. 2.1. Photograph of Luigi Dallapiccola. Courtesy of Sugarmusic SpA — Milano

CHAPTER 2

Luigi Dallapiccola's *Ulisse* (1960–68)

Dallapiccola: Works and Method

Luigi Dallapiccola (1904–75) studied at the Cherubini Conservatory in Florence, where he joined the teaching staff in 1934. Making Florence his home-town, he taught at the Conservatory until 1967, but frequently travelled abroad especially to the USA, both as a concert pianist and as a teacher and internationally recognized lecturer.[1]

In addition to the writing of three operas (*Volo di notte*, 1937–39; *Il prigioniero*, 1944–48; and *Ulisse*, 1960–68) Dallapiccola has produced a mystery play, a ballet, an oratorio, a number of songs, choral pieces, pieces for piano, pieces for cello, and a multitude of compositions for orchestra, chorus and orchestra, ensemble, and solo voice and ensemble (see bibliography, pp. 274–75). Musically, his work contains a curious mixture of experimentalism and traditionalism. As explained in Chapter 1, with *Divertimento*, written in 1934, he first displayed an attraction for the dodecaphonic method, and although relatively speaking this might seem quite late (Schoenberg having 'created' the system in 1924) it was, in fact, much earlier than his Italian contemporaries — Nono, Maderna, Berio, and Manzoni — who only began to practice serialism in the post-war, avant-garde years. However, while being known as the most distinguished Italian twelve-tone composer, Dallapiccola's compositions often bear the heavy influence of early Italian music. Some of his works combine this interest in the old and the new. While the first two of the *Sei cori di Michelangelo Buonarotti il Giovane* (1933–36), for example, have been noticeably influenced by the Italian madrigalists, the remaining four find their inspiration in Busoni. Furthermore, Dallapiccola's brand of Serialism was never the purely academic variety. Rather he imbued the 'Germanic' serial methods with a singing lyricism and an 'Italian' feel for melody, and he sometimes even applied tonal devices within the framework of the dodecaphonic system.

The predominant theme of his libretti — all of which he wrote himself — is liberty. This preoccupation with liberty, or its related opposite, imprisonment, is suggested in many of the titles of his works (e.g. *Canti di prigionia*, 1938–41, *Il prigioniero*, 1944–48, *Canti di liberazione*, 1951–55), and it surfaced in Dallapiccola's teens. At the time of his birth, his native town, Pisino in Istria, was a piece of disputed territory under the Austro-Hungarian Empire (it was eventually transferred to Italy in 1918). In 1917, Dallapiccola's father, who was the headmaster of the only Italian language school in Pisino, was suspected by the Austrian authorities of Italian nationalism, and under the accusation of running a subversive school, was forcibly moved with his family to Graz, where for a period they remained interned. This incident also accounts for the political associations sometimes attached to Dallapiccola's treatment of 'liberty'. The *Canti di prigionia*, for example (whose libretto is made up of Latin texts by Savonarola and Boethius, and of prayers by Mary, Queen of Scots written during one of the last years of her imprisonment) was composed in protest against Mussolini's call for an anti-Semitic campaign in Italy, and is a fervent denunciation of war. *Il prigioniero* focuses on the illusory nature of freedom, and was inspired by Dallapiccola's reading of the short story *La Torture par l'espérance,* 1891, by Villiers de l'Isle-Adam. Both the story and the libretto have as their background the religious wars of the Spanish Inquisition. In the libretto an anonymous prisoner, condemned to death by the Inquisition, is cruelly tricked by his gaoler into believing that he is being released. The prisoner offers no resistance as he is 'recaptured' and led to the stake, muttering only the words 'la libertà?' [liberty?].

Ulisse: 'opera "non attuale"'?

In view of the 'engaged' nature of these well-known compositions by Dallapiccola, and the political associations of others (such as the last two choruses of the *Sei cori,* and the *Tre laudi,* see pp. 14–15), the audience at the Berlin premiere of *Ulisse* (29 September, 1968) remained shocked by his new opera's very personal treatment of the Ulysses myth, and its apparent lack of relation to any political or social issues. The date chosen for the premiere was not exactly a timely one, for a few months earlier there had been protests in American universities against the Vietnam War, followed by the student uprisings in Paris in May 1968. For its 'pura esposizione di convinzioni private e personali' [mere exposition of private and personal convictions] Dallapiccola's *Ulisse* was condemned as an 'opera "non attuale"' [an opera of no topical interest].[2] It was this criticism which the composer attempted to address in his programme notes for the first performance of the opera at La Scala (13 January, 1970) (*Appunti,* pp. 189–91). Here he quotes from an article by Saul Bellow, published a few days before the Berlin premiere, in the Hamburg weekly *Die Zeit.* Discussing the situation of contemporary literature, Bellow complains that the art of narrating has been substituted by social and political journalism, with authors taking as their material political campaigns, political scandal, wars, youth movements, racial disorder etc. All such themes, according to Bellow, take precedence over subjects such as religion, philosophy, personal feelings, and love. The story-teller relates 'events'; he no longer has any personal philosophy or inner 'truth' to share with his readers. Dallapiccola claims that his opera is a 'narrative' work of the type favoured by Bellow, offering a personal philosophy of life rather than a comment upon social or political 'events'; and that in this troubled world, the former is to be desired and sought after more than the latter. His Ulysses is 'l'uomo alla ricerca di se stesso e del significato della vita' (*Appunti,* p. 190) [man searching for himself and the meaning of life], and the liberty Ulysses achieves at the end of his opera is a psychological one. Given that man across the ages has always been searching for a life-philosophy, Dallapiccola argues that his *Ulisse* can also be considered 'in chiave di attualità' (*Appunti,* p. 191) [in a topical light].

The libretto: influences and inspirations

Another problem for the audience at the Berlin premiere of *Ulisse* was, according to Dallapiccola, its lack of familiarity with Dante's interpretation of Ulysses. Reviews mentioned Hamlet and Faust, but none of them spoke of Dante, and, as the composer explained, 'il mio personaggio prende, in parte, le mosse da quello di Dante' (*Appunti*, p. 190) [my character is partly modelled on Dante's]. Obviously, none of the critics present at the Berlin premiere had heard or read Dallapiccola's paper entitled 'The Birth of a Libretto' presented in English on 4 October, 1967 at Ann Arbor, on the occasion of the composer being awarded a doctorate of music from the University of Michigan. In 1968, a German version appeared in the August edition of the journal *Melos,* and in 1970 an Italian rendition, entitled 'Nascita di un libretto d'opera', was published in *Appunti* (pp. 171–87) mentioning the part played by Dante in shaping the libretto: 'Bisogna tener conto che a noi, italiani, il personaggio di Ulisse è arrivato filtrato attraverso l'interpretazione dantesca' ('Nascita', p. 179) [One has to take into account that, for us Italians, the character of Ulysses was filtered down through Dante's interpretation]. In addition, he lists (but does not address his reasons for choosing) a rich variety of other authors spanning the medieval and the modern age who, in different ways, also inspired *Ulisse*: Aeschylus, St Augustine, Hölderlin, Tennyson, Nietzsche, Cavafy, Pascoli, Machado, Mann, and Joyce. While the quotation from St Augustine (a *postscriptum* to the libretto) is presented in its original Latin, all of the other writers are briefly quoted or paraphrased in Italian translation, and incorporated unobtrusively into the text of the libretto which is in verse, sometimes rhyming, and sometimes not. As Dallapiccola remarks, the catalogue of sources listed above is not exhaustive ('e con ciò non penso affatto di aver esaurito l'elenco delle fonti del mio libretto', 'Nascita', p. 186) [and that is certainly not an exhaustive list of the sources of my libretto], and indeed most of the abundant literary influences, apart from Dante and Tennyson, are spread thinly across the text, for it was Dallapiccola's intention to create a monumental work of the twentieth century, incorporating as vast and as varied a literary panorama as possible.[3] It is for this reason that this chapter, while focusing upon Dante and Tennyson, will include some consideration of most of the influences listed in 'Nascita', exploring how they fit together, and how they contribute to the composer's interpretation of the Ulysses myth — something which no criticism to date has attempted to address.[4]

Before any interpretative process can begin, however, some attempt must be made to summarize Dallapiccola's opera. The bow-shaped, annotated diagram, included by Dallapiccola himself in 'Nascita', and which highlights the symmetrical division of the opera into thirteen episodes, helps to clarify the picture (see Figure 2.2; for further explication of Figure 2.2, see pp. 55–56). The summary here will be accompanied by a brief indication of the literary influences, and where exactly they occur. The remainder of this chapter will focus upon certain of these influences and explain how they are used by Dallapiccola to carve out the image of a tormented Ulysses who symbolizes modern man, and for whom Dallapiccola posits a religious answer to the problems of existence.

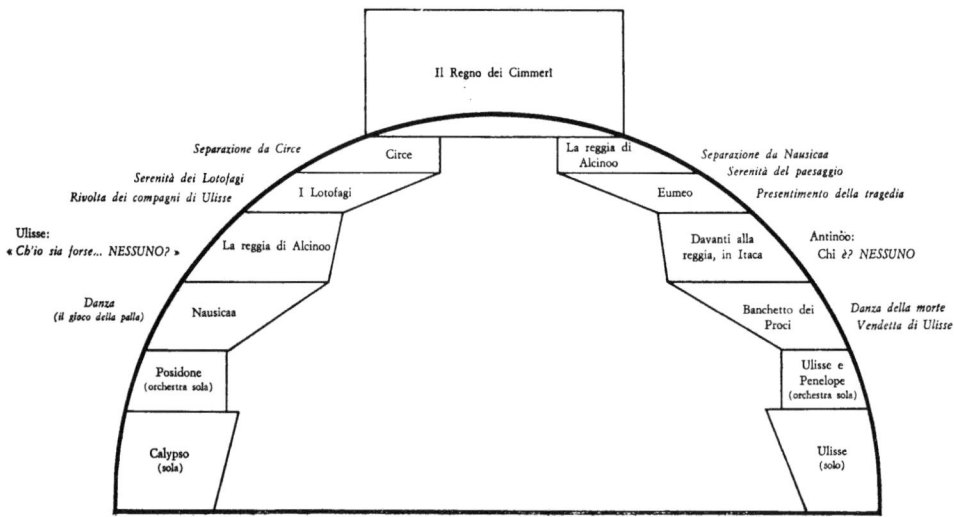

FIG. 2.2. Diagram by Luigi Dallapiccola illustrating the structure of *Ulisse*.
From L. Dallapiccola, 'Nascita di un libretto d'opera',
in *Appunti, Incontri, Meditazioni* (Milan: Suvini Zerboni, 1970), pp. 171–87 (p. 183).
Courtesy of Sugarmusic SpA — Milano.

The opera: a synopsis, and indications of intertextuality

Dallapiccola's *Ulisse* offers a reduced version of the events recounted by Homer in Books v to xxiv of *The Odyssey* (Books i to iv are omitted). Although the text spoken by characters within these episodes differs a great deal from that found in Homer, and most episodes are imbued with the multi-cultural influences already mentioned, the work, from an episodic point of view, is more or less Homeric. Whereas this study will have cause to touch upon certain aspects of Homer (not discussed in 'Nascita'), comparing and contrasting them with Dallapiccola's text, it is not intended as a full comparative study of Homer's *The Odyssey* and Dallapiccola's *Ulisse*.

Ulisse opens with the Calypso episode of Book v of Homer's *The Odyssey,* and Dallapiccola uses it as the first of three scenes in a Prologue. The goddess Calypso (soprano), who has kept Ulysses captive on the island of Ogygia for seven years, stands lonely and weeping on the shore, lamenting that the hero has now left her, in spite of the fact that she offered to make him immortal. Recognizing Ulysses' craving for the sea and solitude, her monologue opens and closes with the simple but poignant sentence 'Son soli, un'altra volta,/ il tuo cuore e il mare' [your heart and the sea/ are alone again], a line, as Dallapiccola explains ('Nascita', p.185), based on a phrase from poem cxix in Machado's *Campos de Castilla*, 1912, to be discussed later: 'Señor, ya estámos solos mi corazón y el mar' [Lord, now my heart and the sea are alone].[5] However, in a motif which becomes central to the whole of the opera, she claims not to understand the nature of Ulysses' endless searching: '*Guardare, meravigliarsi,/ e tornar a guardare*' [To look, to marvel,/ and look again].

The second episode of the Prologue is a piece for orchestra alone, entitled 'Posidone'. It depicts the angry persecution of Ulysses by Poseidon, the god of the sea, in the form of perilous storms which prevent his homecoming.

The Prologue ends with the Nausicaa episode (*The Odyssey,* Book vi). On a wooded beach on the island of Phaeacia, Nausicaa (high soprano), daughter of Alcinous, the King of the Phaeacians, lies apart from her frolicking companions. When asked why she is so silent and unwilling to join in the ball game, she recounts how her future husband, whom she did not recognize, appeared and spoke to her in a dream, hailing her in the following words: '"Luce sei che squarcia un velo / di fitte nubi; bianco giglio sei/ sull'acque in furia: vollero gli Dei/ far di te rosa sorta in mezzo al gelo/ d'inverno"' [You are sunlight that pierces a veil / of thick clouds; you are a white lily/ on turbulent water; the Gods ordained you/ to be a rose blooming among the frosts/ of winter] (the lines are a paraphrase of a religious inscription Dallapiccola spotted in the Duomo in Florence: 'Quasi arcus refulgens inter nebulas,/ Quasi flos rosarum in diebus vernis/ Quasi lilia in transitu aquae', 'Like a light ripping open a veil of thick cloud,/ A rose blossoming in the midst of winter's ice/ And a white lily on furious waters', 'Nascita', p. 187). Ulysses (baritone) emerges from the wood, and Nausicaa recognizes him as the man of her dream. He kneels before the princess, marvelling at her peerless beauty, and she orders him to rise and leads him to her father's palace.

Act i has five scenes and hinges on events spanning Books vii to xii in Homer. Scenes i and v mirror each other in that they both take place in the palace of

Alcinous, and they act as a framework for the scenes in-between in which Ulysses recounts his seafaring adventures. The drama inherent in the adventures is reinforced by singing and speaking choirs amplified by strategically placed loudspeakers in the dome, in the auditorium, and near the stage.

In scene I Ulysses arrives in Alcinous's palace as a large banquet is underway, and the blind but visionary bard, Demodocus (tenor), is singing with his lyre of the hardships encountered by the Greeks after the fall of Troy. He predicts the murder of Agamemnon by Aegisthus, the lover of Agamemnon's wife, Clytaemnestra (Dallapiccola, as will be shown later, here draws on Aeschylus's *Agamemnon*, 458 B.C.), and speaks of blood and remorse. He foretells Ulysses's return to Ithaca where no one would recognize him anymore (the word 'nessuno' [nobody], which is to constitute another leitmotif in the work, is repeated by Demodocus and the choir several times). Ulysses is moved to tears by Demodocus's song, and his weeping attracts the attention of Alcinous who asks him his name. 'Io sono ... Ulisse' [I am ...Ulysses], he answers, but adds almost immediately, 'Ch'io sia forse ... Nessuno?' [Perhaps I am ...Nobody?] (thereby echoing the Cyclops's episode in Homer). Disregarding Ulysses' self-deprecation, Alcinous hails him as a great and glorious hero and invites him to recount his adventures at sea.

Scene II depicts Ulysses' ship as it approaches the island of the Lotus-eaters (boys' voices). It is morning time. Ulysses exhorts his timorous men to take courage, and avoids a mutiny by appealing to their sense of manhood. The song of the Lotus-eaters can be heard in the distance, composed of idyllic images of nature drawn from Tennyson's poem of 1832, 'The Lotos-Eaters' (the spelling is Tennyson's), to be examined later. Then the islanders appear. Drugged through their eating of the lotus fruit, they proffer their fruit in an attempt to entice Ulysses' men away from their world of toil and obligation toward one of dreams and sensual escape. In a sequence where Dallapiccola paraphrases two lines from Hölderlin's 'Hyperions Schiksaalslied', 1800 ('Hyperion's Song of Fate') ('Nascita', p.186) they promote their condition of unconscious happiness: 'Prendetene con noi..., senza destino/ vi sentirete inconsciamente lieti,/ come quando, bambini, dormivate' [Come share it with us ...you will feel free from ill fortune,/ unconsciously happy,/ like when babies you lay asleep] (in Hölderlin 'Schiksaallos, wie der schlafende/ Säugling, athmen die Himmlischen', 'Fateless the Heavenly breathe,/ like an unweaned infant asleep').[6] In spite of Ulysses' orders to his men not to touch the fruit, a few of them are won over. The others hastily re-embark with their leader, and as the Lotus-eaters once again intone their song, the stage darkens over.

After an orchestral interlude, scene III opens on the luxurious island of Aeaea, home to Circe who is lying asleep on the grass, while Ulysses stares longingly out to sea. When Ulysses announces his intention to leave, she attempts to stop him with a series of statements which are alternately wily, elusive, and seductive. When these tactics fail, she resorts to revenge by bestowing upon Ulysses an awareness of the fact that the monsters and tempests he encountered on his journeys were mere embodiments of his own inner nature: 'porti in te stesso tutte le tempeste; e la coscienza d'esse che ti ho dato/ sia la vendetta della Maga' [you carry all the tempests within yourself; and may this awareness of them that I have given you /

be the revenge of the sorceress]. The idea is a crucial one for an understanding of the opera as a whole (as will be seen later), and, as explained in 'Nascita' (p.176), is inspired by Cavafy's poem 'Ithaka', 1911 ('Ithaca') in which the poet informs the reader that on the voyage to Ithaca, symbolic of the journey of life, 'Laistrygonians and Cyclops,/ wild Poseidon– you won't encounter them/ unless you bring them along inside your soul,/ unless your soul sets them up in front of you'.[7] The scene ends with Circe predicting that Ulysses will reach Ithaca but that, old and dissatisfied, he will set sail once more (as in Tennyson's 'Ulysses').

In scene IV Ulysses descends to Hell to question the ghost of the seer, Teiresias, about his future destiny. On a desolate riverbank the shades of the Underworld wander, locked in a mindless repetitive chant: 'Pianto, rimorso, eterno soffrire .../ Pianto, lacrime .../ Sempre il buio; mai la luce. Sempre soffrire; mai sperare ...' [Weeping, repenting, eternal suffering ... / Weeping, tears ... / For ever the darkness; never the light. Always suffering; never to hope]. Their 'Sempre [...] mai' refrain deliberately echoes the 'ever [...] never' repetition in the terrifying hell-fire sermon delivered by Fr Arnall in Joyce's *A Portrait of the Artist as a Young Man,* 1916 (see 'Nascita', p. 186). Here, after the formula of Ignatius Loyola, the priest coldly and systematically describes the odours, sights and sounds of hell and of all of its pains: 'ever, never; ever, never. Ever to be in hell, never to be in heaven; ever to be shut off from the presence of God, never to enjoy the beatific vision'.[8] Unexpectedly, Ulysses encounters his mother Anticleia (soprano) who blames her son's departure from Ithaca for her heartache, anxiety, and subsequent death (in his writing of this scene Dallapiccola claims to have been influenced by Mont-kaw's deathbed speech to Jacob in Thomas Mann's *Joseph und seine Brüder,* 1933–42 (*Joseph and his Brothers*), to be discussed later). Ulysses attempts to embrace her, but her intangible shadow escapes his arms and fades away, at which point, in a line which echoes Nietzsche (*Beyond Good and Evil,* 1886), the protagonist proclaims his sense of utter loneliness: 'Solo. Son solo. Un uomo/ che guarda nel fondo dell'abisso...' [Alone. I am alone. A man/ gazing into the depths of the abyss...] (in Nietzsche, 'And when you gaze long into an abyss, the abyss also gazes into you').[9] Teiresias (tenor, doubling Demodocus) comes forth and, like Circe, foretells that Ulysses will eventually reach home and see his wife and son, but his homecoming will be bloody, and he will push his boat out once more.

Scene V returns to Alcinous's palace. Ulysses concludes his narrative with brief references to Scylla, Charybdis, and his men's fatal slaughter of the cattle of the sun god, Hyperion. Alcinous promises Ulysses a safe escort back to Ithaca, and Ulysses and Nausicaa bid each other a poignant farewell.

In Act II is set in Ithaca, and hinges on Books XII to XXIV of Homer. In Scene I, three of Penelope's suitors, Antinous (baritone), Eurymachus (tenor), and Peisander (baritone) have arranged to have Ulysses' son, Telemachus, killed on his return from Sparta. On the mountain-tops they wait expectantly for news of his death. When they leave, Ulysses, disguised as a beggar, enters and receives hospitality from Eumaeus (tenor), his old and faithful swineherd. Eumaeus vents his spleen against Eurymachus's lover, Melantho (mezzo-soprano, doubling Circe), who, terrified by Ulysses' eyes, hastens back to the palace. Telemachus rushes in, describing his escape, but does not recognize his father.

Scene II depicts a courtyard before the palace. Ulysses, whose original bow can be seen hanging from a column, hides in the shadows and meditates on the disillusionment of return: 'Tristezza del ritorno' [the sadness of return]. Melantho, obsessed by the beggar with the terrifying eyes, tries to convince Antinous that some terrible danger threatens, but the latter dismisses Ulysses as 'un vecchio,/ un senza nome' [an old,/ nameless man']. Together they mock Penelope (soprano, doubling Calypso) who, from inside the palace, can be heard singing and weaving. Their jeering provokes Ulysses who emerges from his hiding place. Melantho is once again panic-stricken by his eyes in which she reads hatred, revenge, and their condemnation, but Antinous dismisses Ulysses as an animal incapable of human emotions. Ulysses in a monologue swears his revenge.

Scene III opens with the suitors banqueting, and Antinous toasting the 'death' of Telemachus. Melantho is asked to dance and is given Ulysses' bow as inspiration. As her lascivious dancing reaches a climax the string of the bow becomes twisted around her neck, provoking her to scream. As she screams, Telemachus enters, followed closely by Ulysses who has abandoned his beggar's disguise, and reveals his identity. He orders the servants to hang Melantho; then strings the bow that only he can use, and kills the suitors one by one, starting with Antinous. As the crowds race for the doors, Penelope suddenly appears, calling Ulysses' name, and they stare at each other intently.

After a symphonic intermezzo, the Epilogue sees Ulysses alone on a tiny boat in the middle of the sea, far from Ithaca. It is a starry night. Now, he remarks, there are no furies or sea-gods to take revenge on him for those he has murdered; rather, as Circe predicted, the monsters that gnaw at his heart are within him. In all of his wanderings, he has gained neither peace nor knowledge, and invoking the stars that he contemplated under so many different skies, he prays for a Word, Name, or Voice that would clarify his misdirected life. The opera ends with Ulysses being suddenly accorded a prophetic vision of God. Reversing the words with which Calypso opens the opera, he proclaims: 'Signore! Non più soli sono/ il mio cuore e il mare!' [Almighty one! My heart and the sea/ are no longer alone!]. The libretto (as Dallapiccola explains in 'Nascita', p.187) closes with a 'post scriptum', a quotation from St Augustine's *Confessions*, A.D. 397: 'Fecisti nos ad te et inquietum est cor nostrum, donec requiescat in te' [You made us in your image, and our hearts are restless until they find their peace in thee'].[10]

Dallapiccola's religious vision

This is a far cry from Homer's pagan Odysseus, and, at first sight, the influence of Dante (to be discussed in depth shortly) is not entirely apparent either. For whereas Dante's Ulysses (*Inferno*, XXVI), was condemned partly for his hubris or his challenging of God (symbolized in his attempt to go beyond the Pillars of Hercules), Dallapiccola's Ulysses discovers God, and is, presumably, redeemed. Religious interpretations of the Ulysses myth do not, of course, begin with Dallapiccola. As explained in Stanford's *The Ulysses Theme*,[11] Christian readings or new Christian versions of the *Odyssey* date as far back as the seventeenth century. In 1655 Jacopo

Ugone claimed that in the second half of the *Odyssey* Odysseus represented St Peter, while Penelope stood for the Mother Church, menaced by Reformers in the guise of her suitors. Chapman, in the preface to his translation of the *Odyssey* published in 1616, interprets Homer's Odysseus as 'the most sustaining, patient, heavenly man [...] the wise and God-observing man [...] whose genius turns, through many and various ways, towards the truth' (Stanford, p. 184). Calderón de la Barca's *Los encantos de la culpa*, 1635, makes his Ulysses undergo arduous theological disputations with Circe, the personification of sin, and after much confession and repentance, he becomes fully christianized and sails away toward his salvation.

Unlike Calderón, however, Dallapiccola does not present one with the picture of a God-like or God-fearing man, striving morally and virtuously after the truth. Rather what one sees is mostly a tortured, guilt-ridden, existentialist, anti-hero. Apart from the Epilogue where Ulysses has his vision of God, there is nothing about Dallapiccola's work which is overtly religious; even the revelation itself is sudden and completely unexpected, so that, like Ulysses, the reader-spectator experiences it as, precisely, a revelation. Nevertheless, that the libretto has a religious slant would seem to be suggested by the list of writers who played some part in its creation. The majority of them are preoccupied in some manner or other with the question of religion, and could be divided into three categories: those who have indicated clear religious beliefs in their writings (St Augustine, Dante, Tennyson); those noted for their anti-religious stances (Nietzsche); and those who occupy a middle ground, adopting a questioning view vis-à-vis religion (Hölderlin, Cavafy, Machado, Mann, and Joyce). Like Penelope weaving her textiles, Dallapiccola manages to thread together these seemingly disconnected writers writing in different, disconnected ages to provide a modern image of man and man's life, symbolized by Ulysses. He also manages to make allusions to 'anti-religious' or religiously sceptical writers rest unobtrusively beside references to strongly religious ones. This very process of weaving *connections*, as we shall see later, underlines a fundamental aspect of Dallapiccola's religious vision, and it is an aspect that is considered in both Tennyson's and Dante's texts on Ulysses, namely a belief in the value and primacy of *interaction* over isolation and the glorification of the isolated self — interaction between men, and between men and God. It is precisely this concept of interacting and connecting which is emphasized in the opera's final line. Here the detachment and loneliness which characterized Ulysses after the Circe episode, and which are suggested in Calypso's opening comment on him — '*Son soli*, un'altra volta,/ il tuo cuore e il mare'– are inverted in Ulysses' final exclamation: 'Signore!/ *Non più soli* sono/ il mio cuore e il mare' (the italics are mine).

On the whole it would be true to say that the libretto, in spite of its diverse influences, is grounded in existentialist thought. In fact, the religious element in the libretto and the existentialist attitude of the protagonist come together in the allusions which the opera seems to make to the philosophical writings of Kierkegaard (1813–55) whose work became increasingly influential in Central Europe during and immediately after the First World War, and eventually acquired international importance through its associations with existentialism which emerged as a major philosophical movement in the 1930s and 1940s.[12] Although *Ulisse* contains no actual quotations from Kierkegaard, it emphasizes his insistence on the importance of subjectivity and inwardness (*inderlighed*) in the quest for religious truth; and Ulysses' religious revelation in the Epilogue is in exact accordance with Kierkegaard's thesis that one gains knowledge of God, not through rational philosophy or theology, but through a 'leap of faith' or moment of enlightenment.

It is to be emphasized, however, that although Dallapiccola's vision seems to be influenced by Kierkegaard's belief in the miraculous character of religious faith, it is not, unlike Kierkegaard's, a strictly Christian vision, nor, for that matter, a Catholic one. This becomes evident in Dallapiccola's diary entry of 3 October, 1968, when, referring to the newspaper reviews of the Berlin premiere of *Ulisse*, he writes 'Ho dato un'occhiata a qualche critica. Resto sorpreso nel vedere come non uno abbia capito che la scoperta di Dio del mio Ulisse non significa affatto che sia diventato cristiano cattolico apostolico romano' [*Saggi*, p. 136] [I've glanced at some of the reviews. I am surprised to see that not one critic has understood that the discovery of God on the part of my Ulysses does not in any way mean that he has become a Catholic, Apostolic, Roman Christian]. Moreover, none of the criticism in articles or book-length publications on Dallapiccola specifies or labels Dallapiccola's religiousness in any way: Wolf Eberhard von Lewinski, for example, speaks of the opera's '*professione di fede* in cui confluiscono, in gran copia, riflessione filosofica, cultura e saggezza' (*Saggi*, p. 29); [profession of faith in which there meets in great abundance philosophical reflexion, culture, and wisdom] while Giuseppe Magnani remarks how 'l'intera vicenda dell'*Ulisse* appaia delinearsi quale progressiva *manifestazione di una essenza divina*, in origine nascosta e inaccessibile'[13] (the italics are mine) [the whole action of *Ulysses* seems to unfold as a progressive manifestation of a divine essence, originally hidden and inaccessible].

Before and after Circe: The Ulysses of Homer and Dante, versus the Modern Existentialist

Crucial to an understanding of Dallapiccola's opera is his version of the Circe episode. For it is Circe's strange vendetta — her bestowing upon Ulysses an awareness or consciousness of how his inner nature can effect his own life, and going hand in hand with that consciousness, a moral and religious conscience (her use of the term 'coscienza' is to be interpreted in both senses) — which transforms Ulysses from the self-important and remorseless man of action to be found in Homer, to a 'modern', self-doubting figure, full of searching and existentialist questioning. After Circe, Ulysses suffers from 'an unrest, an inner strife, a disharmony [...] an anxiety about himself' (*SD*, p. 22) — the Kierkegaardian definition of *Angst*. Speaking of Circe's curse, Dallapiccola himself says 'Da questo momento Ulisse sembra diventare definitivamente un'altra persona' ('Nascita', p. 177) [From that moment Ulysses seems definitely to become another person]. This transformation in character is even announced by Dallapiccola's protagonist himself when, in revealing his identity to Alcinous, he juxtaposes what he once was with what he now considers himself to be: 'Io sono Ulisse./ Eroe glorioso fui: ora son polvere./ Sovrano, or mi vedete ramingare./ Chi'io sia forse ... *Nessuno*?' (I, i) [I am Ulysses./ I once was a famous hero: now I am dust./ I once was a king, now you see before you a wanderer./ Perhaps I am ... Nobody?]. That Ulysses's depiction of himself as he was in the past — a glorious hero and king — is meant to concur with the classical portrait of the hero described in Homer, is reinforced by a comparison with Odysseus's boastful revelation of his identity to Alcinous in Homer's Odyssey: 'I am Odysseus, Laertes's son. The whole world talks of my stratagems, and my fame has reached the heavens'.[14] This is the scheming, vainglorious, and slightly self-righteous hero of *The Odyssey*; the Odysseus who, having cold-bloodedly blinded Polyphemus with a burning stake, and tricked him and his fellow Cyclops by calling himself 'Nobody', can, with typical self-approbation, 'laugh at the way in which 'his' cunning notion of a false name had taken them in' (p. 136); and who, having slain the suitors, remorselessly claims that it was 'their transgressions' which 'brought them to this ignominious death' (p. 341). To reinforce the transition from this classical figure to its modern inversion, Dallapiccola cleverly makes his Ulysses also refer to himself as 'Nobody', but whereas in Homer the term reinforces Odysseus's cunning, in Dallapiccola it only underlines Ulysses' spiritual destitution and his existentialist sense of unimportance. As Ulysses himself puts it in Act II, Scene II: 'Il mio nome che un giorno trasformai/ per astuzia, ritorna a me per scherno' [My name which I altered so cunningly one day,/ comes back to mock me'].

In fact there is only one scene — that of the Lotus-eaters — in Dallapiccola's opera which, recounted by Ulysses in the palace of Alcinous, pre-dates Ulysses' encounter with Circe, and where, prior to Circe's curse, one sees the classic Ulysses at work. The Ulysses of the Lotus-eaters is Homer's wily Ulysses, but also Dante's false counsellor, who has used his high mental gifts for guile, exhorting and beguiling his men to do something which *he* wishes (in Dallapiccola, disembark on the island of the Lotus-eaters; in Dante, go beyond the pillars of Hercules) and which is against *their* will and interests. Although in 'Nascita di un libretto d'opera', Dallapiccola does not provide one with any detailed indications of the influence of Dante on his libretto, he has obviously been influenced by Ulysses' speech in *Inferno* which displays a mastery in the art of persuasion, and he employs three of the techniques used by Dante's Ulysses to overcome his men's diffidence. In Dante, Ulysses begins by humouring his men, addressing them as 'frati' [brothers] in an attempt to make them feel not inferior, but on a par with him. He then proceeds to ask them not to deny the experience of 'the senses', to be interpreted both in its literal meaning, and symbolically as a request not to reject the possibility of gaining further wisdom and learning. In doing so, he manages to tempt their thirst for knowledge:

> A questa tanto picciola vigilia
> de' nostri sensi ch'è del rimanente,
> non vogliate negar l'esperienza.[15]

> [Do not choose to deny the experience/ of this so little vigil/ of the senses which remains.]

Finally, he presents their need to explore the 'mondo sanza gente' [unpopulated world] as a moral imperative (linking together 'virtute' [virtue] and 'canoscenza' [knowledge]) by reminding them of their superiority over animals:

> Considerate la vostra semenza:
> fatti non foste a viver come bruti,
> ma per seguir virtute e canoscenza. (118–20)

> [Consider the seed from which you were born:/ you were not made to live like brutes,/ but to follow virtue and knowledge.]

Dallapiccola's Ulysses, who begins his exhortation with the esclamatory 'Coraggio!' [Courage!], also flatters his men with friendly terms: guilefully, he calls them 'amici' [friends], and his speech is marked 'insinuante' [wheedling]. He appeals, in rhetorical fashion, first to their senses (smelling and hearing):

> È una tortura per le vostre nari
> l'odor del mare?
> [...]
> È tortura
> del mare udir le mille voci?

> [Do you suffer when you smell/ the scent of the sea?/ Do you suffer/ when you hear the thousand voices of the sea?]

And, as in Dante, he continues to suggest that this exploration of the senses acts as a metaphor for the seeking of knowledge itself (his use of the word 'guardare' echoes the aforementioned motif used in the opera to symbolize this quest: 'Guardare, meravigliarsi, e tornar a guardare'): Forse... forse è tortura anche guardare? [Perhaps... perhaps you suffer even to look?]. By ironically referring to this quest for knowledge as a 'torture', he arouses their indignation and incites them to pursue the quest further. Exactly like Dante's Ulysses, he concludes by reminding them that they are 'men', thereby provoking their sense of 'manhood': 'Allora/ ditemi pur ch'è tortura esser uomini!' [Then/ tell me that you even suffer to be men!]. When, having landed, some of Ulysses' men are seduced by the Lotus-eaters' promise of unconscious happiness and sensual escape, Ulysses attacks them precisely for their lack of manliness which has associated qualities of psychological strength and will power: 'Perduti! Sciagurati!/ Uomini voi non siete!' [You are lost! Foolish wretches!/ You are not men!]. That he, by contrast, owns these qualities, is then suggested in the decisive imperative he utters to the rest of his men — 'Seguitemi!' [Follow me!] — which harks back to the two imperatives with which he ordered his men to land on the island in the first place: 'Ascoltate!' [Listen!] (in reference to the Lotus-eaters' song), 'Approdiamo!' [Let us go ashore!]. These imperatives tally with the strong adverbs and adjectives used to describe Ulysses throughout the whole of the Lotus-eaters' episode: 'arditamente' [boldly], 'prorompendo' [in an outburst], 'decisamente' [decisively], and 'calmo' [calmly]. In the post-Circean scenes, by contrast, the most recurrent epithets are 'cupo' [dark], 'meditabondo' [meditating] (Act I, v), 'tormentato' [tormented], 'stanco' [tired] (Epilogue); and in Act I, Scene v, Ulysses even defines himself as 'fra tutti i mortali il più infelice' [the most unhappy of all mortals].

   In the Lotus-eaters' episode, therefore, Ulysses is still the self-confident and wily hero associated with Homer and Dante, free of the restrictions of a 'coscienza' [conscience]. In the post-Circean episodes, by contrast, he becomes diffident and inward-looking, and plagued by the stinging of conscience. Significantly, the scene which follows the Circe episode is Ulysses' descent into Hell, and it is to be interpreted not only literally, but also metaphorically as Ulysses' descent into his troubled psyche.

This, then, is Dallapiccola's modern Ulysses, epitomizing modern man: introverted ('cupo'), and conscience-stricken ('tormentato'); one who in his pursuit of knowledge and truth, thinks about life more than he acts upon it ('meditabondo'). The whole of the opera is a poetic reinforcement of this straightforward portrait of the modern condition. Against the portrait Dallapiccola pits the opposite image of Classical man: active, remorseless, and focussed on 'outer' rather than 'inner' realities such as sensual pleasures and material possessions. It is an opposition which bears similarity to Kierkegaard's presentation in *Either/Or* of two different ways of life, and his invitation to the reader to choose between them: the (preferred) 'ethical' route, on the one hand, which responds to the call of the spiritual and the transcendental, and which makes itself felt to the individual as *Angst*; and, on the other hand, the 'aesthetic', denoting the immediate life of the senses (epitomized by the figure of Don Juan), and an existence reliant upon 'external' factors, such as possessions or power. Like Kierkegaard in *Either/Or*, Dallapiccola's comparison between the meditative life in pursuit of truth, and the active life in pursuit of sensual pleasures allows the composer to offer his personal vision of a just and morally correct way of living for both man and the artist in society. It is a vision which, while promoting certain aspects of the modern condition — in particular, the development of an inner, self-critical nature — warns against the excessive solitude of that condition, a solitude which is posited as typifying the artist in society on his lonely crusade for knowledge. Elaborating upon themes already addressed by Tennyson and Dante, Dallapiccola promotes the pursuit of knowledge and truth (and condemns a lazy relinquishing of the same) but one wherein the pursuer maintains his links with family and society, and, acknowledging the dangers of hubris, recognizes his limitations and the greater all-knowingness of God. The Epilogue posits absolute knowledge to be none other than knowledge of God himself. The self-critical and conscience-stricken nature of Ulysses' personality is presented in the opera as a necessary prerequisite to the final attainment of religious enlightenment, a view once again consistent with Kierkegaard, who has remarked that, in this way, man may come, ironically, to regard sorrow, not pleasure, as the meaning of his life (*SD*, p. 51).

Agnosticism (Machado and Pascoli) repudiated

As explained earlier, Dallapiccola's religious vision only becomes readily apparent in the concluding lines of the opera when Ulysses has a Kierkegaardian moment of enlightenment in which he experiences God: 'Signore!/ Non più soli sono/ il mio cuore e il mare', and the line he utters operates as a positive antithesis to Calypso's opening comment regarding Ulysses' departure: 'Son soli, un'altra volta,/ il tuo cuore e il mare'. As mentioned also, these two quotations are variations on the final line of a poem by Machado in *Campos de Castilla*. An examination of Machado's entire poem reveals Dallapiccola's clear religious intention:

Señor, ya me arrancaste lo que yo más quería,
Oye otra vez, Dios mío, mi corazón clamar.
Tu voluntad se hizo, Señor, contra la mía.
Señor, ya estamos solos mi corazón y el mar. (CXIX)

[Lord, you have now taken from me what I most loved,/ Listen once again
to my heart call out, my Lord,/ May your will be done, Lord, against mine,/
Lord, my heart and the sea are now alone.]

Here, the agnostic Machado is lamenting the death of his young wife, Leonor,
and making an ironic invocation to an all-powerful God who is capable of taking
away both human life and the poet's happiness. The irony can be felt in the echo of
the Lord's Prayer in line 3 where God's will is said to be done 'against' that of the
poet. Machado's 'heart' and the 'sea' (the latter, coterminous in the Leonor poems
with 'death') are now alone.[16] Reproach, therefore, is mingled with an element
of sad resignation in the last line of Machado's poem, emotions identical to those
experienced by Calypso when, following Ulysses' departure, she echoes the line in
the Prologue. But the ironic condemnation of God that is to be found in Machado
is deliberately turned on its head in Dallapiccola's Epilogue. In order to reinforce his
religious vision, the composer reverses the meaning of the final line of Machado's
poem, and extrapolating it from its anti-religious context, he inserts it in a new
setting of religious revelation.

   This religious revelation also stands in stark contrast to the conclusion of Pascoli's
'L'ultimo viaggio' [The last journey] of 1904, a long poem based on the Ulysses
myth. 'L'ultimo viaggio' is another agnostic composition that Dallapiccola seems
anxious to repudiate. At the end of Pascoli's poem, Odysseus, who has returned to
Ithaca and set sail again in a *recherche du temps perdu*, beseeches the Sirens to reveal
to him the truth about mankind and himself:

Vi prego!
Ditemi almeno chi sono io! chi ero![17]

[I beg you!/ Tell me at least who I am, who I was!]

This desire for self-knowledge is clearly echoed in Dallapiccola's Epilogue when
Ulysses, too, yearns for some answers to the meaning of his existence: 'Trovar potessi
il Nome, pronunciar la Parola/ che chiarisca a me stesso/ così ansioso cercare;/ che
giustifichi questa mia vita' [If only I could find the Name, pronounce the Word/
that would clarify for me/ my anxious searching;/ that would justify the life I have
lived]. But whereas Dallapiccola's Ulysses finds the answers to these questions in
God, in Pascoli they remained unanswered. Odysseus's ship is shattered on the reef
of the Siren's island from whence his body is carried by the waves to Ogygia. There,
weeping over his dead body, it is Calypso who voices Pascoli's nihilistic vision: it
would have been better if man had never been born; better not to have existed at
all than to have lived and died.[18] The final lines of 'L'ultimo viaggio' read:

Ed ella avvolse l'uomo nella nube
dei suoi capelli; ed ululò sul flutto
sterile, dove non l'udia nessuno.
– Non esser mai! non esser mai! più nulla,
ma meno morte, che non esser più! (p. 996)

[And she enveloped the man in the cloud/ of her hair; and wailed upon the sterile/ waves, where nobody heard her./ 'Never to have been! Never to have been! Nothing more,/ but less dead than not living anymore!']

The conclusion of Dallapiccola's opera, startling in its religious orientation, is clearly attempting to defy and repudiate such late-nineteenth-century scepticism. Even the verbal echo between the final two lines of Pascoli's and Dallapiccola's compositions, both of which take the form of an exclamation — Pascoli: 'Che *non* esser *più*!'; Dallapiccola: '*Non più* soli*!'* (my italics) — draws one's attention toward a link based on oppositional difference.

Attention to 'Inner' and 'Outer' Realities: A Modern versus a Homeric Sense of Self

One of the ways in which the opera reinforces Ulysses' introspective personality is in the emphasis it gives to an inner vision; and the fact that the looking inwards is being presented as a positive thing which helps Ulysses to attain his salvation, is suggested by the fact that the blind characters of the opera are visionary ones: the bard, Demodocus, and the prophet, Teiresias. When recounting the adventures of the Greeks after the fall of Troy, Demodocus specifically juxtaposes his eyes that do not see with his spirit that sees everything: 'Passano innanzi agli occhi miei, che non vedono, navi gagliarde:/ passano nel mio spirito, che tanto vede, lunghe vicende di orrori' (I, i) [Before my sightless eyes, proud ships pass by:/ before my spirit, which sees so much, endless horrors]. In the kingdom of the Cimmerians, Tiresias is hailed by the chorus as a 'cieco veggente più che ogni veggente' (I, iv) [blind seer who sees more than the sighted], and following the prophet's accurate prediction of Ulysses's fate, the latter reflects: 'Nel mio futuro, come vide chiaro/ Tiresia, il cieco tebano!' (I, v) [How clearly he saw my future/ Tiresias, the blind Theban!]. Indeed, when in Act II, Scene III, Dallapiccola makes a reference to the possible blinding of Ulysses (Antinous threatens to pluck out his eyes, rather than listen to Melantho's constant refrain about how terrifying they are) what he is really hinting at is the visionary enlightenment that Ulysses will experience one scene later, in the Epilogue:

MELANTO:	Antinoo..., e gli occhi di quel vecchio?
ANTINOO:	Gli saran strappati, domani.
[MELANTHO:	Antinous..., and that old man's eyes?
ANTINOUS:	They will be plucked out, tomorrow.]

Antinous too is presented as being (figuratively) 'blind', but his 'blindness' (Melantho asks him 'Sei cieco, Antinoo, o tu non vuoi vedere?' [Are you blind, Antinous, or don't you want to see?]) is the opposite of an inner vision, and denounced by the composer. Devoid of a moral conscience, and incapable of any spiritual or psychological investigation, his vision, like that of the other Suitors, is an Epicurean (or in Kierkegaard's terms, 'aesthetic') one, focused 'outwards' on a material and pleasure-orientated universe of food, drink, and sensual delights. In the banquet scene of Act II, Scene III, the words most often on his lips are 'All'allegrezza! Alla gioia! Al piacere!' [To merriment! To joy! To pleasure!] and 'Mescete del vino!' [Pour us more wine!], and Melantho dances her lascivious dance only at his behest. Elsewhere he shows an impervious disregard, even scorn, for Penelope's grief, and promises an adulterous relationship with Melantho when he and Penelope are wed (II, ii). When the audience meets Antinous for the first time at the beginning of Act II, Dallapiccola has him utter the word 'nulla' [nothing] seven times in the space of one scene in an attempt to underline the empty obtuseness of this character whose sense of self is based solely on his relations with the external world, rather than on any relation with his own internal reality.

This fundamental difference between a 'Classical' and a 'modern' sense of self is one of the things which Dallapiccola would seem to want to emphasize in his 'recognition' scenes, which are linked, to some extent, with the 'seeing' and 'blindness' motifs. Homer's *The Odyssey* abounds in 'recognition' scenes, that is scenes where Odysseus and other characters are asked to reveal their identities, after which they are 'recognized' — 'recognized' also in the sense of being afforded respect and regard, and, consequently, given hospitality ('xenia'). However, in order for this recognition-respect to be guaranteed, the revealing of one's identity should involve a listing of one or more of the following: one's wealth, material possessions, heritage, fine lineage, and social privileges. In Homer, therefore, identity is bound up with honour and prestige, and one's sense of identity is determined by one's valuation in other eyes.[19] Antinous (in both Homer and Dallapiccola) completely conforms to this view. Hence, he can afford only disdain for the powerless persona of an old and homeless beggar:

MELANTO:	Esser chi può quel vecchio?
ANTINOO:	Giovane, bella, bella come sei,
	perchè degnare d'un sol sguardo un vecchio,
	un senza nome?
[...]	
ANTINOO:	Quel relitto
	non è un uomo.
MELANTO:	Cos 'è?
ANTINOO:	Chi è? Nessuno (II, ii).
[MELANTHO:	Who can that old man be?
ANTINOUS:	Beautiful young girl, lovely as you are,/ why should you
	deign to give even one look/ to an old nameless man?
ANTINOUS:	That wreck/ isn't a man.
MELANTHO:	*What* is he then?
ANTINOUS:	*Who* is he? Nobody.]

In fact, in Homer Odysseus does not relish the 'beggar' identity thrust upon him by Athene, precisely because of the lack of 'recognition' that goes with it. For that reason, when Eumaeus bombards him with the usual questions concerning his identity ('Who are you? Where do you come from? What is your city? Who are your family?', p. 212) Odysseus answers with a myriad lies aimed at convincing the swineherd that he was once a rich, respectable man who has fallen on hard times: 'I am [...] the son of a rich man [...] I had nine times my own command and led a well-found fleet [...] large quantities of loot fell into my hands [...] my estate increased rapidly, and my fellow countrymen soon learned to fear and to respect me' (pp. 213–14).

Dallapiccola's opera also abounds with (post-Circean) queries about Ulysses' identity: 'Chi era? Che cercava?' [Who was he? What was he searching for?] (Nausicaa); 'qual'è il tuo nome?' [What is your name?] (Alcinous); 'Chi siete? Donde venite?' [Who are you? Where do you come from?] (Lotus-eaters); 'Chi sei, straniero?' [Who are you, stranger?] (The Shades in Hell); 'Chi sei?' [Who are you?] (Melantho). But instead of the boasts that one finds in answer to similar questions in Homer, in Dallapiccola Ulysses either offers pejorative statements about himself: 'affanno [...], questo,/ questo è il mio nome', I, i [heart-break, that,/ that is my name], gives evasive answers: 'Perchè dirvi il mio nome?' I, iv [Why should I tell you my name?], or does not answer at all. The latter is in fact the case with Eumaeus's questioning. In spite of having befriended Eumaeus on his return to Ithaca, Dallapiccola's Ulysses has revealed so little about himself that when Telemachus asks who the beggar man is, Eumaeus can only reply 'Non so chi sia, nè donde venga,/ nè so che cerchi', II, i [I do not know who he is, nor where he comes from,/ nor what he is looking for]. Dallapiccola would seem to be reinforcing not only the anonymity of modern man, but also, and more importantly, how a sense of self is no longer that uncomplicated issue determined by one's wealth, ancestry, or by one's valuation in other eyes. Rather, one determines one's own value through a gazing upon the abyss of the self with the same intensity with which Odysseus stared unflinchingly into the abyss of Charybdis or into Polyphemus's burning eye. So when in Hell Ulysses pronounces the words 'Solo. Son solo. Un uomo/ che guarda nel fondo dell'abisso' [Alone. I am alone. A man/ gazing into the depths of the abyss], he is expressing not only his loneliness at the disappearance of Anticleia, but is also indicating the solitary scenario of man alone with himself and his own conscience, as indicated by the phrases which follow, where the identity questions typical of Homer are now self-directed: 'Chi sono? Che cerco?' [Who am I? What am I searching for?]. He is, as Kierkegaard advocated, confronting the fact that he is accountable to himself for his life, character, and outlook (as opposed to taking refuge in an impersonal and anonymous mode of consciousness), and, in his quest for truth and knowledge, plunging himself into his own subjectivity, for 'truth *is* subjectivity' [*CUP*, p. 116]. Hence, as Anticleia's shade departs, Ulysses, alone, is left to wrestle with her accusations, and consider the degree to which he can be held accountable for her sadness and death.

Isolation and the Artist-Outsider: Echoes of Mann, Joyce, and Kazantzakis

Dallapiccola's Ulysses is, therefore, characterized by solitude, and it is, of course, his self-consciousness which creates this solitude. (Hölderlin's *Hyperion* deals precisely with the same theme of how consciousness precipitates humans into isolation: in a line which could be significant for Dallapiccola's interpretation of Ulysses' beggarly disguise, the protagonist of *Hyperion* exclaims 'man is a *beggar* when he *reflects*' (*Selected Poems*, p.xxvi; the italics are mine)). Loneliness is never an attribute of Homer's Odysseus. When the latter returns to Ithaca, there is a gradual reanimation of past relationships. By contrast, Ulysses in Dallapiccola's opera remains to the end locked in his own isolation. Speaking of Telemachus he laments 'Neppur mio figlio m'ha riconosciuto', II, ii [Not even my son recognized me]; and in stark contrast to the embracing and kissing between the reunited Odysseus and Penelope in the *Odyssey* ('Bursting into tears she (Penelope) ran up to Odysseus, threw her arms round his neck and kissed his head', p. 349), Penelope in *Ulisse* merely stands with outstretched arms, and from either end of the stage she and her husband 'si guardano intensamente', II, iii [gaze intensely at each other]. There is no physical contact. Rather, their reunion exactly mirrors the farewell scene between Ulysses and Nausicaa, thereby already prefiguring Ulysses' imminent parting from his wife: 'Nausicaa tende le braccia a Ulisse e Ulisse le tende a Nausicaa: ma non si toccano nemmeno', I, v [Nausicaa stretches out her arms to Ulysses, and Ulysses stretches out his to Nausicaa; but they do not even touch each other].

Ulysses' encounters with the other three of the five women he meets on his journeys are also characterized by a lack of communication. Anticleia, as already seen, cannot be embraced, and disappears before his eyes 'quale ombra, qual sogno', I, iv [like a shadow or a dream]. Circe is portrayed as she is about to be abandoned:

> CIRCE: (si avvicina a Ulisse per abbracciarlo)
>   (con passione)
>   Ulisse! Vieni a me, Ulisse! Vieni!
> ULISSE: Non più. (I, iii)

> [CIRCE: (She approaches Ulysses to embrace him)/ (passionately)/ Ulysses!
>   Come to me, Ulysses! Come!
> ULYSSES: No more.]

And Calypso in the Prologue already speaks from a position of rejection: 'Desolata ti piange/ Calypso, la Dea senza amore' [Desolate Calypso, the unloved goddess,/ mourns you].

Dallapiccola once claimed: 'il mio Ulisse [...] non agisce in modo provocatorio: è un essere che riceve, che non dà. Interroga se stesso, gli uomini, la natura' ('Nascita', p. 190) [my Ulysses does not act in a provocative way: he is a being who 'receives', who does not 'give'. He questions himself, men, and nature], and his solitary Ulysses who questions life more than he acts upon it stands not just for modern, existential man in general but also for the artist-outsider in society who 'suffers' from intellectual curiosity. It is this which Calypso hints at in the opening minutes of the opera: 'Altra cosa/ cercavi e tal che mai/ mi riuscì penetrare./ *Guardare, meravigliarsi, e tornar a guardare*' [You were searching for something else/ something/ I could never understand./ *To look, to marvel, and look again*]. The thinker or artist in isolation is, of course, a theme common to at least three of the writers by whom Dallapiccola has been inspired in the creation of *Ulisse*: Thomas Mann, James Joyce, and Nikos Kazantzakis. The biblical Joseph and his brothers in Mann's *Joseph and his Brothers* are commonly recognized to symbolize, respectively, 'the old antithesis of artist and bourgeois, genius and commonplace, disguised in old-world garments and old-world phraseology'.[20] One learns in Joyce's *A Portrait* that Stephen Dedalus suffers from 'the cold silence of intellectual revolt' (p. 152), and that 'To merge his

life in the common tide of other lives was harder for him than any fasting or prayers'
(p. 153). Similarly Bloom in Joyce's *Ulysses,* 1922, a polymath nicknamed 'Mister
Knowall', is sneered at and persecuted into isolation because of his knowledge and
his 'jawbreakers about phenomenon and science and this phenomenon and the other
phenomenon'. [21] In fact, both Joyce's *Ulysses* and *The Odyssey* of Kazantzakis, 1938 [22]
would seem to be evoked in Dallapiccola's Epilogue to underscore the image of the
solitary knowledge-seeker, removed from his fellow men. The atmosphere created
in the Epilogue is distinctly chilly. Ulysses, not having found the knowledge he was
searching for, and lacking the human warmth he sacrificed in aid of his search, feels
a cold and lonely disappointment intensified by the icy gaze of the stars:

> Quanto
> e cosa appresi? Fole.
> Dopo fatiche inani,
> briciole di sapere, vani
> balbettamenti, sillabe soltanto
> mi sono rimaste invece di parole.
> (Guarda in alto)
> Stelle!: quanto mai volte interrogai
> i vostri sguardi tersi,
> luce sperando aver da voi, saggezza! (Epilogue)

[How much / and what did I learn? Fairy-tales./ After vain efforts,/ all I have
been left with are/ scraps of knowledge, futile/ stammerings, and syllables
instead of words./ (He looks up)/ Stars!: how many times did I question/ your
limpid gaze,/ hoping to gain light and knowledge from you!]

Apart from the 'positive' allusion to Dante which is apparent in the reference to
'stars' and symbolic of a drawing near to the divine (see p. 67) one is reminded
of Joyce's friendless Bloom who, deserted by Stephen with whom he had striven
so hard for a long-lasting intellectual relationship, feels 'a lonechill' like 'the cold
of interstellar space, thousands of degrees below freezing point' (*Ulysses*, p. 827).
Similarly, Kazantzakis's Odysseus, referred to frequently by the Greek writer as 'the
lonely one', finds himself at the end of his travels in icy Antarctica: his quest for
absolute knowledge and absolute freedom has brought him only absolute separation
from his fellow men, in a cold, unpopulated land.

In view of this negative sense of loneliness, Dallapiccola would not seem to be
condoning the isolated self on a quest for learning. However, a closer examination
of the Lotus-eaters' chorus, and a greater scrutiny of the Epilogue (the two, as now
demonstrated, are intrinsically linked), show that, as was indeed also the case for
Tennyson and Dante, Dallapiccola has mixed feelings regarding the lonely crusade
for knowledge and truth.

Dallapiccola and Tennyson: Lotus-Eaters Condoned or Condemned?

Dallapiccola chooses not Homer's version of the Lotus-eaters (Book IX, lines
82–104), but that of Tennyson. In Homer, Odysseus brings his weeping men back
by force to the ship where he binds them to their places. The imagery is essentially

active, a violent breaking away from the temptations of lethargy and inertia. Tennyson, on the other hand, chooses from the story the theme of inertia itself, and he elaborates the image of the escapist Lotus-eaters who, drawn towards drug and dream, away from toil, and obligation (the 'fatiche inani' which Dallapiccola's Ulysses alludes to in the Epilogue), seek to evade the hazards and responsibilities of human life. The song of the 'Lotofaghi' in Dallapiccola is rich in similarities with the 'Choric Song' from Tennyson's 'The Lotos-Eaters':[23]

La luna piena sopra la valle,	1
il sole, perenne, nel cielo...	
ruscelli che scorrono cantando...	3
La loro musica scende	
qual sonno, da cieli beati	5
su noi, sulle palpebre stanche,	
sui nostri stanchi occhi...	7
Tanta fatica? Perchè faticare?	
La nostra terra ci dona dei frutti:	9
prendétene con noi... senza destino	
vi sentirete, inconsciamente lieti,	11
come quando, bambini, dormivate.	
Vivrete senza téma del futuro,	13
senza rimpianto per ciò ch'è passato...	
senza sapere che cos'è il dolore,	15
senza sapere che cos'è la morte. (I , ii)	

[The full moon hanging over the valley,/ the sun for ever in the sky .../ streams that sing as they flow .../ Their music descends/ from blissful skies, like slumber/ upon us, upon our weary eyelids,/ our weary eyes .../ Your great labours? But why should you labour?/ Our land gives us plentiful fruit:/ come share it with us ... you will feel/ free from destiny, unconsciously happy,/ like when babies you lay asleep./ You shall live without fearing the future,/ with no regret for the past .../ without knowing what suffering is,/ without knowing what death is.]

These Lotus-eaters have turned their back on a pursuit of knowledge and truth (denoted by the repetition of 'senza sapere' in the final two lines) and all of the hardships — 'dolore', 'morte' — which that pursuit and life itself may throw in their way. The existence they have chosen is a changeless, monotonous one: the sun and the moon in their landscape, as indicated in lines 1 to 2, are always simultaneously present, thereby evoking Tennyson's 'A land where all things always seem'd the same', (I, 24). Their life is devoid of stress and endeavour: to line 8 could be compared Tennyson's 'why should we toil alone/ we only toil?' (II, 4–5); and 'Ah, why/ should life all labour be?' (IV, 3–4). It is full of sleepy abandon: lines 11 and 12 echo Tennyson's 'tir'd eyelids upon tir'd eyes' (I, 6); and 'Surely, surely slumber is more sweet than toil' (VIII, 34). Self-indulgent and reliant on material comforts from the land which always bestows on them eternal fruit (line 9), reminiscent of Tennyson's 'flower [...] in the fruitful soil' (III, 14), they live an anxiety-free life, for the here and now, fearless of the future and harbouring no regret for the past (lines 13–14).

One's initial assumption is that Dallapiccola echoes Tennyson's 'Choric Song' because he shares the English poet's negative attitude toward the Lotus-eaters' escapism. However, as criticism has shown, Tennyson's poem is ambivalent; there is in fact nothing in it which points unequivocally to the poet's out-and-out condemnation of his Lotos-Eaters. Kincaid[24] even suggests that Tennyson shared their vision of life as pointless toil ending in death: the Lotos-Eaters speak of mankind as 'an ill-used race of men' who 'cleave the soil,/ Sow the seed, and reap the harvest with enduring toil, [...] Till they perish and they suffer — some, 'tis whispered — down in hell' (VIII, 26–31). Tired of progressing and battling the storms of life, Tennyson, Kincaid argues, especially after the death of his friend, Hallam, also dreamed of 'regressing', and could be expressing admiration for the Lotos-Eaters who have courageously chosen their 'Innisfree', and responded to what they heard 'in the deep heart's core'. However, arguments can also be drawn up in favour of Tennyson's condemnation of the Lotos-Eaters.[25] One could, for example, draw attention to how Tennyson's poem opens with Ulysses' energetic 'Courage!' (as already mentioned, Dallapiccola's Lotus-eaters' episode opens with the same exhortation). This word then rings throughout the subsequent lines of Tennyson's composition, helping to promote the concept of energy and action over 'mild-eyed melancholy' and inertia. Also, it is to be presumed that, as a Victorian man, writing for a Victorian audience, Tennyson would have been likely to criticize and judge the Lotos-Eaters as guilty of evasion of duty and responsibility. This argument can be supported by a statement from his *Memoir*:

> Man [...] should develop his true self by not shirking responsibility, by casting aside all maudlin and introspective morbidities, and by using his powers cheerfully in accordance with the obvious dictates of his *moral consciousness* (my italics). [26]

Perhaps what Dallapiccola saw and liked in Tennyson's poem was an unresolved ambivalence towards the Lotos-Eaters. For, on the one hand, Dallapiccola seems to recognize the allure of a dream world where there is no harsh reality, and no difficult pursuit of knowledge, an allure embodied by his Nausicaa. Nausicaa repeats the words 'sogno' [dream] or variants of the verb 'sognare' [to dream] five times in the course of her scene, and, like the *lotofaghi*, she is described as being 'quasi assente' [almost lost in thought] and 'trasognata' [dreamy]. But in reference to her Dallapiccola uses the terms 'meraviglia' [marvel] and 'incanto' [charm]. On the other hand, he also seems to condemn an escapist dream world in accordance with the 'dictates of his moral consciousness'. Hence, one of Nausicaa's maids chastises her dreaming, and calls her firmly and disapprovingly back to reality — 'cercando di richiamare Nausicaa alla realtà' [trying to call Nausicaa back to reality] — with the reminder that 'Son foli i sogni: rimani serena' [Dreams are fairy-tales: be calm and forget them]. Furthermore, in an attempt to suggest Nausicaa's lack of knowledge, Dallapiccola peppers her speech with a series of unanswered questions: 'Chi era?' [Who was he?], 'Che cercava?' [What was he looking for?], 'e forse ciò l'amore?' [can this be love?], and negations: 'Non era' [He was not], 'Non ci fu neanche' [There was not even], 'Non so' [I do not know]. 'Non so' — a specific allusion to Nausicaa's lack of knowledge — is immediately repeated in an echo effect by a number of her servants.

It is also noteworthy that in the Epilogue where the moral and didactic purposes of Dallapiccola's work are realized, Dallapiccola lends to the Ulysses who is about to discover God, all the opposite characteristics of the Lotus-eaters: the latter have abandoned the quest for knowledge ('senza sapere') and Ulysses is still searching and questioning: 'Trovar potessi il Nome' [If only I could find the Name], 'quante mai volte interrogai'; the *lotofaghi* harbour no remorse for the past ('senza rimpianto per ciò ch'è passato'), while Ulysses is overcome by 'memorie dolorose' [painful memories], and suffers from the weariness and the toil — the 'fatiche inani' — which the islanders have deliberately relinquished ('Perchè faticare?'). The implication is that, in line with Kierkegaard's equation between 'truth' and 'subjectivity', Ulysses discovers God precisely *because* of his questioning, his self-reflectiveness, and his toiling after knowledge. Moreover, and most significantly, the *communication* that Ulysses feels with God and the rediscovery of mankind which accompanies his prophetic vision, leaving him no longer alone ('Non più soli sono/ il mio cuore e il mare'), operates as a positive antithesis to the Lotus-eaters' severing of all links with mankind. Like Tennyson's 'Lotos-Eaters' who give very little thought to the appeal of home and family and dismiss the idea of ever returning to either ('all hath suffer'd change;/ For surely now our household hearths are cold:/ Our sons inherit us: our looks are strange:/ And we should come like ghosts to trouble joy', VI, 3–6), Dallapiccola's *lotofaghi* cannot even remember what or where their native land is: 'La Patria? Che cos'è?' [The Homeland? What is that?]. In both compositions the Lotus-eaters are guilty of the supreme social insult: they have turned their backs on their families and the world at large, and although in their new communities they sing in chorus and speak of 'we', theirs is not a proper community, embracing and integrating diversity, but one which has made a single personality out of many. In their land where 'all things always seem the same', they also speak and think the same; and they speak and think (like Dallapiccola's Antinous) only of self-indulgence and self-gratification.

Tennyson's and Dante's Ulysses, and the Importance of Social Ties

This promotion of integration and communication over and above the isolated self and the safe-guarding of the interests of the self that one finds in Dallapiccola, is also a subject which emerges in Dante's canto on Ulysses in *Inferno* XXVI, and in Tennyson's 'Ulysses'. Both Dante and Tennyson concur in their promotion of the interests of family and society over and above those of the individual, and it is this similarity in attitude between the two poets that allows Dallapiccola to make textual allusions to both of them in his libretto, especially in the Epilogue. Since, however, this 'promotion' on the part of Dante and Tennyson is a subtle one which is never clearly spelled out for the reader, but rather (as will be shown) heavily suggested in the language and style of each, there are no specific quotations from either of these two authors which Dallapiccola can echo in order to draw obvious attention to the theme in question. For this reason, he makes general allusions to different parts of Tennyson's and Dante's texts on Ulysses.

For example, the passage in which Dante brings to light (through the use of the repetitive 'debito' and 'dovea') Ulysses' self-avowed callousness and *lack of duty* to his son, father, and wife:

> Nè dolcezza di figlio, nè la pièta
> del vecchio padre, nè 'l debito amore
> lo quale dovea Penelopè far lieta,
> vincer poter dentro da me l'ardore
> ch'i'ebbi a divenir del mondo esperto,
> e delli vizi umani e del valore. (lines 94–99)

[Not fondness for my son, nor compassion/ for my old father, nor the love I owed/ Penelope which should have made her happy,/ could overcome the passion I had within me/ to become an expert of the world,/ of human vices and merits.]

is evoked in the opera in Calypso's accusations that Ulysses had feigned nostalgia and a sense of duty toward his son, native land, father, and wife in order to escape her: 'Era menzogna/ la nostalgia del figlio,/ della patria, del vecchio/ padre, della tua sposa' [The nostalgia you professed for your son,/ your homeland, your old/ father, your wife/ — it was all a lie]. And Ulysses' reasons in Dante (given above) for abandoning his familial duties — namely that these duties were not enough to quell his desire to become an expert in human vices and merits — is alluded to in Ulysses' first words to Nausicaa in the opera: 'Nell'uomo scrutar volli il bene e il male' [I wanted to study good and evil in mankind]. Furthermore, Dante, disapproving of Ulysses' hubris, his magnification of his ego, and his neglect of duties toward his family, makes him suffer a quick and ignoble drowning: [27]

> Noi ci allegrammo, e tosto tornò in pianto;
> chè della nova terra un turbo nacque,
> e percosse del legno il primo canto.
> Tre volte il fè girar con tutte l'acque:
> alla quarta levar la poppa in suso
> e la prora ire in giù, com'altrui piacque,
> infin che 'l mar fu sovra noi richiuso. (lines 136–42)

[We rejoiced, and soon the rejoicing turned to tears;/ for from the new land a storm arose,/ and struck the front side of the ship./ Three times it turned it round with all the waters;/ the fourth time it lifted the stern on high/ and plunged the prow below, as was pleasing to Him,/ until the sea closed over us again.]

This unheroic end, reflected in the passage above in the sudden transition from happiness to sorrow; the inexorable engulfing of the boat; and the absence of any fighting or demonstrations of bravery from one who has just boasted to Dante of the 'cento milia/ perigli' [hundred thousand/ perils] he had survived at sea, is also evoked in Dallapiccola's opera when Demodocus, in the palace of Alcinous, posits Ulysses' swift death by drowning 'nei gorghi cupi' [in the dark vortexes], emphasizing in the process Ulysses' current feelings of insignificance and anonymity, (conveyed through the repetition of 'nessuno') which is concordant with the anti-heroism implicit in the *Inferno* extract above:

> Nei gorghi cupi lo volle forse il Dio del mare.
> Fu risparmiato lo strazio al fiero suo cuore
> di tornare alla reggia, ove nessuno
> più l'avrìa conosciuto . . .
> ove il suo grande oprare non rammenta nessuno...; ove il suo arco glorioso
> non doma ormai nessuno. (I, i)

> [Perhaps the God of the sea called him down to his dark vortexes./ His proud heart was spared the torment/ of returning to his kingdom, where nobody/ would have recognized him anymore/ where his great achievements are remembered by nobody; where nobody can master/ his glorious bow.]

Dante's canto on Ulysses is also evoked on a more general level in Dallapiccola's stage directions for the opera's final scene. In *Inferno* Ulysses recounts to Dante and Virgil how, after leaving Circe's island, he took off (the italics are mine) 'per l'alto *mare aperto*/ *sol* con un legno e con quella compagna/ *picciola* dalla qual non fui diserto' (lines 100–03) [across the high, *open sea*; *alone* with a boat and that *little*/ company by whom I was not deserted]; and that when he and his men entered the 'mondo sanza gente' [unpopulated world] the sky was filled not with the familiar stars of the North Pole, but with the unfamiliar ones of the South Pole: '*Tutte le stelle* già dell'altro polo/ vedea la notte' [The night was already filled with/ *all the stars* of the other pole]. The final scene of Dallapiccola's opera opens with the direction (the italics are mine) '*Mare aperto*. Ulisse, *solo*, su una *piccola* imbarcazione. *Notte stellata*' [*The open sea*. Ulysses, *alone*, on a *little* boat. *A starry night*]. The unfamiliarity of the stars is something that is stressed in Dallapiccola too. Ulysses remarks that although he had gazed on them during all of his travels, on that particular night they looked foreign: 'Perchè tanto diverse m'apparite / in questa notte?' [Why do you appear so different /tonight?].

These overt reminiscences of Dante's canto on Ulysses are married, in the Epilogue, to clear echoes of Tennyson's 'Ulysses'. There are striking similarities between these pronouncements made by the protagonist of the latter poem:

> All times I have suffer'd greatly.   7
>
> Always roaming with a hungry heart
> Much have I seen and known.   12–13

and the following made by Dallapiccola's Ulysses :

> soffrii pene infinite
> [...]
> il lungo errare
> [...]
> Un uomo sono, un uomo che ha guardato
> il mondo nelle foggie più diverse. (Epilogue)

> [I suffered endless torments/ my long years of wandering/ I am only mortal, a man who has gazed/ at the world in all of its myriad forms.]

As with the 'Lotos-Eaters', critics' interpretations of Tennyson's 'Ulysses' have oscillated between two extremes: there are those who claim that Tennyson is approving of Ulysses's heroic desire to achieve great things in life, and those who emphasize Tennyson's condemnation of Ulysses's selfishness.[28] The view taken here is in agreement with the latter opinion. Tennyson would seem to be condemning Ulysses as a hard, self-absorbed individual (altogether in the poem there are fourteen uses of the personal pronoun, 'I', and eleven uses of 'me', 'myself', and 'my' or 'mine') whose devotion to the intellect makes him contemptuous of his people and, like Dante's Ulysses, neglectful of his duties toward the rest of society. Along with connubial insensitivity ('match'd with an aged wife'), he demonstrates a contemptuous sense of superiority ('it little profits', 'I mete and dole') over the 'savage race' of which he is king, and the mundane routine of ordinary, civilized life (the 'hoarding', 'sleeping', and 'feeding'):

> It little profits that an idle king,
> By this still hearth, among these barren crags,
> Match'd with an aged wife, I mete and dole
> Unequal laws unto a savage race,
> That hoard, and sleep, and feed, and know not me. (1–5)

As opposed to this life of inferior, 'common duties', which in patronizing tones, he leaves to the 'slow prudence' of his 'most blameless' son to organize, he exalts the gratification of his own enthusiasms and desires: to 'drink/ Life to the lees'; to experience 'Life piled on life'; and 'To follow knowledge like a sinking star,/ Beyond the utmost bound of human thought'.

The reason why Dallapiccola echoes both Dante and Tennyson in the Epilogue must lie with what he sees to be a vision of Ulysses shared by both authors and by himself: an Ulysses who, although heroic in his courage and determination to brave the struggles of life (a positive antithesis to the Lotus-eaters) is a man of misdirected energies. For courage and determination are to be valued only if they are exercised for the improvement, not of the individual, but of society as a whole. Like Dante's Ulysses who attempts to go beyond the pillars of Hercules, and know the unknowable (discover the 'mondo sanza gente'), Tennyson's Ulysses is also guilty of hubris, for what he will not 'yield' to when he famously proclaims 'To strive, to seek, to find, and not to yield!' is, presumably, the limitations of his intellect and/or a superior being within a recognized hierarchical system: God and God's all-knowingness. In short, Dallapiccola makes allusions simultaneously to both Tennyson and Dante in an effort to reinforce the message of his Epilogue, a message present both in Tennyson's poem and in Dante's canto: communication and integration with others are to be valued more highly than isolation and a preoccupation with the betterment of the self alone. The concluding line of the opera which unequivocally promotes the concept of communication with God and mankind over isolation ('Signore! Non più soli sono/ il mio cuore e il mare') harks back to, and operates as a positive negation of, a whole spate of crucial instances in the work as a whole: not just the narcissistic self-interest of the Lotus-eaters (I, ii) but also Ulysses' aforementioned failure to communicate with members of his family (Anticleia, I, iv; Telemachus, II, iii; Penelope, II, iii), and women acquaintances or lovers (Calypso, Prologue; Circe, I, iii; and Nausicaa, I, iv). It also intentionally inverts not only the very opening line of the opera where Calypso comments on Ulysses' lonely crusade, but also the line which occurs exactly in the middle of the opera — Ulysses' Nietzschean paraphrase proclaiming his utter solitude as he gazes onto the abyss of Hades: 'Solo. Son solo. Un uomo/ che guarda nel fondo dell'abisso' (I, iv). This cultivation of a social self in addition to the 'ethical' man's need for self-development is fully compatible with Kierkegaard's view in *Either/Or* that 'the self which it is the task of the ethical individual to develop must not be thought of as existing "in isolation", in the manner envisaged by certain "mystical" doctrines; he stands in "reciprocal relations" with his public surroundings and conditions of life, the self he seeks to realize being "a social and a civic self"' (Gardiner, *Kierkegaard*, p. 52).

Hubris Filtered through Aeschylus, Joyce, and Mann

The aforementioned subject of hubris is an important one for Dallapiccola (he describes the theme of his ballet, *Marsia*, as 'l'immane sforzo umano di avvicinare Dio' [man's enormous effort to be on a par with God])[29] and the parts played not only by Tennyson and Dante, but also by Aeschylus and Thomas Mann in the libretto of *Ulisse* can be explained in the light of this theme. Aeschylus's *Agamemnon*[30] is evoked in Act I, Scene I, when Demodocus, singing at Alcinous's palace of the hardships encountered by the Greeks after the fall of Troy, predicts how Agamemnon will be murdered by Aegisthus, the lover of Agamemnon's wife, Clytaemnestra:

DEMODOCO: Dolce come canto
è il sorriso di Clitennestra che accoglie lo sposo:
su purpurei tappeti
essa lo spinge a inceder, simile a un Dio.
Agamennone, indugi? Perchè indugi?
Gli occhi dell'anima mia contemplano alzata
lama lucente: la scure d'Egisto s'abbatte
sul capo dell'eroe. Sangue d'intorno...
sangue vuol sangue e chiama altro sangue...
E dopo il sangue, il rimorso.

[Demodocus: As sweet as song/ is the smile of Clytemnestra, welcoming her husband:/ on purple carpets/ she urges him to enter like a God./ Agamemnon, do you hesitate? Why do you hesitate?/ My inner sight can see/ a shining blade lifted on high: the axe of Aegisthus falls down/ on the head of the hero. Blood all around .../ bloodshed claims bloodshed and calls for more bloodshed./ And after the blood, remorse.]

Although he does not explain or discuss his choice of Aeschylus in 'Nascita', Dallapiccola has obviously opted for the dramatist's version of the murder of Agamemnon rather than that of Homer in an attempt to suggest the topic of hubris which is very evident in Aeschylus, but altogether missing from Homer's version of events.[31] The detail of the purple carpets is important (it is, again, absent in Homer's account). They were fabrics died with the blood-red dye of the murex snail and held to be sacred to the gods. Clytaemnestra spreads them before Agamemnon on his return home and encourages him to walk on them into the palace (where Aegisthus is waiting to kill him). To walk on them would be to imitate and therefore insult the gods (note Dallapiccola's 'simile a un Dio'), and Agamemnon, recognizing the threat of hubris, hesitates (note Dallapiccola's 'Agamennone, indugi? Perchè indugi?') and at first rejects the queen's temptation:

> Never — only the gods deserve the pomps of honour
> and the stiff brocades of fame. To walk on them...
> I am human, and it makes my pulses stir
> with dread.
> Give me the tributes of a man
> and not a god, a little earth to walk on,
> not this gorgeous work. (*Agamemnon,* 915–20, pp. 137–38)

However, with language similar to Dallapiccola's Circe in its wiliness, Clytaemnestra eventually persuades her husband to walk on the tapestries, and Agamemnon, who feels that the war has, in a sense, 'deified' him, in an idle hope of appeasing the gods, takes off his boots. As he 'tramples' on the gods, he reactivates the curse of the house of Atreus, a curse which, for generations, has been forcing its members to take revenge for acts of revenge. Clytaemnestra, in having Agamemnon killed, is, in fact, avenging her husband's slaughtering of his own daughter, Iphigeneia (another detail omitted in Homer), and for this blood feud, Clytaemnestra will die by the hand of her own son. It is this relentless perpetration of crime to which Dallapiccola alludes with the phrase 'Sangue vuol sangue e chiama altro sangue'. Although Demodocus is recounting the hubris committed by Agamemnon, his prophetic powers allow him to see the relevance of the Agamemnon episode to Ulysses' condition. This relevance is suggested by the fact that Ulysses enters on stage with Nausicaa as Demodocus is actually relating the Agamemnon story, and that the visionary bard, aware of Ulysses' presence in spite of his blindness, stretches out his right arm in the direction of Ulysses as he speaks (as indicated in the stage directions). It is only in the Epilogue that Ulysses comes to recognize how he is guilty of hubris. Here he defines his obsession with 'learning' ('cosa appresi?'), 'contemplating' ('Quante mai volte contemplai?'), and searching ('cercando') with a desire to obtain 'La Parola, il Nome' [The Word, the Name']. These two words are, of course, coterminous in the bible with God (see, for example, John 1. 1; Luke 10. 20; Psalms 69. 36; 115. 1; Isaiah 42. 8), but Dallapiccola chooses them to suggest not God (who is never mentioned by Ulysses in the course of the whole opera) but 'truth' or the absolute *knowledge* known only to God. That 'La Parola' and 'Il Nome' stand for absolute knowledge is made apparent when Ulysses sadly laments the actual results of all of his searching to date: not any supreme knowledge, but mere 'briciole di *sapere*' [scraps of *knowledge*] (my italics). Instead, as the revelation scene at the end of the opera makes clear, supreme knowledge is posited as none other than knowledge of God himself, before whom man is a 'nessuno', 'un senza nome' (Act II, ii). It is to reinforce this point that Dallapiccola repeats the word 'nessuno' thirteen times in the libretto. Furthermore, man's 'wisdom' lies in his recognition of his humble, powerless, and 'beggarly' state. Consequently, Eumeus, when addressing Ulysses in his *beggarly* disguise, uses the terms 'saggio' [wise] and 'saggezza' [wisdom] in reference to him: 'Saggio tu sei, mendico. Dimmi: dove/ tanta saggezza apprendesti?' [You are wise, beggar. Tell me: where/ did you learn such wisdom?] (Act II, i). There are also echoes in this part of the Epilogue to Joyce's *Ulysses* (not, however, indicated in 'Nascita'), and a link based on oppositional difference. When Stephen Dedalus 'meets' his mother in Hell, he, like Dallapiccola's Ulysses, invokes 'the word': 'Stephen (*eagerly*): Tell me the word, mother, if you know now. The word known to all men' (p. 682). The reply, as in Dallapiccola's *Ulisse*, also has a religious orientation, with Stephen's mother suggesting that God *is* the word when she answers: 'Repent, Stephen [...]. I pray for you in my other world' (p. 682). The difference, however, lies in the fact that whereas the conversion of Dallapiccola's Ulysses is complete, Stephen Dedalus refuses to take heed of his mother's warning. Like Tennyson's Ulysses, he refuses to sacrifice the pursuit of knowledge (what Stephen calls 'the intellectual imagination') to family desires, and the clear echo to Lucifer underlines his defiance and his hubris: 'Stephen: *Ah, non par exemple!* The intellectual imagination! With me all or not at all. *Non serviam!*' (p. 682).

In spite of these clear echoes of Joyce's *Ulysses*, Dallapiccola claims to have been influenced in the writing of Anticleia's speech by the chapter entitled 'Account of Mont-Kaw's simple passing' in Thomas Mann's *Joseph and his Brothers*.[32] (In a letter to his wife, following a meeting with Mann, Dallapiccola speaks of the similarities he finds between Mann's novel and Joyce's *Ulysses. Saggi,* p. 127). At first sight there are no apparent similarities between the speech in Dallapiccola and Mann's chapter. Anticleia voices her anguish at Ulysses's departure, and how she died of a broken heart; Mont-Kaw, who is dying of kidney failure, and whose physical deterioration (vomiting, blindness, and spasms), as well as attempted cures (lizard's blood, porcupines' excrement, and urine), are dwelt upon heavily in the course of the chapter, praises Joseph, his servant, for his solicitude towards him, and indirectly offers him some worldly-wise advice on how to lead his life. However, the clue to the link between Anticleia's speech and Mann's chapter would seem to lie in Anticleia's name. In Greek it means 'against glory' (*anti-kleos*), and behind Anticleia's recriminations lie, precisely, her condemnation of Ulysses' desertion of her, his mother, for the purposes of achieving glory and of satisfying his hubristic impulses. The condemnation is even suggested in Dallapiccola's indication that Anticleia should speak, not emotionally but 'con voce ferma e con espressione contenuta':

> Tanti la morte coglie
> con levità e li porta all'altra riva
> liberi da inquietudini e da dubbi:
> e gli occhi loro niuno chiuder deve
> perchè il sonno li chiuse dolcemente....
> Non fu così per me, figliolo mio:
> L'ansia, l'affanno per te che il destino
> spingeva lontano sul mare; l'angoscia
> struggente per te che il mio cuore sentiva in periglio...
> e l'accorato amor che a te portai
> il mio corpo distrussero. (I, iv)

[Death carries away many/ gently, and brings them to that other shore/ free from worries and doubts;/ and no one has to close their eyes/ because sleep closed them sweetly .../ It was not like that for me, my son:/ torment and heartache for you whom destiny/ drove far over the sea; consuming/ anguish for you whom my heart felt to be in danger .../ and the desperate love I bore you,/ destroyed my body.]

Similarly, Mont-Kaw is fully aware that Joseph (like Ulysses) is over-preoccupied with the self, and as if implicitly warning him against this, he speaks in favour of family bonds. He recognizes the 'sin of over-weening blind self-confidence' which had incurred the hatred of Joseph's brothers, and had 'weighed down Joseph', giving rise to 'the mangling and the pit' (p. 269). He also alludes to Joseph's hubristic tendencies, and speaks of how the latter 'measures "himself" boldly against higher things' (p. 274), even God himself whom Joseph 'put to the test' by trying 'all human means of combatting' Mont-Kaw's disease (p. 266). Mont-Kaw himself, by contrast, had 'no use for higher or speculative matters' (p. 262). The importance of life for him lies in family ties, and the involvement with, and service to, others. He recounts his grief to Joseph on the death of his dear wife (p. 271); claims to love Joseph as his own son (p. 271); and explains how, as Petepre's oldest servant, he had 'no thought save for his home that it might flourish' (p. 272).

By alluding to Aeschylus, Joyce, and Mann and their emphasis upon the damage caused to the family and society by submitting to the temptations of hubris, Dallapiccola intends ultimately to reinforce the Dantesque message of his libretto, while also showing how he conceives of the essential problems facing man as timeless ones, spanning the classical, medieval, and modern periods.

The Structure of *Ulisse*: Religious Direction and Self-Definition

Verbal structures

As has been clearly indicated by the composer himself in the diagram accompanying 'Nascita' (Figure 2.2), *Ulisse* is structured as a large, symmetrical arch or bow at the centre of which there is Ulysses' descent into Hades. The idea of man's journey through life as following the shape of an arch could have been inspired by Hölderlin, who in his ode 'Lebenslaug' ('The Course of Life') depicted his life as 'an arch-shaped course' — 'des Lebens/ Bogen' — a sheer ascent followed by a sheer descent (*Selected Poems*, pp. 10–11). More possibly, Dallapiccola may have found his inspiration in Dante's *Convivio*:

> Tornando dunque a la nostra [vita], sola de la quale al presente s'intende, sì dico ch'ella procede a imagine di questo arco, montando e discendendo. (IV, xxiii, 6–7)[33]

> [Coming back therefore to the subject of our life, which is the only one which concerns us at present, yes, I can say/ that it proceeds in the shape of this arch, rising and descending.]

The most striking feature of Dallapiccola's diagram lies in its symmetries. Indeed, all 13 episodes of the opera are heavily characterized by a series of parallels and contrasts, some of which Dallapiccola draws attention to in his notes written outside the diagram. In scenes 1 and 13 both the protagonists (Calypso and Ulysses, respectively) are alone by the sea, and both episodes are flanked by an orchestral interlude. Scenes 3 and 11 have contrasting elements: the playful ball game which takes the form of a dance in 3 contrasts with Melanto's dance of death in 11; and to the serenity of the Feaci beach and dignity of Nausicaa (3) are opposed the violence

> Non è la terra che si sta cercando.
> Non è la terra che ci può dar pace. (I, i)

[It is not the land we are searching for./ It is not the land that can give us peace].

> senza sapere che cos'è dolore,
> senza sapere che cos'è la morte. (I, ii)

[without knowing what suffering is/ without knowing what death is.]

> Sempre soffrire; mai sperare.
> Sempre il buio; mai la luce. (I, iv)

[Always suffering; never to hope./ For ever the darkness; never the light.]

> Ogni pianta, ogni sterpo, e ogni sasso riconoscea
> sul mio cammino, e tutto a me
> parlava del tempo lontano. (II, ii)

[I recognized every plant, every thorn-bush, and every stone/ on my path, and everything/ spoke to me of times gone by.]

> Perchè, perchè volli tanto vedere?
> Perchè tutto alla mente mi ritorna?
> Perchè non volli accettare l'oblìo? (II, ii)

[Why, why did I long to see so much?/ Why does it all come back to mind now?/ Why did I not want to accept oblivion?]

> Dopo fatiche inani,
> briciole di sapere, vani
> balbettamenti. (Epilogue)

[After vain efforts,/ scraps of knowledge, futile/ stammerings.]

> Trovar potessi il Nome, pronunciar la Parola
> *che chiarisca* a me stesso così ansioso cercare;
> *che giustifichi* questa mia vita, il lungo errare;
> *che rasséreni* l'ora che rapida s'invola. (Epilogue, my emphases)

[If only I could find the Name, pronounce the Word/ *that would clarify* for me my anxious searching;/ *that would justify* the life I have lived, and my long years of wandering;/ *that would calm* the swiftly fleeting passage of time.]

The reason for the overriding presence of the symmetries created between episodes and verbal sequences in the opera has never been elucidated in any critical study of the work. That Dallapiccola is somewhat obsessed with structure and symmetry becomes apparent in many of his musical writings. One needs only glance at the large and intricate diagram accompanying his analysis of the verbal and musical 'macrostrutture e microstrutture' [macrostructures and microstructures] in Verdi's operas (*Appunti*, p. 24) to gain some insight into, what Contini calls, the 'temperamento razionale, matematico e formalizzatore' (*Saggi*, pp. 55–56) [rational, mathematical and formalizing temperament] from which Dallapiccola's desire to discover and create structures derives. In fact, this same article offers the best clue to discovering the reason for Dallapiccola's predilection for structures, particularly symmetrical ones. In it Dallapiccola quotes from St. Thomas of Aquinas's definition of beauty: 'Ad pulchritudinem tria requiruntur: integritas, consonantia, claritas' (p. 25) [Three things are required to make beauty: wholeness, harmony, radiance][34] and goes on to give a personal definition of the three requirements:

UNITÀ: cioè il disegno nel suo complesso;
CONSONANZA: l'equilibrio tra le parti che lo costituiscono;
CHIAREZZA: l'espressione essenziale di quanto si ha da dire.

[Wholeness: that is to say, the design in its entirety; Harmony: balance between the parts of the whole; Radiance: the essential expression of what it has to say.]

'Harmony' is thus interpreted as 'balance between the parts of the whole', and Dallapiccola agrees with St. Thomas Aquinas that balance is an essential constituent of a 'beautiful' work of art. One can therefore presume that the carefully created structures of *Ulisse* are tied in with Dallapiccola's conception of beauty. But they could be said to owe their presence to other factors too. When put in relation to the content of the work, they can be seen to reinforce the 'structure' that Ulysses is searching for in his life in opposition to, what he recognizes in the Epilogue to be, his 'wandering' and 'erroneous' existence: 'questa mia vita, il lungo errare' (the verb 'errare' is obviously intended to resonate with two meanings here — that of 'to wander aimlessly', but also 'to make a mistake'). This search for a defining structure in life — which is eventually provided by the knowledge of God — in opposition to a purposeless drifting, has, most probably, strong autobiographical implications for Dallapiccola (in 'Nascita' he insists that the theme of Ulysses' travels 'chose' him, and not vice-versa: 'non siamo sempre noi a scegliere i nostri testi; ma i testi, venendoci incontro, scelgono noi', p. 172 [it is not always we who choose our texts; but rather the texts, coming before us, choose us]). It could be argued that Dallapiccola's need for 'structure' derives from the lack of 'definition' and belonging he felt in life and which is frequently referred to in writings on the composer (see, for example, Smith Brindle). His origins in some remote part of Yugoslavia, his father's persecution for being and teaching Italian, Dallapiccola's marriage to a Jew, and his treatment as an outcast at the Conservatory of Florence for simply not being Florentine, and for an attachment to Schoenberg's serialism within an institution which in 1934 was unprogressive and anti-Germanic in its musical tastes — all these things contributed to a feeling of insecurity which the preoccupation with structure in Dallapiccola's works, and the creation of symmetry, balance, parallels, and binary and tripartite patterns in *Ulisse,* attempts, as it were, to rectify. Fundamentally, all of these structures, in their turn, underline the concept of a life directed by the purpose and meaning afforded by religious faith, and belief in the existence of God.

Musical Structures

It was, in fact, as W. E. Von Lewinski explains, the order and structure inherent in the dodecaphonic system (see pp. 17–19) that attracted Dallapiccola to it (whereas other avant-garde composers, like Berg, found it unattractive for precisely the same reasons). In the twelve-tone system Dallapiccola found a way to 'legare il suo *melos*' [structure his *melos*]:

Ciò che semmai angustiava Berg nel sistema dodecafonico, cioè un ordine troppo severo che minacciava di restringere la sfera d'azione della fantasia, era ciò che allettava Dallapiccola: egli aveva bisogno proprio della severità di un sistema per legare il suo *melos*. In questo senso rimase sempre un classico: teso tra i due poli ordine-libertà, senza mai rinunciare all'uno per amore dell'altro. (*Saggi*, p. 28)

[That which troubled Berg about the dodecaphonic system, namely a much too severe order which threatened to restrict the range of his fantasy, was what attracted Dallapiccola to it: he needed precisely the rigour of the system to structure his *melos*. In this sense he always remained a classic: torn betwen the two poles of order and liberty, without ever renouncing one for the love of the other.]

In *Ulisse* Dallapiccola uses the tone row in all of its four variations: in its original form, as well as in its retrograde, inverted, and retrograde inverted forms. The original tone row is called 'Mare I' [Sea I], and all four versions together constitute the 'Serie del Mare I' ['Sea I Series']:

O = Original; R = Retrograde; I = Inversion; RI = Retrograde Inversion.

The four different themes which the 'Mare I' Series gives rise to are, in fact, doubled in the work by the splitting of each theme into two (dividing the tone-row into six rather than twelve notes), and parts of these themes are transposed to different pitches to be incorporated into new themes. For example, while the first six notes of the original tone row of 'Mare I' form the basis for the 'Serie del Mare II' ['Sea II Series'], the retrograde inverted form of 'Mare I' in the sixth position, form the last six notes of the 'Mare II' original tone row:

As well as the 'sea', each of the characters in *Ulisse* is given their own tone row which becomes, as it were, their theme tune. These musical themes then interrelate in accordance with how the characters themselves interrelate, so that all of the symmetries — the comparisons and contrasts — that were evident on the level of episodes and characters, also exist on the level of the music. Ulysses's theme is, as one would expect, closely linked to that of the sea: the first six notes are the inversion of those of the original 'Mare II' theme; the second six notes are the retrograde form of the second half of 'Mare II':

The Lotus-eaters' theme, meanwhile, is the retrograde form of Ulysses's theme, transposed down a semitone:

Dallapiccola obviously chooses the *retrograde* variation in order to underline how the Lotus-eaters' philosophy of sleepy indulgence is the total *opposite* of Ulysses's quest — his never-ending 'looking' and 'marvelling' — just as their stultifying of the senses acts as an antithesis to the arousal of the senses offered by the sea (its 'odor' [smell] and its 'mille voci', I, ii [thousand voices]). Similarly, Penelope and Calypso, alike in their reclusiveness, and in their singing, weaving, and waiting, sing the same melancholic motif, the only difference being that Penelope's is transposed a third under that of Calypso. And Antinous's recurrent refrain, announcing his Epicurean abandon — 'lieta, gaia, lieta, gaia,' [happy, merry, happy, merry] — while being semantically opposed to the 'Pianto, lacrime, rimorso' [Weeping, tears, remorse] motif of the Cimmerians is, once again, musically identical to it, thereby emphasizing how Antinous will soon be joining the Cimmerian numbers in Hell.

These few examples bear witness to how, in the words of M. Venuti, *Ulisse* is 'un'opera [...] calcolata nei particolari' [35] [an opera [...] whose details have been carefully calculated]. In fact, as well as dodecaphonic theme tunes for characters, it also contains a number of different rhythms which are attached to characters and which operate structurally. The 'ritmo principale' [main rhythm] associated with Ulysses, underlines, in its 3/2 time signature and its use of triplets, the concentric, never-ending nature of Ulysses's search (his 'guardare, meravigliarsi, e tornar a guardare'):

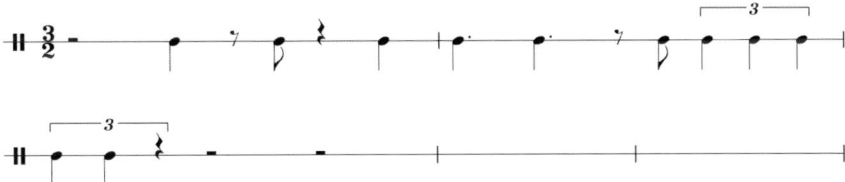

Used at various points throughout the whole opera, it surfaces for the last time at the very end (bar 1023), after the entire orchestra is united on a triple *forte*, and just before Ulysses's revelation and the words 'Signore! Non più soli sono il mio cuore e il mare'. Here, however, Ulysses's rhythm is transferred into pauses. Dallapiccola asks for an 'interruzione improvvisa del suono' [a sudden interruption of the sound] on the triple *forte*, and a 'scrupolosa esattezza dei valori ritmici' (Kämper, p. 263)

FIG. 2.3: Luigi Dallapiccola's *Ulisse* (Milan: Suvini Zerboni, 1968), pp. 406–07
Courtesy of Sugarmusic SpA — Milano

Ulis. cuo — re e il ma — — re.
heart and the sea.

1030

Ulis.

♩ = 48

Arpa. Cel.

Tr. c. s.

Solo Vl.

Cl. picc.

Solo Vla.

Cor. c. s.

Fl.

(+ Arpa. Cel.)

Cl. B.

SIPARIO LENTO
SLOW CURTAIN + Vl.

♩ = 40

lunghissima

Cel.

Vl., Xilo.

lunghissima

Legni

Archi (trem.)

FINE DELL'OPERA
END OF OPERA

*Fecisti nos ad te et inquietum
est cor nostrum, donec reque-
scat in te.
(Sancti Aurelii Augustini "Confessionum" Liber I Caput I)*

S. 6910 Z.

[meticulous precision in the time signatures]. This enables the 'ritmo principale' to be better heard within the silence. The very fact that Ulysses' 'concentric' rhythm has now been converted into silence, a silence which precedes the word 'Signore!', seems to reinforce how his never-ending search is at an end, Ulysses having now found 'God' (see Figure 2.3). Bars 1025 to 1030 in Figure 2.3 also demonstrate the visual aspect of Dallapiccola's music, where the musical signs which denote spoken rather than sung notes aim to reproduce graphically the stars which, as previously explained, have a Dantesque and religious symbolism in all of Dallapiccola's works; while the six minims on the word 'mare' [sea], in their close proximity to each other on the chromatic scale, are visually evocative of the gentle rolling motion of the sea.

Intertextuality and Self-Quotation

The carefully planned verbal and musical structures of *Ulisse* accentuate the heavy intellectualism of Dallapiccola's opera. Giving added emphasis to this aspect are its intertextual references to other opera libretti. As Kämper has observed (Kämper, p. 267), Ulysses's exclamation in the Epilogue, 'Trovar potessi il Nome, pronunciar la Parola' is meant to echo Busoni's *Doktor Faust*, where Faust, at the end of the opera proclaims 'O pregare, pregare! Dove trovare le parole?' [Oh, to be able to pray, to pray! Where do I find the words?], while also alluding to the final words of Moses at the end of the second act of Schoenberg's *Moses und Aron*: 'O Wort, du Wort, daß mir fehlt' [O Word, you Word, which fails me]. *Ulisse* also occasionally hints at celebrated moments in the traditional repertoire. Thus Nausicaa's concluding remark in the account of her dream 'Ditemi, amiche, è forse ciò l'amore?' (I, i) [Tell me, friends, could this be love?'] is clearly meant to evoke Cherubino's aria 'Voi che sapete che cosa è amor' [You who know what love is] from Mozart's *Le nozze di Figaro*. Similarly, those well-known scenes of deliberate insult common to traditional opera, which act as a springboard for most of the ensuing drama (for example, Don Giovanni's invitation to dinner of the statue of the Commendatore in Mozart's *Don Giovanni*; or Rigoletto's mocking of Monterone whose daughter has been seduced by the Duke in Verdi's *Rigoletto*) find their correlative in Melantho's irreverent gesture in Act II, scene 3, when she dances provocatively with Ulysses' bow. There are Wagnerian touches too. The bow, which only Ulysses can string and bend, corresponds to Wotan's sword in Wagner's *Die Walküre* which only Siegmund can extract from the oak tree in which it is embedded; and when in the kingdom of Alcinous Ulysses is asked his name and replies 'Odio, affanno, desío di vendetta: questo, quest'è il mio nome' (I, i) [Hatred, heart-break, and hunger for revenge: these, these are my names], there is an echo to Siegmund's reference to himself as 'Wehwalt' (for further examples, see Mila, *Saggi*, p. 39).

However, even more than nodding in the direction of other opera composers, *Ulisse* endulges in the abundant self-quotation which is characteristic of the majority of Dallapiccola's work.[36] For example, the climax of Melantho's dance (bar 727) when the bow-string twists itself around her neck (thereby prefiguring her imminent hanging) makes a musical allusion to the third movement of Dallapiccola's

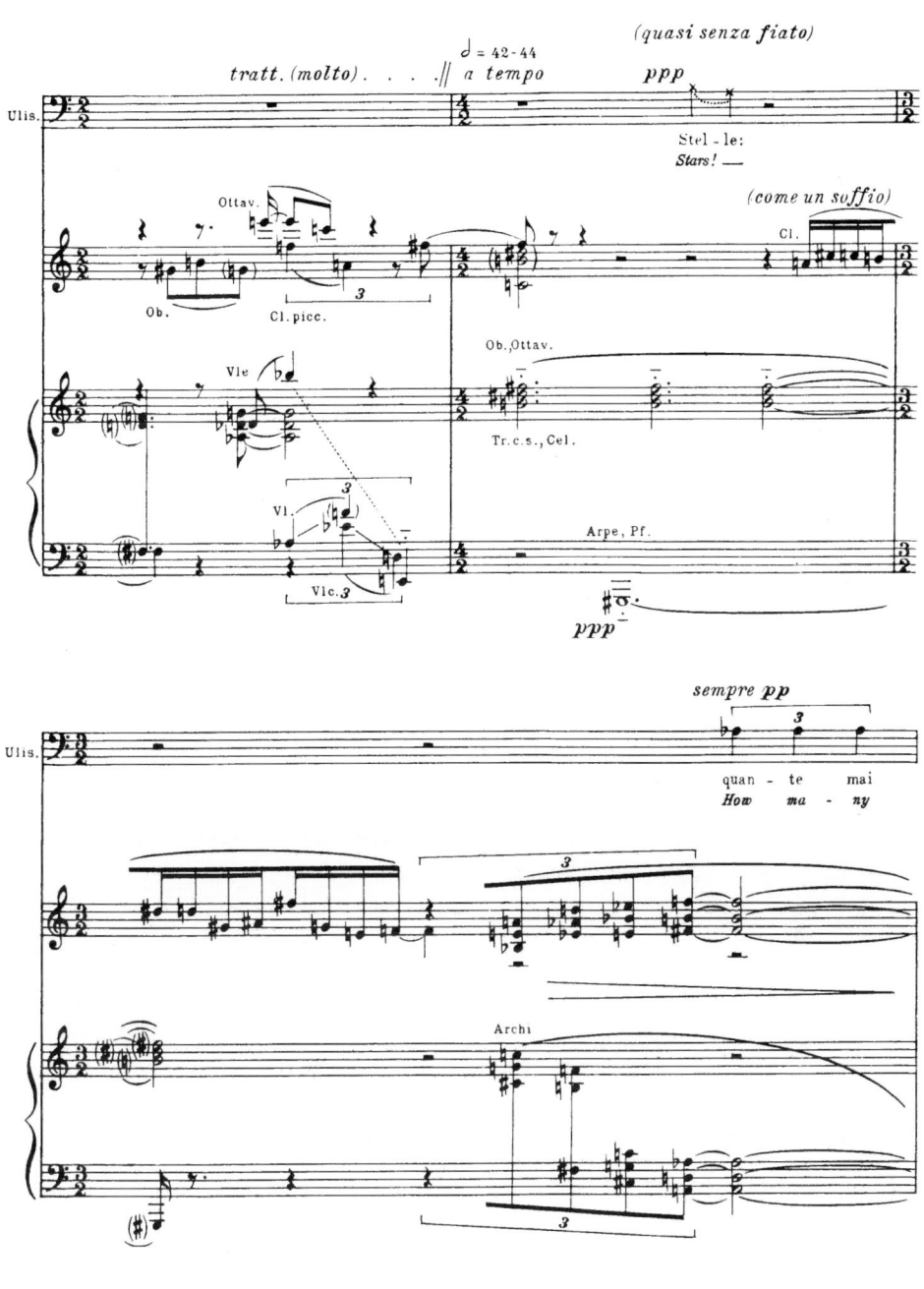

FIG. 2.4. Luigi Dallapiccola's *Ulisse*, p. 393
Courtesy of Sugarmusic SpA — Milano

Fig. 2.5. Luigi Dallapiccola's *Volo di notte* (Milan: Ricordi, 1938), p. 198
Courtesy of G. Ricordi & C. — SpA — Milano)

An Mathilde. In his notes to *An Mathilde* Dallapiccola cites the first line of the Heine poem on which the third movement is based — 'Das ist der böse Thanatos' [That is evil Death] — and underlines the word 'Thanatos'. The musical allusion to *An Mathilde* thereby reinforces how Melantho's dance is a dance of death. Similarly, the intervallic differences in the first three notes of the 'Serie del Mare I' (a falling semitone followed by a rising tone) find their origin in Dallapiccola's *Goethe-Lieder* where they were used to accompany the question 'Ist's möglich?' ('Is it possible?'). In *Ulisse* they become a musical symbol suggesting different contexts of uncertainty or elusiveness. They occur whenever Ulysses either has his identity questioned by others or questions it himself, for example, at the beginning of Act 1, Scene 4 when the Cimmerians enquire of him 'Chi sei? Che cerchi?' [Who are you? What are you searching for?], and towards the end of the same scene when Ulysses poses himself the same questions 'Chi sono? Che cerco?' [Who am I? What am I searching for?]. They also appear on the mentioning of the key word 'Nessuno' to reinforce all of the existential doubt and uncertainty that the word evokes in the opera.

But it is in the Epilogue, after Ulysses utters the phrase 'nell'alma le memorie farsi sembran più dense' [in my soul memories seem to accumulate] that there follows a whole chain of auto-citation. Dallapiccola is clearly identifying himself with Ulysses contemplating and reviewing his life. On Ulysses' exclamation 'Stelle' [Stars] (bar 953, marked 'ppp' and 'quasi senza fiato') there is an ethereal-sounding B major triad, followed by twelve (rhythmically compressed) notes on the clarinet (see Figure 2.4). This same B major triad accompanied the phrase 'Scorgo le stelle' [I can see the stars] in Dallapiccola's opera *Volo di notte*, when the pilot, Fabien, drove his aeroplane out of the hurricane, above the clouds and towards the stars (see Figure 2.5):

> Scorgo le stelle! A costo di non poter ridiscendere voglio raggiungerle. Tutto si fa luminoso: le mie mani, le mie vesti, le mie ali! Troppo bello. Sotto di me... tutto è chiuso.
>
> [I can see the stars! I want to reach them even if it means never being able to come down again. Everything is gleaming: my hands, my clothes, my wings. So beautiful. Beneath me ... everything is closed.]

The twelve notes on the clarinet accompanying the B major triad in *Ulisse* also constituted the original note-row at the basis of *Volo di notte,* and from *Volo di notte* they had been borrowed, in their turn, for the first of Dallapiccola's *Tre Laudi*. The B major triad occurs again on the ecstatically proclaimed 'Le stelle! Il cielo!' of *Il Prigioniero*, where the prisoner, having escaped from his cell, crawls along subterranean passages eventually to see the night-sky. On all three occasions — in *Ulisse*, *Volo di notte*, and *Il Prigioniero* — the stars and the B major triad have a religious symbolism: they announce Ulysses's discovery of God; they hail Fabien's unearthly joy as he leaves this world and enters the next; and they accompany the prisoner's appreciation of the immense value of freedom, for which he praises God. The religious connotations of Dallapiccola's stars are even further emphasized by their appearance at the *end* of his three operas, thereby creating a parallel with Dante's three *cantiche*, each of which ends with the key word 'stelle' — symbol of the ultimate destination of man: his ascent to heaven and to God.

Conclusion

In view of the intricate nature of the musical and literary intertextual references in Dallapiccola's *Ulisse*, it is not surprising that the critics at the Berlin premiere of the opera did not react positively. Indeed, *Ulisse* has been criticized by Venuti as a cerebral opera which leaves one emotionally cold, and which in order to be appreciated fully needs to be analysed and studied prior to any attendance at a performance:

> L'opera risulta perfino troppo levigata [...] tanto da poter generare più freddezza che emotività nello spettatore impreparato, poiché si trasforma in un'opera che ha costituzionalmente bisogno di una preparazione adeguata per essere veramente compresa e amata. (Venuti, p. 109)

> [The opera is even too polished [...] so much so that rather than arousing emotion in the unprepared spectator, it is capable of leaving him cold. This is because it is an opera which, in order to be really understood and appreciated, needs an adequate preparation on the part of the spectator.]

Venuti is indeed right when he proclaims that merely to act as a spectator to *Ulisse* will leave one emotionally cold. Unless, for example, one recognizes the Kierkegaardian associations of the opera, and is aware of Kierkegaard's theory that knowledge of God is obtained through a 'leap of faith' or moment of enlightenment, then Ulysses' sudden and final conversion may seem totally implausible and something in fact which kills the opera dramatically. But this is not an opera for the casual or uninformed theatre-goer, and indeed the point of the opera is that passive, casual looking is never enough. Like Ulysses who, in the Epilogue, contemplated the stars in a *different* way on the night of his religious revelation, the reader-spectator must also commune closely with the work, and observe in greater detail: '*Guardare* [...] *e tornar a guardare*'. The libretto, when compared to that of Berio's *Laborintus II* or Manzoni's *Parole da Becket* (see Chapters 3 and 5), may seem old-fashioned and, in its allusions to classical and medieval literature, out of sync with contemporary poetry. However, what the libretto aims to do is to invite the reader-listener to make *connections*, to discover relationships between literary fragments bridging classical, medieval, and modern times, thereby highlighting that the problems facing man, as exemplified by Ulysses, are timeless ones. Only by engaging in the inter- and extra-textual work that the opera demands, and only by discovering, in that way, its total reliance upon the principle of interaction, does one transcend the Joycean 'lonechill' that Venuti suggests that the opera might cause, and instead feel part of Dallapiccola's vision of a better modern man: no longer alone, fragmented, in a culturally fragmented world, but in a world where devotion to intellect is exercised only for the betterment of society as a whole, and where in that society man's aimless drifting is replaced by the purpose and meaning afforded by religious belief.

Notes to Chapter 1

1. Dallapiccola's academic writings have been collected together in *Parole e musica*, ed. by Fiamma Nicolodi (Milan: Il Saggiatore, 1980). Many of these essays have been published in English in *Dallapiccola on Opera*, trans. and ed. by Rudy Shackelford (London: Toccata, 1987).

2. Quoted by Dallapiccola in 'Nota per il programma della prima esecuzione italiana di *Ulisse* al Teatro alla Scala (13.1.1970)', in *Luigi Dallapiccola: appunti, incontri, meditazioni* (Milan: Suvini Zerboni, 1970), pp. 189–91 (p. 191). Dallapiccola does not say who made this critical comment.

3. See *Enciclopedia Garzanti della Musica* (Milan: Garzanti, 1974), p. 151.

4. There have been, to date, two other studies of *Ulisse* which include a consideration of the libretto: Massimo Mila, 'L'*Ulisse*: opera a due dimensioni', in *Luigi Dallapiccola, Saggi, Testimonianze, Carteggio, Biografia, e Bibliografia*, ed. by Fiamma Nicolodi (Milan: Suvini Zerboni, 1975), pp. 31–43; and Pierluigi Petrobelli, 'Dallapiccola and *Ulisse*', *Cambridge Opera Journal* 1–2 (1989–90), 239–49. Mila tends to repeat what Dallapiccola tells one of the libretto in 'Nascita'; Petrobelli explains Dante's version of Ulysses's death in the *Inferno*, and recounts a 'few anecdotes' which illustrate Dallapiccola's 'constant enthusiasm for Dante'.

5. Machado, *Poesías completas*, ed. by G. Savidis (Madrid: Espasa-Calpe, 1971), p. 133.

6. In *Friedrich Hölderlin. Selected Poems and Fragments* (bilingual text), trans. by M. Hamburger, ed. by J. Adler (London: Penguin, 1998), pp. 24–27.

7. 'Ithaka', in *C. P. Cavafy. Collected Poems*, trans. by E. Keeley and P. Sherrard (Princeton: Princeton University Press, 1992), pp. 36–37.

8. James Joyce, *A Portrait of the Artist as a Young Man*, ed. by J. Johnson (Oxford: Oxford University Press, 2000), pp. 100–14 (p. 112).

9. Friedrich Nietzsche, *Beyond Good and Evil*, trans. by R. J. Hollingdale (London: Penguin, 1990), p. 102.

10. Augustine, *Confessions*, ed. by J. J. O'Donnell (Oxford: Clarendon Press, 1992), I, 10.

11. W. B. Stanford, *The Ulysses Theme. A Study in the Adaptability of a Traditional Hero* (Oxford: Blackwell, 1954), pp. 184–94.

12. See in particular *Either/Or,* 1843 (hereafter *EO*), trans. by D. F. and L. M. Swenson and W. Lowrie, 2 vols (Princeton: Princeton University Press, 1959); *The Concept of Anxiety,* 1844 (hereafter *CA*), trans. by R. Thomte and A. B. Anderson (Princeton: Princeton University Press, 1980); *Concluding Unscientific Postscript,* 1846 (hereafter *CUP*), trans. by D. F. Swenson and W. Lowrie (Princeton: Princeton University Press, 1941); and *The Sickness unto Death,* 1849 (hereafter *SD*), trans. by H. V. and E. H. Hong (Princeton: Princeton University Press, 1967). For a full bibliography of Kierkegaard's works, see Patrick Gardiner, *Kierkegaard* (Oxford: Oxford University Press, 1988), p. 1 and p. 117. For criticism on Kierkegaard's writings, see, in addition to Gardiner, James Collins, *The Mind of Kierkegaard* (Princeton: Princeton University Press, 1953); Louis Mackey, *Kierkegaard: A Kind of Poet* (Philadelphia: University of Pennsylvania Press, 1971); and Alastair Hannay, *Kierkegaard* (London: Routledge and Kegan Paul, 1982). For further writings about Kierkegaard's philosophy, and his relationship to existentialism, see Gardiner, pp. 117–18.

13. Giuseppe Magnani, '*Ulisse*: per un'analisi antropologico-musicale', in *Studi su Luigi Dallapiccola,* ed. by Arrigo Quattrocchi (Lucca: Libreria Musicale Italiana Editrice, 1993), pp. 103–28 (p. 121).

14. Homer, *The Odyssey*, trans. by E. V. Rieu (London: Penguin, 1991), p. 124.

15. Dante, *La Divina Commedia, Inferno* (London, Oxford, New York: Oxford University Press, 1975), p. 326. Canto XXVI (lines 114–16).

16. See A. Terry, *Antonio Machado. Campos de Castilla* (London: Grant and Cutler, 1973), pp. 53–63.

17. Giovanni Pascoli, 'L'ultimo viaggio', *Poesie, con due saggi critici di Gianfranco Contini e una nota bio-bibliografica*, 3 vols (Milan: Mondadori, 1974), II, 954–96.

18. For an interesting reading of Pascoli's 'L'ultimo viaggio', emphasizing nineteenth- century man's futile desire for total knowledge, see Piero Boitani, *The Shadow of Ulysses. Figures of a Myth* (Oxford: Clarendon Press, 1994), pp. 128–30. In his book, Boitani explores the varying interpretations (philosophical, ethical, political) of the Ulysses myth by different cultures. There is, however, only a passing reference to Dallapiccola's *Ulisse*.

19. For further information on this aspect of Homer, see S. Murnaghan, *Disguise and Recognition in the Odyssey* (Princeton: Princeton University Press, 1987).

20. R. J. Hollingdale, *Thomas Mann: A Critical Study* (London: Rupert Hart-Davis, 1971), p. 114.

21. James Joyce, *Ulysses* (London: Penguin, 1992), p. 394.

22. N. Kazantzakis, *The Odyssey. A Modern Sequel*, trans. by K. Friar (New York: Simon and Schuster, 1958).

23. Alfred Tennyson, 'The Lotos-Eaters', in *Selections from Tennyson*, ed. by J. H. Jagger (London, Toronto, New York: J. M. Dent and Sons, 1928), pp. 129–35.

24. J. R. Kincaid, *Tennyson's Major Poems* (New Haven and London: Yale University Press, 1975), pp. 39–45.

25. See, for example, E. E. Smith, *The Two Voices. A Tennyson Study* (Lincoln: University of Nebraska Press, 1964), pp. 30–33.

26. See *Critical Essays on the Poetry of Tennyson*, ed. by J. Killham (London: Routledge and Kegan Paul, 1960), p. 167.

27. For a reading of the Ulysses canto which reinforces how Ulysses's end results from Dante's didactic intention, see G. Singh, '*Inferno* XXVI: A Personal Appreciation', in *Dante Commentaries. Eight Studies of the Divine Comedy*, ed. by D. Nolan (Dublin: Irish Academic Press, 1977), pp. 43–62.

28. For readings which emphasize Ulysses's heroic presentation in Tennyson, see Kincaid, pp. 41–45; and Dorothy Sayers, 'The Eighth Bolgia', in *Further Papers on Dante* (London: Methuen, 1957), pp. 114–20. For a reading which highlights Tennyson's disapproval of Ulysses, see E. J. Chiasson, 'Tennyson's "Ulysses" — A Re-interpretation', in *Critical Essays on the Poetry of Tennyson*, ed. by J. Killham (London: Routledge, 1960), pp. 164–73.

29. Quoted in Kämper, p. 88. Marsyas, the flautist, challenges Apollo, the lyre-player, to a music competition to determine who plays the best. Apollo wins, and Marsyas expiates his hubris with a cruel death.

30. Aeschylus, *Agamemnon, The Oresteia*, trans. by R. Fagles (London: Penguin Books, 1977), pp. 99–173.

31. The two versions of Agamemnon's death differ. For Homer's version see Book XI, 405–39. In Homer, Aegisthus invites Agamemnon to the palace, feasts him, and then has him killed 'as a man fells an ox at its manger' (p. 171).

32. Thomas Mann, *Joseph and his Brothers*, translated by H. T. Lowe-Porter, 3 vols (London: Sphere, 1968), III, 259–78.

33. Dante, *Il Convivio*, Vol. II (Florence: Le Monnier, 1937), 292

34. The term 'claritas' has been translated here in English as 'radiance' and in Italian as 'chiarezza'. The Italian version is Dallapiccola's own; the English translation is that given in James Joyce's *A Portrait of an Artist*, p. 178–79, where Stephen Dedalus discusses Aquinas's 'claritas'. This English version has been used because of the influence of Joyce in *Ulisse*.

35. M. Venuti, *Il teatro di Dallapiccola* (Milan: Suvini Zerboni, 1985). The other major study of the musical aspects of *Ulisse* is the aforementioned article by G. Magnani.

36. For Dallapiccola's use of self-quotation, see R. Brown, 'Dallapiccola's use of symbolic self-quotation', *Studi musicali*, no. 4 (1975), 277–304.

Fig. 3.1. Photograph of Luciano Berio
Courtesy of Sugarmusic SpA — Milano

CHAPTER 3

Luciano Berio's *Laborintus II* (1965)

In 1963 the ORTF (French Radio) commissioned the composer Luciano Berio and the poet Edoardo Sanguineti to write a work celebrating the seven hundredth anniversary of Dante's birth. The result was *Laborintus II*,[1] a piece of musical theatre named after Sanguineti's original *Laborintus* (1951–54) — a long prose poem which was instrumental in sparking off the Neo-Avant-garde movement in Italy (see Introduction, p. 4). Like much of the literature produced by the Neo-Avant-garde, *Laborintus II* condemns the new capitalist values of 1960s' Italy (see p. 3), and Sanguineti uses Dante and Dante's critique of usury in the *Inferno* as the focal point of the libretto. Around that nucleus he intertwines a sequence of other motifs which aim to underscore the perpetuation of cycles of sin and evil from the 'beginning' of time (the original Fall, the pre-diluvial and post-diluvial era) through to, literally, the 'middle' ages, and the 'end' period (the modern, existentialist one, and the neo-capitalist 1960s during which Sanguineti was composing his libretto). The concept of 'beginnings', 'middles', and 'ends' is used to frame the work as a whole. Against the kaleidoscopic visions of 'sin' presented, Sanguineti pits the opposite and simple concept of 'godliness'. Hence the structure of the work is very much based on binary antitheses, but within the antitheses lie also analogies. In fact the 'labyrinth' of the title refers to a multitude of labyrinthine connections between the following: a tape of pre-recorded, electronic music and the live performance; a group of voices (one solo male speaker, three female singers, and a chorus of eight actor-singers) and the tape; the soloists and the instruments (a jazz orchestra and a small string ensemble); the libretto and the music; and, last but not least, the various and widely differing extracts used to make up the libretto. This chapter will address the question of 'connections' 'between the words and the music, and, in particular, the connections between the various parts of the libretto. Whereas the former — the words-music connection — has received some critical attention in the only comprehensive study that exists of *Laborintus II* to date (a doctoral thesis by P. Stacey, submitted to the University of East Anglia in 1984),[2] the latter area — the fascinating and often ingenious links between the extracts that make up the libretto — has not, as yet, been the object of any research.

The libretto, put together by Sanguineti, consists of a montage of citations from early medieval, late medieval, and modern works. The early medieval work quoted is Isidore of Seville's *Etymologiarum sive Originum*. In the *Etymologiae* the Spanish encyclopaedist, theologian, and historian (*c.* 560–636) catalogued in twenty volumes all knowledge accessible to him from previous encyclopaedists, specialists, and Latin writers on the Bible, the liberal arts, medicine, law, history, anthropology, and zoology. The citations used in *Laborintus II* are drawn from sections on the Old Testament. The late medieval component is provided by Dante's *Vita Nuova*, the *Inferno* (cantos I, III, VII, and XI), and the *Convivio*. The modern texts used are ones that were in some way inspired by Dante: Ezra Pound's 'Canto XLV', subtitled 'With Usura' (*Cantos*); T. S. Eliot's 'East Coker' (*Four Quartets*); and Sanguineti's own previous work — the original *Laborintus* — quotations from which are, for the most part, intermingled with new lyrics that Sanguineti composed especially for the libretto.[3]

In order, more easily, to guide the reader through the maze of sources and their ramifications and relationships to each other, this chapter will divide the libretto of *Laborintus II* into fourteen small parts, although it goes without saying that these divisions are nowhere to be found in the work itself.

Part 1: Isidore of Seville's *Etymologiae*, Book XV

The source of the opening phrase from *Laborintus II* is a sentence from Book XV of Isidore's *Etymologiae*. Book XV, entitled 'De Aedificiis et Agris', discusses the origins of pre-diluvial and post-diluvial towns and lands. Isidore explains how, before the flood, Cain founded the first city in the land of Naid, calling it Enoch after his son (the most common spelling for 'Naid' is 'Nod'):

> Primus ante diluvium Cain civitatem Enoch ex nomine filii sui in Naid condidit. (*Etym.* XV. i. 3)

> [First before the flood, Cain founded the city of Enoch named after his son in the land of Naid.]

Sanguineti edits and abridges Isidore's text to focus exclusively upon the city of Enoch:

> A civitate Enoch in Naid. (score, p. 1)
> [From the city of Enoch in Naid.]

This phrase is sung by an incisive, high-pitched, and rather terrifying female voice, around which two other female voices 'experiment' with the phonetic qualities of the line, picking up its predominant vowel sounds, and either enunciating them by themselves or combining them with consonants to create phonemes, which in themselves function as rudimentary musical elements, and sound to the listener like elementary child language: 'be', 'ce', and 'da'. On a musical level, the emphasis would therefore seem to be on *origins*, and this is also true on a textual level. The line 'a civitate Enoch in Naid' has obvious biblical connotations, and multiple references to *beginnings*: not only to the first city, but also, as Isidore's text makes clear, to Cain. Cain was the first born of the first human beings (Adam and Eve) who committed the first murder (of his brother Abel). It is to the first city that Sanguineti's quotation makes precise reference, but the implicit references are in fact more significant from the thematic point of view of the libretto: the beginnings of the human race, the start of civilization, and, with civilization, the inception of evil and violence in the world (which, of course, had already begun, in an orthodox sense, with the 'original sin' committed by Adam and Eve). In *Laborintus II* Berio and Sanguineti will denounce the evil and violence of civilization, from its earliest days, evoked in the quotation from Isidore, to the present age. The didactic and moralizing intentions of the work have already been firmly established.

Part 2: Dante's *Vita nuova*, Chapters I, II

Shortly after the three females have begun singing, the solo male speaker begins to read extracts from the *Vita nuova*. The calm of his voice immediately offers a contrast to the terrifying nature of the singing above it, and, on a textual level too, the whole of the *Vita nuova* section operates in terms of contrasts and analogies with that from Isidore. Sanguineti has in fact altered Dante's text. He has extrapolated short and dislocated phrase units from Chapters I and II of the *Vita nuova*, sometimes embroidering them and sometimes slightly altering them, to create a new and largely coherent text. In the original, the first lines of the *Vita nuova* read:

> In quella parte del libro de la mia memoria dinanzi a la quale poco si potrebbe leggere, si trova una rubrica la quale dice: *Incipit vita nova*. (*Vn*. I, p. 51)

> [In that part of the book of my memory before which little could be read, there is a rubric which says: *The new life begins*.]

Of the first phrase Sanguineti has effectively created a sequence characterized by accumulative repetition:

> In quella parte; in quella parte della mia memoria; in quella parte del libro; in quella parte del libro della mia memoria incipit vita nova. (score, p. 1)

> [In that part; in that part of my memory; in that part of the book; in that part of the book of my memory the new life begins.]

The text moves backwards more than it moves forwards, constantly returning to repeat the initial phrase ('in quella parte') or words that have been gradually added to it ('memoria' and 'libro') . The emphasis therefore, as in the section from Isidore, would seem to be on 'beginnings', further underscored by Sanguineti skipping over the next two and a half phrases in the Dante line to arrive at the key term announcing a *new start*: 'incipit vita nova'. But whereas the 'beginnings' in the section from Isidore were associated with original sin, and a procreation which gave way to murder and ungodliness, the 'vita nova' in Sanguineti's reworking of Dante appears clothed in a 'noble ', 'modest', 'pure', and 'sanguine' colour; and it is Love ('Deus') who is the ruling power:

> Incipit vita nova: e apparve vestita di nobilissimo colore, umile e onesto, sanguigno: ecce Deus, ecce Deus fortior me: dominabitur mihi. (score, p. 1)

> [The new life begins: and she appeared clothed in a most noble, humble and sanguine colour: behold God, behold God stronger than me: ruling over me.]

In the original Dante, the 'vita nova' is, of course, also a felicitous phenomenon, signifying (as the rest of chapter II in the *Vita nuova* clarifies) the 'new life' which began for Dante when he first saw 'la gloriosa donna [...] Beatrice' [the glorious woman [...] Beatrice]. The direct reference to Beatrice is excluded in the Sanguineti text, so that it is the 'new life' itself which has the qualities of 'nobility', 'modesty', and so on listed above — in Dante the four adjectives 'nobilissimo', 'umile', 'onesto', and 'sanguigno' refer literally to the 'colour' of Beatrice's dress — but the Beatrice reference is surely implied, together with all of its positive connotations which act as an antithesis to the negative ones suggested in Isidore's quotation. To the reference to original sin is opposed courtly (non-sexual) love; and to the allusion to murder and ungodliness is opposed Beatrice as an allegorical figure (in Dante's later works) representing theology, and leading man to a contemplation of God and the attainment of Paradise. By leaving the reference to Beatrice as an implicit one, the suggestive qualities of the text are increased, so that, when read in relation to Isidore's extract which is being sung simultaneously with the Dante, one is tempted to see the 'vita nova' as referring to the 'original creation' — the 'first', 'marvellous' life, the state of living as God intended it to be *before* the 'original sin' of Adam and Eve and the ensuing transgression of man. Significantly, 'nova', from 'novus', as well as meaning 'new' in Latin, can also mean 'first', as well as 'wonderful' or 'marvellous'.

Part 3: Isidore's *Etymologiae*, Book XV

The next part of the libretto is half sung, half spoken by the eight actor-singers. The text is once again Book XV of Isidore's *Etymologiae*, where Isidore has moved on to a discussion of the post-diluvial towns — Babylon and Jerusalem. From the text below, Sanguineti has taken and, again, occasionally edited, a number of short, fragmentary words and phrases — those italicized:

> Primus post diluvium Nembroth gigans *Babylonem-urbem* Mesopotamiae fundavit. Hanc Semiramis regina Assyriorum ampliavit, murumque urbis bitumine et cocto latere fecit. Vocabulum autem sumpsit a confusione, eo quod ibi confusae sint atque permixtae linguae aedificantium turrem. Iudaei asserunt Sem, filium Noe, quem dicunt Melchisedech, primum post diluvium *in Syria* condidisse *urbem Salem*, in qua regnum fuit eiusdem Melchisedech. Hanc postea tenuerunt Iebusaei, ex quibus et sortita vocabulum est Iebus; sicque duobus nominibus copulatis *Iebus et Salem vocata est Hierusalem*, quae postea a Salomone Hierosolyma quasi Hierosolomonia dicta est. Haec et corrupte a poetis *Solyma nuncupata est*, et postmodum ab Aelio Hadriano *Aelia vocitata est*. [In] Ipsa est et *Sion*, quae Hebraice interpretatur *speculatio*, eo quod in sublimi constructa sit, et de longe venientia contempletur. *Hierusalem* [autem] *pacifica* in nostro sermone transfertur. (*Etym.* XV. i. 4–6)

> [First after the flood, the giant Nimrod founded the city of Babylon in Mesopotamia. Queen Semiramis of the Assyrians increased this city in size, and made the city wall out of bitumen and terracotta. But the city took its name from confusion, since the languages of those who built the tower were confused and mixed together there. The Jews claim that Sem, son of Noah, whom they call Melchizedek, was the first after the flood to found the city of Salem in Syria, in which was situated the kingdom of the same Melchizedek. Later, the Jebusites held this city, and they also gave it the name Iebus; and so, with the two names, Iebus and Salem, joined together, the city came to be called Hierusalem, and subsequently was named Hierosolyma by Solomon

(i.e. Hierosolomonia). This name was also wrongly called Solyma by the poets, and afterwards Aelius Hadrianus called it Aelia. The city is also known by the name of Sion, which in Hebrew means observation point, because it was built on high ground and from it one could view all things coming from afar. In our language, the city means peaceful Hierusalem.]

Sanguineti omits all of Isidore's detailed etymological *explanations*, and homes in on the name references to the two cities, Babylon and Jerusalem. He changes Isidore's 'Babylonem-urbem' to 'a Babylone urbe' [from the city of Babylon], adds a further reference to Babylon not cited in Isidore's text — 'a Babylone urbe ab urbe' — and juxtaposes these allusions with the majority of the terms denoting Jerusalem listed by Isidore in his etymological tracing of the city's name: Salem, Iebus, Hierusalem, Solyma, Aelia, and Sion:

> Sion speculatio
> a Babylone urbe
> vocata vocata est Hierusalem
> ab urbe Salem in Syria
> et Iebus et Salem vocata est Hierusalem
> Solyma noncupata est
> Aelia vocitata est
> Hierusalem pacifica
> a Babylone urbe ab urbe. (score pp. 2–3)

> [Sion observation point/ from the city of Babylon/ is called is called Hierusalem/ from the city of Salem in Syria/ and Iebus and Salem is called Hierusalem/ it is not called Solyma/ it is called Aelia/ peaceful Hierusalem/ from the city of Babylon from the city.]

Each of these fragments is repeated many times, and the musical technique used here is a sort of fugue, with the first of the actor-singers singing a group of the quotations to a musical theme which is then successively taken up by the other seven actor-singers, and developed by a certain amount of interweaving of parts. The interweaving creates the effect of a Babylonian confusion. It is a technique akin to the accumulative repetition that characterized Sanguineti's earlier rewriting of the opening lines of Dante's *Vita nuova*. Musically, therefore, the emphasis is again upon repetition. Textually the quotations from Isidore allow Sanguineti to underline the evil / good polarity that has already been established between parts 1 and 2 of the libretto. Zion (or Jerusalem) as a symbol of God, and Babylon as a symbol of evil was first established by the Old Testament prophet, Isaiah, and it is these symbolic meanings which are implicit in the libretto. According to Isaiah Zion was to be a city where 'The wolf [...] shall dwell with the lamb, and the leopard shall lie down with the kid' (Isaiah, 11. 6); where 'they shall not hurt nor destroy' (11. 9); and he prophesizes how God would destroy the Gentile army who would dare 'shake his hand against the mount of the daughter of Zion, the hill of Jerusalem' (10. 32). Babylon, in fact, symbolizes the Gentiles, or the Gentile world system — a system of corrupt power and corrupted religion, apostate Christianity, headed by 'the Beast'. (In Revelation 17. 5, Babylon assumes a different but equally negative symbolism: 'Babylon, the great, the mother of Harlots and abomination of the earth'). Isaiah describes the destruction of Babylon by God in apocalyptic terms (13. 10: 'the sun shall be darkened in his going forth, and the moon shall not cause her light to shine'), and presents it as the 'golden city' (14. 4) which worships the false god of wealth (13. 17: 'Behold, I will stir up the Medes against them, which shall not regard silver; and as for gold, they shall not delight in it'). This association of 'sin' and wealth is an important theme to be developed very forcefully later in the libretto through Sanguineti's use of quotations in which Dante and Pound make a critique of usury and, more obliquely, in the next stage of the libretto where Dante and Eliot are fused. However, the blatant link between part 3 of the libretto, and the Dante / Eliot section is the 'babel' or confusion of languages that God created in Babylon.

Part 4: Dante's Inferno I, Eliot's 'East Coker'

Part 4 is introduced by a short section on percussion instruments, marked 'tempo jazz'. Jazz immediately suggests a modern context. In fact, as Stacey has noted (p. 253), throughout the whole of *Laborintus II* 'jazz music is associated with the sins of the flesh, the night-club, drink and drug abuse — in short, the sins of the modern world'. This musical reference, indicating modernity, is however blatantly juxtaposed with an allusion to perhaps the most famous 'labyrinth' in medieval literature. The eight actor-singers literally shout out dislocated (and, once again, slightly altered) words and phrases from Dante's *Inferno*, canto I, evoking the 'savage and harsh wood' — 'selvaggia selva e aspra' (in Dante, line 5, 'selva selvaggia e aspra') — where Dante had lost his way (see Figure 3.2). Of the three animals which Dante meets and which deter him from ascending the sunny hill — the leopard (symbolizing lust), the lion (symbolizing pride), and the she-wolf — it is the wolf which Sanguineti chooses to refer to: 'ed una lupa [...] una lupa [...] ma questa bestia uccide [...] uccide' [and a wolf [...] a wolf [...] but this beast kills [...] kills] (in Dante 'Ed una lupa' (49); 'ché questa bestia'; (94); 'uccide' (96)). The covetousness or greed that the wolf symbolizes — Virgil says of it 'mai non empie la bramosa voglia,/ e dopo 'l pasto ha più fame che pria' (98–99) [her greedy appetite is never satiated,/ and after eating she is hungrier than before] — is mainly the greed for wealth; Virgil prophesizes how eventually the 'hound' (sometimes interpreted as standing for Can Grande della Scala) will come and kill the wolf, and how '*he* will not feed on land or riches,/ but on wisdom, love, and virtue' ('Questi non ciberà terra né peltro,/ ma sapienza, amore e virtute' (103–04)). By choosing to focus on the 'wood' and the 'wolf', Sanguineti manages to conjure up not only the 'evil' but also the 'good' in the evil/good polarity around which the libretto has so far taken shape, for it was Dante's personal 'losing' of himself which gave rise to his aspirations for a better life (see *Inf.* I, 8 — 'ma per trattar del ben ch'io vi trovai' [but to give an account of the good which I found there]) pictured in his attempts to climb the sunny hill (the 'sun' — ''l sol'– being a symbol of God).

All of this happened, according to the *Inferno*, in the 'middle' of Dante's life. In fact Sanguineti begins the *Inferno* quotations with the phrase 'e nel mezzo' [and in the middle] (in Dante, line 1, 'Nel mezzo del cammin' [in the middle of the path]).

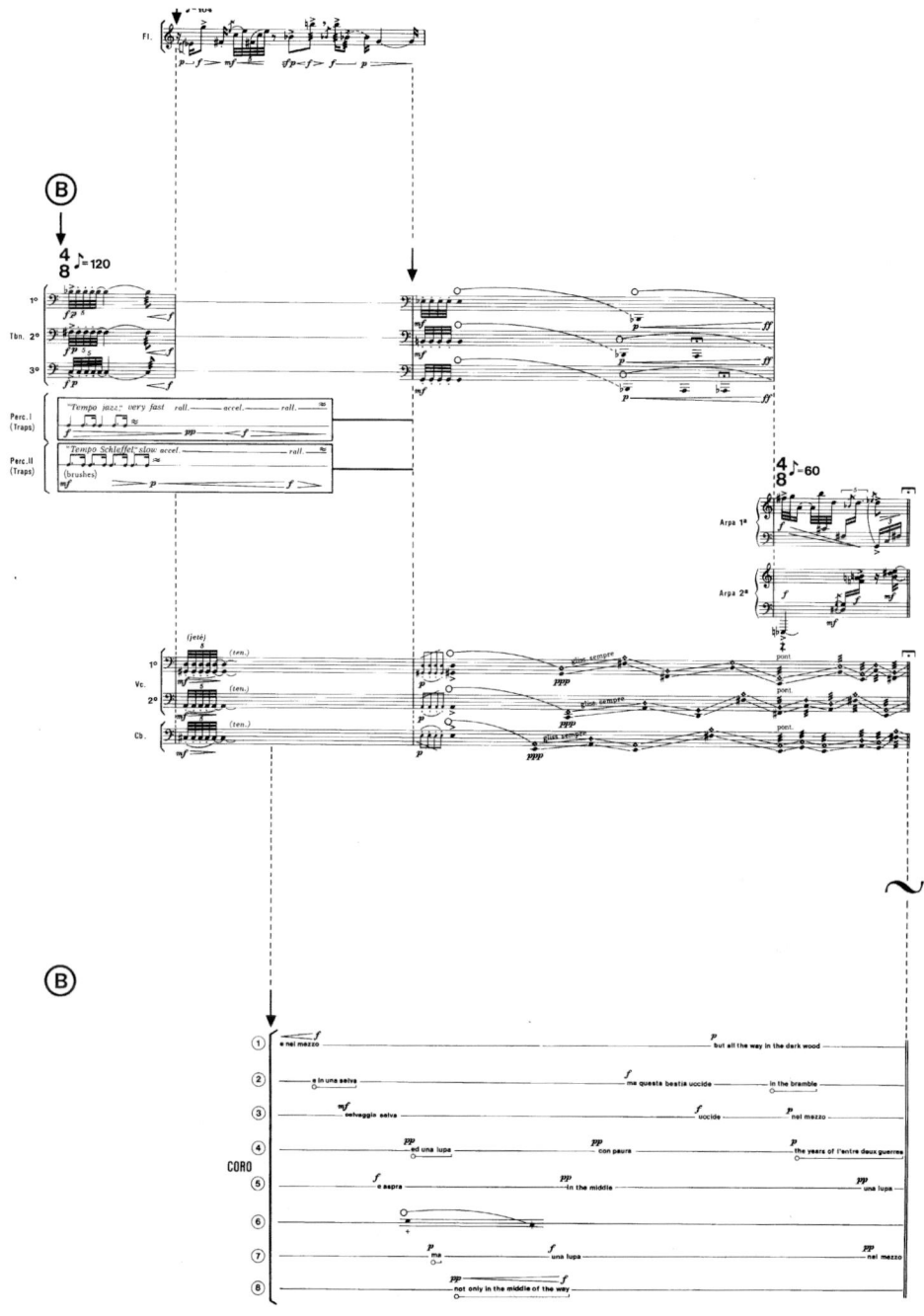

Fɪɢ. 3.2. Luciano Berio's *Laborintus II* (London: Universal Edition Ltd., 1965), p. 5.
Courtesy of Universal Editions Ltd

The emphasis in the libretto has now changed from 'beginnings' (as in parts 1 and 2) to 'middles'; as also evinced by the citations from Eliot's 'East Coker' which are intermingled with the Dante quotations: 'not only in the middle of the way [...] in the middle [...] but all the way in the dark wood [...] in the bramble [...] the years of *l'entre deux guerres*' (score, p. 5). Obviously Eliot's poem has been inspired by Dante[4] (with its references to 'the middle of the way', the 'dark wood', and, although this phrase is not quoted by Sanguineti, the poet-protagonist being 'menaced by monsters' (II, line 43)). The quotations which Sanguineti has selected from 'East Coker' are to be found in sections II and V of the poem. The relevant parts in the original text read as follows:

> In the middle, not only in the middle of the way
> But all the way, in a dark wood, in a bramble,
> On the edge of a grimpen, where there is no secure foothold
> And menaced by monsters. ('East Coker', II, p. 18)

> So here I am, in the middle way, having had twenty years —
> Twenty years largely wasted, the years of *l'entre deux guerres* –
> Trying to learn to use words, and every attempt
> Is a wholly new start, and a different kind of failure. ('East Coker', V, p. 21)

By combining Dante and Eliot, Sanguineti manages to convey the notion of a fusion of medieval disorientation and modern, existential disorientation. Section III of Eliot's poem lists — using the 'catalogue' technique which characterizes both 'East Coker' and *Laborintus II* on the musical and textual level — the 'captains, merchant bankers, eminent men of letters, / The generous patrons of art, the statesmen and the rulers, / Distinguished civil servants' — all of whom 'go into the dark' (pp. 18–19). Eliot's poem is largely about the vanity of all things human on earth where life appears to be no more than a succession of meaningless events ending in death.

So, along with the notion of 'middles' in Eliot, there is also that of 'ends' (and 'death' as opposed to 'new life'). 'Ends' will constitute another theme in the libretto (see part 12), complementing the motifs of 'beginnings' and 'middles' already met, and reinforcing the notion of a cycle, or things cyclical. The idea of things cyclical has in fact already been introduced on a technical, rather than semantic, level in the libretto, through the use of accumulative repetition in Sanguineti's rewriting of the opening section of the *Vita nuova*, and through the repetition of the quotations from Isidore sung by the eight actor-singers in the style of a fugue. It does not, therefore, seem gratuitous that Sanguineti has chosen to quote from an Eliot poem which reinforces the notion of the cyclical nature of all experience, and how, despite the appearance of linear progression, time is really circular. Section I of 'East Coker', for example, talks about old stone houses which are used to construct new houses which in turn crumble back to the earth; and whereas the poem opens with the motto of Mary Queen of Scots — 'In my beginning is my end'– it closes with an inversion of the same statement — 'In my end is my beginning'. Indeed, it is precisely the notion of cycles which Sanguineti is trying to suggest by juxtaposing 'old' and modern literature in the libretto, and this same juxtaposition, employed with the same intention of suggesting cycles, is another feature of Eliot's 'East Coker'. Like

Sanguineti's text, 'East Coker' makes great use of biblical quotations. It imitates the rhythm of a famous passage from Ecclesiastes (3. 1–8) which presents time as a cumulative repetition: 'there is a time for building/ And a time for living and for generation/ And a time for the wind to break the loosened pane' (p. 15). Another insertion of 'old' literature within the modern occurs in section I where Eliot has a dream vision of a country dance which he describes by copying, as if from his own 'libro della memoria', the exact words of *The Governor* — a poem written by his sixteenth-century ancestor, Sir Thomas Elyot: 'In daunsinge, signifying matrimonie — / [...] Two and two, necessayre coniunction' (p. 16).

There are, furthermore, two other connections between Eliot's poem and Sanguineti's libretto. First, whereas Eliot thought of life on earth as a 'dark wood', devoid of sense, he was, like Dante, extremely religious, and firmly believed in the supernal life, or Paradise, as the only reality giving meaning, after death, to an un-Christian world doomed to decay — a belief intimated in the aforementioned line which concludes 'East Coker': 'In my end is my beginning'. It would seem plausible that Sanguineti has therefore also fused Dante and Eliot with a view to suggesting once again the progress from ungodliness to godliness that has pervaded the preceding sections of the libretto.

The second connection between Eliot's poem and the libretto concerns language. Part 3 of Sanguineti's libretto has already made reference to Babylon, in connection with the Gentiles, apostate religion, and the 'sin' of wealth. For a neo-avant-garde poet, like Sanguineti, whose poetical works are characterized by *plurilinguismo* [plurilingualism], Babylon surely carries with it allusions to the tower of Babel, according to *Genesis* (11. 1–9), the tower of the city of Shinar, built by the sons of Noah in order that its top 'may reach unto heaven'; and the 'babel' or confusion of tongues (see Isidore's text cited in part 3) that God created in the city because its inhabitants had attempted to rebel against his authority. This confusion of tongues is very much evident in the libretto of *Laborintus II*; so far one has encountered Latin, Italian, English, and French, and it will be even more evident at a later stage when Sanguineti quotes from his original *Laborintus*. This presentation of language as a 'babel' by Sanguineti (due to the belief, which he shared with other Neo-Avant-garde writers, that ordinary, communicative language had limited possibilities for giving out information) is something which Eliot had in common with him. Eliot's preoccupation with language in 'East Coker' is intimated in the reference cited in the libretto to 'the years of *l'entre deux guerres*', for, as the above quotation from section V elucidates, these were years spent 'trying to learn to use words', and where every attempt to do so resulted in 'a different kind of failure'. His concept of language is best expressed in 'Burnt Norton' (also from *Four Quartets*) where he claims that 'Words strain,/ Crack and sometimes break, under the burden,/ Under the tension, slip, slide, perish,/ [...] Will not stay still' (p. 12). The characters of the 'Waste Land' in the poem of that name speak a Babylonish dialect, including English cockney, French, Provençal, and Sanskrit — a confusion of tongues suggesting nervous breakdowns and Eliot's self-definition as 'a mad poet residing in the ruined tower of Babel'.[5] The theme of madness and nervous breakdowns inherent in the use of a Babylonish language will emerge later in Sanguineti's libretto too. But even

the dishevelled women saying 'tu pur morrai [...] tu se' morto' [yet you will die [...] you are dead]); and once more back to Beatrice, when, in his imagination, Dante's friend pronounces Beatrice dead ('la tua mirabile donna è partita di questo secolo' [your wondrous lady has departed from this world]). All of this culminates in Dante's invocation of death ('Dolcissima Morte, vieni a me'), which, in the words of Sanguineti, 'chiude circolarmente il disegno dell'episodio' (p. 38) [closes, in circular fashion, the design of the episode]. What Sanguineti has done in the libretto is to quote from the beginning and end of this circular episode, which does not seem to be without reason in view of his aforementioned preoccupation in the libretto with beginnings, ends, and middles, the 'circle' being also, of course, related to the notion of 'middles'. One could also note that, so far, Sanguineti's quotations from the *Vita nuova* have been taken from the beginning of the work (chapters I and II) and, roughly, its middle (chapter XXIII), while the next quotations will come from the last chapter (XLII); afterwards he quotes once again from the beginning (III), middle (XXIII), and end (XLII).

Part 6: Dante's *Vita nuova*, Chapter XLII

The citations from chapter XLII of the *Vita nuova* develop a metapoetic theme that was intimated in Eliot's reference to 'the years of *l'entre deux guerres*' in part 4 of the libretto. As already explained, these were the years in which Eliot 'attempted' and 'failed' to 'learn to use words'. Chapter XLII of the *Vita Nuova* is one where Dante has a vision in which he saw things that made him determined not to write any more of Beatrice until such times as he could do so more worthily. The italicized words in the following quotations from the original text are the ones which are relevant to the libretto: 'apparve a me una mirabile visione, ne la quale *io vidi cose che mi fecero proporre di non dire* piú di questa benedetta infino a tanto che io potesse piú degnamente trattare di lei' [there appeared to me a wondrous vision, wherein I saw things *which made me determined to speak no more* of this blessed one until such times as I could treat of her more worthily]. To this end he intends to 'study' as much as he can, and hopes '*di dicer di lei quello che mai non fue detto d'alcuna*' (p. 153) [*to write of her what has never been written of any woman*]. Like Eliot in 'East Coker', therefore, Dante is talking about the difficulties of writing poetry, acknowledging his present linguistic 'failure' (as yet he cannot 'use' the right 'words' to do justice to Beatrice), but announcing an 'attempt', through further study, to compose better poetry about Beatrice in the future. In his preface to the *Vita nuova* Sanguineti in fact emphasizes the 'modern', 'metapoetic' aspect of the work — 'La *Vita nuova* è spiegabile, al sentimento dei moderni, come storia di una vocazione poetica' (p. 13) [The *Vita nuova* can be appreciated more by modern thinking if one explains it as a story on the subject of poetic vocation] — highlighting, in the process, chapter XLII; and it is clear from his choice of phrases from that chapter in the libretto, and the manner in which he has juxtaposed them, that it is the notions of poetic 'failure' and future poetic 'attempts' that he is accentuating. The section is characterized musically by two cellos and a double bass sliding in a glissando effect upwards and downwards from one chord to another, as if in an attempt to find the right 'notes':

Io vidi cose: che mi fecero proporre di non dire, io vidi cose: io spero di dicer
quello che mai non fue detto: mi fecero proporre di non dire di lei: io spero di
dicer di lei quello che mai non fue detto d'alcuna. (score, p. 11)

[I saw things: which made me vow not to speak, I saw things: I hope to say
what has never been said: they made me vow not to speak of her: I hope to say
of her what has never been said of any woman.]

Although the element of negation is already present in the original Dante ('non
dire'; 'mai non fue detto'), Sanguineti makes it more evident through the repetition
of these phrases in the libretto, and he also labours the antithetical aspects of
chapter XLII; as noted above, he believed that negation and antithesis were essential
characteristics of the *Vita nuova*. Whereas in the original Dante only one antithesis
is immediately evident ('spero di dicer di lei quello che mai non fue detto'), in the
libretto Sanguineti makes another stand out (that of 'not saying' and 'hoping to say')
by choosing to bring together two phrases which in Dante are four lines apart: 'di
non dire', and 'io spero di dicer'.

Part 7: Dante's *Vita nuova*, Chapter III

Antithesis is very much present in the original Dante version of this chapter which,
following the account of Beatrice's greeting, can be summarized as follows: Dante
recounts how he fell into 'a gentle sleep' ('uno soave sonno') in which he had 'a
marvellous vision' ('una maravigliosa visione') — a fiery coloured cloud appeared
in his room, within which he could make out the figure of 'a man' ('uno segnore')
who was 'frightening to behold' ('di pauroso aspetto'), and yet seemed to be filled
'with a great joy' ('con tanta letizia'). He said many things to Dante, among which
Dante only understood the words 'Ego dominus tuus' [I am your lord]. In his arms
the lord carried a sleeping woman whom Dante realized to be Beatrice, and in one
hand he held something which was burning and pronounced the words 'Vide cor
tuum' [Behold your heart]. Wakening Beatrice, the lord made her eat this heart,
which she did 'doubtfully' ('mangiava dubitosamente'), whereupon the man's
'gladness turned to bitter weeping' ('la sua letizia si convertia in amarissimo pianto'),
and, weeping, he gathered Beatrice up and rose with her heavenward. Dante was
so anguished by this vision ('onde io sostenea sí grande angoscia' [whereupon I
felt such great anguish]) that he woke up and wrote a sonnet about it, in which he
presented the lord of the dream as the personification of 'Love' ('Amor'), and spoke
of how this lord horrifies him to remember ('mi dà orrore' [he horrifies me]), and
yet appeared so happy ('Allegro mi sembrava Amor' [Love seemed happy to me]).

Dante's text could be said to hinge on two antitheses. The first, and main one,
concerns the lord figure — he arouses fear in the beholder, yet he himself is happy;
and this happiness eventually turns to weeping. These contradictory states obviously
emphasize the bitter-sweet nature of 'love' that the lord personifies. The second
antithesis concerns the sleep and the dream, both of which are initially felicitous
('soave' and 'maravigliosa', respectively), but which end up inducing Dante's
anguished state (his 'angoscia'). Although Dante presents the dream (which belongs
to c. 1283) as indecipherable at the time (why should Love weep when Dante's

heart is accepted?), he himself comments that the dream is now, a decade later, clear to everyone: 'Lo verace giudicio del detto sogno non fue veduto allora per alcuno, ma ora è manifestissimo a li piú semplici' (p. 57) [The true interpretation of the said dream was not then seen by anyone, but now it is extremely evident to the most simple]. Presumably Love weeps because Beatrice is to die. So the antitheses surrounding the Lord figure of Dante's dream are intelligible to readers of the *Vita nuova*, just as the 'anguish' Dante suffered on account of this strange and disturbing dream, in a sleep which began peacefully, is comprehensible. Herein lies the difference between Dante's antitheses, and those in Sanguineti's libretto. Sanguineti's antitheses are not intelligible. Sanguineti has, in fact, plundered the Dante text, extracting, in a first set of quotations, references to diverse heightened emotional states (the horror, the happiness, the marvel, the bitter crying, the fearful eating of the burning heart), and, by simply separating them with semicolons, he juxtaposes them in a rather crazed and disjointed list, using once again, therefore, a catalogue technique. Thus the reciter proclaims:

> Mi dà orrore (uno soave sonno); ma allegro; ma con tanta letizia; ma una maravigliosa visione: e di pauroso aspetto; (amore), piangendo, mangiando dubitosamente. (score, p.12)

> [He horrifies me (a gentle sleep); but happy; but with a great joy; but a marvellous vision: and frightening to behold; (love), crying, eating fearfully.]

Sanguineti's second set of quotations catalogues some of the salient features of the Dante chapter — the fiery coloured cloud, the lord figure, the Latin phrases uttered by the lord, the woman; and although the emphasis is no longer on antitheses, the sense of confusion generated by the latter persists, for there is no attempt on Sanguineti's part to explain the relationship between these salient features — they are, as with the emotional states, simply listed. Indeed, some of the details of Dante's story would seem to have been *confused* as well, for whereas in Dante it is the *lord* who is in bitter tears and who draws attention to the burning heart, in the libretto it is the *woman* who is crying and who points out the heart (Sanguineti writes 'e la donna, in amarissimo pianto [...] piangendo vide cor tuum'); and whereas in Dante it is *Dante* himself who is greatly anguished, in the libretto it is the *woman* ('e la donna [...] in grande angoscia'):

> (Una nebula di colore di fuoco): ego dominus, ego dominus tuus; (una figura); (uno segnore, amore); e la donna, in amarissimo pianto in grande angoscia, piangendo vide cor tuum. (score, p. 13)

> [(A firey coloured cloud): I am lord, I am your lord; (a figure); (a lord, love); and the woman, weeping bitterly in great anguish, crying behold your heart.]

In short, Sanguineti has rewritten chapter III of the *Vita nuova* in such a way as to convey a sense of extreme emotional and psychological confusion — a 'medieval' nervous breakdown which complements the modern one suggested in the aforementioned Babylonish confusion of tongues in the libretto.

This sense of psychological instability is also reinforced on a musical level. The music for the two harps and the two cellos which accompany the reciter's voice when he begins to read extracts from the *Vita nuova*, chapter III, is marked triple *piano* ('ppp'); but by the time the reciter has reached the end of the section (on the words 'vide cor tuum'), the percussion instruments have joined the harps and cellos, playing in a jazz 'Afro-Cuban' style, and the volume has soared abruptly to end on a climactic triple *forte* ('fff').

Part 8: Isidore's *Etymologiae*, Book V

The same gradual crescendo effect characterizes section 8 of the libretto. This section consists of a long quotation from Book V of the *Etymologiae*, in which Isidore presents a genealogical enumeration of the first two ages of Adam's descendants up to Zoroastres and his discovery of magic 3,184 years from the creation of Adam. Sanguineti has more or less remained faithful to Isidore's text, while ommitting all its references to time, thereby adding to the dizzy confusion generated by the relentless cataloguing of names. The italicized sections below are the ones used in the libretto (the English translation is of the italicized sections only):

> **Prima aetas**. *Adam* ann. CCXXX *genuit Seth, a quo filii Dei.* [CCXXX]. *Seth* ann. CCV *genuit Enos, qui coepit invocare nomen Domini.* [CCCCXXXV]. *Enos* ann. CXC *genuit Cainan* [DCXXV]. *Cainan* ann. CLXX *genuit Malalehel.* [DCCXCV]. *Malalehel* ann. CLXV *genuit Iareth.* [DCCCCLX]. *Iareth* ann CLXII *genuit Enoc, qui translatus est.* [MCXXII]. *Enoc* ann. CLXV *genuit Matusalam.* [MCCLXXXVII]. *Matusalam* ann. CLXVII *genuit Lamech.* [MCCCCLIV]. *Lamech* ann. CLXXXVIII *genuit Noe. Arca aedificatur.* [MDCXLII]. Noe autem ann. DC factum est diluvium. [IIMCCXLII] [*Noe* vero D cum esset annorum *genuit* tres filios, *Sem, Cham et Iaphet.* Cuius sexcentesimo vitae anno *factum est diluvium.* Sunt autem ab Adam usque ad *cataclismum* anni IIMCCLII]. **Secunda aetas**. *Sem* [cum esset annorum C] ann. II *post diluvium genuit Arfaxat, a quo Chaldaei.* [IIMCCXLIV]. *Arfaxat* ann CXXXV *genuit Sala, a quo Samaritae et Indi.* [IIMCCCLXXIX]. *Sala* ann. CXXX *genuit Heber, a quo Hebraei.* [IIMDIX]. *Heber* ann. CXXXIV *genuit Falec. Turris aedificatur* [hoc tempore *divisae sunt linguae et per orbem terrae facta est dispersio in aedificatione turris*]. [IIMDCXLIII]. *Falec* ann. CXXX *genuit Ragau. Dii primum adorantur.* [IIMDCCLXXIII]. *Ragau* ann.CXXXII *genuit Seruc. Regnum inchoat Scytharum.* [IIMDCCCCV]. *Seruc* ann. CXXX *genuit Nachor. Regnum Aegyptiorum nascitur.* [IIIMXXXV]. *Nachor* ann. LXXIX *genuit Thara. Regnum Assyriorum et Siciniorum exoritur.* [IIIMCXIV]. *Thara* ann. LXX *genuit Abraham. Zoroastres magicam repperit.* [IIIMCLXXXIV]. (*Etym.* V. xxxix. 2–8; score, pp.15 –18)

> [Adam begat Seth, from whom descended the sons of God. Seth begat Enos, who began to call on the name of the Lord. Enos begat Cainan. Cainan begat Mahalaleel. Mahalaleel begat Jared. Jared begat Enoch, who was taken by God. Enoch begat Methuselah. Methuselah begat Lamech. Lamech begat Noah. The ark was built. Noah begat Shem, Ham, and Japheth. There was the flood. Cataclysm. Shem after the flood begat Arphaxad, from whom descended the Chaldees. Arphaxad begat Salah, from whom descended the inhabitants of Samaria and India. Salah begat Eber from whom descended the Hebrews. Eber begat Peleg. The tower was built. Tongues were divided and they who built the tower were scattered upon the face of the earth. Peleg begat Reu. The Gods were worshipped for the first time. Reu begat Serug. The kingdom of the Scythians began. Serug begat Nahor. The kingdom of the Egyptians was born. Nahor begat Terah. The kingdom of the Assyrians and the Scythians began. Terah begat Abraham. Zoroastres discovered magic.]

Whereas the section is initially marked 'semplicemente' [simply], and is recited by three female voices in a pedestrian monotone which suits the monotonous repetition of clauses centred on the verb 'genuit', on the mentioning of 'Noah' and the building of the ark, the tempo accelerates, and the volume and pitch rise to announce the disasters visited by God on man: the Flood and the cataclysm. Thematically, Sanguineti has returned to the opening issue of the libretto — the issue of the beginnings of the human race and the inception of evil and violence in the world, which God sees fit to punish. For, according to the book of Genesis from which Isidore derives his list of the descendants of Adam, it was when God saw the multiplication of man on the earth, and how 'every imagination of the thoughts of his heart was only evil continually' (6. 5), that he repented of his creation, and brought 'a flood of waters upon the earth, to destroy all flesh' (6. 17).

Following the evocation of the Flood and the cataclysm, the three female voices are unexpectedly joined by the choir of eight voices who chant in unison the inventory of Adam's descendants in the post-diluvial days, and accelerate towards the second punishment of God in response to the transgression of man under the Noachic Covenant — the destruction of the tower of Babel, the division of tongues, and the scattering of God's people upon the face of the earth. From then onwards the score is marked 'sempre più rapido e più forte' [increasingly faster and louder], and the section ends with a violent orchestral clash in which seem to be condensed all the fury of the punishments of God recounted in the sequences.

It is section 8's reference to Babel and the confusion of tongues (already intimated in parts 3 and 4 of the libretto) which provides a natural transition to the next part of the work.

Part 9: Sanguineti's Lyrics Composed for the Libretto, and *Laborintus* 10

In this part of the libretto Sanguineti yokes together a series of new lyrics written for the libretto, and a section (lines 25–33) from the poem numbered 10 in his original Neo-Avant-garde collection of poetry, *Laborintus*, first published nine years prior to *Laborintus II* in 1956[7] (see libretto, p. 250). Both sets of lyrics set up structural and thematic links with other parts of the libretto. The new sequence (beginning 'tutto tutto tutto' [all all all], and ending 'alla polvere' [to dust]) maintains the catalogue structure which characterized the quotations from Isidore in part 8, but the diverse elements that are catalogued are now distinctly modern, and one is not told how or why they are bound together; one merely goes from one element to another:

> Dalla biblioteca al babbuino: dal 1265 al 1321: dal cianuro di potassio alla cronaca cittadina: dalla cresima alla corte dei conti: dalla oscurità in cui è sempre immersa la nostra vita alla rendita del 4%. (Nl; score pp. 18–19)

> [From the library to the baboon: from 1265 to 1321: from potassium cyanide to the local news: from confirmation to the Treasury Department: from the darkness in which our lives are constantly immersed to the 4% profit.]

The excess of detail in this section of the libretto, evinced by quotations such as those above, implies a psycho-pathological state which is reminiscent of the 'mad poet' Eliot residing in his 'ruined tower of Babel'. The impression of madness is further underscored by an Italian that is bound together by similarities in sound rather than in sense ('dalla biblioteca al babbuino [...] dal fegato al frigorifero: dal francobollo al formaggio' [from the library to the baboon [...] from the liver to the fridge: from the stamp to the cheese]) and by the literal confusion of tongues which characterizes the quotations from *Laborintus* 10, where Italian is mixed with English ('Paradise Valley'), Latin ('novimus enim tenebras aquas ventos ignem fumum' [we also renew darkness water winds fire smoke]) and French ('quoi qu'elle fasse elle est désir' [whatever she does she is desire]). Furthermore, in keeping with the libretto's semantic emphasis on cycles — beginnings, middles, and ends which are beginnings — conveyed musically through the aforementioned repetitive schemas (in parts 2 and 3), a citation from *Laborintus* 10 reinforces this notion of cyclical time — of how the future presents no change in terms of the past, and hence both past and future can be viewed *together* ('insieme'):

> Vediamo insieme il passato, il futuro. (*Lab.* 10, line 31; score, p. 23)

> [We can see together the past, the future.]

This particular line, as well as evoking the aforementioned preoccupation with time in 'East Coker' seems to bear a specific reference to Eliot's 'Burnt Norton', where the poet claims (the emphases are mine):

> Time present and time past
> Are both perhaps present in time future,
> *And time future contained in time past.* ('Burnt Norton', I, lines 1–3)

Although the links with Eliot are the most apparent ones, echoes back to the Dante sections of the libretto are also suggested. Indeed, Sanguineti's new lyrics actually contain the dates of Dante's birth and death ('dal 1265 al 1321') as well as the date, 1965, indicating the seven hundredth anniversary of Dante's birth which *Laborintus II* is commemorating:

> Dall'elefante di mare, grande foca del Pacifico, fornita di due lunghe zanne al 1965. (Nl; score, p. 20)

> [From the sea-elephant, great seal of the Pacific, with its two long tusks to 1965.]

The most obvious link between this section and Dante is provided by the theme of 'disorientation', which hitherto also yoked Dante with Eliot: Dante's losing of himself in the dark labyrinthine wood ('Nel mezzo del cammin di nostra vita/ mi ritrovai per una selva oscura' [In the middle of the path of our life/ I found myself in a dark wood]); Sanguineti's existential straying in the 'oscurità in cui è sempre immersa la nostra vita' (new lyrics; score, p.19), but two other links are also apparent. First, whereas Dante, as explained earlier (part 6), wrestling with words in chapter XLII of the *Vita nuova*, voiced a resolution not to write any more of Beatrice until he felt he could compose better poetry, and Sanguineti, when quoting from the relevant section of the *Vita nuova,* had chosen to duplicate those Dante quotations which highlighted the notion of *not* being able to write (repeating the phrase 'non dire' and 'mai non fue detto'), Sanguineti's new lyrics in this section hint at an *excess* of 'saying', an inability to stop talking. The long sequence of the new lyrics is totally devoid of full stops, and thirteen of its eighteen phrases, each divided by colons, have the same construction: 'da' [from] plus a noun (and sometimes, explanation of that noun), followed by 'a' [to] plus a noun. The effect is one of relentless gabble. The nine lines from *Laborintus* 10, meanwhile, are written in the same oppressively garrulous fashion, with colons replacing the original line breaks, and six of the lines repetitively structured around main verbs in the perfect tense: 'ho inventato [...] ho liberato [...] ho trascinato [...] ho anche detto [...] ho detto [...] ho detto [...]' [I invented [...] I freed [...] I dragged [...] I also said [...] I said [...] I said]. The verb 'ho detto' is, in fact, repeated in unison first by three choral voices, then by five, and finally, by seven. Given the libretto's aforementioned fusion of the medieval and the modern on the linguistic level, the phrase is obviously intended to be read in a metapoetic sense — 'dire', in old Italian, and indeed in the *Vita nuova* (for example, in XLII, quoted above), meaning 'to compose poetry'.

The second major link between this section and earlier references to Dante occurs under the theme of wealth. The she-wolf that Dante encountered in the dark wood (part 4 of the libretto) symbolized covetousness or greed, especially the greed for wealth; and Sanguineti's *Laborintus II*, written at the onset of neo-capitalist society in Italy, is at pains to denounce the morally unacceptable system of capitalism and profit in contemporary Italy, as demonstrated by ironic references to 'the Treasury Department' and 'the 4% profit'. Sandwiched between these two references is one to the Dantesque wandering in darkness (*Inf.* I, 1–2) which the greed for wealth procures:

> Dalla cresima alla corte dei conti: dalla oscurità in cui è sempre immersa la nostra vita alla rendita del 4%. (Nl; score, p. 19)

Part 10: Dante's *Inferno* XI and Pound's 'Canto XLV'

The sin of wealth, in Dante, is, of course, dealt with much more comprehensively elsewhere in *La Divina Commedia*, notably in *Inferno* XI and XVII. In part 10 of the libretto Sanguineti cites from its first major instance, *Inferno* XI, bunching together phrases and parts of phrases from the canto. The italicized sections below are the ones used by Sanguineti:

> Come *natura lo suo corso prende*
> *da divino intelletto e da sua arte;*
> e se tu ben la tua Fisica note,
> tu troverai, non dopo molte carte,
> che *l'arte vostra quella*, quanto pote,
> *segue, come 'l maestro fa il discente;*
> sì che vostr'arte a Dio quasi è nepote.
> *Da queste due*, se tu ti rechi a mente
> lo Genesi dal principio, *convene*
> *prender sua vita ed avanzar la gente;*
> e perchè *l'usuriere altra via tene,*
> *per sè natura e per la sua seguace*
> *dispregia*, poi ch'in altro pon la spene.
> (*Inf.* XI, 99–111; score, p. 25)

[How *nature takes its course / from divine intellect and its art;/* and if you were to note your Physics well,/ you will find, after the examination of not many pages,/ that *your art follows nature* as much as it can,/ *as the pupil follows the master,/* so that your art is almost a grandchild to God./ *By these two*, if you recall to mind/ the beginning of Genesis, *mankind/ should gain its livelihood and advancement;/* and because *the usurer takes a different route,/ he despises nature both in herself and in her follower,/* putting his hope elsewhere.]

This denunciation of usury by Dante is fused with Pound's indictment of usury in 'Canto XLV', subtitled 'With Usura':

With usura hath no man a house of good stone
[...]
with usura
hath no man a painted paradise on his church wall
harpes et luthes ('Canto XLV', lines 1; 4–6)

Some of the above lines which are derived from Dante are then repeated by isolated voices in the chorus of eight people, and intermingled with more dislocated phrases from Pound's 'Canto XLV' (line 11 in Pound reads 'no picture is made to endure nor to live with'; Sanguineti has substituted the term 'picture' with 'music', presumably in order to make Pound's reference more relevant to *Laborintus II*):

With usura
[...]
no music is made to endure nor to live with
but is made to sell and to sell quickly
with usura, sin against nature,
[...]
with usura the line grows thick. ('Canto XLV', lines 1; 11–13; 17; score p. 28)

This Dante-Pound section on usury, coming directly after Sanguineti's own neo-avant-garde preoccupation with capitalism and profit, would seem to be reinforcing the cyclical nature of the usurious system — its all-pervasiveness across the centuries from Dante's medieval age to the modern one of Pound and Sanguineti. At the time Dante was writing, Florence was undergoing rapid economic change, and there was new demand in the city for capital, leading to an increase in lending and borrowing in trade. It is the moral consequences of this which Dante is considering, and what he seems to be condemning is the practice of oppressive and unscrupulous usury on the part of men of rank and wealth, which, as the quotation in the libretto makes clear, he considers a sin directed against God himself (the 'divino intelletto'), against God's Nature ('natura'), and against human art or industry ('arte'). It is from the latter two — natural resources (in God's creation) and man's own labour — that mankind should gain its livelihood and its advancement ('da queste due convene prender sua vita ed avanzar la gente'), not from the buying and selling of money as though it were a commodity in itself.[8]

Pound's 'Canto XLV', having been (like all of Pound's work)[9] influenced by Dante, is exactly in tune with these ideas. Money, according to Pound, should be 'a ticket for the orderly distribution of what is available',[10] and the usurer who treats it as a commodity which 'breeds' unnaturally is committing a 'sin against nature'; this concept of the *unnatural* breeding of money is also implied in Dante in the manner in which he places Usurers alongside Sodomites in *Inferno* XI and XVII. For Pound, usury stands in the way of adequate housing and food ('with usura hath no man a house of good stone'); it is associated with the degradation of the holy ('with usura/ hath no man a painted paradise on his church wall') and of the arts ('with usura [...] no picture is made to endure nor to live with').[11]

There are also interesting connections between the style of the Pound quotations used in the libretto, and verbal sequences in other sections of *Laborintus II*. The Old Testament style in which Pound denounces usury provides a fusion once again of the old and the new, and this, together with the allusions to usura and religion ('[...] church wall, harpes et luthes') make his voice sound like that of an Old Testament Prophet, denouncing the worship of the Golden Calf. This creates a subtle echo of part 3 of the libretto — the Zion / Babylon section, where Sanguineti implicitly drew upon Isaiah, the Old Testament prophet's interpretation of Babylon as the 'golden city' worshipping the false God of wealth. Furthermore, Pound, who was a composer of several pieces of music, and who wrote an influential treatise on the relationship between music and poetry,[12] distinguished between three kinds of poetry, the third of which he called 'melopoeia' — poetry in which words are invested over and above their literal meaning with some musical property, which indicates the direction of that meaning.[13] The musical property of 'Canto XLV' is obviously that of the fugue — its use of anaphora (the repetition of 'with usura' at the beginning of successive clauses) creating the effect of a tolling bell, or a chant of the dead. It is Pound's 'fugal' poetry which is echoed by Berio at this stage in the score, with four of the eight choral voices shouting out the term 'with usura' one after the other in fugal style (see Figure 3.3). The fugal style reinforces the emphasis placed in the libretto on cycles — a fugue having, ideally, no point of termination, while also consolidating the idea of usury as an incessant 'breeding' of money, and as a timeless evil.

Part II: Dante's *Inferno* III, and *Inferno* VII

The effect of the tolling bell or death chant in the quotations from Pound is then reiterated in the use of the opening lines from Dante's *Inferno*, canto III — the inscription on the doors of Hell. This inscription, with its ominous message, reinforced also through the use of anaphora, sounds, in the words of Sinclair,[14] like 'strokes of doom'. The italicized parts below are used in the libretto:

> PER ME SI VA NELLA CITTA DOLENTE,
> PER ME SI VA NELL'ETTERNO DOLORE,
> PER ME SI VA TRA LA PERDUTA GENTE. (*Inf.* III, 1–3; score, p. 30)
>
> [Through me the way to the mournful city,/ through me the way to eternal pain,/ through me the way to the lost people.]

By omitting the repeated term 'SI VA', Sanguineti has completely depersonalized Dante's lines, making them even more 'inhuman' and frightful than they were. Berio, meanwhile, on the musical level, highlights the anaphora of Dante's

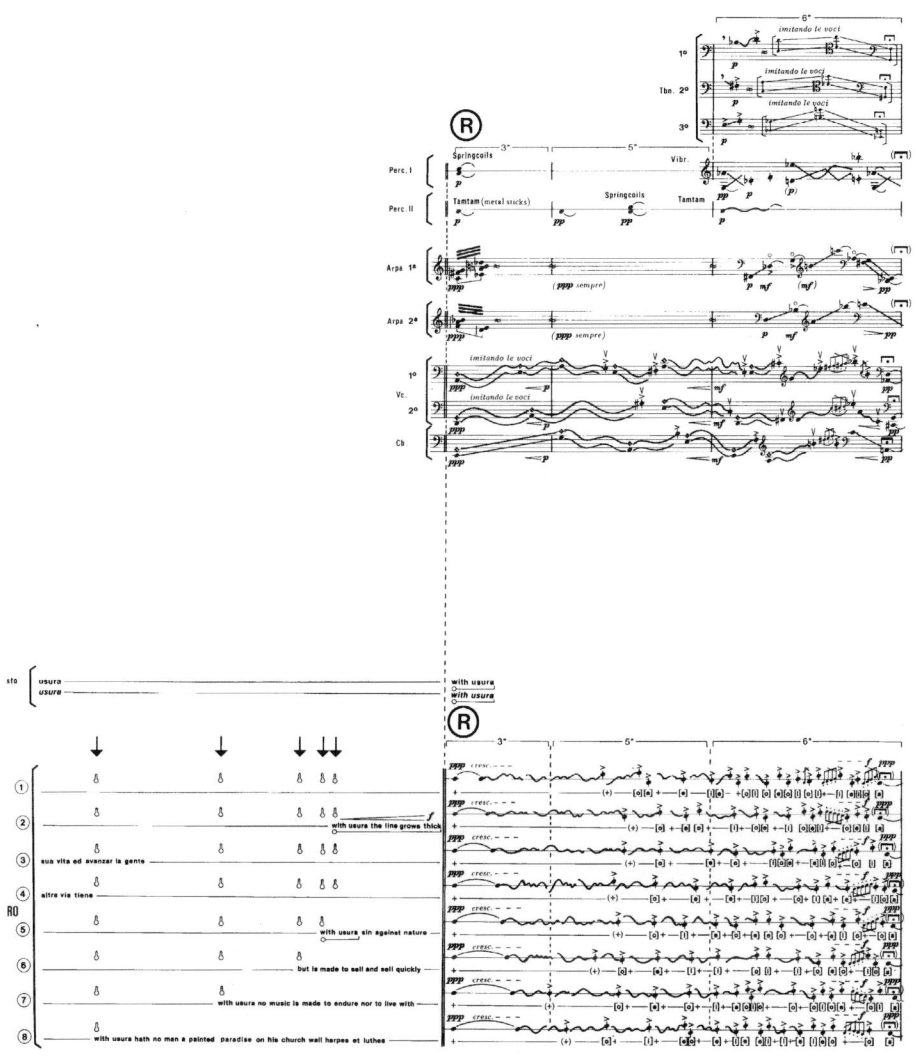

FIG. 3.3. Luciano Berio's *Laborintus II*, p. 28
Courtesy of Universal Edition Ltd

quotation by scoring the words 'PER ME' for seven choral voices (sung 'forte', and then diminishing quickly to 'piano'), and the rest of the three part quotation for a solo speaking voice which alternates with the chorus part and, conversely, starts 'piano' and rises to a 'forte'. One is now in a musical arrangement of Dante's Hell, and not yet free of *Laborintus II*'s trenchant rebuke of the root of all evil, for it is Dante's fourth circle of Hell which Sanguineti now chooses to depict — the circle of the Avaricious and the Prodigal, whose respective hoarding and reckless spending were, in Dante's view, opposite forms of the same sin in relation to the middle way, the correct use of money. In Dante, these sinners butt great stones against one another, and it is the concept of their restlessness that Sanguineti emphasizes, the reciter quoting (making one minimal change to Dante's Italian: 'potrebbe' instead of 'poterebbe') from canto VII, lines 64–66:

> Tutto l'oro ch'è sotto la luna
> e che già fu, di quest'anime stanche
> non potrebbe farne posare una. (score, pp. 31–32)

> [All the gold that is beneath the moon/ and ever was, could never give rest/ to one of these weary souls.]

The futile tussle of these sinners to which there is now no end nor profit would seem to be reflected in the restless contrabassoon line accompanying the reciter's voice, moving up and down the stave in an aimless and dissonant succession of flats, sharps, and naturals. This manic line foreshadows the hysteria with which the section closes. Dante, in canto VII, moves on from the depiction of the Avaricious and the Prodigal to that of the Wrathful whom he groups with the former two under the sins of incontinence; and Sanguineti follows suit, quoting exactly from the original lines:

> [...] Si percotean non pur con mano,
> ma con la testa e col petto e coi piedi,
> troncandosi co' denti a brano a brano. (*Inf.* VII, 112–14; score, pp. 32–33)

> [[...] They were hitting each other not only with their hands,/ but also with their heads, chest, and feet,/ tearing each other apart piece by piece with their teeth.]

Sunk in the bog of the Styx, these wrathful sinners in their uncontrolled temper hit, bite, and kick each other, and their aggressive behaviour and intemperance of spirit 'invites', in Berio's score, an explosion of the percussion ensemble, accompanied by screeching electronic music, while the chorus (much like Plutus, the 'maledetto lupo' [cursed wolf] who personifies wealth in Dante's canto) enunciates meaningless vowel sounds. Musically, the whole score, at this point, suggests chaos and violence — two themes which are strongly present in the next stage of the libretto where Sanguineti inserts another section of lyrics composed specifically for *Laborintus II*, adding to the end of it isolated fragments from poems 1, 2, 3, and 13 of *Laborintus* (see libretto, pp. 376–78).

Lyrics Composed for the Libretto, and *Laborintus* 1, 2, 3, and 13

From Dante's Hell, one now journeys to the modern hell of Western civilization. The section begins 'tutto, tutto, tutto' [all, all, all] and, as with Sanguineti's first catalogue text (part 9), the lists that follow are, for the most part, structured around the prepositions 'da', 'a', and 'di fronte a', so that the reader / listener is thrown 'from', 'to' and 'before' an anomalous mix of the diverse facets that go to make up the *inferno,* or 'Valles Mortis' (*Lab.* 3) [Valley of Death] of Western society. The new set of lyrics make allusions to consumerism ('dalla caramella al miele' [from the sweet to the honey]), war ('dalla guerra di frontiera cino-indiana' [from the Chinese-Indian frontier war]), modern technology ('alla segreteria telefonica' [to the answering machine]), and the mass media ('al *Sunday Times*'). Ironic references to educational establishments and their 'honourable' and powerful presidents and deans ('al magnifico rettore [to the magnificent rector], to the President of the NYU, to the honourable dean of Columbia University') go hand in hand with an emphasis on an insane need and desire for travel (Sanguineti lists the many addresses at which Berio has lived at different stages in his career, in the USA, Germany, Italy, and France: 'a Santa Fé, a Mass. Avenue, a Kastanienallee 34 vierunddreissig, a via Vespucci 25, a via Moscati 7, a Rue Jacob 27'). To these allusions are married the preoccupations of the original *Laborintus*: psychoanalysis ('Palus Putredinis' — Sanguineti's definition in the opening poem of *Laborintus* for the 'stinking swamp' of the psyche prior to analysis), sex (*Lab.* 2: 'dopo la fluida intromissione' [after the fluid intervention]), the nuclear holocaust (*Lab.* 2: 'lunghi funghi fumosi' [long, smokey mushrooms]), and problems of language (Nl: 'mio alfabeto vegetale' [my vegetable alphabet]). The section ends with the words 'di fronte al silenzio' [before the silence] (new lyrics), and the word 'silenzio' is repeated four times, seeming to imply that 'all' ('tutto') of this chaos that constitutes life is ultimately faced with a final 'end' — the silence of death. The similarities between this section and section three of 'East Coker', cited below, are very striking:

> The captains, merchant bankers, eminent men of letters,
> The generous patrons of art, the statesmen and the rulers,
> Distinguished civil servants, chairmen of many committees,
> [...] all go into the dark,
> [...] into the silent funeral. ('East Coker', III, p. 19)

Part 13: Dante's *Convivio* II, xiii

Contrasting with the orchestral cacophony which ended the section depicting the Avaricious, Prodigal, and Wrathful of Dante's Hell, the libretto now switches to a passage from Dante's *Convivio* on *harmony* in music.[15] Sanguineti's text adheres largely to the original version, except for the omission of some phrases (those placed in parentheses below), and the modernization of some archaic constructions (Dante's original constructions are italicized and placed in parentheses — these have been omitted from the English translation below). The passage is preceded by a single strike of a gong, which seems to herald the arrival of something of particular importance, and then declaimed by the reciter without any interference from the chorus or instruments:

La Musica, (la quale) è tutta relativa, come (*sì come*) si vede nelle (*ne le*) parole armonizzate e nei (*ne li*) canti, (de' quali) tanto più dolce armonia resulta, quanto più la relazione è bella: (la quale in essa scienza massimamente è bella) perché massimamente in essa s'intende. Ancora, la Musica trae a sé gli (*li*) spiriti umani, che quasi sono principalmente vapori del cuore, sí che quasi cessano da ogni operazione: sí è l'anima intera, quando l'ode, e la virtù di tutti quasi corre allo (*a lo*) spirito sensibile, che riceve lo suono. (*Conv.* II. xiii. 23–25; score, p. 48)

[Music (which) consists entirely of relations, as one can see from harmonized words and songs (whose) harmony is so much the sweeter the more the relation is beautiful, because a lot is to be understood in the relation. Furthermore, Music attracts to itself the human spirits, which are mainly, as it were, heart-vapours, so that they almost cease all other activity: this is how the whole heart is when it hears music, and the virtue of all of them runs, as it were, to the spirit of sense which receives the sound.]

Although there is very little harmony in the traditional musical sense of the word in Berio's score (most of the music sounding, in fact, extremely dissonant), Dante's passage on music, and the relationship of words to music, slots neatly and harmonically into the context of a musico-poetic work celebrating the medieval poet. Indeed the gong which announces the passage, and the absence of any musical accompaniment to the lyrics, which means that the listener's attention is concentrated exclusively on the latter, serves to remind one that Dante is, indeed, the focal point of the entire work, and that the work is intended as a *celebration* of the poet. The main emphasis therefore is upon eulogizing Dante, the man, and his *oeuvre*.

However, there are phrases and concepts expressed in the *Convivio* passage which also seem to have more specific links with *Laborintus II* as a whole. Dante's phrase 'parole armonizzate', which refers to the idea of a musical composition where the words are put well and convincingly to music, seems particularly relevant to *Laborintus II*. No one, on examining the latter, could fail to recognize the effort on the part of Sanguineti and Berio to create a harmony of this kind between the libretto and the score. From the jazz sections conveying the sins of the night club and the modern world, to the Renaissance-style 'canzonetta' accompanying the references to suffering and death in the second quotation from the *Vita nuova*, and the chaotic mixture of percussion, electronic, and choral sounds evoking the uncontrolled temper of the Wrathful in Dante's Hell — the music is consistently in tune with the mood of the lyrics. Indeed the phrase 'parole armonizzate' from the *Convivio* passage has a further resonance to it. Considering it out of Dante's context and applying it solely to *Laborintus II*, one is reminded of the harmonious relationships set up between the words of widely different lyrical extracts, and they are indeed 'beautiful relationships' in the sense that Dante defines a 'relazione [...] bella' — they are rich and proliferating, or, to paraphrase Dante, a 'lot' is to be 'understood' in 'them' ('perché massimamente in essa s'intende').

Dante's discourse in the latter half of the passage is also pertinent to *Laborintus II*. Here Dante is discussing the 'vital spirits' of medieval physiology, which all travel to the sense of hearing, so that the soul is entirely engrossed in the music, and unaware of other sensations. The only other blatant reference to music in the libretto of

Laborintus II occurs in the quotations from Pound's 'Canto XLV': 'with usura no music is', where Sanguineti had substituted Pound's use of the term 'picture' with 'music'. This quotation reminds one of how under the neo-capitalist ideology of the mid 1960s, even works of art, musical compositions included, became part of the world of consumerism. Berio and Sanguineti would seem to be saying, through Pound, that no serious artist could contemplate entering the consumer market place; and similarly, through Dante, that an engrossing music of 'relations' cannot exist with usury. By composing in the eccentric and unorthodox manner in which they do, Berio and Sanguineti are disdainfully and heroically taking a stance against neo-capitalism with its emphasis on selling and profit making.

Part 14: Sanguineti: Lyrics Composed for the Libretto

The sense of peace and respite which surrounds the *Convivio* section is continued through until the end of the work which is composed of another set of lyrics written especially for *Laborintus II* by Sanguineti. This section is, for the most part, whispered by the eight choral voices, and whereas the Sanguineti section (part 12) which preceded the *Convivio* citations ended on the concept of the end of life, with 'all' of the frenzy of modern living sinking inevitably into the 'silence' of the grave, *Laborintus II* concludes on the subject of the beginning of life, and is suffused with images suggesting innocence and hope: chattering and dreaming babies, and sunshine among the trees:

> Ma seguimi,
> ma vedi i bambini che parlano sognando
> ma seguimi oramai,
> ma vedi il fango che ci sta alle spalle
> e il sole
> e il sole in mezzo agli alberi
> e i bambini che dormono
> che sognano
> che parlano sognando
> ma così inquieti. (score, pp. 50–52)

> [But follow me / but see the babies, chattering as they dream/ but follow me at this point,/ but see the mud at our backs/ and the sun/ and the sun between the trees/ and the babies asleep/ dreaming/ chattering as they dream/ but so restless.]

However, a sudden and intrusive disturbance on the musical and lyrical level serves to remind the listener of the negative aspects of life to which these innocent beings will soon succumb: among the whispering, the first of the eight voices rises for an instant from a double 'piano' on the repetition of 'che parlano sognando', to a 'mezzo forte' on the disquieting phrase 'ma così inquieti', sung in a *glissando* style on four dissonant notes, before resuming the whispered motif of the sleeping and dreaming infants. This motif then gradually decreases in volume so that by the final page of the score, among the four terms 'sognando', 'i bambini', 'adesso', and 'dormendo', which are repeated in various different combinations by the eight voices, only the sibilants of 'sognando' and 'adesso' are audible:

Sognando i bambini adesso
adesso sognando i bambini
dormendo adesso sognando
adesso dormendo dormendo
adesso adesso adesso. (score, p. 53)

[Dreaming babies now/ now dreaming babies/ sleeping now dreaming/ now
sleeping sleeping/ now now now.]

The worrying intrusion of the phrase 'ma così inquieti' acts as a reminder of the
forces of evil and suffering to be reckoned with by all human beings in the course
of living, as well as the inclination to depravity held to be common to all as the
consequence of the Fall. In spite of this spoiling of the optimism of the last section,
the final emphasis on, and repetition of, the word 'adesso' would seem to suggest a
utopian desire to start afresh from the here and the now, and the innocent dreams
of the children, and to eradicate once and for all the cycle of sin and evil which has
persisted from the beginning of time to the modern age, and which it has been the
aim of the work to expose and to denounce.

Notes to Chapter 3

1. *Laborintus II* (London: Universal Edition, 1965).
2. P. Stacey, *Contemporary Tendencies in the Relationship of Music and Text, with Special Reference to
   'Pli selon Pli' (Boulez) and 'Laborintus II' (Berio)* (doctoral thesis, University of East Anglia, 1984).
   Published by Garland (New York, London, 1989) in the series 'Outstanding Dissertations in
   Music from British Universities'.
3. The following editions of (St) Isidore of Seville, Dante, E. Pound, T. S. Eliot, and E. Sanguineti
   have been used (all page numbers refer to these editions). Isidore of Seville: *Etymologiarum sive
   Originum*, ed. by W. M. Lindsay, 2 vols (Oxford: Clarendon Press, 1911). Dante: *Inferno*, ed.
   by N. Sapegno (Florence: La Nuova Italia, 1955); *Vita nuova* (Milan: Lerici, 1965); *Convivio*
   (Milan: Rizzoli, 1952). E. Pound: *The Cantos 1–95* (New York: New Directions, 1956). T.
   S. Eliot: *Four Quartets* (London: Faber and Faber, 1946); *The Waste Land* in *Collected Poems
   1909–1962* (London, Boston: Faber and Faber, 1963). E. Sanguineti: *Laborintus*, in *Opus Metricum
   1951–59* (Milan: Rusconi e Paolazzi, 1960). The following abbreviations have been used: *Etym*:
   Etymologiarum sive Originum; *Vn*: *Vita nuova*, *Inf*: *Inferno*, *Conv*: *Convivio*; *Lab*: *Laborintus*, Nl: new
   lyrics composed by Sanguineti for *Laborintus II*.
4. For studies on the influence of Dante on Eliot's work, see D. Manganiello, *T. S. Eliot and
   Dante* (London: Macmillan, 1989); and S. Ellis, *Dante and English Poetry: Shelley to T. S. Eliot*
   (Cambridge: Cambridge University Press, 1983).
5. Manganiello, *T. S. Eliot and Dante*, p. 54.
6. E. Sanguineti, 'Per una lettura della Vita nuova', in *Vita nuova*, pp. 9–47 (14–17).
7. E. Sanguineti, *Laborintus II* (Milan: Magenta, 1956).
8. For other references to usury in Dante, see *Enciclopedia Dantesca* (Rome: Istituto della
   Enciclopedia Italiana, 1970–71): 'usura' (O. Capitani), 'usurai' (S. Jacomuzzi),'usuriere' (A.
   Bufano). For a discussion of Dante's attitude towards wealth, avarice, and usury, see P. Armour,
   'Gold, Silver, and True Treasure: Economic Imagery in Dante', *Romance Studies*, 23 (spring
   1994), 7–30.
9. For studies on the relationship between Pound and Dante, see J. Wilhelm, *Il miglior fabbro: The
   Cult of the Difficult in Daniel, Dante, and Pound* (Maine: National Poetry Foundation, University
   of Maine, 1982); S. Y. Mc Dougal, 'Dreaming a Renaissance: Pound's Dantean Inheritance',
   in *Ezra Pound among the Poets*, ed. by G. Bornstein (Chicago, London: University of Chicago
   Press, 1985), pp. 63–81; and R. Bush, *The Genesis of Ezra Pound's Cantos* (Princeton: Princeton
   University Press, 1976).

10. W. Cookson, *A Guide to The Cantos of Ezra Pound* (London, Sydney: Croom Helm, 1985), pp. 48–49.

11. Other poems in which Pound denounces *usura* include 'Canto XLII', 'Canto XLIII', and 'Canto 92'. Much like Sanguineti who is at pains to establish *usura* as a timeless vice, Pound, in 'Canto 92' observes how the immoral practices of the usurer have been going on for 'two thousand years'.

12. E. Pound, *Antheil and the Treatise on Harmony* (Paris: Three Mountains Press, 1924).

13. The other two were logopoeia — poetry of ideas and accurate expression; and phanopoeia — poetry of images. For a discussion of Pound and music, see M. Schafer, 'Ezra Pound and Music', in *Ezra Pound. A Collection of Critical Essays*, ed. by W. Sutton (New Jersey: Prentice-Hall, 1963), pp. 129–42.

14. *Inferno*, with translation and commentary by J. D. Sinclair (Oxford, New York: Oxford University Press, 1948), p. 54.

15. For other references to music in the *Convivio*, see *Enciclopedia Dantesca*: 'musica' (A. Niccoli). For writings on Dante and music, see A. Bonaventura, *Dante e la musica* (Livorno: Raffaellol Giusti, 1904); and R. Monterosso, 'Problemi musicali danteschi', *Cultura e Scuola*, 13–14 (1965), 207–12.

FIG. 4.1 Photograph of Armando Gentilucci
Courtesy of Archivio Storico Ricordi, Milano

CHAPTER 4

Armando Gentilucci's
Strofe di Ungaretti (1967)

Armando Gentilucci (1939–89), son of the composer, Ottorino Gentilucci, was born in Lecce, and received his early musical education at the Milan Conservatory. There he was taught by Franco Donatoni and Bruno Bettinelli, and took diplomas in the piano (1961), choral music, conducting (1962), and composition (1963). From 1964 to 1969 he taught at the Conservatories of Bolzano and Milan, and held the post of director of the Istituto Musicale of Reggio Emilia until 1989. Gentilucci is best known for his operatic version of Melville's novel, *Moby Dick*, written between 1986 and 1988. His other compositions, of which there are ninety-three in all (see bibliography), include two ballets, orchestral works, string and chamber ensembles, duets and pieces for solo instruments, and a large number of vocal works, including the mixed sextet, *Strofe di Ungaretti*, which will be the subject of examination in this chapter. In addition to his activity as a composer, Gentilucci in 1970 inaugurated a project entitled *Musica/Realtà* [Music/Reality], aimed at experimenting with new forms of musical communication for all sectors of society. To it was linked a musical journal of the same name, founded and edited by the composer himself. From 1970 onwards, Gentilucci also worked for many years as a free-lance collaborator with the publisher, Ricordi, and published essays and articles on twentieth-century music, including three major books: *Guida all'ascolto della musica contemporanea* (1969); *Introduzione alla musica elettronica* (1972); and *Oltre l'avanguardia: un invito al molteplice* (1980).[1] According to G. Ferrari, the latter, during the 1980s 'became a reference point of musical theory for the new generation of Italian composers'.[2] The influence behind Gentilucci's music lies with a group of composers who, in his view, do not fit neatly into either of the two fields posited by Adorno as characterizing the musical avant-garde of the first half of the twentieth century: Schoenberg and the Expressionism of the First Viennese School on the one hand, and Stravinsky and Neo-Classicism, on the other (for the First Viennese School and Neo-Classicism, see Chapter 1, p. 11 and pp. 8–10, respectively). The composers who influenced him are Janácek, Bartók, Prokofiev, Shostakovich, Ives, Varèse, Malipiero, and Dallapiccola, and, according to Gentilucci, their music lies outside the two movements indicated by Adorno in that these composers, while sometimes borrowing techniques associated with one or the other movement, also display autonomous characteristics (*Guida*, pp. 17–18). Hence, they have a freer, less regulated approach to the writing of music than that practised by either Expressionism or Neo-Classicism, and each composer possesses individual qualities which set them apart from each other. If they have a feature in common, it is a recognition of the disintegration of tonal aesthetics.

Gentilucci, however, was extremely critical of the aesthetics of negativism in music. While representing the *problems* confronting post-war man, his vision always allowed for *optimism,* and progressive, life-affirmative instincts. Hence, of the six composers whose names are most often associated with the Darmstadt school of the 50s (see Chapter 1, pp. 15–18) — Nono, Stockhausen, Boulez, Pousseur, Maderna, and Berio — it is with Nono that Gentilucci feels the greatest affinity for his 'intento violentemente esortativo' [violently exhortative intention], and his 'passione morale' [moral passion] (*Guida*, p. 34). Nono, in Gentilucci's view, while iconoclastically breaking with the musical past, was also progressive in the emphasis he placed on the need for expression and communication:

> Va sottolineato come la linea di sviluppo della musica di Nono si configuri da un lato come 'rottura' nei confronti del passato, dall'altra come progressivo reinserimento in una curva storica che si fonda sul fondamentale concetto di espressione e comunicazione. (*Guida*, p. 286)

> [It needs to be stressed how the line of development in Nono's music on the one hand takes the form of a 'rupture' with the past, and, on the other hand, it acts as a progressive reinsertion into an historical curve which is founded on the fundamental concept of expression and communication.]

In fact, it was in response to Nono's morally 'engaged' works, such as *Il canto sospeso* (1956) (a cantata whose libretto is composed of the words of condemned political prisoners) and *Intolleranza* (1960) (a choral opera on the subject on 'intolerance' toward immigrants), that Gentilucci also imbued his works of the 70s with political and social themes. Thus *Canti di Majakovski* (1970), dedicated to Nono, denounces the new, capitalist society generated by the sixties 'boom period' in Italy; while *Cile* (1973) is Gentilucci's personal statement on the military coup in Chile. But it was Nono's compositions for the human voice, written after 1955, that Gentilucci most admired. These vocal compositions were based mostly on literary but also on documentary texts. The most well-known of them include the choral work, *Cori di Didone* (1958) (where the lyrics are taken from Ungaretti's 'Cori descrittivi di stati d'animo di Didone'), *La Terra e la Compagna* (1958) (based on poems from Pavese's *Verrà la morte e avrà i tuoi occhi*); and *A Floresta é jovem e cheja de vida* (1966) (whose libretto consists of letters, law-court depositions, newspaper articles, and documents relating to the working class struggle in capitalist countries). What Gentilucci admired in them was, again, their communicative thrust: the manner in which, rather than conjuring up some vague sense of post-war crisis, they presented 'una precisa situazione umana e sociale' [a precise human and social situation] (*Guida*, p. 35), while also proposing definite views with regard to this human and social state:

> È per esempio molto indicativo che attorno al 1955 Nono abbia recuperato la voce umana rivolgendo la sua attenzione sempre a testi che abbiano inoltre un diretto valore di documento di una certa situazione esistenziale ed esprimano una precisa coscienza umana e una presa di posizione rispetto alla vita: tale

gesto ha rappresentato in quegli anni un vero e proprio atto di coraggio, anche
se oggi si stenta a crederlo. (*Guida*, p. 286)

[It is, for example, very indicative that around 1955 Nono had started using
the human voice always turning his attention towards texts which, moreover,
document in a direct and valuable way a certain existential situation, and
express a precise human consciousness and a point of view *vis-à-vis* life. Such a
gesture represented in those years a real act of courage, even if that is hard to
believe today.]

Gentilucci once more followed Nono's example, setting, between 1965 and 1989,
a wide-ranging choice of literature to vocal music: poems by Neruda (in *Canti da
Estravagario*, 1965), Ungaretti (*Strofe di Ungaretti*, 1967), Novalis (*Siamo prossimi al
risveglio*, 1968), Foscolo (*Le segrete vie*, 1980–81), Dante (*Ramo di foglia verde*, 1982),
and Cvetaeva (*Frammenti poetici di Marina Cvetaeva*, 1989).

Strofe di Ungaretti — a sextet for two sopranos, one contralto, two tenors, and a
bass — demonstrates best the Nonian traits which Gentilucci indicates above: the
texts chosen from Ungaretti give voice to 'a precise situation which is both human
and social' in their presentation of a family tragedy and private bereavement, set
against the universal tragedy of war, and the grief of the Italian people and the
world at large in the bewildering arena of World War II. The libretto with its,
for the most part, discursive tone, and its use of imperatives, vocatives, and the
collective pronoun 'ci' [us], has a strong, communicative thrust, and demonstrates
a 'positive aesthetics' in the speaker's injunction to himself and to others to cast
away tragic thoughts and embrace a new beginning. The lyrics comprise three
poems by Ungaretti: 'L'angelo del povero' [The poor man's angel], 'Silenzio stellato
(1932)' [Starry silence (1932)], and 'Non gridate più' [Do not shout anymore].
Two of the three sections of 'L'angelo del povero' are used, while the latter two
poems are presented in their entirety. The three compositions are 'sung' one after
the other in the order presented above, with no superimpositions. 'L'angelo del
povero' and 'Non gridate più' both occur in the sixth section of the collection
Il Dolore [Grief] (1937–46), entitled 'I ricordi (1942–46)' [Memories (1942–46)],
while 'Silenzio stellato (1932)' is the last poem of Ungaretti's preceding collection,
Sentimento del tempo [A Feeling for Time] (1919–35), occurring in the section
entitled 'L'amore'.[3]

Il Dolore was written largely during the Second World War. The first section,
'Tutto ho perduto' [I have lost everything], consists of poems commemorating the
death in 1937 of the poet's only brother, Costantino; while the following three
sections, 'Giorno per giorno' [Day by day], 1940–46; 'Il tempo è muto' [Time is
mute], 1940–45, and 'Incontro a un pino' [Meeting at a pine-tree], 1943, evoke the
last days and moments in the life of Ungaretti's nine year old son, Antonietto, who
died in 1939 in Brazil from a badly-treated case of appendicitis. Section 5 of the
collection, 'Roma occupata' [Occupied Rome], 1943–44, written in the shadows
of the German occupation, deals with the invasion of Italy, and the world at war.
The final section, 'I ricordi', laments both the poet's domestic tragedies and the
tragedy of a whole nation; in short, it 'remembers' all 'the dead', and personal and
communal grief now become indistinguishable. Gentilucci, in his use of two poems

from the 'I ricordi' section — the first to open his work, and the second to close it — clearly intends to highlight one man's tragedy and the tragedy of a whole nation. The 'middle' composition from *Sentimento del tempo*, by contrast, reverts to an earlier, serene, and pre-tragic stage in the poet's life, thereby aiming to set the subsequent tragedies in greater relief. Its style and imagery is remarkably different from that of the two poems from *Il Dolore*.

Both 'L'angelo del povero' and 'Non gridate più' have a discursive tone. It is a tone which breaks with the 'Hermeticism' for which Ungaretti became famous, 'Hermeticism' being a term derived from Hermes Trismegistus — reputedly the author of occult works on astrology, magic, and alchemy — and popularized by Francesco Flora in his study *La poesia ermetica*,[4] where Flora used it to describe, (pejoratively), the symbolic language and subjective imagery of Ungaretti's early poems which left them hermetically 'sealed'. More in keeping with the diaristic collective title given to Ungaretti's complete works — *Vita d'un uomo* [The Life of a Man] — the two poems chosen by Gentilucci from *Il Dolore* have a declarative forthrightness, and a 'naturalness' about them which communicates a spontaneous and intensely felt outpouring of grief. This is how the two poems are presented in the libretto accompanying Gentilucci's score:

'L'angelo del povero'

Ora che invade le oscurate menti
Più aspra pietà del sangue e della terra,
Ora che ci misura ad ogni palpito
Il silenzio di tante ingiuste morti,

Ora si svegli l'angelo del povero,
gentilezza superstite dell'anima...
. . . .
(Da 'I ricordi' di Giuseppe Ungaretti, 1942–46)

[Now that darkened minds are invaded/ by a most bitter compassion for blood and land,/ Now that the silence of so many unjustly dead people/ Measures us with every heartbeat,/ Now may the poor man's angel/ — the surviving kindness of the soul — awaken.]

'Non gridate più'

Cessate d'uccidere i morti,
Non gridate più, non gridate
Se li volete ancora udire,
Se sperate di non perire.

Hanno l'impercettibile sussurro,
Non fanno più rumore
Del crescere dell'erba,
Lieta dove non passa l'uomo.
(Da 'I ricordi' di Giuseppe Ungaretti, 1942–46)

[Stop killing the dead,/ Do not shout anymore, do not shout/ If you still want to hear them,/ If you hope not to perish./ They whisper imperceptibly,/ They make no more sound/ Than the growing of the grass,/ The happy grass where man does not tread.]

Both sequences have a rhetorical and obsessively repetitive style: 'Ora che', 'Ora che', 'Ora' ('L'angelo'); 'Non gridate', 'non gridate', 'Se [...] volete', 'Se sperate' ('Non gridate più'). Even the title of both poems is repeated in their respective texts, and rhythm also is without variation: that of 'L'angelo' is a hammering-like interchange between two minimally different verse lengths — hendecasyllables and dodecasyllables; while the whole of the first section of 'Non gridate più' consists of four consecutive *novenari* [lines of nine syllables]. This repetitiveness, together with the poems' rhetorical style conveys feelings of explosive rage and torment.

Paradoxically, however, the message of each component is a call for an end to self-destructive emotions such as anger and grief, and an awareness of a need for a new beginning. The first section of 'L'angelo' presents an impassioned assessment of the situation at present (conveyed in the use of 'ora' followed by present tense verbs: 'invade', 'ci misura'): the mind of the poet and contemporary man (Ungaretti uses the collective 'ci') have been 'darkened over' by tragedy and haunted by compassion ('pietà') for the dead: the reference to 'blood' and 'land' specifically evokes the *bloodshed* in the poet's *homeland* i.e. the national tragedy of war, but, as explained earlier, Ungaretti's own personal tragedies, especially the death of Antonietto, are also intended. The silence of these unjustly dead people 'measures' the living with every heartbeat of the latter, that is to say, makes them feel guilty for being alive, and almost responsible for their deaths. But in the second section, Ungaretti's repetition of 'Ora', now followed by a subjunctive verb ('Ora si svegli') expresses a desire for a change in this situation, a new 'awakening'. He prays that, whatever goodness or 'kindheartedness' ('gentilezza') that 'survives' in man's soul — personified by the 'poor man's angel' — may be awakened and, as the rest of Ungaretti's poem makes clear, reign supreme over the 'shadows' of death, as has been the case for centuries (the last section, not quoted by Gentilucci, reads 'Col gesto inestinguibile dei secoli / Discenda a capo del suo vecchio popolo, / In mezzo alle ombre...' [With the inextinguishable gesture of the centuries, / May he descend at the head of his old people, / In the midst of the shadows]). In other words, Ungaretti is saying that the time has come for positive emotions such as kindheartedness, and the hope that is implicit in his use of subjunctives, to replace grief, guilt and injustice; and he wishes that the life-affirmative instincts which, since time immemorial, have always returned in the wake of tragedies to ensure the continuation and preservation of civilization, will now reassert themselves. Similarly, in 'Non gridate più' a connection is made between showing more respect for the dead and *not* mourning them: mourning them is made synonymous with 'killing' them ('Cessate d'uccidere i morti'), and the poet calls for an end to lamentations ('Non gridate più, non gridate') which only enfeeble those who lament ('Se sperate di non perire'), and muffle the memory of those who have died ('Se li volete ancora udire').

The antithesis between the *tone* of both poems, which conveys a mixture of impotent rage and torment, and their *content*, which calls for an end to such destructive emotions, is reinforced by imagery which communicates a pull of opposites: the Petrarchan 'aspra pietà'; the 'silence' of the 'dead' versus the 'heartbeat' of the living; the noun-adjective contrast, 'morti', 'superstite', ('L'angelo'); the oxymoronic 'killing' of the 'dead'; the poet's injunction to listen to the *voices* of the *dead*; and his prediction that the *living* who do not do so, will themselves *perish* ('Non gridate più'). The most blatant antithesis belongs, however, to 'L'angelo'. It occurs in the recurrent use of the word 'Ora', underscoring the need for change in the *here and the now*, and its contrast with the sectional title of the poem: 'I ricordi' (added by Gentilucci after the extract in the libretto). That Ungaretti fails in his attempt to forget tragedy and free himself from the negative emotions which consume him is made clear in two stylistic features of the libretto, the first of which is the use of the negation 'non'.

The word 'non' is a feature of both the second and third poem of the libretto, and occurs seven times in all. Its recurrence cannot be considered incidental. In view of the libretto's preoccupation with the concepts of memory and time (evinced by the choice of two poems from a section of *Il Dolore* called 'I ricordi', and the third from a collection entitled *Sentimento del tempo*) the high frequency of the use of negation would seem to be linked to Henri Bergson's writings on the same within his philosophical works on the concept of time. Ungaretti attended Bergson's lectures at the Collège de France in Paris from January 1913 to March 1914, and recalls these lectures in three short articles on Bergson.[5] Bergson had a major influence on his writing, and, as he explains below, helped him formulate his own 'feeling for time':

> Je crois que Bergson est un grand philosophe romantique, le plus grand philosophe de son temps. J'ai beaucoup appris de ses leçons, [...]. Je crois que ma poésie lui a une grande dette. C'est par ses leçons que mon sentiment du temps s'est précisé.[6]

> [I think that Bergson is a great romantic philosopher, the greatest philosopher of his time. I learned a lot from his lessons [...]. I believe that my poetry owes him a huge debt. It was through his lessons that my feeling for time took shape.]

In *L'existence et le néant* [Existence and Nothingness] Bergson explains the self-reflexiveness of 'negation' in relation to time. He argues that since in negation, the thing being negated is not substituted by its opposite or by something else, the negated object is merely reaffirmed and reinforced (for example, saying that something is 'not white' does not inform one of its real colour; it merely emphasizes the notion of 'whiteness'):

> Ce qui donne à la négation son caractère subjectif, c'est précisément que, dans la constatation d'un remplacement, elle ne tient compte que du remplacé et ne s'occupe pas du remplaçant.[7]

> [That which gives negation its subjective character is precisely this: in the recording of a substitution, it only takes into account the thing being replaced, and is not interested in the replacement.]

It follows therefore that negation is not forward-looking (it does not replace the 'old' object being negated with something 'new'), but backward-looking, and being backward-looking, it is linked to the past and memory:

> C'est ce qu'on fait quand on nie. On constate le changement, ou plus généralement la substitution, come verrait le trajet de la voiture un voyageur

qui regarderait en arrière et ne voudrait connaître à chaque instant que le point
où il a cessé d'être; il ne déterminerait jamais sa postion actuelle que par rapport
à celle qu'il vient de quitter au lieu de l'exprimer en fonction d'elle-même.
(*L'existence et le néant*, p. 743)

[It is what one does when one negates. One states the change, or more
generally, the substitution, as a traveller would see the route of a car journey if
he were looking backwards, and was only interested, every second, in the point
where he had ceased to be. He would only ever establish his present position
in relationship to the one he had just left, rather than expressing that position
in and for itself.]

Ungaretti's negations, therefore, as well as obviously emphasizing a sense of absence
and loss (the loss of the poet's family members and compatriots), are also to be
considered in Bergsonian terms. Ungaretti has consciously used Bergson's ideas on
negation to highlight his inability to move on with his life. He attempts to move
forward but fails. He is like Bergson's traveller who gazes backwards while moving
forwards. He might desire an end to grieving ('Non gridate più, non gridate'); an
end to memories of dying and perishing ('non perire'); a universe free of war-faring
men ('dove non passa l'uomo'); and peace from the psychological havoc engendered
by 'unjust' deaths ('Non si muovono più', 'Non fanno più rumore'), but grief, and
images of war and death still manage to crowd his consciousness. They are not,
as yet, substituted by their opposites; the poet is still helplessly tied to the past and
memory.

 This state of being bound to the past is also something which is underlined in
the *Strofe* through the use of ellipsis. In the following extract from the libretto, the
ellipsis after 'anima' is present in the original version of Ungaretti's poem, but the
further series of suspension points has been added by Gentilucci himself:

  Gentilezza superstite dell'anima ...
  . . . .

Ellipsis — a feature of the whole of the 'I ricordi' section of Ungaretti's *Il Dolore*, as
well as of poems from other sections recalling the last, painful days in the life of the
poet's son, in particular 'Giorno per giorno' — indicates (as noted by Cary, p. 197)
the mind's uncontrollable shifting backwards in time from the here and now into
the dark recesses of memory with all of its concomitant pain. The poet's ineluctable
falling into the abyss of memory, or being shipwrecked, helplessly, on its waves (two
metaphors used in 'Il tempo è muto'), is something which Gentilucci obviously
wishes to underscore not only in the libretto of *Strofe*, but also in its music. He does
it, in fact, through operating a type of musical ellipsis. At the point in the score
where the singers enunciate the words 'Gentilezza superstite dell'anima...', there is
an attempt at a type of musical ellipsis on the final vowel of 'anima'. Here each of
the voices sings a tied note, and the darker the voice colour, the longer it is held:
hence, the second voice holds it for longer than the first, the third, for longer than
the second, etc. The result is that the notes themselves operate visually like a series
of suspension points (see Figure 4.2).

 Besides memory, ellipsis in 'L'angelo' is also used to convey the related
phenomenon of unspeakable, as opposed to 'shouted' suffering. This is made clear

Fig. 4.2. Armando Gentilucci's *Strofe di Ungaretti* (Milan: Ricordi, 1969), p. 7
Courtesy of G. Ricordi & C. SpA Milano

in the opening poem of *Il Dolore*, 'Tutto ho perduto', where the poet speaks of a paralysing type of suffering, where 'stony' cries remain locked in his throat, resulting in silence:

> Disperazione che incessante aumenta.
> La vita non mi è più,
> Arrestata in fondo alla gola,
> Che una roccia di gridi.

> [Desperation which incessantly increases./ My life, halted at the back of my throat,/ Is nothing more/ Than a rock of cries.]

Similar imagery is employed in Ungaretti's brief 'Note' to *Il Dolore*, where instead of discussing the collection, he talks about the pain and the impropriety of discussing it:

> *Il Dolore* è il libro che di più amo, il libro che ho scritto negli anni orribili, stretto alla gola. Se ne parlassi mi parrebbe d'essere impudico. (*Tutte le poesie*, p. 543)

> [*Il Dolore* is the book I love most, the book I wrote in those horrible years, with a tightened throat. To speak of it would seem to me to be improper.]

Gentilucci is obviously familiar with *Il Dolore's* key motif of excessive emotionalism and muted grief, of shouting and silence, as it becomes a major musical feature of his score with rapid and unexpected juxtapositions of *piano*s and *forte*s. After the first soprano sings a soft and lyrical rendition of the opening phrase from 'L'angelo' (reminiscent of the beginning of the 'Liriche Greche' by Dallapiccola), the second soprano and contralto take up the vowel sound 'o' from 'Ora', and holding it (the soprano for six beats and the contralto for three) swell, respectively, from *pianissimo* to *mezzo forte* and back to *pianissimo,* and from *pianissimo* to *forte* and back to *piano*. The second phrase, sung by the men, begins on a *mezzo forte*, but the volume increases to a *forte* on the words 'e della terra', sung '*marcato*', immediately after which the last syllable 'ra' of 'terra' is repeated *piano*, and diminishes over a space of three bars to a double *piano*. The most startling juxtaposition occurs between the third and fourth lines of the lyrics. Underneath the sopranos who sing the word 'palpita' on a double *piano* (the arrangement of their notes in quintuplets and triplets suggest the irregular heartbeat of which they sing, while the slight intervallic increases in the music as it proceeds are visually reminiscent of an electrocardiograph reading) the tenors and basses, in a technique known as *sprächgesang*, invented by Schoenberg, speak, rather than sing the phrase 'ad ogni palpito'. Their speaking is marked triple piano and 'un mormorio' [a murmur]. This quiet and 'murmuring', however, erupts without warning into a curious composition for the phrase 'il silenzio', uttered syllabically as 'il — si — len — en — zi — o', with each of the syllables sung by a different voice. The first three syllables, 'il — si — len' are marked *fortissimo* and *marcato*, and the colour of the voices which sing them 'rises' from dark to light (first tenor, contralto, and second soprano, respectively); while the last three syllables 'en — zi — o', in shocking contrast, move from a triple *piano* to a *mezzo piano*, and like the volume, the colour of the voices which sing them 'falls' (contralto, followed by bass) (see Figure 4.3). That Gentilucci means these juxtapositions in volume to

FIG. 4.3. Armando Gentilucci's *Strofe di Ungaretti*, p. 4
Courtesy of G. Ricordi & C. SpA Milano

FIG. 4.4. Armando Gentilucci's *Strofe di Ungaretti*, pp. 13–14
Courtesy of G. Ricordi & C. SpA Milano

concord with the shouting and silence motif indicated in the two extracts from 'I ricordi' and present in the poems of *Il Dolore* as a whole, is made evident by the fact that he chooses to organize exaggerated differences in volume around the word 'silence', and that the first three syllables of 'silenzio' are, paradoxically, practically 'shouted'.

The second component from 'I ricordi' demonstrates similar extremes in volume, with the opening imperative 'Cessate d'uccidere i morti' (sung in the repetitive musical style of a canon, and, in fact, repeated three times, thereby highlighting Ungaretti's aforementioned 'obsessive repetitiveness', symptomatic of his rage and torment) sung *fortissimo* and *marcato* by all six voices. The double *forte* jumps kaleidoscopically to a triple *piano* on the following phrase, 'Non gridate più', and the rest of the first section of the poem moves between *piano*, *pianissimo*, and triple *piano*. Hence, while in 'L'angelo' the first three syllables of 'silenzio' were sung double *forte*, here there is a reverse procedure, where the word 'gridate' is sung triple *piano*. Graphically too, the score reinforces this inversion and, as a consequence, the interrelatedness of 'silence' and 'shouting', for whereas the colour of the voices singing each syllable of 'il — si — len — en — zi — o' grows lighter and then darker, so that the music rises and falls across the staves; those on the phrase 'non gridate', darken and then lighten, so that, conversely, the music traverses the staves first in a descending, and then in an ascending motion (see Figure 4.4). The dotted lines connecting the notes on both occasions draw attention to this type of musical chiasmus.

Perhaps the most radical feature of the music for 'Non gridate', however, occurs in the second section of the lyrics. Here sound, in the sense of music, is reduced to a limit which approximates, as much as possible, silence. This is indicated not only by the composer's directions 'Parlato [...] — sempre P — come sussurrato' [Spoken, [...] — always softly — as if whispered], but also by the extremist gesture of erasing the majority of the musical staves, and replacing them with words which speak of whispering, noiselessness, and imperceptibility (Figure 4.5). Graphically, this creates a strong link with Ungaretti, for it produces a typographical feature immediately evocative of Ungaretti's early compositional style in *L'Allegria*: the isolation and accentuation of short phrases, and often individual words, set against the white background of the page. This method has been compared, to some extent, with Japanese Haiku poetry, with the 'frammenti' or 'fragment'-style poetry practised by contributors to the Florentine periodical, *La Voce*, and even with Mallarmé's words, born out of the 'blanche agonie' [white agony] of the page. But above all it owes its inspiration to techniques associated with Cubism and the 'Parole in libertà' [Free words] of the Futurists — two avant-garde movements from which Ungaretti drew inspiration during his residence in Paris from 1912 to 1914.[8] Ungaretti's dissection of the musical flow of traditional metres — for the most part *endecasillabi* [hendecasyllables], *novenari* [lines of nine syllables], and *settenari* [lines of seven syllables] into short, clipped segments, evokes, on the one hand, the manner in which Picasso and Braque replaced the curvilinear style of traditional painting with an angular faceting which lent their paintings an effect of dislocation; and on the other hand, it recalls Futurist 'Free Words', set randomly on the page or

FIG. 4.9. Armando Gentilucci's *Strofe di Ungaretti*, p. 10
Courtesy of G. Ricordi & C. SpA Milano

stellato', therefore, may look anomalous in *Sentimento del tempo*, but it is related to the rest of the collection through the concept of time and memory. It is a 'happy' memory, and has the positive effect of releasing the poet from mechanical time. Its positioning within the collection is crucial. For although there are many other poems in *Sentimento del tempo* dated 1934, 'Silenzio stellato', dated 1932, is placed last. It is therefore the poem which precedes *Il Dolore* in *Vita d'un uomo*, and the opening section of *Il Dolore* is, as mentioned previously, significantly called 'Tutto ho perduto'. The juxtaposition of happiness and utter despair is intentional. The first poem of *Il Dolore*, also called 'Tutto ho perduto', speaks of the death of the poet's brother, and with his death, the poet's own 'childhood', by which he means, his ability to see the world through the innocent eyes of a child, and consequently conjure up a serene, and pleasant vision of it such as that evoked in 'Silenzio stellato'. It is inferred that, with the death of a member of family, innocence too dies, and one's vision of the world is irrevocably altered. 'Memories' become a 'useless infinite' in the midst of infinite 'death-rattles': 'I ricordi, un inutile infinito, [...] In mezzo a rantoli infiniti...' ('I Ricordi', *Il Dolore*). In an implicit reference back to the sweetness of recollection in 'Silenzio stellato', 'Tutto ho perduto' alludes to memory as something from which one now only 'unburdens' oneself ('smemorarmi') with the 'shouted' suffering mentioned previously, and which in this particular poem Ungaretti feels incapable of, overcome as he is by a more numbing kind of grief:

> Tutto ho perduto dell'infanzia
> E non potrò mai più
> Smemorarmi in un grido. (p. 201)

> [I have lost everything from my childhood/ And I can never again/ Unburden my memory with a cry.]

That Gentilucci is aware of 'Silenzio stellato''s associations with the concepts of time and memory is demonstrated by two things: the dates of the compositions are added, thereby illustrating that the middle poem of the libretto was composed at least a decade before the first and the third, so that in terms of 'L'angelo' and 'Non gridate', 'Silenzio stellato' operates as a distant memory; and the composer sandwiches 'Silenzio stellato' between two others from the section of *Il Dolore* called 'I ricordi'. This positioning of the poem in the libretto, as in Ungaretti's oeuvre, is deliberately and effectively designed to evoke, through juxtapositions with 'darker' poems of great despair, feelings of pathos and tragedy.

In fact, taken out of its original context of *Sentimento del tempo*, and examined within the context of Gentilucci's score, the imagery of 'Silenzio stellato' takes on a whole new intentional meaning and relevance. Its childish constructions and its naive, story-book imagery, when considered alongside the 'unjust' death of Ungaretti's son which looms behind the two poems quoted from 'I ricordi', cannot fail to evoke the 'memory' of the dead child. Once that association has been made, the poem activates the reader/listener's cultural memory, and becomes resonant with all kinds of poignant, extra-textual overtones, which interact with other parts of the libretto. The final word of 'Silenzio stellato', 'nidi', calls to mind the birds which are a recurrent feature of the poem 'Giorno per giorno', commemorating the last days in the life of the poet's son. In the first section of this poem Ungaretti talks of how he would put crumbs on the window sill of his child's bedroom so that the feeding sparrows would distract the dying child (the gesture encapsulates something of the 'aspra pietà' felt by the poet in 'L'angelo del povero'):

> E il volto già scomparso
> Ma gli occhi ancora vivi
> Dal guanciale volgeva alla finestra.
> E riempivano passeri la stanza
> Verso le briciole dal babbo sparse
> Per distrarre il suo bimbo... (p. 205)

> [And he would turn his already dead face,/ But with eyes still alive/ From the pillow to the window./ And sparrows filled the room/ Coming down for the crumbs scattered by the father/ To distract his little boy... .]

Besides sparrows, swallows also occur in section eleven of 'Giorno per giorno' where their passing is linked to the end of summer and the arrival of winter, old age and death:

> Passa la rondine e con essa estate,
> E anchi'io, mi dico, passerò... (p. 207)

> [The swallow passes and with it, summer,/ And I too, I tell myself, will pass away ... .]

Perhaps most significant of all, however, is the reference to the 'drunken swift' in section sixteen. This reference occurs amidst a kaleidoscopic bombardment of rather grotesque, 'baroque' imagery (Jones, *Modern Italian Lyric*, p. 385) used to describe the violent and inhuman landscape of Brazil where the poet remembers his son play, and which will always be associated with his death (a similar landscape is evoked in 'Tu ti spezzasti'):

> Agli abbagli che squillano dai vetri
> Squadra un riflesso alla tovaglia l'ombra,
> Tornano al lustro labile d'un orcio
> Gonfie ortensie dall'aiuola, un rondone ebbro,
> Il grattacielo in vampe delle nuvole,
> Sull'albero, saltelli d'un bimbetto... (p. 208)

> [In the dazzle which shrieks from the window-panes/ The shade frames a reflexion on the tablecloth,/ Swollen hydrangeas from the flowerbed reappear/ In the faint shining of a pot; a drunken swift,/ The skyscraper in a blaze of clouds,/ On a tree the capering of a young child... .]

This drunken bird in a terrifying landscape contrasts starkly with the nesting birds in the quiet, gentle, and therapeutic landscape evoked in 'Silenzio stellato', where the reference to slight movements in nests connotes, not death, but new life, and the warm 'love' from which that new life is born (as Gentilucci indicates in the libretto, 'Silenzio stellato' occurs in the section of *Sentimento del tempo* called 'L'amore' [Love]).

Besides allusions to *Il Dolore*, the libretto's lyrics recall other compositions by Ungaretti as well. Just like the 'movement' of the libretto which travels backwards in time (from 1942–46 to 1932) and then forwards again (from 1932 to 1942–46) the 'aspra pietà' of 'L'angelo del povero' points backwards in the direction of 'La Pietà' [Compassion] (1928) — a famous crisis-hymn from the section called 'Inni' [Hymns] in *Sentimento del tempo*; while the title 'Non gridate più' looks forward to the later collection *Un grido e paesaggi* [A Cry and Landscapes] (1939–52) and its main composition — 'Gridasti: soffoco' [You cried: I am suffocating]. The reminders which the *Strofe*'s lyrics make to both these poems, render the libretto more pregnant with dark despair. 'La Pietà' voices existential anguish, caused by a feeling of 'incomunicabilità tra gli uomini, e le crescenti condizioni politiche di inevitabili orrori' (*Tutte le poesie*, p. 530) [a lack of communication between men, and the growing political conditions laden with inevitable horrors] — horrors that resulted precisely in the 'tante ingiuste morti' of World War II referred to in 'L'angelo del povero'. The poem takes the form of impassioned questions directed at a God who remains, throughout, a silent, remote, unmoved addressee. His silence is embodied in the blank spaces between the indignant, staccato questions. Jones (*Giuseppe Ungaretti*, p. 108) makes the point that the whole atmosphere of the poem is similar to that experienced by Christ in the garden of Gethsemane when Christ appeals to an unresponsive God to deliver him from his anguish:

> E mi sento esiliato in mezzo agli uomini.
> Ma per essi sto in pena.
> Dio, guarda la nostra debolezza.
> Vorremmo una certezza.
> Di noi nemmeno più ridi?
> E compiangici dunque, crudeltà.

> [And I feel exiled amongst men./ But for them I am in anguish./ God, look on our weaknesses./ We desire some certainty./ Don't you even laugh at us any more?/ Pity us then, cruel one.]

'Gridasti: soffoco' was originally written as part of 'Giorno per giorno', but contains blacker and more harrowing descriptions than those of the latter poem — of Antonietto's dilating eyes, contorted mouth, pale, dry hands, breathlessness, and his final utterance, 'Soffoco' (Ungaretti, in fact, did not originally publish this section of the poem with 'Giorno per giorno' considering the detail within to be too personal to him[14]). Two sequences from 'Gridasti: soffoco' also serve to explain some features of 'L'angelo del povero':

> Sconto, sopravvivendoti, l'orrore
> Degli anni che t'usurpo,
> E che ai tuoi anni aggiungo,
> Demente di rimorso... .(p. 264)

> [I expiate, surviving you, the horror/ Of the years I usurp from you,/ And which, mad with remorse / I add to your years.]

> Cielo sordo, che scende senza un soffio,
> Sordo che udrò continuamente opprimere
> Mani tese a scansarlo... . (p. 264)

> [Deaf sky, falling without a breath,/ Deaf sky that I will always hear pressing/ On hands held up to fend it off... .]

The reference in the first extract to the weight of the years unlived by Ungaretti's son, wearing down the poet, filling him with remorse, and expiating the guilt he feels at surviving him, concurs with and throws light on the concept of the silence of the dead, measuring the heartbeat of the guilt-ridden living that one finds in lines 3 and 4 of 'L'angelo'; while the second extract (the concluding lines of 'Gridasti: soffoco') with its horrifying allusion to the protesting child being 'suffocated' by death allows one to appreciate fully the sense of 'injustice' surrounding his decease.

In addition to sparking off memories of other poems in *Vita d'un uomo* which serve to aid one's appreciation and understanding of the lyrics in the libretto, *Strofe* also activates a number of allusions to prominent names in the literary tradition. The manner in which 'Silenzio stellato' echoes, through relationships of contrast, 'Giorno per giorno' with its sparrows, swallows, and swift, brings to mind Leopardi's famous 'Il passero solitario' (*Canti*) [The lonely sparrow, *Poems*] where Leopardi used the solitary bird as a symbol of his own feelings of loneliness and separation from the rest of society. These feelings of separation and loneliness are tacitly expressed in 'Non gridate più' when Ungaretti calls for an end to 'shouting' so that the 'whisperings' of the dead (his son) can be heard. More than to Leopardi, however, the 'nidi' of 'Silenzio stellato' generate an allusion to Pascoli. That Gentilucci intends this allusion to be felt is reinforced by the references to family deaths in the two poems with which he 'envelops' 'Silenzio stellato' — Pascoli being profoundly disturbed by the deaths of his father, mother, sister, and two brothers during his childhood, deaths which gave rise to the recurrent motif of the 'nest' in his poetry, a symbol of the home, family love and unity. It is precisely these concepts which the nests in 'Silenzio stellato' seem to symbolize: the tiny shuffling within them, said to be the only perceptible movement in this still and starry night, evokes a sense of warm security. And for that reason, the poem in fact reads like a positive counterpart, or an inverted image of Pascoli's famous 'X Agosto' [10 August], which draws an analogy between the senseless killing of a swallow on its way back to the nest to feed its young, and the death of the poet's father who was also murdered on his way home, carrying presents for his children. Importantly also, there are stars in Pascoli's poem too, but they are stars which join with the earth in weeping at the wretchedness of violence:

> Ritornava una rondine al tetto:
> l'uccisero; cadde tra spini:
> ella aveva nel becco un insetto:
> la cena dei suoi rondinini.
> [...]
> Anche un uomo tornava al suo nido:
> l'uccisero: disse: perdono;
> e restò negli aperti occhi un grido:
> portava due bambole in dono...
> [...]
> E tu, Cielo, dall'alto dei mondi
> sereni, infinito, immortale,
> oh! d'un pianto di stelle lo inondi
> quest'atomo opaco del Male![15]

[A swallow was returning to the roof:/ they killed it; it fell among thorns:/ it had an insect in its beak:/ a meal for its young [...]./ A man was also returning to his nest:/ they killed him: he said: Forgiveness!;/ and a cry remained in his open eyes; / he was carrying two dolls as presents... [...]./ And you, infinite, immortal Heaven,/ from the height of the peaceful worlds,/ oh, this opaque atom of Evil/ flood it with the crying of stars!]

That a number of key words here — not only 'nido', but also 'l'uccisero' (used twice) and 'grido' — are present in the poems of the libretto — 'nidi', 'uccidere', 'gridate' (repeated three times) — also seems evidence of the fact that Pascoli's poem was present in Gentilucci's mind when choosing the poems for his *Strofe*. Apart from the domestic tragedies which befell both poets, there are a number of other reasons why Gentilucci should want to evoke Pascoli. Ungaretti himself echoes the poet many times both in *L'Allegria* and *Sentimento del tempo*,[16] but mostly in the former collection where the simplicity of his lexical register — recalled in 'Silenzio stellato' — finds, to some extent, a precedent in Pascoli's use of child, and sometimes, baby language,[17] which goes hand in hand with the cult of a child's innocent vision of the world, proposed by Pascoli in his essay 'Il fanciullino'[18] [The young boy]. This childish, anti-literary style is clearly exemplified by the extract from 'X Agosto'. Also pertinent to Ungaretti's vision is Pascoli's view of the human condition where death, grief, and violence are posited as the enemies of man, and man is encouraged to reject all forms of vengeance and unite in brotherhood:

Pace, fratelli! e fate che le braccia
ch'ora o poi tenderete ai più vicini,
non sappiano la lotta e la minaccia.
E buoni veda voi dormir nei lini
placidi e bianchi, quando non intesa,
quando non vista, sopra voi si chini
la Morte con la sua lampada accesa. ('I due fanciulli', *Poesie*, p. 267)

[Peace, my brothers! And see to it that your arms/ which either today or tomorrow you will stretch out to your closest friends,/ know nothing of battle and menace./ And when Death with his burning lamp/ unseen and unheard bends over you,/ may he see you to be good people, asleep/ in your peaceful, white linen sheets. ('The two young boys').]

Something of that same exhortation is, of course, present in Ungaretti's 'Non gridate più' where behind his imperative to stop killing the dead, there lies implicit a message to stop killing the living, and where his injunction to 'cease shouting' could be meant to be directed also at the heated rhetoric of politicians.

The power and inevitability of literature to awaken resonances with literature of the past (and, indeed, when compared to music, its lesser ability to sever links with tradition) is something that has been discussed by Gentilucci in a section of his *Guida*: 'La "rottura" completa con il passato è negata in letteratura dal potere semantico della letteratura stessa' (p. 32) [The complete 'rupture' with the past is not possible in literature on account of the semantic power of literature itself]. By choosing and arranging poems which activate a whole plethora of extra-textual references — to other poems in *Il Dolore*, other poems in Ungaretti's oeuvre as a whole, and major voices in the Italian literary tradition — Gentilucci has created a work which imitates what Flora called, Ungaretti's 'impressionismo atomico' [atomic impressionism]: the ability of his Hermetic poems to emit suggestive overtones and radiate an abundance of meanings through the power of linguistic association. The libretto in itself is, in many respects, therefore, one large Hermetic composition.

Looking at the libretto as one rather than as three individual compositions also exposes one final, important feature of the work. The whole of Ungaretti's poetic output is characterized by a transcendental impulse, a desire for an unearthly realm, which, on more than one occasion he has referred to as 'un paese innocente'[19] [an innocent country]. In view of the poet's early influence by the French Symbolist poets, this impulse could be inspired by Transcendental Symbolism and its theory of 'vertical correspondences', or it could be one of religious orientation. Very probably it is a fusion of both. In the following quotation, taken from the 'Notes' to *Sentimento del tempo*, Ungaretti expresses this cult of an otherworldly dimension more in religious terms as a vision of pre-Adamic innocence:

> Nel *Sentimento del tempo*, come in qualsiasi altro momento della mia poesia sino ad oggi, quest'uomo ch'io sono, prigioniero nella propria libertà, poiché come ogni altro essere vivente è colpito dall'espiazione d'un'oscura colpa, non ha potuto non fare sorgere la presenza d'un sogno d'innocenza. Di innocenza preadamitica, quella dell'universo prima dell'uomo. [...] non si sa quale altro battesimo potrebbe riscattarci, togliendoci di dosso la persecuzione della memoria. (*Tutte le poesie*, p. 535–36)

> [In the *Sentimento del tempo*, as in any other phase of my poetry up until the present, this man that I am, a prisoner in his own liberty — since like every other living being he is persecuted by the expiation of a dark sense of guilt –, could not help but create the presence of a dream of innocence. A dream of pre-Adamic innocence: of the universe before the existence of man. [...] one cannot think of any other baptism that could redeem us, removing from us the persecution of memory.]

This quotation, in fact, touches upon a number of concepts which have been shown to be fundamental to the two poems from *Il Dolore* quoted in Gentilucci's libretto: the idea of man expiating a sense of guilt (present in lines 3 and 4 of 'L'angelo del povero') and which in the citation above seems to be acquainted with a 'Catholic' sense of Original Sin (Ungaretti, whose poetry, from the onset, hovers ambivalently between a secular and religious vision, made a full conversion to Catholicism in 1928); the 'persecution' caused by memory (recalling the painful memories, present in the two poems quoted from *Il Dolore,* of the poet's dead son, brother, and those who have perished in the war); and the concept of an innocent, man-free universe (alluded to in the final lines of 'Non gridate più' with its reference to 'happy', untrodden grass).What Ungaretti's 'Note' serves to do is to consolidate the religious dimension behind the poems in the libretto, felt as a shadowy presence through the use of vaguely religious vocabulary such as 'pietà', 'l'angelo'; and the two Dantean echoes: the first in the phrase 'Se sperate di non perire' where the juxtaposition of 'hope' and 'perishing' recalls the line written on the gates of Dante's Hell: 'LASCIATE OGNI SPERANZA, VOI CH'ENTRATE' [Abandon hope, all you who enter here]; and the second in the term 'Lieta', an adjective frequently used to describe Beatrice in Dante's *Paradiso*.[20] In fact the whole of the libretto demonstrates an attempt to move away from this world and the present moment in time, to a more ethereal and happier dimension. The weighty, emphatic opening of the libretto — 'Ora' — repeated twice thereafter, together with references to darkness, land, and death ('oscurate', 'terra', 'morti') firmly announce a linkage with the 'here and now' on this earth. The second component steers away from the heavy earth towards the weightless sky, and the darkness of the earth is replaced by the luminosity of stars. The verbs of movement yoked to the adverbs of time in the first sequence ('Ora che invade', 'Ora che ci misura', 'Ora si svegli') are substituted by a lack of movement ('Non si muovono più'), and the progression from 'business' to a more peaceful sense of stasis is even reflected grammatically ('E (...) e', 'Non (...) più', 'Se non') and rhythmically, in the retreating lengths of each line (7, 6, and 5 syllables, respectively). The 'negative' silence that was first associated with the deceased within the earth ('il silenzio di tante ingiuste morti'), is transferred into the more 'positive' 'whispering' of the dead in the third component ('positive' because it is compared to the whispering of 'happy' grass), indicating life after death in a peaceful, abstract, 'imperceptible' realm, where, as 'Gridasti: soffoco' puts it, 'il vivere è calma, è senza morte...' [living is calm, is deathless...]. This desired progression from the 'here and now' indicated at the beginning of the libretto ('Ora'), to the more abstract and, possibly, religious dimension alluded to at the end, imitates a pattern common to the early compositions of Ungaretti, often characterized by a play of antithesis between a terminology stressing the present moment in time — the use of words such as 'ora' [now], 'a quest'ora' [at this hour], 'stanotte' [tonight], 'stamani' [this morning] — and a 'metaphysical' vocabulary — 'infinito' [infinite], 'spazio' [space], 'universo' [universe], 'immenso' [immense]. The juxtaposition is most pronounced in Ungaretti's best-known compositions, which could be considered acts of 'intuition', in Bergson's sense of the term (discussed in *L'évolution créatrice*): an intuitive communing with the *élan vital,* with the eternally creative source of being, or the divine impulse in evolution which is ultimately God himself. In these poems 'Ora' is followed closely by references to abstract concepts of space and universality, as, for example, in 'La notte bella' [The beautiful night], *L'Allegria*:

> Ora mordo
> come un bambino la mammella
> lo spazio
> Ora sono ubriaco
> d'universo. (p. 48)

> [Now I bite/ at space/ as a child bites the breast/ Now I am drunk/ with universe.]

Judging by the titles of many of Gentilucci's compositions, the composer would seem to share Ungaretti's interest in metaphysical phenomena such as space (with its related concepts of stars and silence), universality, time, and memory:

> Tempo-spazio [Time-space] (1977)
> In alto, le stelle [High above, the Stars] (1981)
> Voci dal silenzio [Voices from the Silence] (1981)

Nei quieti silenzi [In the Quiet Silences] (1983)
Lied senza parole [Song without Words] (1977)
Oh, voce che mi sfuggi [Oh, Voice which Escapes me] (1981)
Intervalli del tempo [Intervals of Time] (1981)
Al telaio del tempo [At the Loom of Time] (1983)
Metafore del tempo [Metaphors of Time] (1984)
Specchi della memoria [Mirrors of Memory] (1984)

However, if the metaphysical dimension invoked in the poems by Ungaretti used in the *Strofe* is of a strictly religious orientation, then it is doubtful whether Gentilucci who, like Nono, his musical 'maestro', was of Marxist persuasion, identified with that religious vision. In fact, in his musical writings, Gentilucci constantly equates the loss of tonality with the contesting of a centripetal and harmonious vision of the universe with God as its centre:

> Alla base della concezione [del sistema tonale] sta infatti il criterio centripeto secondo il quale tutto muove da un punto unificatore e ad esso continuamente rinvia [...]. L'idea di una musica legata a una concezione meccanicistica dell'Universo, fondata su una ricerca a-priori dell'*affinità* dei suoni tra loro e con espunzione o subordinazione degli elementi di contrasto armonicamente *dissonanti*, entra in definitiva crisi nel '900 per vari motivi: dal logorio interno di un sistema organico ridotto ormai a prontuario di luoghi comuni, alla volontà di contestare l'ordine di una musica a perfetta somiglianza di Dio e quindi dell'Autorità, per suggerire invece una piú imprevedibile, a volte aspra vita dei suoni. (*Un invito,* p. 14)

> [At the basis of the conception (of the tonal system) there is, in fact, the centripetal criterion according to which everything moves from and continually returns to a unifying point [...]. The idea of a music bound to a mechanistic conception of the Universe, founded on a prior investigation into the affinities of sounds with each other, and involving expunction or subordination of contrasting elements which are harmonically dissonant, comes to a definite crisis point in the twentieth century for various reasons — because of the internal strain on an organic system which has been reduced by this stage to a handbook of clichés; because of a willingness to contest the order inherent in music which has a perfect resemblance to God, and therefore, Authority — and music comes to suggest, instead, a more unpredictable, and sometimes, bitter, life of sounds.]

In fact, as already seen, by isolating the word 'l'uomo' at the end of *Strofe* Gentilucci reverses the emphasis from the non-human or divine in Ungaretti ('dove non passa l'uomo') to the human. The last page of the *Strofe* sets to music only the words 'lieta' and 'l'uomo', and 'l'uomo' is sung on two notes (d and f sharp) which together constitute a rising major third (Figure 4.10). This is an interval at the basis of all chords in the *tonal* (not atonal) system. From this becomes apparent the main difference between Ungaretti and Gentilucci. Ungaretti's poems move out of an expression of anger, grief, and the general 'dissonance' caused by domestic and national tragedy, into 'consonance', where 'consonance' is posited as a Godly, not human, state of being; the dissonance expressed in Gentilucci's music is one which tacitly contests God and his authority, and the consonance that it reaches in the last two bars of the composition is categorically associated with man. The word 'man' is, importantly, isolated from the rest of the music by 'paused' rests, and

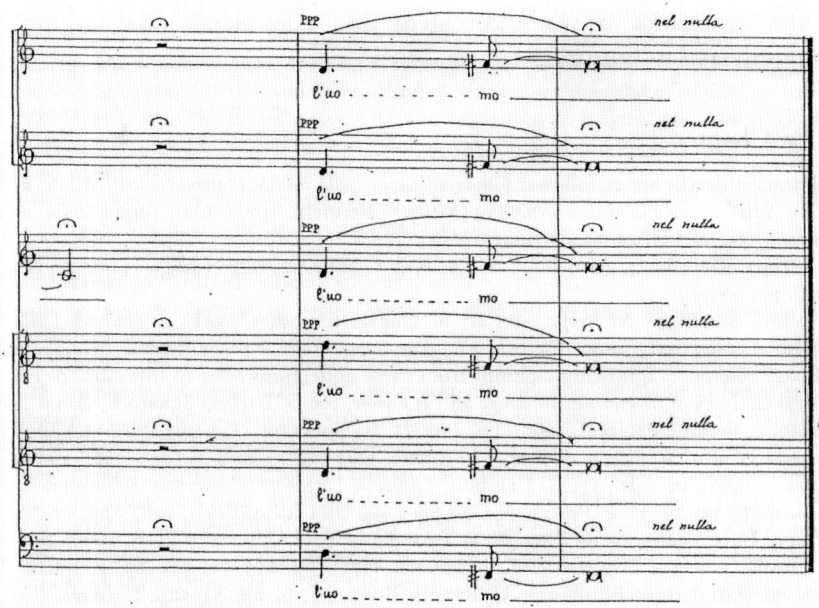

FIG. 4.10. Armando Gentilucci's *Strofe di Ungaretti*, p. 18
Courtesy of G. Ricordi & C. SpA Milano

FIG. 5.1. Photograph of Giacomo Manzoni
Courtesy of Archivio Storico Ricordi, Milano

CHAPTER 5

Giacomo Manzoni's *Parole da Beckett* (1970)

Currently residing in Milan where he was born in 1932, Giacomo Manzoni's formal musical education began at the age of sixteen when he became a student of composition in Messina, and later at the Conservatory of Milan. At the age of twenty-three he gained a degree in foreign languages and literature from the Bocconi University of Milan, and then started a career as an orchestral player and choral director. As well as teaching harmony, counterpoint, and composition at the Conservatoires of Milan and Bologna, he has travelled extensively throughout Europe giving musical seminars and courses, is a member of several editorial boards, and has worked as music critic for the newspaper, *L'Unità,* from 1958–66. Besides being a prolific composer, he has also written four book-length studies, a plethora of articles on composers ranging from Monteverdi and Brahms to Dallapiccola, Schoenberg and Stockhausen, and has translated into Italian most of Adorno's and Schoenberg's didactic works (see bibliography, pp. 282–84).

When he began writing in the 1950s Manzoni's work, like that of Berio, Nono, and Maderna, was rooted mostly, but not exclusively, in a Marxist ideology. The social and political climate at the end of the Second World War drove him to tackle *engagé* issues, and Manzoni's early works, as well as focussing upon historical and political themes — for example, the Chinese Revolution of 1948, the atomic bomb, and Robespierre and the French Revolution in, respectively, his first three operas *La Sentenza* (1960), *Atomtod* (1965), and *Per Massimiliano Robespierre* (1975) — are also, for the most part, charged with messages of solidarity and responsibility.

From the very start, however, he was also composing pieces which were personal and intimate and had very little in common with so-called *engagement* or commitment. In an interview with Francesco Degrada,[1] he quotes the example of 'Preludio — "Grave" di Waring Cuney — Finale' — a piece composed in 1956, based on a poem by the Black American poet, Waring Cuney, which far from concentrating upon issues of race, had a sombre, funereal character. Moreover, in the same interview he voices the opinion that the liveliness of ideas and the great network of relationships and possibilities that existed in Italy from the 1960s to the beginning of the 1980s, have obviously diminished, thereby forcing all Italian artists, whether they like it or not, to fall back into a dimension that is individual and personal: 'Certo, oggi, bisogna fare molto di più i conti soltanto di fronte a se stessi' [Certainly, today, one's reckoning is much more with the self alone].

This perhaps explains why a large part of Manzoni's compositions in the 1980s and 1990s were inspired by literary texts, rather than by social or political events, although some literary influence can also be found in works of the late 1950s and early 1960s.

Poems set to music, throughout his entire *oeuvre,* include those by Éluard, Hölderlin, Bachmann, Cuney, Tsvetaeva, Rilke, and Emily Dickinson. Other literary influences have been Thomas Mann, Francesco Leonetti, and, of course, Samuel Beckett. *Parole da Beckett* was composed in 1970, first conducted by Bruno Maderna at Rome on 21 May 1971 with the Rai orchestra and chorus, and awarded a UNESCO prize in 1973. Manzoni himself includes it among one of his more personal compositions. Indeed the difference between *Parole da Beckett* and his more ideologically inspired works could hardly be more complete. Whereas in the latter Manzoni was concerned with projecting explicit 'messages', the *Parole,* by contrast, as David Osmond-Smith has put it, is 'a monument to the limits of articulacy, or more accurately, of what it is worth articulating'.[2]

The work was initially conceived as a theatrical project. As the composer himself has said: 'quella componente di desolazione, di allucinazione che si esprime nell'opera come una venatura sotterranea sembrava volesse affermarsi più apertamente in un nuovo lavoro teatrale, basato appunto su testi beckettiani' [that component of desolation, of hallucination which runs underneath the opera in, as it were, its veins, seemed initially to want to voice itself more explicitly in a new theatrical work, based precisely on Becketts' texts].[3] However, the music eventually evolved as a composition for two choirs (one with between twenty-four and thirty-two choristers; the other with sixty-four to eighty-three), three groups of instruments (nine brass, seventeen strings, and a chamber ensemble of twenty members) and a tape (some choral sections being recorded and electronically elaborated in advance at the Rai Electronic Music Studio). In spite of this change in the original conception of the piece, Manzoni still manages to instil into it a theatrical element, largely through the strategic positioning of the choirs and the various other components (which include a mixer and six loudspeakers, see Figure 5.2), which means that a constant interaction of various diverse patterns of sound reaches the audience from different directions). The actual 'parole' consist of a montage of fragments taken from Beckett's *Molloy, How it is, Happy Days, Waiting for Godot, All That Fall,* and *Poems in English.* These lyrics (translated into Italian) are sung, spoken, murmured, or yelled by the choir, thereby adding further to the theatrical atmosphere.

Viewed as a whole, the overriding themes that emerge from these 'parole' are the typical Beckettian ones of death and/or life as a tiresome, living death: 'tired of dying' ('Eneug II'), 'peering out of my deadlight' ('Four Poems', no. 3), 'vivas puellas mortui incurrrrsant boves'[the live girls frequently run through the dead oxen] ('Sanies II'), 'Die I may die I shall die' (*How it is*); the absurdity of routine: 'Would I do what I did yesterday and the day before'('Four Poems', no. 3), 'From sleep I come to sleep return between the two there is all the doing suffering failing bungling achieving until the mud yawns again'(*How it is*); limbo existences: 'peering [...] looking for another wandering like me eddying far from all the living' ('Four Poems', no. 3); the haunting, incomprehensible voices which constantly plague

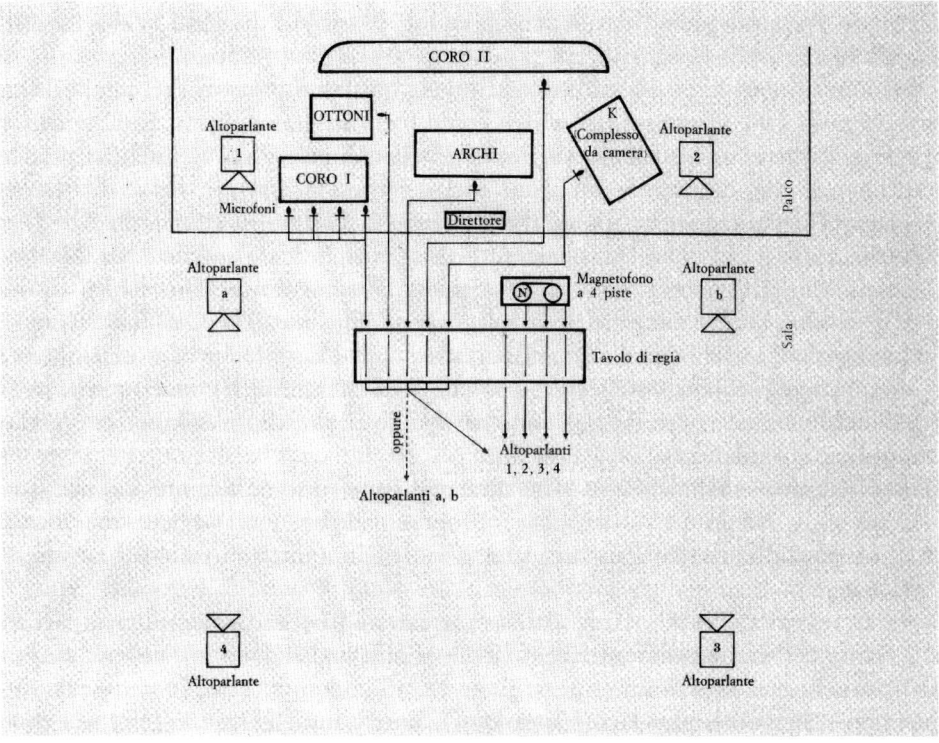

Fig. 5.2. Diagram by Giacomo Manzoni illustrating the layout of choruses, instrumental groups, tape recorders and amplifiers for *Parole da Beckett*. Pictured on the cover sleeve of the recording of *Parole da Beckett* and *Ode* by the Rai orchestra and chorus, conducted by Bruno Maderna (Italian Fonit Cetra Spa: 1983)

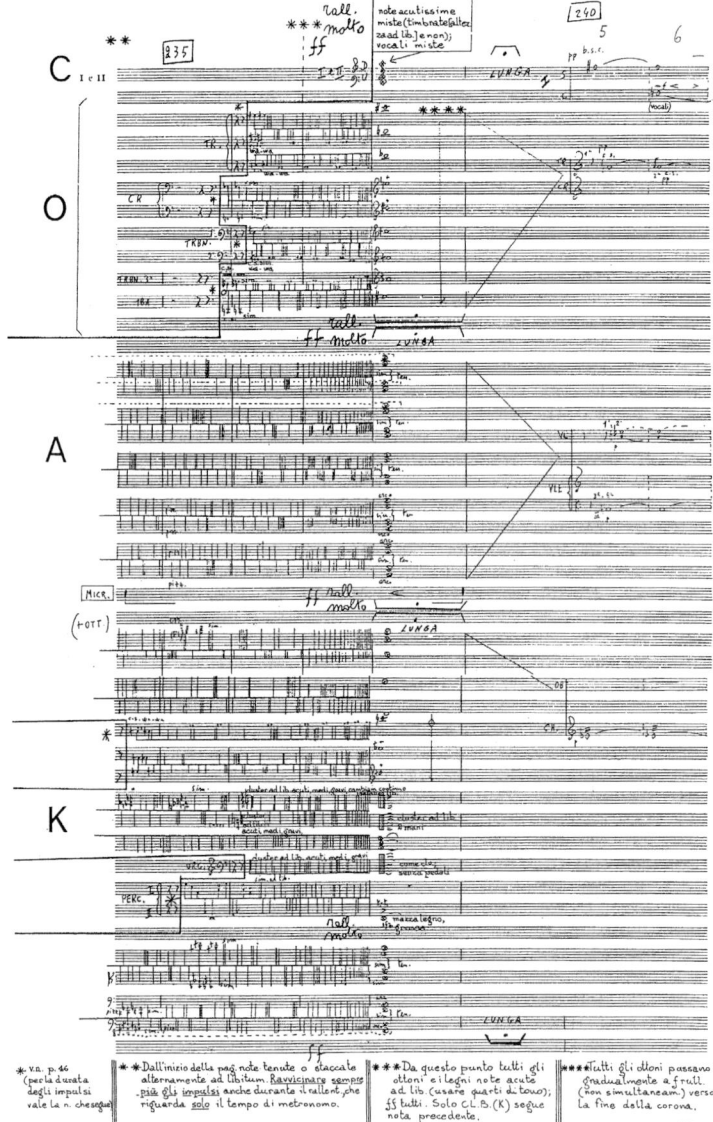

FIG. 5.3. Giacomo Manzoni's *Parole da Beckett* (Milan: Ricordi, 1971), p. 47
Courtesy of G. Ricordi & C. SpA Milano

stole a crust of bread./ Then cook up with a ladle/ And beat him till he was dead', etc. The recording of his voice has been passed through filters, thereby removing different frequencies in its sound, and the resulting distortion works well, in that it produces a sound which is, at one and the same time, slightly grotesque and comic, conjuring up something of the tragicomic atmosphere of the play as a whole.

Another antithesis in the composition is that involving comprehensibility and incomprehensibility on the listener's part. One of the best examples of comprehensibility is provided by a fragment at the end of the piece, where a line from *How it is* — 'so things may change end I may choke sink the dark trouble the peace no more the silence die' — spoken softly but clearly by one voice, is broken up by another which literally shouts the phrase which follows in the Beckett text — 'Die I may die I shall die'. Equally comprehensible is the pre-taped voice (of the actor Ottavio Fanfani) reading from the opening paragraph of *Molloy*, Part II: 'My son is sleeping. Let him sleep. The night will come when he too, unable to sleep, will get up and go to his desk. I shall be forgotten.' The clarity and, indeed, the soothing quality of this voice stand in stark contrast to those sections of the work which are pronounced by the chorus in an unintelligible manner, where the text is deformed through the treatment of individual syllables as raw sound, giving rise to long, prolonged vowels or consonants, and *glissandi*. It is a technique which creates an impression of aphasia, reinforced in other of the Beckett extracts, notably a further quotation from *Molloy*: 'Not to want to say, not to know what you want to say, not to be able to say what you think you want to say.' But more importantly, in these particular sections of deformed text Manzoni is clearly revoking the traditional idea that, in vocal music, the music must always be at the service of the word; that the words must be clearly enunciated and emotively expressed so that their meaning remains intelligible. Here Beckett's lyrics have clearly not been 'set to music'; rather, by highlighting their phonetic characteristics, the composer has transformed them into pure, elementary 'music', into, what he himself has called, 'parole come musica'[7] (as will be discussed below).

A further effect involved in Manzoni's project of creating antithesis is the howling and shouting which is very deliberately juxtaposed with whispers and murmurs, as at the beginning of the piece, where the phrase 'tired of dying' from 'Eneug II', enunciated furiously and with a biting rhythm, is followed abruptly by the chorus's breathy tones, imitating the text which speaks of living 'in a convulsive space among the voices, voiceless' ('Four Poems', no. 3). Indeed, this shouting and whispering which runs, to a greater or lesser extent, right through the composition, is the predominant motif of the Beckett text which Manzoni cites from at greatest length in the *Parole* — *How* it is. In *How* it is, the speaker is lying face-downwards in an endless pool of mud, through which he pulls himself forward, a yard or so at a time, dragging after him a coal-sack which is attached to his neck by a rope and contains rations, mostly tins of sardines and a tin-opener (a situation evoked in the sixth fragment of the *Parole*: 'The wet the dragging the rubbing the hugging the ages old coal-sack [...] the tins the opener an opener and no tins'). As he edges himself forward, he mutters phrases which could be appropriately used to describe many sections of Manzoni. On the one hand there is the motif of murmuring:

> Murmur it in bits and scraps
> this semi-castrate mutter
> I can't make out the words the mud muffles
> bits and scraps barely audible certainly distorted.
> On the other hand, the motif of howling and megaphones:
> Here howls good
> mouth howls good
> a choir [...] quaqua meaning on all sides
> megaphones possibly technique, something wrong there.

This last phrase — 'possibly technique, something wrong there' — seems to be echoed by a statement made in a review of *Parole da Beckett* by Massimo Mila:

> Il profano che metta questo disco sul giradischi e poi si sieda in poltrona ad ascoltare, probabilmente dopo un paio di minuti si alza per andare a vedere cos'è successo al suo apparecchio.[8]

> [The novice who puts on this record, and then sits down in his armchair to listen to it, would probably get up after a couple of minutes to see what had gone wrong with his record player.]

Mila was referring to the hissing and sucking sounds which open the composition, and which, generated by oscillators, are known in the language of electronic music as 'white noise' or 'sine waves' (see Chapter One, pp. 20–21). There are other informal passages like this too, such as when each player is allowed to improvise on a few given pitches with rhythmic freedom, thereby destroying the notion of the performer as the intermediary between the music and the audience. The performer now becomes a collaborator; the music is not something that is totally ready-made, but rather to *be* made (See section on 'aleatory', Chapter One, pp. 17–18). These aleatoric parts in Manzoni stand out once again in antithesis to some brief areas which are almost conventional in style in their melodiousness: such as a phrase played on wind instruments towards the beginning of the composition and, later, another on the double bass. All in all, it is the quick succession of these densely contrasting, almost kaleidoscopic bands of sound which gives to the *Parole* the austere, existentialist atmosphere solicited by the Beckett texts.

However, to say that the *Parole* merely evoke a Beckettian atmosphere would be too simplistic, for on closer inspection, Manzoni's relationship with Beckett's lyrics appears to be complex and multifaceted. On the one hand, the music assumes a certain autonomy over the text, for, as previously stated, Beckett's words are, to a large extent, treated as raw, elementary sound, and the actual text is often unintelligible. In this respect it is significant that Manzoni chose to call his work *Parole da Beckett*, and not *Parole di Beckett*. The chosen title shifts the emphasis from 'Beckett' to 'words', displaying Manzoni's desire for his work to be seen largely as a free experimentation with the phonic qualities of individual words, rather than as a musical rendering of the Beckett fragments which remain faithful to the meaning of the phrase.

One example of this preoccupation with the 'word' rather than with the 'phrase', and the autonomy which the music holds over the Beckett texts, occurs towards the end of the composition. The libretto at this point consists of a parenthesized section of lyrics, composed of ten lines from three different Beckett works: line 1 from *How it is*; lines 2–4 from *Happy Days*; and lines 5–10 from *Molloy*:

	Beckett	Translation
1	the murmurs	bisbigli
2	not a day goes by	non passa quasi giorno
3	my story of course	sempre la mia storia
4	this will have been	questo sarà stato
5	when 1 am asked something	mi si chieda qualcosa
6	to know what	...sapere cosa sia
7	my raglimp stasis	stasi da straccio
8	then flaming and extinguished	nascono
9	as fire by filth and martyrs	si estinguono ... spazzature di santi
10	to open under me	si aprisse sotto di me

The lines chosen from *Happy Days* are totally unconnected in Beckett, and, in fact, occur at a distance of some pages. The same applies to the lines from *Molloy*. The reason for Manzoni's choice of these particular lines to constitute one individual section of libretto becomes obvious when one examines how they have been translated into Italian. According to the composer, the translations he availed himself of were those used in the 'Einaudi e Sugar' editions of Beckett.[9] In the Italian, each line contains at least one sibilant (line 9 contains as many as five) so that, put together as a section, its abundance of sibilants helps to accentuate one of the major motifs of Manzoni's composition — that of whispering and murmuring (and, indeed, a note by Manzoni at the head of the libretto indicates that parenthesized sections should be whispered by the chorus). In other words, these particular ten lines would seem to have been selected by Manzoni, not for the semantic value they carry in Beckett, but for the phonetic qualities they possess in translation, thus confirming that one of Manzoni's main compositional aims in writing the *Parole* was to promote the musical qualities naturally inherent in speech-sounds.

On the other hand, one could equally argue that this lack of emphasis upon the meaning of the phrase is, paradoxically, one of the ways in which Manzoni's music is attuned to the experimental style of the two prose works quoted in the *Parole*: *Molloy*, and *How it is* (citations from these together constitute approximately one third of the libretto). In these two works Beckett employs two radically different, in fact, oppositional styles; but both are styles in which the traditional, 'meaningful' phrase does not exist. *Molloy* is composed of an endless torrent of sentences which are not paragraphed, but punctuated and syntactically coherent. The effect of this relentless onslaught of phrases, no one of which seems to carry more semantic weight than any of the others, is that the meaning of each individual phrase is largely lost, and what is conveyed is only an atmosphere, or the essence of a situation. Conversely, in *How it is* there are 'blocks' of words (rather than traditional paragraphs), but punctuation and syntax have been totally discarded. Without them, there is nothing to indicate where a sentence should begin, and where it should end, so that 'the phrase', as such, does not exist, and the 'blocking' of words is superfluous, since the absence of phrases results in an absence of any logical continuity of thought. In short, the two opposing styles in these prose works create the same effect — the reader is more conscious of reading words than he or she is of reading phrases, and it could well be this stylistic feature which Manzoni is imitating when choosing not to set to music the Beckett 'phrase', but to experiment with individual words within the 'phrase'.

There are many other aspects of the *Parole* which reinforce how Manzoni has not only a comprehensive knowledge of Beckett, but is also very much attuned to Beckett's idiosyncratic vision of the world, and is anxious to reinforce it. He could have chosen as a libretto one single text by Beckett. The fact that he chose instead to create a libretto composed of twenty-three extracts from six different works — ranging from well-known prose and drama (like *Molloy* and *Waiting for Godot*, respectively) to a less well-known poetry collection (*Poems in English*) — is evidence in itself of his close familiarity with Beckett's oeuvre. The twenty-three fragments also offer a more global vision of Beckett than that which could have been achieved if Manzoni had vased his libretto on just one text.

The collage technique adopted by Manzoni also seems to serve another purpose. The most characteristic feature of Beckett's style is its lack of narrative and continuity. By choosing to 'cut and paste' together a large number of diverse extracts, Manzoni is magnifying that stylistic feature — the libretto jumps in an apparently unstructured fashion from one context to another, with few or no linking threads between them. In this way, it exaggerates the style of any one Beckett text and brings one closer to the 'spirit' of Beckett, where discontinuity and an absence of linear development accentuate the author's vision of a world devoid of meaning and direction.

It is important to note, however, that the libretto only *apparently* lacks a structure. Although the overall impression is one of a disordered and casual form, on closer inspection the quotations are tentatively held together by three motifs — birth, journeying, and death: the beginning, middle, and end of life. In this way too, the libretto cleverly imitates Beckett, since all of Beckett's works are, to a greater or lesser extent, variations on the problems of mortality, and the absurdity of our three-stage existence. In *Molloy*, for example, life is described ironically as 'a handsome little sum, with a beginning, a middle, and an end, as in the well-built phrase'. The references to birth are poetically disguised by Beckett, and for that reason, not fully evident on a first reading. In the sixth citation in Manzoni's libretto (taken from *How it is*) the 'ages old coal-sack' ('vecchio sacco da carbone'), which is being 'dragged' along by the protagonist through the mud ('l'umidità il trascinio l'abrasione' [the wet the dragging the rubbing]), tied, as it is, at the mouth by a rope which is in turn attached to the protagonist's neck, is highly suggestive of the placental sack and the umbilical cord. While in the thirteenth citation (from 'Serena II', *Poems in English*) the 'earth' is depicted in terms of a woman in labour: 'clonic' (from 'clonus', a pathological term denoting a spasm with alternate muscular contractions and relaxations), 'periodically blurred in sleep', 'fat', and 'half dead':

> Questa terra clonica
> periodicamente offuscata dal sonno
> è grassa mezzo morta

The allusions to journeying are more conspicuous in the Italian translations than in the English texts (due, possibly, to the translator's attempts to stamp more definite meaning onto some of Beckett's obscure terminology). In this respect, since the lyrics are sung in Italian, and Manzoni was working largely, if not exclusively, with the Italian versions, the theme of journeying was almost certainly intended to play an integral part in the conception and make-up of the libretto. The nineteenth quotation in the *Parole* (from *All That Fall*) speaks of a journey possibly nearing its end: 'e può darsi che non sia ancora alla fine del mio viaggio' (a translation of 'and perhaps my course is not yet fully run', where Beckett's ambiguous term, 'course', has been replaced by the less equivocal 'viaggio'). Ship imagery occurs in the third quotation (from 'Four Poems', no. 3) with the reference to an 'oblò', used to translate 'deadlight' (the choice of the Italian word may have been dictated in part by the allusion, a few words later in Beckett, to 'eddying'). 'Oblò' then has an internal association with the *'shipwrecked* mind' of the seventeenth fragment — 'e la mente annullata/ naufraga del vento' ('and the mind annulled/ wrecked in wind' ['Eneug I', *Poems in English*]). And, as a final example of the theme of journeying, there is the quotation (which Manzoni has left in its original French version) which speaks of walking towards light, with its Dantesque overtones of the lights of *Paradiso*: 'puis les pas vers les vieilles lumières' [then the steps towards the old lights; in the libretto's translation 'then the steps toward the lighted town', 'Dieppe', *Poems in English*]. The allusion to Dante would seem to be underscored by the fact that in the line which Manzoni cites directly after his use of the quotation from 'Dieppe' — 'un altro giorno divino' [another divine day; in the libretto's translation, 'another happy day'] — the Dantesque word 'divino' has been used as a translation for 'happy'. That Manzoni's choice of word is deliberate at this point in the libretto is made evident by the fact that at the end of the *Parole,* he has used a more literal translation of the same line — 'un altro giorno *felice*' (the emphasis is mine).[10]

The references to death are the most apparent and the most frequent of the three motifs, and seem to have been placed strategically by Manzoni at the beginning ('tired of dying'), middle ('tired of dying', 'dying', the 'dead' dog and the 'tomb', from Vladimir's song), and end of the libretto ('DIE I MAY DIE I SHALL DIE'). Two further quotations link the concepts of life and death: '*vivas* puellas *mortui* incurrrrsant boves'; 'thirst abating humanity regained' (a reference, it would seem, to the *salvation* of mankind through Christ's *death,* his 'thirst', on the cross). The circular structure of the *Parole,* beginning with an allusion to death and ending with the same, is also a Beckettian trait. One has only to think of the final line of *How it is* in its original French version, with its pun on *Comment c'est (commencez!)* [How it is (begin!)] to give the effect of the protagonist bound upon a Dantesque circle, caught up in an inferno-like repetition which typifies Beckett's vision of the human condition as Hell-on-earth.

How it is is indeed one of Beckett's most Dantesque works, and the fact that it is the most frequently quoted one in the *Parole* does not seem coincidental, especially in view of the fact that Manzoni's contrasting panels of sound create the effect of drawing the listener through a harsh, convulsed — in a word, infernal — landscape. In the course of *How it is,* the protagonist compares himself to the lethargic Belacqua of *Purgatorio IV.* Although Manzoni has not cited the precise section of *How it is* where the name Belacqua occurs, he has chosen to quote a passage where Beckett was clearly underscoring the allusion to Belacqua through references to sleeping, yawning, and the boredom of having to 'do' and to 'achieve':

> From sleep I come to sleep return between the two there is all all the doing suffering failing bungling achieving until the mud yawns again.

What is more interesting is the fact that Beckett has placed his protagonist in an endless pool of mud — a condition which is immediately (and probably, deliberately) evocative of the contrapasso of the wrathful in *Inferno* VII — the 'genti fangose' [muddy people]. Indeed, given Belacqua's lethargy, one is reminded in particular of the 'slow' wrathful, or 'tristi', those who bore in their hearts an 'accidioso fummo' [sluggish smoke], and who now remain 'fitti nel limo'[fixed in the slime], 'nella belletta negra' [in the black mud]. It would be highly unlikely that Beckett's allusions to Dante could have escaped Manzoni, especially since references to mud are frequent in the phrases he chooses to quote: 'before the mud yawns again'; 'barely audible in the mud'; 'the face in the mud the mouth open the mud in the mouth' (a sequence which is especially reminiscent of Dante's description of the aforementioned 'tristi', 'gurgling' a hymn in their throats, unable to articulate the words because of the mud in their mouths: 'Quest'inno si gorgoglian nella strozza,/ ché dir nol posson con parola integra' [They gurgle this hymn in their throats,/ for they cannot get the words out clearly]). Towards the end of the *Parole* a reference to mud has even been added in the Italian where it did not exist in the Beckett version: 'non insozzare più, il fango' [do not dirty any more, the mud].

'Mud in the mouth' is also evocative of *Inferno* VI, where Virgil fires fistfuls of earth into the gullet of Cerberus before he and Dante encounter Ciacco who also suffers from 'la dannosa colpa della gola' [the harmful fault of gluttony]. The protagonist of *How it is* reflects something of Ciacco's gluttony in that, as Manzoni's sixth extract serves to highlight, he drags his provisions around with him.

In Beckett the inter-textual references to Dante are, of course, partially there to negate the Dantesque notion of a divinely coherent universe ruled by an inexorable, yet just, God. Suffering on Beckett's 'earth', unlike that in Dante's *Inferno*, is causeless and gratuitous; and waiting, unlike that in *Purgatorio*, is a mere *ennui*, bereft of any hopeful expectation. Like Beckett, Manzoni is not animated by any religious faith, and there are three indications of this in the *Parole,* the first two of them suggested by the manner in which Manzoni has chosen to juxtapose certain lyrics. First, whereas on the one hand, the choice of the word 'divino' as a translation of 'happy' in the previously mentioned phrase from *Happy Days* — 'un altro giorno divino' — appears to underscore the allusion to *Paradiso* in the preceding line from 'Dieppe' — 'e puis les pas vers les [...] lumières' — on the other hand, it actually cancels the 'religious' optimism of the allusion, since the line 'another happy day' is clearly ironic, and being one of Beckett's most famous, cannot be pronounced without conjuring up the mixture of sarcasm and anguish inherent in his vision. Secondly, the positive connotations one might attach to the phrase alluding to the salvation of mankind — 'humanity regained' — are deflated by the abrupt statement which follows immediately in Manzoni's libretto — 'dying'. It would also seem significant that the longest quotation in the *Parole* is from *Waiting for Godot*, where Vladimir and Estragon observe how Godot has failed to turn up yet again — an emblematic passage which (if one adheres to a superficial, yet very common interpretation of the play) reinforces how God (Godot) is absent, dead, or never existed in the first place.

There are, however, two ways in which Beckett and Manzoni would seem to be at variance. The first lies with the composer's more humanist temperament. Neither artist may have any religious faith, but Manzoni, unlike Beckett, sees man as a social animal, and believes in his ability to love, and to interact positively with others. An example of this difference in outlook is provided by the penultimate quotation from the *Parole*. It is a passage from *How it is* which Manzoni has edited. In Beckett, the lines read:

> So things may change no answer end no answer I may choke no answer sink no answer the dark no answer trouble the peace no more no answer the silence no answer die no answer [...].

In Manzoni's version, Beckett's eight uses of the phrase 'no answer' have been removed, the composer's more philanthropic attitude obviously finding itself at odds with the reinforced cynicism and the absence of dialogue implied in Beckett's 'no answer':

> Allora può cambiare, finire, potrei soffocare, inabissarmi, non insozzare più, il fango, il buio, non turbare più, il silenzio, crepare [...].

Similarly, it is interesting to note that Manzoni chooses to follow his ninth quotation in the libretto (from *Molloy*), ending, 'I shall be forgotten', with a line from 'Cascando' (*Poems in English*): 'unless they love you'. The juxtaposition, which makes the line from 'Cascando' operate as a reply to Molloy's statement, can only be intentional. Manzoni is pitting the power of love and communication against the loveless universe of Beckett, wherein characters are solitaries, or, where paired (Pozzo and Lucky, Hamm and Clov, etc.), are unable to communicate, their egos expressing themselves only in grotesque monologues.

Indeed, besides 'Cascando', there are, among the *Parole*, quotations from other less well-known poems by Beckett which (uncharacteristically for Beckett) touch upon the subject of love, and the fact that Manzoni has included them in his libretto seems further indicative of his humanist sensibility:

> Mourning the first and the last to love me ('Four Poems', no. 4)
> And the mind annulled/ wrecked in wind ('Four Poems', 'Eneug I')
> Tired of dying ('Four Poems', 'Eneug II').

In the fourth of the 'Four Poems', 'the first and the last to love "Beckett"' is his mother, and the poem is a lament for his mother's impending death. The 'Eneugs' outline Beckett's suffering as he impotently waits for his loved one to die in a private hospital in Dublin. She is believed to be the girl he affectionately called Smeraldina (a name clearly evoking the Emerald Isle) for this girl had, reputedly, green eyes, wore only green, and was very Irish.

The second major contrast between Manzoni and Beckett lies in the way in which both artists use stark, austere techniques, but for very different reasons. Paolo

Petazzi was indicating this difference when he wrote:

> Beckett vede nella perdita di senso o nella riduzione delle parole a gesti un processo di annullamento umano. Inversamente, le stesse cose Manzoni avverte nella musica come la realizzazione del concreto. Mentre lo scrittore vi addita un principio di morte, il musicista vi individua un principio di vita.[11]

> [Beckett sees in the loss of meaning, or the reduction of words to gestures, a cancellation of the human element. Inversely, in music Manzoni regards the same things are the realization of something concrete. While the writer uses them to denote the beginnings of death, the musician recognizes in them the beginnings of life.]

In other words, Manzoni's reduction of singing to speaking, of words to phonemes and elementary vocal effects is not intended to convey the universal 'shrinking and dwindling' of which Vladimir speaks. On the contrary, *Parole da Beckett* demonstrates a display of faith in the renewal of musical linguistics. The efforts of post-Webern composers, concerned no longer with the relationship of notes to each other but rather with the physical make-up of musical sounds themselves, are, after all, a musical counterpart to the preoccupations with the very nature of words and the functioning of language which pervades present day literature.

Notes to Chapter 5

1. Degrada, F., 'Colloquio con Giacomo Manzoni', in *Omaggio a Giacomo Manzoni* (Milan: Ricordi, 1992), pp. 4–19.
2. Osmond-Smith, D., 'Something rich and strange: from words to music in the work of Giacomo Manzoni', in *Omaggio a Giacomo Manzoni*, pp. 20–25.
3. Quoted in the booklet accompanying the record of *Parole da Beckett* and *Ode*.
4. See V. Mercier's chapter entitled 'Painting/ Music', in *Beckett/ Beckett* (Oxford: Oxford University Press, 1977).
5. Alvarez, A., *Beckett* (Glasgow: Fontana Modern Masters, 1973), p. 56.
6. Coe, R. N., *Samuel Beckett* (Edinburgh, London: Oliver and Boyd, 1968), p. 54.
7. The title of an article by Manzoni in *Giacomo Manzoni. Scritti*, ed. by C. Tempo (Florence: La Nuova Italia, 1991), pp. 59–64.
8. Mila, M., 'Parole da Beckett', in *Omaggio a Giacomo Manzoni* , p. 40.
9. Communicated in Manzoni's letter to me, dated 20 August 1994.
10. Manzoni has claimed (reference as in n. 9 above) that, when putting together the Italian version of his libretto, he very occasionally made some minimal adjustments to the translations of Beckett found in the 'Einaudi e Sugar' editions. It would seem likely that this substitution of 'divino' for 'felice', in the eighth quotation from the libretto, constitutes one of those minimal adjustments.
11. Reference as in n. 3 above.

Fig. 6.1. Photograph of Bruno Maderna
Courtesy of Archivio Storico Ricordi, Milano

CHAPTER 6

Bruno Maderna's *Ausstrahlung* (1971)

Bruno Maderna (1920–73) was widely acknowledged as one of the world's foremost conductors of twentieth-century music, and a particularly engaging and approachable personality in the rather alienating world of total serialism and the 'dodecaphonic police'.[1] These qualities were developed in spite of a difficult, albeit, in some respects, colourful, childhood. Born of illegitimate origin in Sant' Anna di Chioggia near Venice, Maderna, following the death of his mother, Caroline Maderna, was raised by his alleged father, Umberto Grossato, who reputedly exploited Bruno's musical genius in a self-created band — the 'Happy Grossato Company Band' — which played in hotels, cabarets, and the like. At the age of twelve, Bruno conducted the La Scala orchestra to great acclaim, and went on to conduct in nearly every major Italian city, before being separated from his 'father' by the Fascist authorities in 1933, and displayed as a prodigy of the Fascist regime. He eventually went to live with Irma Manfredi, a well-known dressmaker from Verona, where he had private tutelage in a range of subjects, including music. On the recommendation of Cardinal Montini, the future Pope Paul VI, Maderna was sent to be educated at the Rome Conservatory of Music from which he graduated in 1940. From 1941–42 he studied composition under Malipiero who was instrumental in obtaining for Maderna a teaching position at the Venice Conservatory — a post he held until 1952. He served in the Italian Army during World War II, eventually joining the Partisan forces against the Fascists. After the war, he studied conducting with Hermann Scherchen in Darmstadt. In 1955 he set up, together with Berio and others, the Studio di Fonologia Musicale della RAI in Milan, as well as an ensemble and a musical periodical, *Incontri Musicali* [Musical Encounters], both devoted to the promotion and advancement of contemporary music (see 'The Darmstadt School and total serialism', Chapter One, pp. 15–18).

Maderna's music stands out among that of his Darmstadt colleagues for the manner in which it combines the strict mathematical procedures of serial music with a considerable degree of fantasy and lyricism. Speaking, for example, of Maderna's *Serenata per undici strumenti* (1954) Luciano Berio proclaimed 'sul volto corrugato e intento della "musica seriale", appare per la prima volta un sorriso' [on the wrinkled and concentrating face of 'serial music', a smile appears for the first time] (*Dialogo*, p. 210). This element of fantasy also displays itself in Maderna's use of aleatory and *opera aperta* aesthetics (see Chapter One, pp. 17–18). As M. Romito points out, these were devices which also guaranteed the maximum of creativity and freedom on the part of the composer and conductor: 'Alla tecnica aleatoria

Maderna affidava le possibilità "altre" della materia sonora, possibilità (...) che in parte egli si riservava di scoprire, di reinventare, di ricomporre al momento di preparare l'orchestra, nel contatto vivo e diretto con gli strumentisti, con l'ambiente, assecondando l'illuminarsi di nuove intuizioni, di nuove prospettive, di nuove possibilità di organizzazione' (*Dialogo*, pp. 128–29) [Maderna entrusted to aleatory 'other' possibilities of sonorous material, possibilities which, in part, he proposed to discover, reinvent, and rearrange according to how he felt inspired by new intuitions, and new ways of looking at and organizing things, at the very moment when he was preparing the orchestra, and when the contact with the instrumentalists and his surroundings was alive and direct]. *Ausstrahlung* (1971), a work for female voice, orchestra, tape-recording, solo flute and solo oboe (of which, to date, there has been no detailed study, either of the libretto or of the music) provides a good example of how Maderna manages to combine a brand of lyrical serialism, aleatory, and an 'open work' aesthetics. The vocal part testifies to a moving away from the strict vocal serialism of Schoenberg and Viennese Expressionism in general, and adopts more the style of the vocal writing employed by Dallapiccola (see Chapter One, pp. 11–15), where the 'Germanic' serial method is imbued with a singing lyricism, and tonal devices are even sometimes used within the framework of the dodecaphonic system. Hence, *Ausstrahlung*'s brand of vocal serialism is more lyrical than the purely academic variety. The use of aleatory, as well as being highlighted at various stages in the actual score, with the employment of terms like 'in questo caso gli strumenti dovranno [...] "inventare" dinamiche e fraseggi' (p. 15) [in this case, the instruments will have to 'invent' dynamics and phrasing], and 'cesura *ad libitum* — si può anche non osservarla' (p. 27), [an ad-lib caesura, but one can equally ignore it] was best demonstrated by Maderna himself when he conducted the premiere of *Ausstrahlung* at Persepolis on 4th September, 1971, using the manuscript score only as a base for an extempore improvisation. Furthermore, the seven parts in to which the piece is divided (Maderna called them seven *Ausstrahlungen*) can, in accordance with the 'open work' philosophy, be combined in any manner possible, and similarly, the separate tape recording can be placed wherever the conductor sees fit. The version of *Ausstrahlung* examined in this study follows the printed score of the work published by Ricordi whose structure was suggested by Maderna's widow who had been present at the Persepolis premiere.

Maderna's interest in the endless creative possibilities of art which manifests itself through his use of a modified vocal serialism, aleatory, and *opera aperta* techniques, is linked up with a concern with the notions of 'creation' in general — the creation, indeed, the origins, of musical sound and language. This concern translates into an emphasis upon the concept of 'song', for the origins of sound, in Maderna, *is* 'song'. Hence, like the music for the female voice in *Ausstrahlung*, much of Maderna's writing for solo instruments has an expansive, singing quality: the flute in *Hyperion*, the violin in *Concerto per violino* (1969), the oboe in the three oboe concertos of 1962, 1967, and 1973. In fact, the flute and oboe both assume a certain importance for the composer, for the purity of their monodic lines are felt to be evocative of ancient Greece (a constant thematic presence in Maderna) and the very origins of music. The three pieces which best demonstrate Maderna's interest in origins and creation are *Grande Aulodia* (1970), *Ausstrahlung* (1971), and *Aura* (1972), which together, as suggested by their similar sounding titles, form a type of trilogy. Maderna himself has explained the title 'Aura' as denoting for him 'l'essenza del suono, e l'irradiarsi di ogni possibile consequenza sonora da un nucleo centrale' (*Dialogo*, p. 215) [the essence of sound, and the radiation of every possible sonorous consequence from a central nucleus], and this 'essence of sound' is evoked symbolically at the opening of the work by the very gradual, and successive entries of fifty-four strings divided into six groups, increasing slowly, by degrees, in intensity and pitch, and creating a distinctly ethereal effect. At the beginning of *Grande Aulodia,* meanwhile, the oboe, against the silence of the orchestra, intones a long 'la', which, as M. Mila has observed, is meant to symbolize 'l'origine stessa della musica, l'*Ur-Ton* o suono originario'(*Dialogo*, p. 149) [the very origins of music, the *Ur-Ton* or original sound]. Similarly, in the opening moments of *Ausstrahlung*, the female voice, along with a flute solo rise above a babel of indistinct mutterings to pronounce a quotation from Dandin's *Kavyadarsa* which evokes the Biblical creation and God's replacing of darkness with light. In fact, what makes *Ausstrahlung* stand out in the trilogy is that, more than being concerned, like *Grande Aulodia* and *Aura* with the origins of musical sound, it is preoccupied with the origins of language and literature and the relationship of both of these things to the divine.

As already mentioned, the premiere of *Ausstrahlung* was performed in the ancient Persian city of Persepolis in 1971. The reason for this strange venue was the commissioning of the work for the celebrations in Persepolis to commemorate the birth of Cyrus, the Great, considered to be the founder of the Persian Empire. This anachronistic subject gave Maderna the opportunity to explore the topic of origins through an exploration of ancient Indian and Persian texts. Fragments from the latter are juxtaposed in the libretto in the form of a collage which throws into relief different visions and interpretations of the divine. Among the Indian sources there are quotations from Dandin's (A.D. c665–710) *Kavyadarsa*; Book 4 — the *Bhagavadgita* — of the Indian epic, the *Mahabharata,* written in the first or second century A.D.; and the *Atharvaveda,* or sacred text of the Indo-Aryans, the majority of which was believed to have been composed by 1500 B.C., within the second phase of Vedic creativity — the classic mantra period that followed the Rigvedic period. To these texts are married verses from celebrated Persian poets: Rudaki (A.D. c858–941), Khayyam (A.D. c1050–1125), and Sadi (A.D. c1184–1291), as well as a passage from the *Avesta* — the sacred writings of Zoroastrianism, the religion founded by the Iranian prophet, Zoroaster, in the sixth century B.C.[2] Some of the literature quoted, therefore, dates from before Christianity; some was written after Christianity. Roughly, the extracts span the sixteenth century B.C. and the thirteenth century A.D., and do not in the libretto follow in any chronological sequence. The sequences cited are translated into English, French, Italian, and German, with, it would seem, the intention of highlighting a common, remote cultural and linguistic matrix in languages of Indo-European origin.

The link between language, earliest forms of literature, and the divine is clearly established from the onset of *Ausstrahlung*. The female voice, as previously mentioned, reciting a passage from the beginning of the *Kavyadarsa* — Dandin's treatise on the nature of Sanskrit poetics[3] — rises above the babel of mutterings to denote the possibility of clear articulation and the emergence of language. This voice, moreover, speaks of the creation of the 'Word' at the beginning of time, and the manner in which the *Kavyadarsa* evokes both the biblical creation in Genesis, and the start of the Gospel according to St. John[4] clearly underlines a fundamental association between the linguistic and the divine, which, moreover, is spelled out clearly by Dandin in Chapter I, paragraph 33: 'The Sanskrit is indeed the speech divine':[5]

> All these worlds
> would have been a dense darkness,
> if the light,
> called Word
> had not shone
> from the beginning of the world. (*Kavyadarsa,* I, 4)

The passage is significant from another point of view as well. Maderna himself has explained the title *Ausstrahlung* as meaning 'irradiazione'[6] [radiation], that is to say, the emission of light and warmth in all directions, and connoting, by extension, the concept of diffusion and propagation (there are similarities with the aforementioned definition of *Aura*). The 'Word' in this passage is called a 'light' which shines, and the passage itself demonstrates how the Christian 'Word' has become diffused, in this case to the extent that it has influenced an Indian concept of origins. Feelings of 'divinity' and creative 'diffusion' also pervade aspects of the music in this section. The flute melody is accompanied by six groups of strings (marked, in the score, A to F), five of which are muted, and all of which play 'sempre il più delicato possibile' [as delicately as possible all the time], creating an otherworldly effect. At bar 15 the strings in group F have a 'da capo', as do the group E strings at bar 16, and the strings in groups A to D in bar 17. In aleatoric fashion, they repeat all of their material alone without being conducted, and as Maderna indicates, 'Non devono esservi preoccupazioni di sincronismi; al contrario una certa libertà di suonare "rubato" è permessa' (p. 3) [One should not worry about synchronizing; on the contrary, one can exercise some freedom in playing 'rubato'], so that the effect is one of a swarming proliferation of sound.

The theistic concerns of the first extract in the libretto are continued in the second. Indeed here Maderna quotes from, what Alduous Huxley has called,[7] 'the Gospel of India': the *Bhagavadgita*. One of the greatest of the Hindu scriptures, originally written in Sanskrit, but translated here into French,[8] the *Bhagavadgita* forms Book VI of the Indian epic the *Mahabharata*. The work is in the form of a dialogue between the warrior, Prince Arjuna, and his charioteer, Krishna, who is also, unbeknownst to Arjuna, the god, Vishnu, incarnate. Maderna cites at length from the first of the eighteen chapters of the work, and the scene depicted is that of the battlefield of Kuruksetra (a sacred place of pilgrimage from the immemorial time of the Vedic age), just as the great war between the Pandavas and the Kurus is about to begin. Both the Pandavas, whose Prince is Arjuna, and the Kurus belong to the same family (they are all sons of Dhrtarastra), but the Pandavas were all pious sons since birth, whereas Dhrtarastra and the Kurus are bereft of spiritual vision. Dhrtarastra has claimed only the Kurus as his sons, and separated the Pandavas from the family heritage. It is Arjuna's duty, as a warrior, to avenge this wrong, and reclaim the kingdom that he had originally inherited from his father. The two armies, four million soldiers in all, stand opposing each other. Maderna's extract begins where the battle scene is painted with vivid local colour: archers, burning with a desire to fight, stand erect on chariots harnessed to white horses, and the battlefield resounds with the deafening noise of conch-shell horns, drums, and trumpets, which Maderna conveys musically through a 'battle' of percussion and brass instruments, the first of which must sound 'brutali e drammatiche' [brutal and dramatic], the second, 'eroici e minacciosi' [heroic and menacing]. The quotation is spoken on a pre-recorded tape by the female speaker, whose voice is accompanied by the piercing strains of a musette (a bagpipe played with bellows, once common in the seventeenth to eighteenth-century French court):

> Sur le champ les hommes se sont assemblés
> brûlants de combattre.
> Debout sur leurs grands chars de guerre,
> attelés à des coursiers blancs,
> les puissants archers sont des héros,
> prêts à donner leur vie,
> tous maîtres dans l'art du combat.
> Aussitôt résonnèrent les conques et les tambours,
> les cors et les trompettes
> et ce fut un tumulte immense,
> qui retentit comme rugissement du lion.

> [The men have assembled on the battle field,/ burning with a desire to fight./ Standing up on their huge war chariots/ harnessed to white chargers,/ the powerful archers are heroes,/ ready to give up their lives,/ all masters in the art of battle./ As soon as the conch-shells, drums,/ horns, and trumpets rang out,/ there was an immense commotion/ which resounded like the roaring of a lion.]

However, on seeing so many of his friends and relatives lined up on the opposing, enemy side, Prince Arjuna hesitates. His limbs begin to quiver, and his mouth dries up. According to the commentary provided by A.C. Bhaktivedanta Swami Prabhupāda 'such symptoms in Arjuna were not due to weakness but to his soft-heartedness, a characteristic of a pure devotee of the Lord'.[9] Arjuna's compassion for his community and family members is such that rather than kill them for political reasons, he would rather forgive them on the grounds of religion and saintly behaviour. He does not consider killing them profitable simply on the grounds of material possessions, and, he claims, it would not be justified even if he became king of three kingdoms. And so, throwing aside his bow and arrow, he voices his desire to be slain by his relatives rather than engage in a cruel, but just war:

> En voyant dans les rangs mes parents
> brûlants de combattre,
> mes jambes fléchissent, et ma bouche

se dessèche; [...].
Je ne voudrais pas les tuer, même si cela
devait me rendre souverain des trois mondes.
Les précepteurs, les pères, les fils
et les grands-pères, les oncles, les beaux-pères,
les gendres et tous les parents
si, les armes à la main,
ils allaient me tuer dans la bataille,
moi, je ne veux pas résister.

Ayant ainsi parlé sur le champ de la bataille, Arjuna,
le coeur percé de douleur,
retomba sur le siège de son char
et jeta loin de soi l'arc et la flèche.

[Seeing, among the ranks, my relatives/ burning with a desire to fight,/ my
legs begin to quiver, and my mouth/ dries up; [...]/ I would not like to kill
them, even if that/ should make me king of the three worlds./ Teachers,
fathers, sons/ and grand-parents, uncles, father-in-laws,/ son-in-laws, and all
my relations,/ if, armed with weapons,/ they were going to kill me in battle,/
I would not resist./ Having spoken thus on the battle field, Arjuna,/ his heart
pierced with sorrow,/ fell down on the seat of his chariot,/ and threw his bow
and arrow far away from him.]

On hearing this, Krishna rebukes Arjuna for his shameful lack of courage, unworthy
of an Aryan, and explains that there is nothing more desirable for an Aryan than
a just war:

D'où te vient, Arjuna, en cette heure de danger
ce honteux découragement
indigne d'un Aryen?
[...]
En vérité, pour un Aryen il n'y a rien
de plus désirable qu'un juste combat.

[Where does this shameful lack of courage,/ unworthy of an Aryan,/ come
from, Arjuna, in this hour of danger? [...]/ In truth, for an Aryan there is
nothing/ more desirable than a just war.]

What the literary extract is highlighting, therefore, is the relationship between
warfare and religious belief. Krishna's words may seem to favour violence over
religious compassion but, as commentaries make clear (Prabhupāda, p. 12), according
to Vedic injunctions the killing of aggressors is right and proper, and no sin is
incurred thereby. Moreover, although a religiously inclined person, like Arjuna, may
not want to retaliate against a wrongdoer, the Lord excuses no one who has harmed
his devotees, in this case Arjuna and his brothers. For this reason, Krishna reminds
Arjuna of his sense of duty as a warrior, and points out to him that the proper course
of action is the dispassionate discharge of his duty, performed in the name of God.
Hence, according to Vedic philosophy, it is entirely feasible that justified violence
may be exercised by someone of a compassionate and religious temperament, and
this is indeed emphasized in Krishna's reference, on two occasions, to Arjuna as
an 'Aryan' for whom cowardice is an unworthy attribute, and a just war is highly

desirable: the word 'Aryan' being applicable to persons whose life is based on spiritual and religious, rather than material, values, and whose ultimate realization is Vishnu or Absolute Truth. Consequently, whereas Dandin's *Kavyadarsa* displayed evidence of having been influenced by Christian doctrine, this Indian text, far from promoting the Christian forgiveness of trespasses, preaches that it is as important to punish the wicked as it is to be good to the good. The god, Vishnu, is not a god of mercy; he is a god of justice.

However, moderating somewhat Krishna's thesis on the killing of wrongdoers is his belief in the Hindu theory of the doctrine of reincarnation. Maderna quotes the passage where Krishna proceeds to explain to Arjuna that he should not feel sorrow at the thought of dying relatives and friends, for man cannot kill nor be killed: having been created, he can no longer cease to be. Only the material body dies; the soul is indestructible ('permanent, eternal, ancient'), for it there is neither birth nor death. Furthermore, (as Krishna goes on to explain in the section following that quoted by Maderna) the soul, in transmigrating from one body to another upon the death of the body, rejuvenates its energy, and this is a cause for rejoicing, not lamentation. With its emphasis upon the perpetuity of creation, and the soul's infinite possibilities for regeneration and renewal, Krishna provides an essential detail to his doctrine concerning the validity of waging war with an aggressor:

> Celui qui croit qu'il peut tuer et
> celui qui croit qui'il peut être tué,
> tous les deux sont ignorants.
> Il ne peut ni tuer, ni être tué
> il ne naît, ni ne meurt.
> Ayant été, il ne peut plus cesser d'être.
> Non-né, permanent, éternel, ancien,
> il n'est pas détruit
> quand le corps est tué.
> Les armes ne peuvent le percer,
> ni le feu le brûler,
> ni les eaux le mouiller,
> ni le vent le sécher!
> Celui qui habite le corps
> est toujours invulnérable.
> Tu ne dois donc t'affliger pour aucune créature,
> tu ne dois pas trembler, Arjuna.

> [He who thinks he can kill, and/ he who thinks he can be killed,/ both are wrong./ He cannot either kill nor be killed,/ he is not born, and he does not die./ Having been, he cannot cease to be./ Unborn, permanent, eternal, ancient,/ he is not destroyed when the body is killed./ Weapons cannot pierce him,/ nor fire burn him,/ nor water soak him,/ nor wind dry him up!/ He who lives in the body/ is always invulnerable./ You must not therefore grieve for any human being,/ you should not tremble, Arjuna.]

One further point needs to be made about the *Bhagavadgita* extract which offers an interesting comparison with the sequence from the *Atharvaveda* which follows it. When the divine Krishna speaks to the Aryan, he employs a forceful language with a rhetorical scheme, present also in the original Sanskrit — the use of anaphora (the repetition of a word or phrase at the beginning of successive clauses):

> Celui qui croit qu'il peut tuer et
> celui qui croit qui'il peut être tué
>
> il ne peut ni tuer, ni être tué
> il ne naît, ni ne meurt
>
> ni le feu le brûler,
> ni les eaux le mouiller,
> ni le vent le sécher!
>
> Tu ne dois donc t'affliger pour aucune créature,
> tu ne dois pas trembler, Arjuna.

The repetition here clearly hammers home the content, and has an urgent, declamatory nature which is at odds with Arjuna's more pious and sorrowful disposition (emphasized twice in the *Bhagavadgita* extract: 'ému par la pitié/ et plein du douleur'; 'le coeur percé de douleur'), and his more anti-rhetorical explanation for not wanting to engage in battle, comprising of simple utterances such as 'je ne voudrais pas les tuer', and 'moi, je ne veux pas résister'. Indeed the fact that Krishna's verbal paralellisms are *physically* sensible in the sense that they are audible to the listener and visible to the reader serves to reinforce the physical action that he is promoting over Arjuna's contemplative stance (this non-active, contemplative stance being symbolized in Arjuna's throwing down of arms, and his sitting down again on the seat of his chariot). In short, Krishna alias Vishnu advocates the compatibility of a religious and fighting disposition, and similarly his language, while speaking of the divine and promoting divinity, is active, forceful, and bordering on the aggressive. This is also exactly the case in the quotations which follow, and which take one further back in time than the *Bhagavadgita*, while being fundamentally related to the latter text.

The third extract of the libretto is from the fourth Veda, entitled the *Atharvaveda*.[10] Vedism, that is to say, the religion of the earliest Indo-European peoples who settled in India in the first quarter of the second millennium BC, and who named their sacred texts after themselves, was the first form of Hinduism which subsequently evolved into Brahmanism (deriving its name from the subject of worship — the supreme God, Brahman), and then into the Vaisnavism that is to be found in the *Bhagavadgita,* where Vishnu (and his earthly incarnations, such as Krishna) is regarded as the Supreme Being. Written in Sanskrit, but in Maderna's libretto translated into English,[11] the *Atharvaveda* is mostly a compilation of hymns, one sixth of which are to be found in the earlier *Rigveda*, dedicated to gods of the Vedic religion (gods of fire, water, sky, sun, and moon), and recited by the Atharvan priests at the great Vedic sacrifices. The work is said to derive its name from 'Atharvan', who is spoken of in the *Rigveda* as the first priest who produced fire by attrition, and through his sacrifices was the first to establish ways of communication between men and gods. Unlike the *Rigveda*, however, the *Atharvaveda* is posited by many to belong to the lower levels of Vedic society, whereas the *Rigveda* appears to have been the property of the higher families (this, for example, is the view of Weber, Bloomfield, and

Ragozin).[12] This is because in the *Atharvaveda*, there are, in addition to hymns, curses, charms, magical spells, witchcraft, and sorcery, so that, in the words of Ragozin, 'we sometimes find ourselves in the midst of goblin-worship' where 'worship takes the form of conjuring, not prayer', and ministers seem 'sorcerers, not priests' (Murdoch, p. 6). Maderna quotes from Books II and XIX which contain hymns of a miscellaneous character, not really indicative of the 'ruder' dimensions of the work highlighted by Ragozin and others. The structure of many of these hymns is identical: they take the form of an invocation where the attention of the god is evoked by praise or an enumeration of his great deeds, followed by an exhortation of his help. This schematic form is clearly present in the first extract cited — the Atharvan priests bestow exclamatory praise upon the god, and invoke for themselves those qualities for which he is being praised ('power', 'might', 'strength' etc). Maderna's music is now direct (not pre-recorded), and the liturgical prayer from the *Atharvaveda* is sung 'sempre appassionato' by the soprano to the accompaniment of strings which convey the intensity of the invocation by playing only in the upper registers. The winds join in with gestures of explosive energy just as the singer begins the second extract from Book XIX:

> Power art thou, give me power!
> Might art thou, give me might!
> Strength art thou, give me strength!
> Life art thou, give me life!
> Ear art thou, give me hearing!
> Eye art thou, give me eyes!
> Shield art thou, shield me well! (*Atharvaveda* II, xvii)
>
> May I have voice in my mouth,
> breath in my nostrils,
> sight in my eyes,
> hearing in my ears,
> hair always shining young
> and much strength in my arms! (*Atharvaveda* XIX, lx)

Apart from the clear thematic link with the *Bhagavadgita* by way of the origins of Hinduism, and the preoccupation with gods, one notes here a feature of style common to the *Bhagavadgita* sequence (and, again, present also in the Sanskrit originals) which provides an interesting comparison with subsequent citations in the libretto. Like the rhetorical verbal parallelisms of the *Bhagavadgita* extract, the *Atharvaveda* sequence, as is common with ritual, liturgical language, employs a heavy dosage of foregrounded repetitions of expression: in the first cited extract, epanalepsis, where the initial part of each unit of the line pattern (the words 'Power', 'Might', 'Strength', 'Life', and 'Eyes') is repeated in the final part; and epistrophe in the second cited extract, i.e. the use of final repetition, ('in my mouth', 'in my nostrils', 'in my eyes', 'in my ears', 'in my arms!'). Hence, as in the *Bhagavadgita,* the *Atharvaveda* sequence is speaking of the divine and to the divine, but in an active and physical language which tonally borders on the bellicose. Furthermore, the life-force that is being coveted by the priests is equated with a warrior-like power and strength. This is reinforced by the reference to the 'shield' and the 'strength in the arms', and more heavily by an echo of contrast between this text and the *Bhagavadgita*, and which cannot be deemed to be coincidental: the Atharvan priests ask for 'voice' in their 'mouths' and 'strength' in their 'arms' — 'qualities' which Arjuna, the pacificist and *reluctant warrior*, is without: he is said to have a 'mouth' which 'dries up', 'legs' 'bending' beneath him; and is lacking the strength to stand upstraight ('mes jambes fléchissent, et ma bouche/ se dessèche; je n'ai pas la force/ de me ténir debout'). Maderna also seems deliberately to emphasize the combative nature of the language of the *Atharvaveda* by making the orchestral material grow in density, intensity, and volume as the section reaches a close.

What therefore seems most evident in both the *Bhagavadgita* and the *Atharvaveda* extracts is the presentation of religious philosophies where belligerency is an acceptable ingredient. What follows next in the libretto suggests no longer an approximation of violence and religion, and the spirituality that religion connotes, but rather their separation. Further sections from the *Atharvaveda*, identical to what has come before in their use of a rhetorical, active, and combative style, are juxtaposed with highly lyrical verses of Persian poets which speak quietly of contemplative feeling in relation to idyllic landscapes.

The first Persian poet to be cited is Omar Khayyam, born in the latter half of the eleventh century A.D., and the contrast between his verses and the words of Krishna and the Atharvan priests is immediately apparent. Whereas Arjuna's 'heart' was filled with compassion and sorrow for the thought of his dead relatives ('le coeur percé de douleur'), but Krishna had ordered him to respond to duty rather than feeling, Khayyam's sequence starts with an apostrophe to his own heart:

> O cuore, fingi d'avere tutte le cose del mondo,
> fingi che tutto ti sia giardino delizioso di verde.
> E tu, anima mia, su quell'erba verde
> fingi d'esser rugiada gocciata là nella notte
> e al sorgere dell'alba svanita... .(*Rubaiyat*, Quatrain 103)[13]

> [Oh heart, you pretend to have everything in the world,/ you pretend that everything for you is a delightful, green garden./ And you, my soul, you pretend to be/ a dewdrop which has fallen there in the night on that green grass,/ and disappeared at the rising of dawn.]

The lines are read by the female voice, and in stark contrast to the business and intensity of the music which ended the *Atharvaveda* section, the words are not set to any music; rather they are handwritten graphically across three lines of a stave as if they were themselves music: those words written on the top line of the stave are, as indicated by the composer, to be pronounced in a voice which is 'acuto' ('high'); those in the centre line are spoken in a register which is 'medio' ('middle'), and those on the bottom line, in a voice which is 'grave' ('low-pitched') (see Figure 6.2). Some words are spread out over more than one line, indicating a falling or rising of voice-register across syllables; some are written in a larger and bolder font than others, suggesting they are pronounced in a louder tone; some are more spaced out than others, indicating a slowing of tempo as they are spoken. Presented as music, rather than accompanied by music, standing out against the white background of the page, and flanked on the left by the highly textured, complicated, and above

FIG. 6.2. Bruno Maderna's *Ausstrahlung* (Milan: Ricordi, 1975), p. 14
Courtesy of G. Ricordi & C. SpA Milano

all, active music ending the *Atharvaveda* section, these words induce a sense of quiet stasis, peacefulness, and respite from the urgency of what has preceded them. This effect is underscored by the use of caesuras (in the form of large V-shaped signs between certain words and phrases of Khayyam's extract), indicating the taking of a breath, and/or of a pause.

Semantically too, an antithesis exists with the *Atharvaveda* text. There the priests were coveting and invoking the attributes of the gods: the term 'give me!' is repeated six times in succession in the sequence from Book II, and its harsh, emphatic quality is only toned down slightly in the 'May I have' of the quotations from Book XIX. Khayyam, by contrast, says of his heart that it pretends already to have 'everything in the world', and this 'everything' is posited in simple terms as a 'delightful green garden'. Such contentment with the small and simple, and a desire to blend with nature as one of its smallest components — a drop of dew upon the green grass of the garden — contrasts with the rapacious attitude of the *Atharvaveda* extract. Similarly the desire for self-aggrandizement on the part of the Atharvan priests serves only to foil Khayyam's lonely, self-effacing attitude, implicit in the reference to the 'dewdrop'-heart which at dawn has *melted*,[14] and contrasted again with the desire for collectivity and the force to be found in numbers in a further citation from *Atharvaveda* XIX, placed after the Khayyam quatrain, and accompanied by violent sounds on brass and percussion instruments:

> Let's walk together, speak together,
> may the purpose be common, common the assembly,
> common the mind.
> So be our thoughts united
> may our decision be unanimous. (*Atharvaveda*, XIX, lx)

There is, of course, no explicit reference to god or to the divine in the quatrain from the *Rubaiyat* cited by Maderna, but nevertheless, what seems to be suggested is that the features associated with Khayyam's personality and which are being foregrounded by the libretto — lyricism, quiet contemplation, a communing with nature, humility and self-effacement — connote holiness and an sense of divinity, irrespective of the actual religious standing of Khayyam. Indeed the question of Khayyam's religiousness, in the strict sense of the word, is one which has caused much debate and controversy within literary criticism, and is alluded to in the second citation Maderna uses from Khayyam. Edward Fitzgerald (see note 14) was adamant that in Khayyam there was no preoccupation with the divine, and that he in fact ridiculed the practice of the Sufis by whom he was hated. Although not exorbitant, Khayyam's desires, according to Fitzgerald, were more worldly than otherworldly: 'his Worldly Pleasures are what they profess to be without any pretence at divine allegory: his Wine is the veritable Juice of the Grape: his Tavern, where it was to be had: his Sáki, the Flesh and Blood that poured it our for him: all of which, and where the Roses were in bloom, was all he professed to want of this World or to expect of Paradise' (Fitzgerald, p. ix). Other critics, however, have strongly disagreed with Fitzgerald's view, as, for example, Idries Shah, who argues that Khayyam was a 'practical instructor in Sufism'; that he uses 'the special terminology and allegory of Sufism', and that 'Fitzgerald's interpolation of anti-Sufism propaganda into his rendering of Khayyam cannot be excused'.[15] To a certain extent, the libretto would seem want to highlight Fitzgerald's view. This becomes apparent in a further quotation which emphasizes Khayyam's preoccupation with the transience of life and his own mortality (deliberately juxtaposed with invocations of longevity from the Atharvan priests: 'May we see a hundred years! (XIX, lxvii)):

> Sulla mia tomba ad ogni primavera
> il vento del nord farà piovere fiori. (Khayyam)

> [The north wind will rain down flowers/ on my tomb at every spring.]

These lines are taken from a story by one of Khayyam's acquaintances, Nezami Aruzi of Samarcand, and which is reported by Fitzgerald (pp. vii–viii).[16] Aruzi, while seated with Khayyam one day in a garden, heard the poet pronounce the following words: 'my tomb shall be in a spot, where the north wind may scatter roses over it'. Aruzi, commenting on this statement, said 'I wondered at the words he spoke, but I knew that his were no idle words. Years after, when I chanced to visit Naishápur, I went to his final resting place, and lo! It was just outside a garden, and trees laden with fruit stretched their boughs over the garden wall, and dropped their flowers upon his tomb, so as the stone was hidden under them'. Maderna includes a version of the latter statement two extracts later in the libretto:

> May we live a hundred years!
> May we know a hundred years! (*Atharvaveda*, XIX, lxvii)

> I peri e gli albicocchi
> avevan ricoperto la tomba di fiori. (Nezami Aruzi)

> [The pear and apricot trees/ had covered the tomb with flowers.]

As Fitzgerald explains (p. viii) the significance of Khayyam's utterance lies in the fact that it was taken to be rash and irreligious, for in the Koran it is categorically stated 'No man knows where he shall die'. Significantly, Maderna, aware of the famously irreligious import of Khayyam's utterance, deliberately sets both it and Aruzi's observation to three lines each of medieval plainsong — a type of church music which in its final form, called gregorian chant, became standard in Roman Catholic use in the middle ages. This supports the idea that whereas Khayyam may have been collectively regarded as an outcast because of his hostility to contemporary religious beliefs (as was Fitzgerald's view), the libretto means to underline an aspect of the man and his poetry which is unorthodoxly 'holy'. The libretto would therefore seem to be encouraging a more fluid perception of divinity: promoting the idea that there are aspects and definitions of divinity which lie outside the traditionally orthodox ones.

Maderna does not quote again from Khayyam in the libretto, but the flower motif which was established with the citations from that poet is sustained a little longer in two brief quotations from Sadi — another Persian lyric poet, born approximately sixty years after Khayyam's death. Khayyam and Sadi would seem to be associated in the libretto through the allusions to flower, fruit, and greenery which link them: 'giardino di verde', 'erba verde', 'primavera', 'fiori' (Khayyam), 'i peri e gli albicocchi' (Aruzi in reference to Khayyam); 'Sono tutti verdi i rami'

[The branches are all green], 'È fiorito il giardino' [The garden has flowered], and implied allusions to the *Gulistan* [The Rose Garden] and the *Bustan* [The Orchard] (Sadi).[17] They are also curiously linked by an inversion of the importance normally attributed to each in literary criticism. In contrast to Khayyam, Sadi enjoyed enormous fame in his day, his *Gulistan*[18] attaining a popularity in the East which, according to A. Kadah,[19] has never been reached by any European work in this Western world. A collection of anecdotes, drawn mostly from experiences gleaned from many years of travels, the *Gulistan* contains ethical reflexions and maxims of worldly wisdom, written in prose scattered with numerous poems. In addition to the *Gulistan*, Sadi also wrote the *Bustan*,[20] containing ten chapters in verse on the duties of mankind towards God and towards their fellow-men, and a great many ghazals, or odes. In spite of achieving fame and popularity in his day and subsequently, Maderna gives less room to Sadi's poetry in the libretto than he does to Khayyam's, and indeed he cites two almost insignificant and anonymous sounding verses from Sadi, which are half spoken and half sung by the soprano:

> Sono tutti verdi i rami
> È fiorito il giardino

These lines are not to be found in either the *Gulistan* or the *Bustan*;[21] but they make a clear reference to Sadi's main oeuvre as a whole — their allusions to 'verdant branches', 'flowering', and a 'garden' clearly evoking either Sadi's 'Rose' or 'Orchard' garden, or indeed both.

Unlike for Khayyam, there has been no disagreement in scholarly criticism regarding the religiousness of Sadi. He is considered to be very much a religious poet, and his Preface to the *Gulistan* makes this particularly evident. Subtitled 'In the Name of God, the Merciful, the Compassionate!', it begins 'Praise be to God! (May he be honoured and glorified!) whose worship is the means of drawing close to Him, and in giving thanks to whom is involved an increase of benefits' (*The Rose Garden*, p. 1). For Sadi, divinity is present within nature, as demonstrated by the poet's frequently quoted couplet:

> To pious minds each verdant leaf displays,
> A volume teeming with th' Almighty's praise. (*The Rose Garden*, p. xxviii)

The 'verdant leaf' here obviously bears an affinity with the 'verdant branches' of the libretto's extract.

Sadi's concept of divinity is more closely related to that of Khayyam than to that of the *Bhagavadgita*. Whereas in the latter, as previously demonstrated, aggressors must be punished, and the punisher is seen to be acting out god's will, giving rise to 'just wars', in Sadi's religious philosophy, evil should be requited only with good deeds, as demonstrated by a host of poems and stories in the *Gulistan*, including the following:

> Whenever then
> Thy enemy thee slanders absent, thou
> To his face applaud him. (*The Rose Garden*, p. 57)

> Shew kindness even to thy foes
> The dog's mouth with a morsel close. (*The Rose Garden*, p. 67)

Story IV.
A thief entered the house of a recluse. However much he searched, he found nothing. He turned back sadly and in despair, and was observed by the holy man, who cast the blanket on which he slept in the way of the thief, that he might not be disappointed.

Stanza.
The men of God's true faith, I've heard,
Grieve not the hearts e'en of their foes.
When will this station be conferred
On thee who dost thy friends oppose? (*The Rose Garden*, p. 76)

Similarly, Sadi's promotion of the qualities of humility and contentment (Chapter 3 of the *Gulistan* is entitled 'On the Excellence of Contentment'), and his rejection of the state of powerfulness, blend with those of Khayyam, and clash with the invocations *for* powerfulness in the *Atharvaveda*:

I am the ant which under foot men tread,
And not the hornet whose fierce sting they dread.
How, for this boon, shall I my thanks express?
That I, to injure man, am powerless. (*The Rose Garden*, p. 118)

Sadi's associations with the concepts of divinity, humility, and contentment, are, of course, not clearly spelled out by the libretto itself. But they seem naturally to come to the fore by way of Maderna's linking of Sadi to Khayyam through the flower motif. That Maderna is also creating links of contrast between Sadi and the *Atharvaveda* is also strongly implied on a more direct level in the libretto. It seems rather intentional that the quotation which sums up Sadi and his oeuvre — 'È fiorito il giardino' — is sandwiched between two of the invocations for long life from the Atharvan priests: 'May we assert our existence a hundred years!', and 'Yea, even more than a hundred years!', and in the music is pronounced simultaneously with the former. Here Maderna displays a slight element of humour, for one of the most well-known facts about Sadi is that he reputedly lived well beyond the age of 100.

The discourse on the relationship between nature and divinity which has been established through the quotations from Khayyam and Sadi, is now taken a step further in three more citations from Dandin's *Kavyadarsa*. The first two are taken from Section II of the treatise on Sanskrit poetry, subtitled 'Classification of Sense-Embellishments'; the third, from Section III, subtitled 'Section on Word-Embellishments, and Defects'. All three citations take the form of a short *kavya* lyric,[22] written in the tradition of Sanskrit love poetry. The first one intends to illustrate 'Paronomasia' (a pun or play on words) 'with identical action'; the second 'Paronomasia with two non-contrary actions' (II, 314); the third, 'continuous initial chime' (the repetition of syllabic groups) 'in the first and the second feet'(III. 8, Belvalkar, English translation). In *Ausstrahlung,* all three poems are recited in a very lyrical and expressive fashion on a tape: the first two follow each other in succession; the third is placed after an extract from Rudaki (to be considered later):

Glances to the side,
loving by nature,
announce intense *love*,
when thrown by *loving* maidens,
as messengers to
attract *lovers*. (*Kavyadarsa,* II, 316) (the italics are mine)

The mango tree's bud
fills my heart with strong
desire for my *lover*,
as does the cry of the cuckoos
drunken with *love*. (*Kavyadarsa* II, 317) (the italics are mine)

They say that the spring
must not cause the lovely
movement of your eyes
and the illusion that they
might be two bees... .(*Kavyadarsa* III, 8)

Since neither the puns nor the chime come across in the English translation used by Maderna (the chime — in Sanskrit, *yamaka* — can, however, be very easily identified in the Sanskrit original by someone who does not read Sanskrit[23]), it would seem reasonable to assume that Maderna uses the three *kavya* lyrics here, not so much to illustrate the poetical embellishments possible in Sanskrit poetry, as the tradition of Sanskrit love poetry of which they function as perfect examples. All three poems are on the subject of love and sexual passion, as clearly underlined in the vocabulary (in the first two the word 'love' and its variants occurs six times in all). The concept of mood, *rasa* (which literally means the taste or flavour of something) which governs Indian artistic expression, is also very much to the fore. As J. M. Masson explains,[24] the spring time, cuckoos, and bees are traditionally considered as *uddīpanavibhavas*, that is to say, things that create the right atmosphere for, and which intensify latent feelings of sexual love (in Indian myth, spring is the ally of Kama, the god of love).[25] As in most Sanskrit love verse, atmosphere is also evoked through the sensuous description of the female's movement, form, and behaviour: the 'loving' 'glances to the side' of the maidens in the first poem, and the girl's 'lovely/ movement of your eyes' in the third are simple, and yet subtle and expressive gestures which create a dense atmosphere of passion. The reference to the mango tree in the second poem (with its associations with fleshiness, juicy ripeness, and a tropical atmosphere) exudes the eroticism which is also typical of many Sanskrit love poems. Indeed, these poems traditionally were meant to have evocative and suggestive overtones, so that the 'bees' to which the maiden's eyes are compared in the final lyric (the stock comparison of the woman's eyes was to lotuses) cannot fail to evoke the biting — a conventional aspect of love-making often referred to in Sanskrit poetry — for which the girl's standard excuse the next day was that she had been stung on the lip by a bee. Simultaneously, it is suggestive of the god of love's bow which was said to be strung of bees, whose buzzing represents the twang of the bow-string.[26] These quotations seem a far cry from the very first citation from the *Kavyadarsa* with which Maderna opened his work: the sexual connotations here seem to jar with the biblical nuances of *Kavyadarsa*

I, 4, and the divine qualities attributed to the Word. The apparent incongruity can exist, however, because in *Kavyadarsa* I, 4, Dandin is defining language (the divine 'Word') as giving sense to the world, in line with his definition of poetry as Word and Sense in unity and endowed with beauty. The three short lyrics quoted subsequently by Maderna function in the *Kavyadarsa* as examples of this definition of poetry. However, in addition to this explanation of the co-existence of the sacred and the sensual in the *Kavyadarsa*, there exists another. For whereas to Western ears the merging of the erotic and divine may seem incongruous, it was much less so to the writers of the Indian love lyric. From the earliest known anthology of Sanskrit love poetry, written in the second century A.D., right up until the fourteenth century and beyond, sensual joy and divine love have been intrinsically linked,[27] and desire, union, and the consummation of desire have often been presented as the concrete example of a religious experience. In these works 'the erotic and devotional lyric merge freely, and at times it is impossible to make out whether the free sexual imagery employed is to be taken literally or as an allegory of the human soul courting the love of its god'.[28]

The fact that Dandin's references to love are so very heavily tied to descriptions of nature, and the previous quotations from Khayyam and Sadi emphasized, respectively, the *holiness* of a quiet communing with nature, and the divinity within nature (the 'verdant leaves' which in Sadi, 'teem with th'Almighty's praise') would seem to imply that the libretto does indeed wish to suggest the associations in Dandin between the sensual and the divine.

This implication is further emphasized in the manner in which the Rudaki piece interacts with Dandin. As previously mentioned, a sequence dating from the tenth century by Rudaki[29] is sandwiched between the second and third *kavya* of Dandin. This sequence harks back to the first reference to Dandin's *Kavyadarsa* used at the beginning of the libretto: the allusion to the transformation of 'dense darkness' into divine light — 'the light called Word' which shone 'from the beginning of the world'. In Rudaki there is an inversion of this procedure. Depicting a scene in nature, he describes how the light in the landscape ('*silver*' mountains, a '*golden*' meadow, and '*shining*' water) is suddenly transformed into darkness: 'ma tenebrosa s'è fatta l'aria' ('but the air has become shadowy'). Rudaki then proceeds to make the point that when this divine light disappears from the landscape, nature and its natural music dies: the dove becomes silent; the lark, mute; the orchard is empty; and the garden is bare. Clinching the association between nature, the divine, and sensual love that seemed to be implied in the *kavya* poems by Dandin, Rudaki concludes by making an analogy between the disappearance of divine light in the landscape, the blowing of a cold wind, and the sigh of *parting lovers* at dawn. His use of the word 'amanti' ('lovers') clearly echoes the first *kavya* of Dandin where, as previously mentioned, the word 'love' and its variants occurred no less than 4 times in the space of 6 short lines. The link by inversion between *Kavyadarsa* I, 4, and the Rudaki quotation is also reinforced musically. The former citation, spoken by the female voice, was accompanied by a flute solo; a flute and an oboe solo, imitating the natural sounds of nature (particularly bird song) also accompany the soprano who sings the extract from Rudaki; but at the point where there is mention of the conversion of light into darkness ('ma tenebrosa s'è fatta l'aria') the oboe is substituted by an English horn, and the flute, by a low-pitched flute (Maderna's instructions read; 'Oboe solo cambia in Eng. Hrn; flauto solo cambia in flauto grave', p. 34), and the music decreases in activity and volume, culminating in a long pause which proceeds the 'cold wind' of the final line, sung completely unaccompanied by the soprano:

> Il monte, un altro monte
> d'argento, d'oro è il prato,
> l'acqua ora è lucente,
> ma tenebrosa s'è fatta l'aria.
> Tace la colomba,
> vuoto è il verziere
> muto è l'usignolo
> spoglio è il giardino.
> Un vento freddo
> come sospiro d'amanti all'alba. (Rudaki)

> [The mountain, another silver/ mountain, the meadow is golden,/ the water is now shining,/ but the air has become shadowy./ The dove sings no more,/ the orchard is empty,/ the lark is silent,/ and the garden is bare./ A cold wind blows,/ like the sighing of lovers at dawn.]

Like with the Khayyam citations, the piece which Maderna chooses to quote from in Rudaki's oeuvre manages also to convey something of the character of the poet as reported by chroniclers of his life and times. It is significant that the extract speaks of the transformation of light into darkness, and is placed between two poems by Dandin which emphasize 'eyes' (the 'Glances to the side [...] thrown by loving maidens' of the *Kavyadarsa* II, 316; and the illusion that the eyes of the lady in *Kavyadarsa* III, 8 might be 'two bees'). Most chroniclers of Rudaki's life claim either that he was blind from birth (as does, for example, 'Awfi), or that he lost his vision gradually, perhaps even suddenly (Gerasimov claims that Rudaki was blinded for refusing to follow tradition and write empty praises of the ruler for payment).[30] Also, although the source of the extract is not known, when it speaks of the nightingale falling silent upon the conversion of light to darkness ('muto è l'usignolo'), it echoes the most famous and most often quoted composition by Rudaki, 'Lament in Old Age', where he refers to his own poetry as 'music more appealing than the nightingales'.[31] Finally, the libretto would seem to want to pay tribute to Rudaki's status not only as a poet, but also as a renowned ballad singer poet and musician — he reputedly played the harp and the lute very skilfully, learning music from the famed teacher, Bakhtiar with whom he travelled all around the present day Tajik highlands, singing, playing, and composing. In this respect it is significant that the Rudaki extract is sung live by the soprano (and not pre–recorded as are so many of the other literary extracts), and in the musical score of *Ausstrahlung*, the whole of the Rudaki sequence is repeated to a busier musical texture, where the low-pitched flute and the English horn are accompanied by a counter bassoon, percussion instruments, and, importantly, two harps.

The final extract in *Ausstrahlung* is from the *Avesta*: the sacred book of Zoroastrianism, containing the teachings of the prophet, Zoroaster (Zarathustra), the Iranian religious reformer and very first theologian who founded in the sixth century B.C. the religion that bears his name — Zoroastrianism, or Parsiism, as it is known in India. Whereas most of the literary extracts in the libretto follow each other without any musical break, the *Avesta* passage is preceded by a long musical section punctuated by children's voices (those of Maderna's three daughters) which repeat, at intervals, two words from the actual passage: 'so wunderbar' ('so wonderful'), and it is indeed the 'wondrous' work of the divine which is the prevailing sentiment of the concluding sequence.

Maderna quotes from a German translation[32] of the chief liturgical part of the *Avesta*, entitled the *Yasna*[33] — a section compiled of a number of hymns which contain the rite of the preparation and sacrifice of *haoma* — a sacred plant, considered also to be a god (the son of Ahura Mazdāh) that originally grew in the Iranian mountains and which, apparently, had intoxicating qualities. Maderna quotes from hymn 44, and for the first time in the libretto, 'god' is addressed head on. This god is Zoroaster's god — Ahura Mazdāh — the one, true god from whom all other divinities proceeded. He is questioned about the mystery of Nature. Zoroaster asks him to reveal the secrets of the sidereal and atmospheric skies, and the earth below: the progress of the sun and stars, and the phases of the moon; how the clouds and winds are moved along by invisible steeds; how the earth does not move, and what gives rise to its sparkling waters and blossoming flowers. The questions are rhetorical, and the prophet is clearly not desiring a scientific explanation to all of these mysteries; rather he is marvelling at their wonder: the phrase 'so wunderbar', as well as being used in a leitmotif in the musical section preceding the *Avesta* section, is repeated three times in the actual text in reference to natural phenomena, and the female voice which recites the text does so in a most expressive and arresting fashion, prolonging and almost singing the vowel sounds, and inducing in the listener a sense of 'wonder'. The extract also clearly wishes to establish a relationship between the material order, controlled by god, and the human spirit: 'Unser Geist hat die Augen' ('Our spirit has eyes'):

> Ich frage Dich mein Gott
> gib Du mir Antwort und Verstehen.
> Wie kommt es, daß aller Wahrheit eigen
> diese zeugende Kraft,
> daß die Sonne dort steht
> und die Sterne der Nacht,
> entsprungenes Licht,
> doch gehalten und wandeln in
> stiller Bahn?
> Und der Mond in der Kammer
> der Schlummernden
> so wunderbar ruhe?
> Eine Hand legt sich um uns.
> Nun weicht sie
> so wunderbar
> zurück und sein Licht winkt uns zu.
> Wie geschieht uns so wunderbar.

aggiunte all'edizione Forûghî dall'antico manoscritto Chester Beatty edito da Arberry' [The asterisks indicate quatrains added to the Forûghî edition from the Chester Beatty ancient manuscript edited by Arberry]. From the information available in the archives, it is impossible to tell whether Maderna availed of Bausani's edition of the *Rubaiyat* or whether he used another Italian translation. The Italian translation provided by Bausani is not identical to that offered in Maderna's libretto. It reads: 'O cuore, fa' conto d'avere tutte le cose del mondo,/ Fa' conto che tutto ti sia giardino delizioso di verde,/ E tu su quell'erba verde fa' conto d'esser rugiada/ Gocciata colà nella notte, e al sorger dell'alba svanita' [Oh heart, imagine having everything in the world,/ imagine that everything for you is a delightful, green garden,/ and imagine being a dewdrop/ which has fallen there in the night on that green grass,/ and disappeared at the rising of dawn].

14. All these impressions and nuances surrounding the Khayyam piece — its quiet inward-looking and contemplative nature; its love of nature; its preference for the small and humble are all, reputedly, aspects of Khayyam's character. In his *Rubáiyát of Omar Khayyám* (London: Bernard Quaritch, 1859), pp. iv-vii, Edward Fitzgerald, a Victorian who was the first to translate Khayyam into English, explains how his name, in fact, came to represent the antithesis of the violent man by virtue of its association with two other names in Persian literary history — Nizám al Mulk and Hasan Ben Sabbáh — with whom Khayyam studied as a boy under the illustrious scholar, Imám Mowaffak of Naishápur. It was believed that whoever studied with Mowaffak would attain honour, happiness, and good fortune, and it was Hasan Ben Sabbáh who suggested that whomsoever of the three boys acquired this good fortune would share it equally with the other two. Nizám al Mulk was the fortunate one who rose to be administrator of affairs during the Sultanate of Sultan Alp Arslán, and he kept his word to Sabbáh, obtaining him a place in the government. Sabbáh abused this position, and was disgraced and fell after failing in an attempt to supplant al Mulk himself. He subsequently became part of an evil Persian sect, and murdered Nizám, his old school-boy friend. Khayyam, by contrast with his violent friend, did not request title or office from Nizám during his life time. He is reputed to have said 'the greatest boon you can confer on me is to let me live in a corner under the shadow of your fortune, to spread wide the advantages of Science, and pray for your long life and prosperity' (all things which Nizám granted, along with a yearly pension of 1, 200 *mithkáls* of gold). In this 'shadowy' existence, Khayyam became a leaned scholar of astronomy, was one of the eight men chosen to reform the calendar under the sultanate of Malik Shah, and wrote a treatise on algebra. But he was also author of a plethora of poems, the most famous of which are the *Rubaiyat*, written not for publication but for his own personal enjoyment. In addition he is said to have liked to farm; and as an indication of his innate humility, he adopted as his 'Takhallus' or poetical name, 'Khayyam', meaning 'tent-maker', having once exercised that trade.

15. I. Shah, *The Way of the Sufi* (Harmondsworth: Penguin, 1968), p. 64.

16. Fitzgerald explains how the story, as he reports it, derives from an anonymous preface sometimes prefixed to Khayyam's poems, and printed in Persian in the appendix to Hyde's *Veterum persarum religio*, p. 499. Maderna could have found the reference to this story either in Fitzgerald or in Bausani's Italian edition of the *Rubaiyat, Quartine*, (pp. viii-ix). Here Bausani, referring to the *Antologia persiana di Badî'-oz-Zamâm Khorâsânî* (Teheran: 1316, 1937), pp. 199–200, relates how Nezami Aruzi is reported to have said 'Nell'anno 506 (cioè 1112–13) si trovavano a Balkh, nella via dei venditori di schiavi, nel palazzo dell'amîr Abû Sa'd, l'*imâm* Omar Khayyâm e l'*imâm* Mozaffar Esfzârî, e io anche ero con loro. In una piacevole riunione sentii dire alla "Prova della Verità" Omar: "La mia tomba sarà in un luogo tale, che ad ogni primavera il vento del nord farà piovere fiori sulla terra del corpo mio"' [In the year 506 (that is 1112–13) Omar Khayyam and Mozaffar Esfzari met up at Balkh, in the road where they sold slaves, in Abu Sa'd's palace, and I too was with them. In a pleasant reunion, I heard Omar, in the 'Proof of Truth', say: 'My tomb will be in a place where the north wind will rain down flowers each spring on the land above my body'). However, Bausani does not make reference to Aruzi's visiting of Khayyam's tomb where he found that, as Khayyam had predicted, fruit trees had covered the tomb with flowers — reference to which is also made in the libretto. This makes one suspect that Maderna might have been influenced more by Fitzgerald's English edition than by Bausani's Italian edition of the *Rubaiyat*.

17. A concrete link also existed between the two poets in real life, for Sadi studied at the important Nidhàmiyya College founded by Nizám al Mulk.

18. For an English translation, see *The Rose Garden*, trans. by E. B. Eastwick (London: Octagon Press, 1979).

19. *The Rose garden* (Preface), p. xiii.

20. For an English translation, see *The Bustān of Sadi*, trans. by A. Hart Edwards (London: John Murray, Albemarle Street, 1911).

21. The Fondo Maderna contains an Italian translation of the *Gulistan*: *Il Roseto*, trans. by Pio Filippani-Ronconi (Turin: Boringhieri, 1965). To date, there has been no Italian translation of the *Bustan*.

22. *Kavya* refers to a Sanskrit literary style that arose in the first centuries AD, and dominated Sanskrit literature for over a millennium. The style is characterized by a self-conscious effort on the part of the writer to compose poetry pleasing to both the ear and the mind. It involves elaborate figures of speech, especially metaphor and simile; skilfulness in the use of complicated and varied metres; a tendency for compound nouns; and a display of great learning and erudition in the arts and sciences.

23. The original reads 'Madhuram madhur ambhoja — vadane vada netrayoh / vibhramam bhramarabhrāntyā vidamba yati kim nu te' (the underlining highlights the chime), *Kavyadarsa*. Sanskrit text and English translation by Belvalkar, p. 52.

24. In *Sanskrit Love Poetry*, trans. by W.S. Merwin and J. Moussaieff Masson (New York: Columbia University Press, 1977), p. 32.

25. Other examples of spring, cuckoos, and bees as *uddīpanavibhavas* in Sanskrit love poetry: 'Beautiful branches swaying in/ heavy wind/ beautiful with throat songs of cuckoos' joy/ and singing of bees look/ oh you with beautiful limbs/ at the forest/ hung with bright flowers' (From the *Nātyaśāstra*, c. third century A.D. See *Sanskrit Love Poetry*, pp. 74–75); 'Bāna and Asana trees/ in full flower/ bees shrill from joy/ with drawn bow/ merciless arrow/ moves at his pleasure/ today through the forests / the love god' (From the *Rāmāyana* IV, 30.56, ascribed to Vālmīki, A.D. 100. See *Sanskrit Love Poetry*, pp. 62–63).

26. See *Poems from the Sanskrit*. Trans. and intro. by J. Brough (Baltimore: Penguin Books, 1968), p. 39. For an example of a lyric illustrating this, see note 29: a poem from the *Rāmāyana*.

27. In the last verse of the *Gāhākoso* (*Gāthāsaptaśatī*) of Hāla (stanza no. 697), the earliest available anthology of Prākrit love poems, dating from the second century A.D., even Vishnu himself forgets the evening prayers he ritually performs when he notices the reflection of the lotus-like face of his wife in the ocean (*Sanskrit Love Poetry*, p. 57); in the fifth-century *Kumārasambhava* of Kālidāsa, on whose huge literary achievements Dandin drew inspiration, Shiva, the father of the universe and preserver of the cosmos in a triad with the gods, Brahma and Vishnu, is depicted making love (Chapter 8, line 91): 'Attached to his beloved/ Day and night Shiva made love/ One hundred and fifty seasons — a single night!/ He never tired of sexual pleasure [...]' (*Sanskrit Love Poetry*, p. 35); in Mammata's *Kāvyaprakaśa*, an influential eleventh century work on poetics, line 137, the goddess Laksmi makes love to Vishnu from on top: 'The goddess Laksmi/ loves to make love to Vishnu/ from on top / looking down she sees in his navel a lotus / and on it Brahmā the god [...]' (*Sanskrit Love poetry*, p. 111); in the fifteenth-century anthology *Padyāvalī*, an anthology of verses relating to Krishna, the earthly embodiment of Vishnu, one is told that when the young Krishna played his flute, no woman could resist the call: 'What did you/ feel inside you/ when you heard the flute/ Krishna was playing/ and no woman said no' (*Sanskrit Love Poetry*, p. 157); in the twelfth-century *Gītagovinda* by Jayadeva (a dramatic lyrical poem on the love of Rādhā and Krishna), 'potentially pornographic subject matter becomes the material of aesthetic and religious experience', and 'the aesthetic experience of their love is the means from breaking the imaginary barrier dividing human from divine' (see *Love Song of the Dark Lord*, ed. and trans. by B. Stoler Miller, New York: Columbia University Press, 1977, p. 15); similarly Vidyapati's 500 love songs, composed in the fourteenth century, are 'still sung at marriages, for the love of Krishna and Rādhā was interpreted as an allegory of the love of the soul for the divine, or the love of humans for God, and construed almost as a guide to married love' (see *Love Songs of Vidyapati*, trans. by Deben Bhattacharya, ed. and intro. by W.G. Archer, London 1963, p. 55).

28. *The New Encyclopaedia Britannica* (Chicago: Helen Hemingway Benton Publisher, 1979), 17, 137.

29. Maderna's notes on the libretto of *Ausstrahlung* in the Fondo Maderna, while mentioning that the quotation in question is by Rudaki, do not, however, reveal the source of the quotation, nor of its Italian translation.

30. 'Awfi and Gerasimov's accounts of Rudaki's life are to be found at the web site http://www.angelfire.com/rnb/bashiri/Poets/Rudaki.htm/

31. To be found at source quoted in note 34.

32. *Das Rufen des Zarathustra, die Gathas des Avesta. Ein Versuch, ihren Sinn zu geben,* ed. and trans. by von Paul Eberhardt (Jena: Diederichs, 1920).

33. The *Yasna* contains the religious core of the work — a collection of songs or hymns, called the *Gāthās* — generally ascribed to Zoroaster himself. As well as the *Yasna*, there are four other sections: the *Visp-rat*, a liturgical scripture of lesser importance, containing homage to a number of Zoroastrian spiritual leaders; the *Vendidad*, consisting of Zoroastrian ritual and civil law; the *Yashts*, consisting of twenty-one sacrificial hymns to various angels (*yazatas*) and ancient heroes; and the *Khūrda Avesta*, or 'Little Avesta', a section of minor hymns and prayers for specific occasions.

34. Darmesteter, in the introduction to his French translation of the work, published in the *Annales du Musée Guimet* in 1892, claimed that Zoroaster's ideas and language were so advanced that his *Avesta* must be a forgery: 'how is one to accept that a man (Zoroaster) who lived at least six centuries before our era, far away from Greece, could have expressed his views on God and the world in philosophical language, using abstract notions which recall those of the Gnostics and the neo-Platonists? These discourses must, therefore, be forgeries composed seven or eight centuries after the time of the prophet to whom they are attributed' (Quoted in *The Hymns of Zarathustra*. A translation of the *Gāthās* together with an introduction and commentary by J. Duchesne-Guillemin. Translated from the French by M. Henning (Connecticut: Hyperion Press, Inc: 1952), pp. 2–3). Darmesteter's theory is widely referred to, but also widely discredited in scholarly works on the *Avesta*. See, for example, Duchesne-Guillemin (above), and J. H. Moulton, *Early Religious Poetry of Persia* (Cambridge: Cambridge University Press, 1911), pp. 14–16, both of whom contest the notion of the *Avesta* as a forgery.

CONCLUSION

Impacting with the central-European influences of dodecaphony, the Second Viennese and the Darmstadt Schools, as well as the radicalism of American musical inventions of the 1940s onwards, the iconoclastic music of 1960s Italy represents almost a cult phenomenon and a milestone in Italian musical history. There has been no return to conventional 'tonalism' in music, and nothing is composed in Italy today which does not take stock of the achievements of that period. Profoundly Utopian in its vision of a better world dictated, as has been shown, by spiritual and/or humanitarian principles, music in the decade in question sought to break through the bland facade of happy consensus which characterised bourgeois society, and give expression to the conflicts, uncertainties, and loss of real values which neo-capitalist ideology chose to conceal. In this sense, while being, on the one hand, in harmony with the climate of disaffection registered by students and workers in the latter part of the decade, 1960s music, on the other hand, could not have been further removed from the sense of carefree optimism enjoyed by the bourgeoisie as a result of their new found prosperity. The simpler and easier way of life generated by mass-produced goods and technological advances stood blatantly at odds with the harsh incisiveness and obtuseness of the works written by the composers dealt with in this study, who, like their Neo-Avant-garde counterparts, deliberately eschewed simplicity in favour of the difficult and the highly intellectual. Part of this difficulty lay, as has been shown, with the actual nature of the music — for example, the high jumps of register in dodecaphonic notation, the 'mathematics' of total serialism, or the indeterminacy of the aleatoric method, making pieces notoriously arduous both to write and to perform. But, as has also been illustrated, difficulty was equally inherent in the lyrics of the compositions, for the openness of Italian composers of that period to the literature of other western and eastern nationalities, ranging from Zoroastrianism of the sixth-century B. C. to James Joyce's *Ulysses*, also resulted in the most intricate of collage libretti which no simple nor superficial consideration could render either intelligible or deserving of appreciation. For just as Dallapiccola reinforced in *Ulisse* how passive, casual 'looking' is never enough to understand life, so too the works examined here may seem incomprehensible if not incoherent to any casual observer. Hopefully, however, this study has demonstrated the rich density of ideas that are to be unearthed when the reader-listener is prepared to give close scrutiny to each of the different extracts from, or inspirations behind, the libretti, and trace the often labyrinthine and cross-cultural connections and relations operating between them.

And it is not only for their density and all-embracing eclecticism that these works are to be esteemed. The public money that went into subsidizing high art may have been generated by the economic boom itself, but the emphasis on the difficult and the intricate promoted by this art kept it intentionally out of the arena of commercialism, and guaranteed that it was not in danger of becoming yet another commodity to oil the machinery of the bourgeois-capitalist system. The irony of engaging in artistic warfare against the State while obtaining funding from the State, cannot, of course, be overlooked, and part of the *malaise* expressed in the works examined derives from an awareness of this essential irony. A further contradiction lies in these anti-establishment works now being viewed as part of Italy's artistic canon. And this is more than ever the case today, when something of a cult status is being attributed to 1960s classical music and musicians in Italy. For in a twenty-first century where art and even education is becoming increasingly controlled by financial profit and gain, and little is written, performed, or taught which cannot generate gain, the indisputable anti-commercial orientation of these works makes them distinctive, unique, and commendable, and justifies the respect in which they and their composers are held.

Libretto of
Dallapiccola's *Ulisse* (1960–68)

Prologo

Primo episodio [Calypso]

Sipario. Tratto di spiaggia sull'isola Ogigia. Vasto orizzonte. Calypso è sola sulla scena e sta guardando lontano.

CALYPSO:

Son soli, un'altra volta,   il tuo cuore e il mare.
Desolata ti piange Calypso,   la dea senza amore.
Ti rivelasti a me   momorando in profondo sopore:
Guardare, meravigliarsi,   *e tornar a guardare.*
Compresi. Era menzogna   la nostalgia del figlio,
della patria, del vecchio   padre, della tua sposa:
era menzogna il pianto   che ti scendea dal ciglio,
rigandoti le guancie   e le vesti. Altra cosa
cercavi, e tal che mai   mi riuscì penetrare.
Guardare, meravigliarsi,   *e tornar a guardare.*
Immortal ti voleva,   Ulisse. Tale sorte
non accettasti. A che   il tuo cuore aspirava?
Che bramare può l'uomo   se non sfuggir la morte?
Quanto mistero nello   spirito che anelava
Guardare, meravigliarsi,   *e tornar a guardare.*
Son soli, un'altra volta,   il tuo cuore e il mare.

Cambiamento di scena

Secondo Episodio
Intermezzo sinfonico [Posidone]

Libretto of
Dallapiccola's *Ulisse* (1960–68)

Prologue

First episode [Calypso]

Curtain. A stretch of beach on the island of Ogygia. Wide horizon. Calypso is alone on the stage and gazing into the distance.

CALYPSO:

Your heart and the sea / are alone again.
The unloved goddess, / desolate Calypso, mourns you.
You revealed yourself to me, / murmuring in deep slumber:
To look, to marvel, / *and look again.*
I understood your deceit. / The nostalgia you professed for your son,
your homeland, your old / father, your wife — it was all a lie;
like the tears / that fell from your eyes,
and streamed down your cheeks / and your clothes. You were searching
for something else, something I could / never understand.

To look, to marvel, / *and look again.*
I wanted to make you immortal, / Ulysses. But you would not accept
my offer. What was your heart / aspiring to?
What can man desire / if not to escape death?
How mysterious was / your soul that yearned
To look, to marvel, / *and look again.*
Your heart and the sea / are alone again.

Scene change

Second Episode
Symphonic Intermezzo [Poseidon]

Terzo episodio [Nausicaa]

Tratto di spiaggia sull'isola dei Feaci. Boscaglia nel fondo. Le Ancelle, che hanno appena finito di lavare e di esporre al sole varie tuniche multicolori, con grida di gioia, si apprestano al gioco della palla. Nausicaa è sdraiata sulla spiaggia in disparte; quasi assente.

(Il gioco della palla si svolge intercalato da grida di gioia delle Ancelle. Finito il gioco, queste si volgono a Nausicaa).

ANCELLE:
    Nausicaa! Nausicaa!
I ANCELLA:
    Tu, la più gaia e ciarliera tra noi,
    come e perchè quest'oggi
    sei così appartata e silenziosa?
NAUSICAA:
    Amiche, ho fatto un sogno così strano...
    ne son felice, ma tanto turbata....
II ANCELLA:
    Turbata perchè mai?
NAUSICAA:
    Tu m'apparivi
    nel sonno e m'annunciavi
    prossime nozze....
ANCELLE:
    Nausicaa! Qual sogno...
I ANCELLA:
    Come può un sogno sì bello turbare?
NAUSICAA:
    Ho veduto lo sposo in sogno
    e m'ha parlato.
I ANCELLA:
    Quale egli era dei nobili Feaci?
NAUSICAA:
    Non era uno dei nostri.
ANCELLE:
    Era un eroe? Un principe?
I ANCELLA:
    Era un Re?
NAUSICAA (trasognata)
    Non so chi fosse..
I ANCELLA:
    Non sai chi fosse.. E quale aspetto aveva?

Third Episode [Nausicaa]

A stretch of beach on the island of the Phaeacians. A wood in the background. The maidservants, who have just finished washing various multicoloured tunics and laying them out in the sun, get ready with joyful cries for a ball game. Nausicaa lies stretched out on the beach, apart from the others and lost in thought.

(The ball game takes place, interspersed with the joyful cries of the maidservants. Their game over, they turn to Nausicaa.)

MAIDSERVANTS:
> Nausicaa! Nausicaa!

FIRST MAIDSERVANT:
> You, the gayest and most talkative among us,
> how and why today
> are you so withdrawn and silent?

NAUSICAA:
> My dear friends, I had such a strange dream...
> it made me happy, but also troubled me...

SECOND MAIDSERVANT:
> It troubled you ? But why?

NAUSICAA:
> You appeared to me
> in the dream, and you announced
> that I would be marrying soon...

MAIDSERVANTS:
> Nausicaa! What a dream...

FIRST MAIDSERVANT:
> How could such a lovely dream disturb you?

NAUSICAA:
> I saw my bridegroom in the dream,
> and he spoke to me

FIRST MAIDSERVANT:
> Which of our noble Phaeacians was he?

NAUSICAA:
> He was not one of our people.

MAIDSERVANTS:
> Was he a hero? A prince?

FIRST MAIDSERVANT:
> Was he a King?

NAUSICAA *(dreamily)*
> I do not know who he was...

FIRST MAIDSERVANT:
> You do not know who he was... And what did he look like?

Nausicaa:

>Occhi fondi, provati dal dolore
>un volto che sembrava quel d'un Dio
>aveva l'uomo venuto a me dal mare.
>Guardava al cielo, in alto, interrogante.
>Chi era? Che cercava ? 'O creatura,
>— mi disse — luce sei che squarcia un velo
>di fitte nubi; bianco giglio sei
>sull'acque in furia: vollero gli Dei
>far di te rosa sorta in mezzo al gelo
>d'inverno'. Tutto intorno la natura
>taceva. Ed io tacevo, trepidante.
>Ero così felice di sognare.
>Scomparve. Non ci fu neanche un addio.
>Ditemi, amiche, è forse ciò l'amore ?
>(Rimane assorta)

Ancelle (cercando di richiamare Nausicaa alla realtà):

>Nausicaa! Nausicaa!

I Ancella:

>Strana, fanciulla, la tua domanda!
>Son fole i sogni: rimani serena...

Ancelle:

>Nausicaa! Con noi gioca!

(Nausicaa si unisce al gruppo delle ancelle: viene ripreso il gioco della palla. La palla arriva a Nausicaa; questa la respinge con violenza maldestra, tanto da farla finire nella boscaglia. Al limitare di questa appare Ulisse, sommariamente coperto di frasche: due ancelle in fretta gli mettono indosso una tunica).

Nausicaa (fra sè; trasognata):

>Era questo lo sposo che ho sognato...

(Ulisse avanza di qualche passo... Si ferma)

Ulisse:

>Nell'uomo scrutar volli il bene e il male.
>Questi occhi il mondo e i prodigi suoi
>han contemplato. Ma una volta sola
>miracolo m'apparve che simile
>fosse alla tua bellezza.

Nausicaa (come sopra):

>Ancor sognare
>desidero...

NAUSICAA:

>The man who came to me from the sea
>had deep eyes, wearied by grief,
>and a face like a God.
>He gazed upwards to the heavens, as if questioning.
>Who was he? What was he looking for? 'O lovely being',
>he said to me, 'You are sunlight that pierces a veil
>of thick clouds; you are a white lily
>on turbulent waters; the Gods ordained you
>to be a rose blooming among the frosts of winter'.
>Nature fell silent all around.
>And I too was silent, and trembling.
>I was so happy to be dreaming.
>He disappeared. There was not even a word of farewell.
>Tell me then, my friends, can this be love?
>*(She remains lost in thought.)*

MAIDSERVANTS *(trying to summon Nausicaa back to reality)*

>Nausicaa! Nausicaa!

FIRST MAIDSERVANT:

>Young girl, what a strange question you ask us!
>Dreams are fairy-tales: be calm and forget them...

MAIDSERVANTS:

>Nausicaa! Come and play with us!

(Nausicaa joins the group of maidservants: they start to play with the ball again. The ball is thrown to Nausicaa, and she knocks it away with clumsy violence, so that it ends up in the wood. Ulysses, scantily covered by leafy branches, appears at the edge of the wood: two maidservants hastily throw a tunic over him.)

NAUSICAA *(to herself, dreamily)*:

>This is the bridegroom I dreamed of ...

(Ulysses takes few steps forward....and stops.)

ULYSSES:

>I wanted to study good and evil in mankind.
>These eyes have seen the world
>and all of its marvels. Yet only once
>did I see a miracle that could compare
>with your beauty.

NAUSICAA *(as above)*:

>O let me still
>dream...

Ulisse (che si era interrotto come per richiamare un ricordo):
>   Di palma agile stelo
>   — il vedo! — sorgea da terra all'ara accanto
>   d'Apollo, in Delo. Per la meraviglia
>   tremò il mio spirto. Tu, cui niun somiglia,
>   provar mi fai d'allor lo stesso incanto.
>   Vive Artemide nel tuo bianco velo?

Nausicaa (c.s):
>   È lui che in sogno a me venìa dal mare...

Ulisse:
>   Chi in te si cela con arte sottile?

Nausicaa (c.s)
>   Odo la voce sua, la sua parola...

Ulisse:
>   Da quali cieli sei discesa a noi ?
>   Mi prostro a te, sia tu Dea o mortale.
>   (Si prostra ai pedi di Nausicaa)

Nausicaa:
>   Ti prostrerai dinanzi al Re mio padre.
>   T'alza, Straniero, e segui i passi miei.

(Ulisse si alza. A poco a poco la scena si oscura e si vuota lentamente. Le Ancelle si avviano all'uscita, seguite da Nausicaa. Da ultimo, Ulisse)

Sipario

FINE DEL PROLOGO

ULYSSES (*who had broken off, as if trying to recall a memory*):
> The pliant stem of a palm tree —
> I can see it now! — rose up from the earth by the altar of the temple
> of Apollo in Delos. My soul trembled
> at such a wondrous sight. You, whose beauty is peerless,
> you awaken in my soul that same enchantment.
> Does Artemis herself inhabit your white veil?

NAUSICAA (*as before*):
> It is he who came to me in a dream from the sea...

ULYSSES:
> Who hides in you with subtle magic?

NAUSICAA (*as before*)
> I hear his voice, his words...

ULYSSES:
> From what heaven have you descended to us?
> I kneel before you, be you Goddess or mortal.
> (*He kneels before Nausicaa's feet*)]

NAUSICAA:
> You will kneel before my father, the King.
> Arise, stranger, and follow me.

(*Ulysses rises. The stage slowly darkens and empties. The maidservants start to leave, followed by Nausicaa. Ulysses leaves last*)

Curtain

END OF PROLOGUE

Primo Atto

Prima Scena

Sipario. Vasta sala nella reggia di Alcinoo. In fondo, il mare. Alcinoo siede a una tavola con numerosi convitati: altri stanno sparsi qua e là. Appoggiato a una colonna, alla quale è appesa una cetra, immobile, il cantore Demodoco.

ALCINOO:

Pria che sia tarda notte, Demodoco, vanto
di questa reggia, canta per noi.
È in me scolpito ancora il ricordo
di quanto altra volta il tuo canto evocava
(quasi citando; cadenzato)
'Erano calde ancora le mura di Troia
quando gli argivi eroi presero il mare
per ritrovar la patria...' Che avvenne,
che avvenne poi, Demodoco ?

CORO:

Canta, Demodoco !

DEMODOCO (visionario):

Passano innanzi agli occhi miei, che non vedono, navi gagliarde:
passano nel mio spirito, che tanto vede, lunghe vicende di orrori...

CORO:

Canta, canta, Demodoco !

ALCINOO:

Sia il tuo canto ispirato specchio di grandi eventi !

CORO:

Canta, canta, Demodoco!

(Demodoco impugna la cetra)

DEMODOCO:

Quanto sia amaro il ritorno, ogni ritorno,
era ignoto agli eroi...
Dolce come canto
è il sorriso di Clitennestra cha accoglie lo sposo: su purpurei tappeti
essa lo spinge a inceder, simile a un Dio.
(Segretamente)
Agamennone, indugi ? Perchè indugi ?
Gli occhi dell'anima mia contemplano alzata
lama lucente: la scure d'Egisto s'abbatte
sul capo dell'eroe. Sangue d'intorno ...
sangue vuol sangue e chiama altro sangue...
E dopo il sangue, il rimorso.

Act One

Scene One

Curtain. A great hall in Alcinous' palace. In the background, the sea. Alcinous is sitting at the table with numerous guests; others are standing scattered here and there. Leaning motionless against a pillar, on which hangs his lyre, the bard Demodocus.

ALCINOUS:

> Before night falls upon us, Demodocus,
> sing for us the glory of this kingdom.
> The memory of all your song evoked last time
> is still engraved in me:
> (*almost quoting; sung in cadences*)
> 'The walls of Troy were still hot from burning,
> when the Grecian heroes took to the sea,
> to reach once again their nativeland...' What happened,
> what happened then, Demodocus?

CHOIR:

> Sing, Demodocus!

DEMODOCUS (*in a visionary trance*):

> Before my sightless eyes, proud ships pass by;
> before my spirit which sees so much, endless horrors...

CHOIR:

> Sing, Demodocus! Sing!

ALCINOUS:

> And may your inspired song mirror great adventures!

CHOIR:

> Sing, Demodocus! Sing!

(Demodocus seizes the lyre)

DEMODOCUS:

> None of the heroes knew how bitter was to be their returning,
> each man's returning...
> As sweet as song
> is the smile of Clytemnestra, welcoming her husband: on purple carpets
> she urges him to enter like a God.
> (*Secretly*)
> Agamemnon, do you hesitate? Why do you hesitate?
> My inner sight can see a shining
> blade lifted on high; the axe of Aegisthus falls down
> on the head of the hero. Blood all around...
> bloodshed claims bloodshed, and calls for more bloodshed.
> And after the blood, remorse.

(Alle parole 'sangue d'intorno', — prima apparizione del 'ritmo principale'- Ulisse
è entrato in scena, seguìto da Nausicaa e da alcune Ancelle. Nausicaa si siede quasi
al riparo di una colonna; Ulisse in modo da essere ben visibile al Re Alcinoo)

Demodoco:
>   Forse men crudo il fato d'Ulisse che, su tre navi
>   nere, Ilio lasciò, coi fidi compagni.
>   Chi mai può dire quando, dove,
>   chi può dir come perì?
>   Nei gorghi cupi lo volle forse il Dio del mare.
>   Fu risparmiato lo strazio al fiero suo cuore
>   di tornare alla reggia, ove nessuno
>   piú l'avrìa conosciuto...

(Ulisse, che avrà seguito la narrazione di Demodoco con emozione crescente, si
copre gli occhi e piange)

Coro:
>   Nessuno,
>   Nessuno...

Demodoco:
>   ...ove il suo grande oprare
>   non rammenta nessuno...

Coro (c.s):
>   Nessuno,
>   Nessuno...

Demodoco:
>   Ove il suo arco glorioso
>   non doma ormai nessuno.

(Ulisse alza il capo e guarda a lungo Demodoco)

Demodoco (stende il braccio destro verso Ulisse)
>   Solo gli Aedi san chi tu fosti, Ulisse.

(Ulisse riabbassa il capo: si copre gli occhi).

>   Io, Demodoco,
>   verso la vasta mobile tomba ove tu giaci
>   lancio il mio canto commosso. Non dire, Ulisse,
>   che sulla terra non ti ricorda nessuno.

(Depone la cetra)

(On the words 'Blood everywhere', there is the first appearance of the 'principal rhythm', and Ulysses enters, followed by Nausicaa and a few maidservants. Nausicaa sits down, almost half hidden behind a pillar; Ulysses sits down, fully visible to King Alcinous)

DEMODOCUS:

> Perhaps less harsh was the fate of Ulysses, who, with his faithful companions,
> left Ilium with three black ships.
> Who can say when and where he died;
> who can say how?
> Perhaps the God of the sea called him down to his dark vortexes.
> His proud heart was spared the torment
> of returning to his kingdom, where nobody
> would have recognized him any more...

(Ulysses, who has followed the narration of Demodocus with growing emotion, covers his eyes and weeps)

CHOIR:

> Nobody,
> nobody...

DEMODOCUS:

> ...where his great achievements
> are remembered by nobody

CHOIR (*as above*):

> Nobody,
> nobody...

DEMODOCUS:

> Where no one can master
> his glorious bow

(Ulysses raises his head and looks for a long time at Demodocus)

DEMODOCUS (*stretches his right arm toward Ulysses*):

> Only the Poets know who you once were, Ulysses.

(Ulysses lowers his head again and covers his eyes.)

> I, Demodocus,
> send my heartfelt song
> over the vast and restless waters which entomb you.
> Do not say, Ulysses, that no one remembers you on earth.

(Puts down his lyre)

CORO:

> Sembrava un Nume dettare a te il volo del canto!
> In te spirava il soffio d'Apollo, Demodoco insigne.

ALCINOO (si alza e muove qualche passo verso Ulisse):

> T'ho osservato, Straniero. Mentre l'Aedo cantava,
> lacrime fitte ti rigavan le gote.
> Quale angoscia t'opprime ? E dimmi
> qual'è il tuo nome?

ULISSE (si alza):

> Odio, affanno, desìo di vendetta: questo,
> questo è il mio nome. Io sono... Ulisse.

CORO:

> Ulisse! Ulisse!

ULISSE:

> Eroe glorioso fui: ora son polvere.
> Sovrano, or mi vedete ramingare...

CORO:

> Ulisse! Ulisse!

ULISSE (fra sè):

> Ch'io sia forse... Nessuno?

(In scena la luce si abbassa gradatamente)

ALCINOO (commosso):

> Grande, glorioso eroe, sii fra noi il benvenuto!
> (Con semplicità)
> Vorresti dirci dove
> il destino ti trasse per tant'anni ?

ULISSE:

> M'ascoltate.

Cambiamento di scena

I COMPAGNI DI ULISSE (CORO):

> Terra! Terra! Terra! Ter-...
> Non è la terra che si sta cercando...
> Non è la terra che ci può dar pace...

CHOIR:

      Your winged verses seem to be inspired by a God!

      Apollo's breath breathes within you, renowned Demodocus.

ALCINOUS (*standing up and taking a few steps toward Ulysses*):

      I have observed you, stranger. While our bard was singing,

      heavy tears streamed down your cheeks.

      What anguish grieves you? And tell me,

      what is your name?

ULYSSES (*standing up*):

      Hatred, heartbreak, and hunger for vengeance: these,

      these are my names. I am...Ulysses.

CHOIR:

      Ulysses! Ulysses!

ULYSSES:

      I once was a famous hero: now I am dust.

      I once was a king; now you see before you a wanderer...

CHOIR:

      Ulysses! Ulysses!

ULYSSES (*to himself*):

      Perhaps I am... Nobody?

(The light on stage gradually fades)

ALCINOUS (*moved*):

      Great and glorious hero, you are welcome among us here!

      (*Simply.*)

      Please tell us where

      destiny drove you for so many years.

ULYSSES:

      Listen to me

Scene change

ULYSSES'S COMPANIONS (CHOIR):

      Land ahoy! Land ahoy! Land ahoy! Land! ...

      It is not the land we are searching for...

      It is not the land that can give us peace...

Seconda Scena [I Lotofagi]

Tratto di spiaggia. Collina a destra. La nave di Ulisse sta per approdare. Sulla tolda Ulisse e i suoi compagni. È il mattino.

Ulisse (arditamente):
>   Coraggio, amici! Quest'onda che monta
>   è per noi segno di salvezza...

Coro (con violenza):
>   Ulisse !
>   Uomo di corta memoria, scordasti
>   presto le acute zagaglie dei Cìconi:
>   presto i compagni trafitti copristi d'oblìo...

Ulisse (calmo):
>   Nulla scordai...

Coro (c.s):
>   Non rammenti,
>   alti come la vetta di un monte,
>   i feroci Lestrìgoni ?
>   Non ricordi il Ciclope
>   urlante lapidar le nostre navi ?

Ulisse (calmissimo):
>   Nulla, nulla scordai.
>   (Vibrante)
>   Voi..., non scordate che legati siamo
>   e per la vita e per la morte.

Coro:
>   Ulisse!
>   Da troppo tempo, troppo ci torturi

Ulisse (insinuante):
>   È una tortura per le vostre nari
>   l'odor del mare ?

Coro:
>   D'Itaca le zolle
>   diversamente odorano!

Ulisse:
>   È tortura
>   del mar udir le mille voci ?

Coro:
>   Itaca!
>   Questa, questa è del mar la sola voce!

Ulisse:
>   Forse..., forse è tortura anche guardare?

Scene Two [The Lotus-Eaters]

A stretch of beach. To the right, a hill. Ulysses's ship is about to land. Ulysses and his companions are on deck. It is morning.

ULYSSES (*boldly*):
>Have courage, my friends! This mounting wave
>must surely bring us to salvation!

CHOIR (*violently*):
>Ulysses!
>Man of short memory, you soon forgot
>the sharp spears of the Cicones;
>you soon let your murdered comrades sink into oblivion...

ULYSSES (*calmly*):
>I forgot nothing...

CHOIR (*as above*):
>Do you not remember
>the ferocious Laestrigones,
>towering high as the peak of a mountain?
>Do you not remember the Cyclops
>roaring, as he hurled his rocks at our ships?

ULYSSES (*very calm*):
>Nothing, I have forgotten nothing.
>(*Forcefully*)
>You too..., do not forget that we are bound together
>for the whole of life and the whole of death.

CHOIR:
>Ulysses!
>We have suffered under you for too long, for far too long.

ULYSSES (*wheedling*):
>Do you suffer when you smell
>the scent of the sea?

CHOIR:
>The turf of Ithaca
>has a different smell!

ULYSSES:
>Do you suffer
>when you hear the thousand voices of the sea?

CHOIR:
>Ithaca!
>That, that is the only word the waves call out to us!

ULYSSES:
>Perhaps..., perhaps you suffer even to look?

Coro:

    Troppo questi occhi hanno veduto....

Ulisse (molto teso):

    Allora

    ditemi pure ch' è tortura essere uomini!

(Dall'interno, molto in lontananza, si odono delle voci chiare)

I Lotofagi:

    La luna piena sopra la valle,

    il sole, perenne, nel cielo...

Ulisse:

    Ascoltate..., approdiamo.

I Lotofagi:

    ...ruscelli che scorrono cantando...

    La loro musica scende

    qual sonno, da cieli beati,

    su noi, sulle palpebre stanche,

    sui nostri stanchi occhi...

    (Entrando in scena)

    Felici noi siamo...

(Fanno un gesto di stupore nel vedere Ulisse e i suoi Compagni)

    Chi siete ? Donde venite ?

    Come il dolore vi ha segnato i volti...

Ulisse (cupo):

    Andiam sul mare per trovare la patria.

I Lotofagi:

    La patria ? Che cos'è ?

Ulisse:

    Vogliam tornare là, dove siam nati,

    a dissodare la nost'aspra terra

    che con tanta fatica ci dà frutto.

I Lotofagi:

    Tanta fatica ? Perchè faticare ?

(Cominciano una vera e propria scena di seduzione, che andrà aumentando gradatamente)

    La nostra terra ci dona dei frutti:

    prendètene con noi..., senza destino

    vi sentirete, inconsciamente lieti,

    come quando, bambini, dormivate.

CHOIR:
>Our eyes already have seen too much...

ULYSSES (*very tense*)
>Then
>tell me that you even suffer to be men!

(From off-stage, clear voices can be heard, very far away)

LOTUS-EATERS:
>The full moon hanging over the valley;
>the sun for ever in the sky...

ULYSSES:
>Listen..., let us go ashore.

LOTUS-EATERS:
>...streams that sing as they flow...
>Their music descends
>from blissful skies like slumber upon us,
>upon our weary eyelids,
>our weary eyes...
>*(Entering)*
>How happy we are ...

(They make a gesture of astonishment on seeing Ulysses and his companions)

>Who are you? Where have you come from?
>How your faces are scarred by sorrow...

ULYSSES (*darkly*):
>We are sailing the ocean to find our homeland.

LOTUS-EATERS:
>Your homeland? What is that?

ULYSSES:
>We want to return to where we were born,
>to till the harsh soil,
>and to harvest the fruits of our great labours.

LOTUS-EATERS:
>Of your great labours? But why should you labour?

(The Lotus-eaters begin a real seduction-scene, gradually heightening in intensity.)

>Our land gives us plentiful fruit:
>come share it with us..., you will feel
>free from destiny, unconsciously happy,
>like when babies you lay asleep.

ULISSE:

> Compagni! Non prendete di quel frutto!

(I Lotofagi sembreranno ignorare sia questo che i due successivi interventi di Ulisse)

I LOTOFAGI:

> Quanto son tormentati i vostri volti!
> Guardate i nostri come son sereni...

ULISSE:

> Amici! Ve ne supplico!

I LOTOFAGI:

> Vivrete senza tèma del futuro,
> senza rimpianto per ciò ch'è
> passato...

ULISSE

> Ascoltatemi!

I LOTOFAGI:

> ...senza sapere che cos'è dolore,
> senza sapere che cos'è la morte.

(Alcuni compagni di Ulisse appaiono vinti: si staccano dal gruppo..., prendono il frutto... e si uniscono, sorridenti, ai Lotofagi)

ULISSE (prorompendo):

> Perduti! Sciagurati!
> Uomini non siete!

(Volgendosi di scatto ai compagni rimasti nel suo gruppo)

> Seguìtemi!

(Risalgono in fretta sulla nave)

I LOTOFAGI:

> La luna piena sopra la valle,
> il sole, perenne, nel cielo,
> ruscelli che scorrono cantando...

Cambiamento di Scena

ULYSSES:

    Companions! Do not touch that fruit!

(The Lotus-eaters seem to ignore completely both this and the later interventions of Ulysses)

LOTUS-EATERS:

    How full of torment are your faces!
    Look at ours, how serene they are...

ULYSSES:

    My friends! I implore you!

LOTUS-EATERS:

    You shall live without fearing the future,
    with no regret for the
    past...

ULYSSES

    Listen to me!

LOTUS-EATERS:

    ...without knowing what suffering is;
    without knowing what death is.

(Some of Ulysses's companions appear to have been won over: they move away from the rest..., accept the fruit... and, smiling, join the Lotus-eaters)

ULYSSES *(in an outburst)*:

    You are lost! Foolish wretches!
    You are not men!

(Suddenly turning to the men who have stayed in his group)

    Follow me!

(They hastily re-embark)

LOTUS-EATERS:

    The full moon hanging over the valley;
    the sun for ever in the sky;
    streams that sing as they flow...

Scene change

Terza Scena [Circe]

Lussureggiante paesaggio sull'isola Eèa. Ulisse, in piedi, sta contemplando il mare.
Non lontana da lui, addormentata sull'erba, Circe. È il meriggio.

Ulisse (fra sè, mormorando):
    Guardare, meravigliarsi, e tornare a guardare...
Circe (scuotendosi):
    T'ho udito un'altra volta mormorare
    queste stesse parole...
Ulisse (deciso):
    Circe, debbo
    tornar sul mare...
Circe:
    No! Con me rimani,
    Ulisse...
Ulisse:
    Nuovo tormento sorge
    in me col sorgere di ogni giorno...
Circe:
    No!
    Rimani, Ulisse...
Ulisse (visionario):
    Trascorso è piú di un anno...
    il mare mi richiama a sè; mi vuole...
Circe (fra sè, mormorando):
    Il mare...
    Trascorso è piú di un anno...
    (Come da lontano)
     A me venisti quando
    rari fili d'argento — Ulisse, ancora
    non li avevi notati! —
    s'insinuavano in mezzo ai tuoi capelli.
    (Con espressione molto piú terrena)
    Quanto imperfette furono le donne
    che conoscesti pria di me! Non una
    ti disse mai che l'uomo dai capelli
    grigi abbisogna d'una nuova madre.
    Son io, che con pazienza, con amore,
    un'altra vita, un'altra giovinezza
    ti ho dato...
    (gesto di Ulisse)
    — Nol negare! —
    e un'altra conoscenza.

Scene Three [Circe]

Luxuriant landscape on the island of Aeaea. Ulysses stands contemplating the sea. Near him, sleeping on the grass, is Circe. It is mid-day.

ULYSSES (*murmuring to himself*):
>To look, to marvel, and look again...

CIRCE (*awakening*):
>I have heard you murmur
>these same words before...

ULYSSES (*resolutely*):
>Circe, I must
>return to sea...

CIRCE:
>No! Stay with me,
>Ulysses...

ULYSSES:
>A new pain wells up
>in me with each new day break...

CIRCE:
>No!
>Stay, Ulysses...

ULYSSES (*in a visionary trance*):
>Almost a year has passed...
>the sea is calling me again; it wants me...

CIRCE (*murmuring to herself*):
>The sea ...
>More than a year has passed ...
>(*As if from afar*)
>You came to me when
>a few threads of silver — Ulysses,
>at that time you had not even noticed! —
>were creeping in amongst your hair.
>(*Much more earthy in tone*)
>How imperfect were the women
>you knew before me! Not one of them
>ever told you that the man whose hair is turning
>grey needs a new mother.
>It was I who, with patience and love,
>gave you
>a new life, a new youth...
>(*Ulysses makes a gesture*)
>and — don't deny it! —
>a new consciousness.

Ulisse (oscuro):

 Per me, Circe, tu fosti ognor mistero.
 Non conosco il tuo volto!

Circe (carezzevole):

 Ha un volto solo
 il mare che tant'ami?

Ulisse:

 Non ricordo il colore dei tuoi occhi
 se da te m'allontano...

Circe (sempre piú insinuante):

 Di che colore è l'onda
 che a sé ti attira?

Ulisse:

 Il tuo sguardo mi sembra inafferrabile...

Circe:

 Assai meno mutevole,
 del mare che ti chiama, che ti vuole...

(Si avvicina a Ulisse per abbracciarlo)

 (con passione)
 Ulisse! Vieni a me, Ulisse! Vieni!

Ulisse

 Non piú.

Circe (molto tesa):

 Ma non mi temi?

Ulisse:

 Il richiamo del mare è assai piú forte
 della minaccia, della seduzione.

Circe:

 Ulisse, tu da me tanto apprendesti.
 Accogli ancor l'insegnamento estremo,
 che valga a suggellare il nostro addio.
 Non avresti incontrati, Ulisse, mai
 Ciclopi nè Lestrìgoni,
 se non li avessi avuti già nel cuore.

Ulisse (gridato):

 Circe!

Circe:

 Il tuo cuor, le cui pieghe conosco,
 anche le piú recondite,
 altri mostri racchiude,
 che contro te s'ergeranno dall'onde ...

Ulisse (c.s):

 Taci!

ULYSSES (*darkly*):
>   You have always be an mystery to me, Circe.
>   I do not recognize your face!

CIRCE (*caressingly*):
>   Does the sea you love so much
>   have only one face?

ULYSSES:
>   If I leave you
>   I will not remember the colour of your eyes ...

CIRCE (*more and more persuasively*):
>   What colour is the wave
>   which attracts you?

ULYSSES:
>   Your gaze is elusive...

CIRCE:
>   Much less changeable
>   than that of the sea which calls you, which wants you ...

(She approaches Ulysses to embrace him)

>   (*passionately*)
>   Ulysses! Come to me, Ulysses! Come!

ULYSSES:
>   No more

CIRCE (*very tense*):
>   But do you not fear me?

ULYSSES:
>   The call of the sea is much stronger
>   than threat and seduction.

CIRCE:
>   Ulysses, you have learned a lot from me.
>   Accept one last lesson from me,
>   worthy of sealing our parting.
>   Ulysses, you would never have met
>   Cyclops nor Laestrigones,
>   had you not already possessed them in your heart.

ULYSSES (*crying out*):
>   Circe!

CIRCE:
>   In your heart, whose recesses I know
>   — even its most secret ones —
>   there lurk other monsters
>   which will rise up out of the waves against you...

ULYSSES (*as above*):
>   Be quiet!

CIRCE:

> In Itaca invan cercherà pace
> il tuo cuor tormentato,
> e ancor ti spingerà sul vasto mare...
> ancora, ancora...
> sino all'ultimo giorno. Parti, Ulisse.
> Non temere che scagli sul tuo legno
> folgori, o che scateni tempeste:
> porti in te stesso tutte le tempeste;
> (rimanendo paurosamente immobile)
> e la coscienza d'esse che ti ho dato
> sia la vendetta della Maga.
> (Si scuote)
> L'ultima donna che nominerai
> son io.
> (appassionato)
> Ulisse !
> (Subito con un altro tono)
> Dimmi...,
> (Con raffinata, perfida dolcezza)
> dimmi, non ti sembra
> sul mar d'udir cantare le Sirene ?

Cambiamento di scena

CIRCE:

Your tormented heart
will search in vain for peace in Ithaca,
and will drive you out onto the vast sea again ...
and again and again ...
until your final day. Go, Ulysses.
Do not fear that I shall hurl lightning
at your ship or unleash tempests on you:
you carry the tempests within yourself;
(*keeping frighteningly still*)
and may this awareness of them that I have now given you
be the revenge of the Sorceress.
(*rousing herself*)
I will be
the last woman you will name.
(*passionately*)
Ulysses!
(*suddenly in a different tone*)
Tell me ...,
(*with subtle, treacherous sweetness*)
tell me, can't you seem
to hear the Sirens sing out at sea?

Scene change

Quarta Scena [Il Regno dei Cimmerî]

(Gli altoparlanti trasmettono nella sala i due Cori come provenienti da direzioni opposte)

LE OMBRE (Voci interne):

>   Lacrime ...
>   Pianto, rimorso, eterno soffrire ...
>   Pianto, lacrime ...
>   Sempre il buio; mai la luce ...
>   Sempre soffrire; mai sperare ...
>   Oppressi dal passato
>   siamo genti senza futuro.

L'Ade. La scena è popolata di Ombre. È notte. Unica luce, di tanto in tanto, il riflesso della luna su uno dei tanti fiumi infernali.

CORO:

>   Sempre soffrire; mai sperare...
>   Sempre! Mai !

(Ulisse e alcuni dei suoi Compagni entrano in scena. Con le spade cominciano a scavare una fossa)

CORO:

>   Ritmo eterno dei fiumi d'Averno,
>   onde che frangonsi sulla scogliera,
>   dirci sembrate con voce tremenda:
>   Sempre! Mai!

(Appena in questo momento le Ombre sembrano accorgersi della presenza di Ulisse e dei suoi Compagni)

>   Chi sono quell'Ombre ?
>   Versano latte, versano miele,
>   versano vino soave,
>   fresc'acqua versano...
>   Di farina cospargono la fossa...
>   Non son Ombre! Son Uomini!
>   Sgozzan l'agnello! Ne sprizza il sangue!
>   Soltanto il sangue a noi può dar parvenza di vita:
>   il sangue, il sangue ...
>   A noi, che tanto sangue vedemmo lassú sulla terra,
>   a noi, che tanto sangue spargemmo,
>   pria di cadere nel nostro stesso sangue.

Scene Four [The Kingdom of the Cimmerians]

(The loudspeakers are to relay the sound of the two choirs in the auditorium as if coming from opposite directions.)

THE SHADES (*Off-stage voices*):
> Tears ...
> weeping, repenting, eternal suffering ...
> weeping, tears ...
> For ever the darkness; never the light ...
> Always suffering; never to hope ...
> Oppressed by the past,
> we are people without a future.

Hades. The stage is filled with shades. It is night-time. The only light is that which comes intermittently from the reflection of the moon on one of the many infernal rivers.

CHOIR:
> Always suffering; never to hope ...
> Always! Never!

(Ulysses and some of his companions enter on stage. They begin to dig a trench with their swords)

CHOIR:
> Eternal rhythm of the rivers of Hell,
> waves breaking on the reef;
> your terrifying voice seems to say:
> Always! Never!

(Only now do the Shades seem to be aware of the presence of Ulysses and his Companions)

> Who are those Shades?
> They are pouring out milk and honey;
> they are pouring sweet wine,
> fresh water ...
> They are scattering flour in the ditch ...
> They are not Shades! They are men!
> They are slaughtering a lamb! The blood is spurting from it!
> Only blood can give us the semblance of life:
> blood, blood ...
> we who saw so much bloodshed up on earth,
> we who shed so much blood
> before dying by that same bloodshed.

(Le Ombre sembrano rivolgere intensa attenzione a Ulisse)

Coro:

>   Chi sei, Straniero?
>   Tu, vivo, in questo regno di dolore?
>   Chi sei? Che cerchi?

Ulisse:

>   Tiresia, il vate, vo' interrogare:
>   da lui saper bramo
>   qual destino mi attende.

Coro:

>   Chi sei?

Ulisse:

>   Perchè dirvi il mio nome?

(Un volto di donna appare con particolare rilievo in mezzo alle Ombre: Ulisse sembra non accorgesene)

La Madre (Anticleia):

>   Figlio!
>   (Ulisse si volge di scatto nella direzione della voce)
>   Mio figlio!

Ulisse (quasi senza fiato):

>   Questa voce... No...
>   (A poco a poco le Ombre scompaiono)
>   No, Madre: non pensavo
>   di ritrovarti in questo regno pallido...
>   Ti credevo nell'isola petrosa,
>   nell'angolo del mondo a me piú caro...

La Madre:

>   Itaca ...No ... Tanti la morte coglie
>   con levità e li porta all'altra riva
>   liberi da inquietudini e da dubbi:
>   e gli occhi loro niuno chiuder deve
>   perchè il sonno li chiuse dolcemente ...

Ulisse:

>   Ancora ..., parla ancora...

La Madre:

>   Non fu così per me, figliolo mio:
>   L'ansia, l'affanno per te che il destino
>   spingeva lontano sul mare; l'angoscia
>   struggente per te che il mio cuore sentiva in periglio ...
>   e l'accorato amor che a te portai
>   il mio corpo distrussero.
>   Vedi, men' venni nel regno dell'Ombre,

(The Shades seem to pay great attention to Ulysses)

CHOIR:
>Who are you, Stranger?
>How are you alive in this realm of grief?
>Who are you? What are you searching for?

ULYSSES:
>I want to question Tiresias, the prophet:
>I wish to learn from him
>what destiny has in store for me.

CHOIR:
>Who are you?

ULYSSES:
>Why should I tell you my name?

(The face of a woman stands out among the Shades. Ulysses seems not to notice)

MOTHER (Anticleia):
>Son!
>*(Ulysses turns suddenly in the direction of the voice)*
>My son!

ULYSSES *(almost breathlessly)*
>That voice ...No...
>*(Little by little the Shades disappear)*
>No, Mother: I did not expect
>to find you in this pale realm ...
>I thought you were still on that stony island
>in the corner of the world so dear to me ...

MOTHER:
>Ithaca ... No ... Death carries away many
>gently, and brings them to that other shore
>free from worries and doubts;
>and no one has to close their eyes
>because sleep closed them sweetly ...

ULYSSES:
>Talk ..., keep talking ...

MOTHER:
>It was not like that for me, my son:
>Torment and heartache for you whom destiny
>had driven far over the sea;
>consuming anguish for you whom my heart felt to be in danger ...
>and the desperate love I bore you
>— all of this destroyed me.
>You see, that is how I entered the kingdom of the Shades,

in questo desolato paesaggio,
popolato
d'alberi solitari, di vastissimi fiumi:
là, dove oltre il prato
degli asfodeli pallidi,
s'apre nera, paurosa, la porta dell'Ade.

LE OMBRE:

Pianto ..., lacrime..., rimorso ...

ULISSE:

Pria di cader per sempre
in questo regno oscuro,
che la vicenda ignora
delle stagioni, o Madre,
ti vo' abbracciare!

(muove qualche passo verso la Madre: l'Ombra si allontana)

LA MADRE:

Figlio!
Come ignori la sorte dell'uomo che scende sottoterra ...

CORO: (lontanissimo):

Ritmo eterno dei fiumi d'Averno ...

LA MADRE:

Ombre noi siamo: vaghiamo per l'etere simili a sogno ...

CORO (c.s.):

Onde che frangosi sulla scogliera ...

LA MADRE:

Così son sfuggita all'abbraccio, quale ombra, qual sogno ...
(con grande agitazione; paurosa)
Non odi? Non odi di là della porta
la voce ...

ULISSE:

Che dici?

LA MADRE:

... la voce che debbo seguire ...

ULISSE:

Rimani!

LA MADRE (disperatamente):

Figlio!

(L'Ombra comincia a svanire)

ULISSE (allargando le braccia):

Ah!
Solo. Son solo. Un uomo

this desolate landscape,
inhabited
only by a few lonely trees and great, wide rivers:
there, where beyond the meadow
of pale asphodels,
the gate of Hell yawns open, black and frightening

THE SHADES:
Weeping ..., tears ..., repenting ...

ULYSSES:
Before you sink for ever
into this kingdom of darkness
where seasons never
alternate, dear Mother,
I want to embrace you!

(he takes a few steps toward his mother; the Shade moves away)

MOTHER:
My son!
How ignorant you are of the fate of man who descends below earth ...]

CHOIR (*from very far off*):
Eternal rhythm of the rivers of Hell ...

MOTHER:
We are Shades: we wander through the ether like in a dream ...

CHOIR (*as above*):
Waves that break on the reef ...

MOTHER:
And so I have slipped out of your embrace like a shadow or a dream ...
(*with great agitation; terrified*)
Can't you hear? Can't you hear beyond the door
the voice ...

ULYSSES:
What are you saying?

MOTHER:
... the voice I must follow ...

ULYSSES:
Stay!

MOTHER (*desperately*):
My son!

(The Shade begins to disappear)

ULYSSES (*extending his arms*):
Ah!
Alone. I am alone. A man

che guarda nel fondo dell'abisso ...

(La scena si popola a poco a poco di Ombre)

(smarrito)
Chi sono? Che cerco?

Coro:

Pianto ..., Lacrime ...,
Dolore ..., Rimorso ..., Orrore ...

(Crescente movimento fra le Ombre. Esattamente sulla pausa appare l'ombra di Tiresia. Ha in mano lo scettro d'oro)

Coro

Ecco Tiresia!
Tiresia, sommo vate di Tebe,
cieco veggente più che ogni veggente:
qual'è il destino di quest'uomo?
Lacrime...
Pianto, rimorso, eterno soffrire...

Tiresia:

Ergonsi contro te mostri dall'onde:
sul tuo legno la folgore s'abbatte ...
(dolce)
D'Itaca baci il suolo, ed il figlio e la consorte ...
(con ribrezzo)
Ma quanto sangue intorno ...
Infine,
solo, ancor ti vedo ramingo sul mare:
canuto sei, canuto come il mare.
Ti cullan l'onde ...

Coro:

Ritmo eterno dei fiumi d'Averno ...

Tiresia:

Altro non vedo...
(scompare)

Cambiamento di scena

Coro:

Ritmo eterno dei fiumi d'Averno,
Onde che frangosi sulla scogliera,
dirci sembrate con voce tremenda:
Sempre! Mai!

gazing into the depths of the abyss ...

(Slowly the Shades return to fill the stage)

> (*bewildered*)
> Who am I? What am I searching for?

Choir:
> Weeping ..., Tears ...,
> Grief ..., Remorse ..., Horror ...

(The Shades start to move around more. Exactly in the rest, the shade of Tiresias appears. He carries in his hand the golden sceptre)

Choir:
> Here is Tiresias!
> Tiresias, great prophet of the Thebans,
> blind seer who sees more than the sighted:
> what is this man's destiny?
> Tears ...,
> Weeping, remorse, eternal suffering ...

Tiresias:
> Monsters rise out of the waves to attack you:
> lightning strikes on your boat ...
> (*sweetly*)
> You kiss the ground of Ithaca, and your son and your wife ...
> (*shuddering*)
> But there is so much blood around ...
> Finally,
> I see you alone again, wandering on the sea:
> your hair is white, as white as the foam of the sea.
> The waves rock you ...

Choir:
> Eternal rhythm of the rivers of Hell ...

Tiresias:
> I see nothing else ...
> (*he disappears*)

Scene change

Choir:
> Eternal rhythm of the rivers of Hell,
> waves breaking on the reef;
> your terrifying voice would seem to say:
> Always! Never!

Quinta Scena

Riappare la sala nella reggia di Alcinoo, come al principio dell'atto. I personaggi si trovano nell'identica posizione in cui li abbiamo lasciati alla fine della prima scena.

ULISSE:

    Nel mio futuro come vide chiaro
    Tiresia, il cieco tebano!
    Dal mare che ribolle
    s'ergono contro me due mostri ...

CORO:

    Cariddi!
    Scilla!

ULISSE:

    Poi,
    quando, lasciata l'isola del Sole,
    ci percosse la folgore ...

CORO:

    Infausto sonno il tuo! Di sacrilegio
    si macchiarono tutti i tuoi Compagni!

ULISSE:

    ... un altra volta, e l'ultima non fu,
    solo, disperso, ancora sul mare
    a lottar mi trovai,
    insin che un Nume
    approdare mi fe' su queste rive
    ove il più dolce dei sorrisi
    sul più puro dei volti accoglier volle
    me, fra tutti i mortali il più infelice.

ALCINOO:

    Ulisse, certo i Numi ti condussero a noi:
    e noi domani, con doni,
    ti condurremo in Itaca, tua patria.

ULISSE:

    Grazie, possente Re. Colmino i Numi
    te e la tua terra di bene.

(Le torce vengono tolte: la scena si vuota gradatamente)

(Ulisse è solo, nel mezzo della scena quasi buia. Nausicaa, rimasta finora seminascosta da una colonna, lentamente, furtivamente, muove qualche passo verso Ulisse)

Scene Five

The hall in Alcinous's palace reappears, as at the beginning of the act. The characters are in the exact same position that we left them in at the end of the first scene.

ULYSSES:
> How clearly Tiresias, the blind Theban,
> saw my future!
> From the seething waves
> two monsters rise up to attack me ...

CHOIR:
> Charybdis!
> Scylla!

ULYSSES:
> Then,
> when we had left the island of the Sun,
> lightning struck us ...

CHOIR:
> Ill-omened was that dream of yours!
> All your Companions committed a terrible sacrilege!

ULYSSES:
> ...once more, and it was not the last time,
> I found myself fighting
> alone and lost, still on the sea
> until a God
> made me land on this shore
> where I, the most wretched of all mortals,
> was welcomed by the sweetest of smiles
> on the purest of faces.

ALCINOUS:
> Ulysses, certainly the Gods led you to us:
> and we, tomorrow, will lead you back
> with gifts to Ithaca, your native land.

ULYSSES:
> Thank you, oh great King. May the Gods reward
> you and your land with every blessing.

(The torches are removed: the stage gradually empties)

(Ulysses is alone in the middle of the stage which is almost in darkness. Nausicaa, who up until now has been half hidden by a column, slowly and furtively takes a few steps toward Ulysses)

NAUSICAA (con la più grande tenerezza):
>   Straniero, che tanto hai veduto,
>   Straniero, che tanto hai sofferto ...
>   quando sarai tornato alla patria tua terra
>   pensa a me qualche volta ...

(Nausicaa tende la braccia a Ulisse e Ulisse le tende a Nausicaa; ma non si toccano nemmeno)

ULISSE:
>   Sì, Nausicaa.

FINE DEL PRIMO ATTO

NAUSICAA (*with great tenderness*):
> Stranger, who has seen so much,
> Stranger who has suffered so much ...
> when you have returned to your native land,
> think about me sometimes ...

(Nausicaa stretches out her arms to Ulysses, and Ulysses stretches out his to Nausicaa; but they do not even touch each other)

ULYSSES:
> Yes, Nausicaa.

END OF ACT ONE

Secondo Atto

Prima Scena (Itaca)

Spiazzo in mezzo alle colline. In fondo, Eumeo attizza il fuoco davanti alla sua capanna. In mezzo, al proscenio, vestito di nero, Antinoo, immobile.

Antinoo (fra sè, meditabondo):
     Nulla sul mare ...
Pisandro (entrando in fretta):
     Antinoo! Là, in fondo,
     sul lontano orizzonte
     qualcosa sembra muoversi ...
Eurimaco (entrando in fretta):
     Antinoo! Sul mare
     si profila piú chiara
     d'una nave la sagoma ...
Melanto (entrando in fretta):
     Antinoo! Le vele
     rosse ... Torna da Sparta
     la nave di Telemaco!
Melanto, Eurimaco e Pisandro:
     La nave di Telemaco!
Antinoo:
     Ma dietro al promontorio
     pronta all'attacco, attende
     la nostra nave ...
Melanto:
     Un corpo inanimato
     tra qualche giorno affiorerà dall'acque ...
Eurimaco:
     Del giovinetto il corpo, che — fedele -
     seguí suo padre nel regno dell'Ombre.
Pisandro:
     Abbiamo atteso assai. Ma questa sera
     ci siederemo piú tranquilli a mensa.
Antinoo (voltandosi di scatto verso Eumeo; imperioso)
     Eumeo!
     Nulla manchi al banchetto o son frustate!
     Nulla, ho detto, nulla.
Eumeo (che si è avvicinato timidamente ad Antinoo)
     Avrai quanto desideri, Signore,
     e forse ancor di piú ...

Act Two

Scene One (Ithaca)

An open space in the midst of hills. In the background Eumaeus is tending to the fire in front of his hut. Downstage centre, dressed all in black, Antinous stands motionless.

ANTINOUS (*to himself, meditating*):
> Nothing out at sea ...

PEISANDER (*entering hastily*):
> Antinous! There, in the background,
> on the distant horizon,
> there is something moving ...

EURYMACHUS (*entering hastily*):
> Antinous! Out at sea
> there is now a clearer
> outline of a ship ...

MELANTHO (*entering hastily*):
> Antinous! Red
> sails ... Telemachus's ship
> is returning from Sparta!

MELANTHO, EURYMACHUS and PEISANDER:
> Telemachus's ship!

ANTINOUS:
> But behind the headland,
> our ship waits,
> ready for the attack ...

MELANTHO:
> In a few days a dead body
> will appear at the surface of the water ...

EURYMACHUS:
> The body of the young boy who — faithfully —
> followed his father into the kingdom of the Shades.

PEISANDER:
> We have waited a long time. But this evening
> we will sit more peacefully at table.

ANTINOUS (*turning suddenly towards Eumaeus; in a commanding tone*):
> Eumaeus!
> See to it that our banquet lacks nothing, or fear a whipping!
> Nothing, I warn you, nothing.

EUMAEUS (*who has timidly approached Antinous*):
> You will have all that you desire, Sir,
> and perhaps even more ...

(Ad un gesto di Antinoo, Eumeo ritorna al fondo della scena)

Antinoo:

>   Si ritorni alla reggia.

(Erimaco, Pisandro e Melanto si apprestano ad uscire; ma Antinoo trattiene quest'ultima)

>   Tu, Melanto,
>   rimani un poco ancor quassù. Che nulla
>   sfugga al tuo sguardo ed al tuo orecchio. Nulla ...
>   (quasi fra sè)
>   Nulla.

(Esce, seguito da Eurimaco e da Pisandro. Melanto si avvia al pozzo per attingervi dell'acqua)

Eumeo:

>   Odio feroce aleggia d'intorno.
>   Dimmi ove sei, Ulisse,
>   sovrano giusto, sovrano amato!

(Sono entrati in scena alcuni Pastori e Contadini, che hanno deposto i loro arnesi di lavoro nella capanna di Eumeo)
(Ulisse in veste di mendicante, appare in fondo al sentiero e avanza lentamente)

Ulisse (si è fermato a qualche passo da Eumeo)

>   Uno stanco mendico
>   che tanto ha camminato,
>   vorrebbe riposarsi per brev'ora ...

Eumeo:

>   Amico, siedi, e sosta quanto vuoi.

Melanto (che non ha fatto altro se non guardare Ulisse, con curiosità non disgiunta da inquietudine — fra sè)

>   Nessuno mai vidi che avesse
>   così terribili occhi ...

Eumeo:

>   Melanto!
>   (Melanto si scuote)
>   Prepara un po' di cibo per quest'ospite ...

Melanto:

>   Questo non è il mio compito ...

(At a gesture from Antinous, Eumaeus returns upstage)

ANTINOUS:
>   Let's return to the palace.

(Eurymachus, Peisander and Melantho prepare to leave; but Antinous detains the latter.)

>   You, Melantho,
>   stay up here a little on this hill. Let nothing
>   escape your eye and your ear. Nothing ...
>   *(almost to himself)*
>   Nothing.

(He exits, followed by Eurymachus and Peisander. Melantho moves to the well to draw water)

EUMAEUS:
>   There is fierce hatred in the air.
>   Ulysses, most just and beloved king,
>   tell me where you are!

(Some Shepherds and Peasants have entered on stage, and have left their work-tools in Eumaeus's hut)
(Ulysses, dressed as a beggar, appears upstage on the path, and moves slowly downstage)

ULYSSES *(he has stopped a few paces away from Eumaeus)*:
>   May a weary beggar
>   who has walked for so long
>   rest here for a little while ...
EUMAEUS:
>   My friend, sit down, and rest as much as you like.
MELANTHO *(who has done nothing other than watch Ulysses, with a mixture of curiosity and worry — to herself)*:
>   I have never seen anyone with
>   such terrible eyes ...
EUMAEUS:
>   Melantho!
>   *(Melantho rouses herself)*
>   Prepare some food for this guest ...
MELANTHO:
>   That is not my job ...

EUMEO (con finta indifferenza)
    Sbadato!
    Dimenticavo che da tempo il tuo
    còmpito è un altro...
MELANTO (violenta):
    Come parli? Come parli, porcaro?

(Pastori e Contadini rivolgono lo sguardo alle colline)

CORO:
    Una fiamma sui monti!
    Un'altra fiamma!
    Ed una terza!
EUMEO:
    Vien dall'alto il segno!
    Sei salvo, Telemaco, sei salvo!
MELANTO (si avvicina ad Eumeo. Con tono inquisitorio):
    Perchè quei fuochi sui monti ?
EUMEO (con imbarazzo):
    Son fuochi
    di gioia ...
MELANTO:
    Di gioia?
EUMEO:
    Abbondante raccolto, quest'oggi ...
MELANTO (ripetendo, fra sè):
    Abbondante raccolto ... quest'oggi ...
    Sarà bene che scenda a valle.
    S'avvicina la notte.

(Melanto si carica un'anfora sulle spalle e s'avvia all'uscita)

EUMEO (cominciando con ira repressa e lasciandosi involontariamente trascinare):
    Scendi, scendi a valle
    e narra che sui monti
    c'è qualcun che gioisce!
    Vivere voglio sino a che non vegga
    il tuo bel collo bianco, la delizia
    dei Proci, stretto da una fune,
    sostenere il tuo corpo appeso a un ramo.
ULISSE:
    Pastor, troppo t'irrìti ... :
    Chi s'irrìta non crede alla giustizia.
EUMEO:
    Saggio, tu sei, mendico. Dimmi: dove
    tanta saggezza apprendesti?

EUMAEUS (*with feigned indifference*):
> How absent-minded of me!
> I forgot that for some time now
> your job has been quite a different one ...

MELANTHO (*violently*)
> Watch your tongue! Watch your tongue, you swineherd!

(Shepherds and Peasants turn their gaze towards the hills)

CHOIR:
> A flame on the mountains!
> Another one!
> And a third!

EUMAEUS:
> It is a sign coming from on high!
> You are safe, Telemachus, you are safe!

MELANTHO (*she approaches Eumaeus. In a persistent manner*):
> What do those fires mean on the mountain?

EUMAEUS (*embarrassedly*):
> They are a sign
> of rejoicing ...

MELANTHO:
> Rejoicing?

EUMAEUS:
> There was a full harvest today ...

MELANTHO (*repeating to herself*):
> A full harvest ... today ...
> I should go down into the valley.
> Night is falling.

(Melantho puts a pitcher on her shoulder and approaches the exit)

EUMAEUS (*beginning with repressed anger, and involuntarily letting himself be carried away*):
> Go down, go down to the valley, then,
> and tell everyone that on the mountains
> there is someone rejoicing!
> I want to live until the day I see
> your beautiful white neck, the delight
> of the Suitors, tightly bound by a rope,
> and your body dangling from the branch of a tree.

ULYSSES:
> Shepherd, you are getting too angry ... :
> He who loses his temper does not believe in justice.

EUMAEUS:
> You are a wise man, beggar. Tell me: where
> did you learn such wisdom?

Ulisse:

>Molto ho vagato sul mare.
>Il mare rende saggi ...

Eumeo (come colto da un'idea improvvisa, ma senza sottolineare):

>Il mare ...
>Dimmi se mai t'avvenne d'incontrare ...
>Un uom chiamato Ulisse ...

Ulisse:

>In un porto conobbi un di tal nome:
>anelava, dicea, di tornare in Itaca.

Eumeo:

>Son vent'anni che manca ...

Ulisse:

>Chi potrà riconoscerlo?

Eumeo:

>Nessuno.

(Ansante, entra di corsa Telemaco)

Eumeo:

>Telemaco! Telemaco! Telemaco!

Telemaco:

>Sfuggito
>sono all'agguato infame. Quanto vili
>e spregevoli sono! Tra poco, giù,
>siederò coi miei nemici a mensa.
>Mi credon morto. Attendon essi di vedere
>il mio corpo inanimato affiorare sull'acque ...

Ulisse:

>Giovane, bello al pari d'un Dio ...,
>c'è qualcun ... che ti odia?
>(dimentico per un istante che deve recitare la parte di un mendico)
>Voglio sapere dov'egli si trova ...

Eumeo (fra sè):

>Quest'ira. ..., la domanda che scoppia
>sulle sue labbra ... Quegli occhi ...
>No ... è tutta un'illusione.

Telemaco:

>Chi è quel vecchio?

Eumeo:

>Non so chi sia, nè donde venga,
>nè so che cerchi ...

Ulisse:

>Pastor, dammi un bastone.
>È ancora così lungo il mio cammino (esce)

ULYSSES:

    I have travelled the sea a lot.

    The sea makes you wise ...

EUMAEUS (*as if struck by a sudden thought, but without undue emphasis*):

    The sea ...

    Tell me, did you ever meet ....

    A man called Ulysses ...

ULYSSES:

    I met a man of that name in a port:

    he told me that he was eager to return to Ithaca.

EUMAEUS:

    He has been gone twenty years ...

ULYSSES:

    Who would be able to recognize him?

EUMAEUS:

    No one.

(*Telemachus comes running in, panting*)

EUMAEUS:

    Telemachus! Telemachus! Telemachus!

TELEMACHUS:

    I have escaped

    their treacherous ambush. How cowardly

    and contemptible they are! Soon, down there,

    I shall sit at table with my enemies.

    They think me dead. They are waiting to see

    my dead body appear on the surface of the water ...

ULYSSES:

    Young man, with features as beautiful as a God's ...,

    is there someone ... who hates you?

    (*forgetting for a second that he should play the part of a beggar*)

    I would like to know where this man can be found ...

EUMAEUS (*to himself*):

    That anger ..., the question that bursts

    from his lips ... Those eyes ...

    No ...it is all an illusion.

TELEMACHUS:

    Who is that old man?

EUMAEUS:

    I do not know who he is, nor where he comes from,

    nor what he is looking for ...

ULYSSES:

    Shepherd, give me a stick.

    My journey is still so long (*he exits*).

EUMEO (tra sè; guardando Ulisse che esce):
    Eppur ... quegli occhi ...

Cambiamento di scena

Seconda Scena

Cortile davanti alla reggia. Tra le colonne della costruzione, tende rosse, chiuse.
Una luce sarà sistemata in modo da rendere ben visibile l'arco di Ulisse, con la corda
pendula, appeso a una colonna. È notte. Una sola finestra, in alto, è illuminata
debolmente. Un braciere nell'angolo, a sinistra.
Ulisse entra lentamente ... Guarda attorno a sé ... La sua attenzione sembra essere
attratta dall'arco appeso alla colonna.

ULISSE:
    "Ma quanto sangue intorno..."
    Così mi disse il cieco Tiresia,
    là, nel profondo dell'Ade.
    Sangue non vedo ancora intorno a me:
    intorno a me vive la solitudine.
    Neppure mio figlio mi ha riconosciuto ...
    Tristezza del ritorno ...
    Ogni pianta, ogni sterpo e ogni sasso
    riconoscea sul mio cammino, e tutto
    a me parlava del tempo lontano ...
    Tristezza del ritorno ...
    Perchè, perchè volli tanto vedere?
    Perchè tutto alla mente mi ritorna?
    Perchè non volli accettare l'oblìo?
    Neppur mio figlio mi ha riconosciuto ...

(Dall'interno, come proveniente dalla finestra illuminata, si ode la voce di
Penelope)

PENELOPE:
    Ritorna, Ulisse; ritorna, Ulisse ...
ULISSE (sorpreso, volge lo sguardo alla finestra illuminata):
    Tu canti e tessi come la divina
    Calypso; pura sei come Nausicaa
    e dolce sei come mia madre ...
    Come
    e perchè sembran sorgere di sotterra
    a occupar la mia mente — e proprio in questa notte —
    le donne che incontrai nel lungo errare?

EUMAEUS (*to himself; watching Ulysses leave*):
> And yet ... those eyes ...

Scene change

Scene Two

A courtyard before the palace. Between the pillars of the palace, there are red curtains, drawn. A spotlight should be placed so as to focus attention on Ulysses's bow, hanging on a pillar with its string dangling loose. It is night-time. Only one window, up above, is dimly lit. A brazier in the corner, on the left.
Ulysses slowly enters... He looks around... His attention seems to be caught by the bow hung on the pillar.

ULYSSES:
> 'But there is so much blood around ...'.
> That is what the blind Tiresias told me,
> there, in the depths of Hell.
> I do not yet see blood around me:
> around me there is only loneliness.
> Not even my son recognized me ...
> The sadness of return ...
> I recognized every plant, thorn-bush, and every stone
> on my path, and everything
> spoke of times gone by ...
> The sadness of return ...
> Why, why did I long to see so much?
> Why does it all come back to mind now?
> Why did I not want to accept oblivion?
> Not even my son recognized me ...

(*Offstage, but as if coming from the window that is lit, one can hear Penelope's voice*)

PENELOPE:
> Come back, Ulysses; come back, Ulysses ...

ULYSSES (*surprised, he looks up at the lighted window*):
> You sing and weave like the divine
> Calypso; you are as pure as Nausicaa
> and as sweet as my mother ...
> How
> and why do all the women I met in the course of my wanderings
> seem to rise from underground
> and haunt my mind
> — and why on this very night?

Mi sembra d'averle tutte d'intorno ...
Una, sol una manca:
Circe manca, per opra di magìa
Antinoo (internamente, ma vicino. Con espressione sguaiata):
Lieta, lieta ...

(Ulisse, udita la voce di Antinoo, si rannicchia in fretta al riparo di una colonna, accanto al braciere)

Antinoo (è entrato in scena, alquanto brillo, tenendo Melanto stretta alla vita):
Lieta, gaja sia questa notte ...
Melanto (paurosamente):
Antinoo! ... quelle fiamme, ...
Quelle fiamme sui monti ...
Antinoo:
Nulla, Melanto ...
Melanto:
Esser chi può quel vecchio?
Antinoo:
Giovane, bella, bella come sei,
perchè degnare d'un sol sguardo un vecchio,
un senza nome?
Penelope (internamente):
Ulisse, torna! Ritorna, Ulisse ...
Melanto:
Ascolta: intona la Regina il suo lamento ...
Antinoo:
Lascia che pianga chi piú non ritorna ...
Si parli d'altro.
Melanto (cominciando con semplicità e gradatamente aumentando in sensualità e passione):
Dice il vero Pisandro quando afferma
che tu saresti lo sposo prescelto?
Dice il vero Pisandro?
Antinoo:
T'importa?
Melanto:
Antinoo: re d'Itaca, Melanto
disdegnerai?
Antinoo:
Ti pare?
Melanto:
Dal letto freddo della tua Regina
scivolare potrai nel mio ... non credo
che il mio calore ti dispiaccia ...
(abbraccia Antinoo)

They seem to be all around me ...
Only one is absent:
Circe has used her sorcery to keep away.

ANTINOUS (*offstage, but close by. In a vulgar manner*):
Happy, happy ...

(*Ulysses, having heard Antinous's voice, squats quickly behind a pillar, near the brazier*)

ANTINOUS (*enters, rather drunk, holding Melantho around the waist*):
Happy, merry may this night be ...

MELANTHO (*frightened*):
Antinous! ... those flames, ...
those flames on the mountains ...

ANTINOUS:
They were nothing, Melantho ...

MELANTHO:
Who can that old man be?

ANTINOUS:
Beautiful young girl, lovely as you are,
why should you deign to give even one look to an old,
nameless man?

PENELOPE (*offstage*):
Ulysses, come back! Come back, Ulysses...

MELANTHO:
Listen: the Queen is striking up her lamentations again ...

ANTINOUS:
Let her lament him; he's not coming back ...
Let's talk of something else.

MELANTHO (*starting simply and gradually increasing in sensuality and passion*):
Is Peisander telling the truth when he claims
that you will be the husband she chooses?
Is he telling the truth?

ANTINOUS:
Does it matter to you?

MELANTHO:
Antinous: king of Ithaca, would you spurn
Melantho?

ANTINOUS:
What do you think?

MELANTHO:
From the cold bed of your Queen
you will be able to slip into mine ... I don't think
you would find my warm body disagreeable ...
(*she embraces Antinous*)

Ulisse (prorompendo):
> Hai udito il mio appello, Circe!

(Melanto si stacca da Antinoo: si guarda intorno: fa qualche passo ... si accorge della presenza di Ulisse. Ulisse per darsi un contegno, attizza il fuoco del braciere)

Melanto:
> Chi è là?

Antinoo:
> Chi è là?

Melanto (ad Antinoo: con disgusto):
> Il mendico cencioso che ronza qui intorno ...

(Va verso Ulisse ... si ferma)
(Pauroso)
(Qualche altro passo ... porta il viso all'altezza di Ulisse)

> Ma tu..., chi sei?

(Ritorna accanto ad Antinoo)

> (Fra sè) Che angoscia ...

Antinoo (fra sè):
> Ei tace.

Melanto:
> Sei cieco, Antinoo, o tu non vuoi vedere?
> (a denti stretti)
> Odio vendetta esprimono quegl'occhi:
> in essi ho letto la nostra condanna!

Antinoo (fatuamente; conscio di sé):
> Per odiare, Melanto, per amare
> bisogna essere un uomo. Quel relitto
> non è un uomo.

Melanto:
> Cos'è ?

Antinoo:
> Chi è ? Nessuno.

(Prende Melanto per la vita. Escono)

Ulisse (senza luce):
> *Nessuno.* Tanto in basso sono caduto.
> Ulisse eroe; Re d'Itaca: *Nessuno.*

ULYSSES (*in an outburst*):
>   You have answered my summons, Circe!

(*Melantho breaks away from Antinous; she looks around; takes a few steps ... becomes aware of Ulysses's presence. Ulysses, as if to explain his being there, pokes the fire in the brazier*)

MELANTHO:
>   Who is there?

ANTINOUS:
>   Who is there?

MELANTHO (*to Antinous; with disgust*):
>   The ragged old beggar who is still lurking around here ...

(*She approaches Ulysses ... then stops*)
(*Frightened*)
(*A few more steps ... until her face is level with Ulysses's*)

>   Who *are* you?

(*She goes back to Antinous*)

>   (*to herself*) He terrifies me ...

ANTINOUS (*to himself*):
>   He doesn't utter a word.

MELANTHO:
>   Are you blind, Antinous, or don't you want to see?
>   (*between clenched teeth*)
>   His eyes glow with hate and vengeance:
>   they tell me that we are condemned!

ANTINOUS (*fatuously, and self-consciously*):
>   One needs to be a man
>   before hating or loving, Melantho.
>   That wreck isn't a man.

MELANTHO:
>   What is he then?

ANTINOUS:
>   Who is he? No man.

(*He takes Melantho by the waist. They leave*)

ULYSSES (*disheartened*):
>   *No man.* I have fallen so low.
>   The heroic Ulysses; king of Ithaca: *No man.*

(si alza di scatto)

> Assai ti vendicasti, o Dio del mare.
> Il mio nome che un giorno trasformai
> per astuzia, ritorna a me per scherno.
> (decisamente)
> Si compia quanto compiere si deve
> in questa notte.

(Ulisse mira in alto.)

Scene Three

Si aprono le tende: appare una sala sfarzosamente illuminata. I Proci sono radunati a banchetto: con essi, molte giovani donne. Melanto è seduta in disparte, sola. Ulisse, non appena ha udito le voci dietro le tende, si siede ai piedi della colonna alla quale è appeso l'arco.

Coro:

> Alla gioia! All'allegrezza!
> Alla gioia, al piacere, alla gioventú!
> All'allegrezza!

Antinoo:

> Amici, che avete brindato al piacere, alla gioia
> ed alla giovinezza,
> non disdegnate levare il calice in alto
> a Posìdone dio,
> che l'inquietante Telémaco volle chiamare
> nei gorghi profondi ...

Coro:

> A Posìdone dio!
> All'allegrezza! Alla gioia! Al piacere!
> A Posìdone dio!

(Antinoo guarda con stupore di briaco Melanto che, seduta in disparte, sola, tiene il viso coperto colle mani)

Antinoo:

> Melanto ...,
> perchè qui sola ed estranea alla festa?

Melanto (si alza di scatto; ha gli occhi sbarrati, come fosse in preda a una visione terrificante):

> Quelle fiamme sui monti!

Coro:

> Alla madre Demètria rendevan grazie!

(He jumps up suddenly.)

> You have exacted enough vengeance, Oh god of the sea.
> My name, which I altered so cunningly one day,
> comes back to mock me.
> *(decidedly)*
> Let what needs be done, be done,
> this very night.

(Ulysses looks upwards.)

Scene Three

The curtains open: a brilliantly lit room. The suitors are assembled for a banquet; with them there are many young women. Melantho sits alone and apart. As soon as Ulysses hears the voices behind the curtains, he sits at the foot of the pillar where his bow is hanging.

CHOIR:
> To joy! To merriment!
> To joy, pleasure, and youth!
> To merriment!

ANTINOUS:
> Friends, you have drunk a toast to pleasure, joy,
> and youth;
> now join me in raising your goblets
> to Poseidon, the sea-god,
> who has summoned the bothersome Telemachus
> down to his deepest abysses ...

CHOIR:
> To Poseidon, the sea-god!
> To merriment! To joy! To pleasure!
> To Poseidon, the sea-god!

(Antinous, in a drunken stupor, looks at Melantho who, sits apart and alone, with her hands over her face)

ANTINOUS:
> Melantho ...,
> why are you alone, and not making merry with us?

MELANTHO *(she jumps up; her eyes wide open as if in the grip of a terrifying vision)*:
> Those flames on the mountains!

CHOIR:
> They were fires of thanksgiving to Demeter, our mother!

Melanto (assorta nella sua visione, sembra non aver notato l'interruzione del Coro):

      Antinoo ..., e gli occhi di quel vecchio?

Antinoo:

      Gli saran strappati, domani ...

Melanto:

      Mi fai ribrezzo, Antinoo ...

Coro:

      Al dio Posìdone! a Posìdone dio!

Antinoo (urlato):

      Voi, coppieri, mescete del vino!

(I coppieri eseguono)

Eurimaco (si è avvicinato a Melanto):

      (Con dolcezza; carezzevole)

      Bella Melanto, danza, danza per noi ...

Melanto (ruvidamente):

      No, questa sera.

Pisandro (c.s):

      Bella Melanto, danza, danza per noi...

Melanto (piú decisamente):

      Oggi non danzo.

Pisandro:

      Ma perchè?

Eurimaco:

      Ma perchè?

Melanto (congiunge le mani sopra il capo):

      Come danzare qui, dove nulla,

      nulla m'ispira al volo?

(Allontana le mani giunte, con senso di sconforto. Queste, allontanandosi, disegnano un semicerchio. Antinoo, che ha notato il gesto, si avvicina a Melanto)

Antinoo:

      Nulla? Nulla al volo t'ispira?

      Pure..., il tuo gesto mi dice l'opposto:

      (con sottigliezza demoniaca)

      Ti sento ispirata ... m'intendi?

Melanto:

      No: non t'intendo.

(Antinoo imita il gesto a semicerchio che Melanto ha fatto poco prima)

MELANTHO (*engrossed in her vision, and not seeming to notice the intervention of the Chorus*):

> Antinous ..., and that old man's eyes?

ANTINOUS:

> We shall pluck them out, tomorrow ...

MELANTHO:

> You make me shudder, Antinous ...

CHOIR:

> To Poseidon, the sea-god! To Poseidon, the sea-god!

ANTINOUS (*shouting*):

> You there, servants, pour us more wine here!

(The cup-bearers obey)

EURYMACHUS (*he has approached Melantho*):

> (*sweetly and caressingly*)
> Beautiful Melantho, dance, dance for us ...

MELANTHO (*harshly*):

> No, not this evening.

PEISANDER:

> Beautiful Melantho, dance, dance for us ...

MELANTHO (*more decisively*):

> I am not dancing today.

PEISANDER:

> But why?

EURYMACHUS:

> But why?

MELANTHO (*clasps her hands above her head*):

> How can I dance here, where there is nothing,
> nothing to inspire me?

(She separates her hands, with a feeling of uneasiness. As she separates her hands, they draw a semicircle. Antinous, who has noticed this gesture, approaches Melantho)

ANTINOUS:

> Nothing? Nothing inspires you to dance?
> And yet, the way you moved just now would seem to imply the opposite:
> (*with devilish subtlety*)
> I feel that you *are* inspired ... understand?

MELANTHO:

> No, I don't understand.

(Antinous imitates the gesture — the drawing of the semicircle — made by Melantho shortly before)

Antinoo:

Bella Melanto, ancor non intendi?

Melanto:

No.

Antinoo:

L'arco d' Ulisse!

(Melanto lancia un'urlo di sgomento)

Antinoo (imperioso):

Ci porta, fido Eumeo,
l'arco che da vent'anni è inoperoso.

(Eumeo si avvia verso la colonna ... ne stacca l'arco ... lo consegna ad Antinoo)
(Antinoo esamina l'arco. Eurimaco e Pisandro si sono intanto avvicinati ad Antinoo)

Antinoo (fra sè):

Soltanto Ulisse lo potè piegare ...

Eurimaco e Pisandro:

Soltanto Ulisse ...

Coro:

Danza, bella Melanto! Danza, danza!

(Antinoo si avvicina a Melanto: con decisione le consegna l'arco. Melanto abbassa il capo).
(Comincia la danza di Melanto. Dapprima la danzatrice sembra in cerca d'ispirazione; poi la danza si svolge in modo languido e molle. Infine si fa selvaggia. La danza è arrivata al punto culminante: la corda dell'arco si è attorcigliata attorno al collo di Melanto, che caccia un'urlo terribile. Esattamente nello stesso momento appare in scena Telemaco con la spada al fianco. Un momento di stupore generale. Melanto scioglie la corda che le attorcigliava la gola e getta l'arco, che va a cadere accanto a Ulisse)

Coro:

Telemaco!

Antinoo:

Telemaco! Ben giunto ...
T'aspettavamo proprio questa sera ...

Telemaco:

M'aspettava sul mare
una nave corsara ...

Antinoo:

Quelle navi ...

ANTINOUS:
>Beautiful Melantho, do you still not understand?

MELANTHO:
>No.

ANTINOUS:
>Ulysses's bow!

(Melantho cries out in dismay)

ANTINOUS *(in a commanding tone)*:
>Faithful Eumaeus, bring us
>the bow which has been hanging idle for twenty years now.

(Eumaeus approaches the pillar ... takes down the bow ...and gives it to Antinous)
(Antinous examines the bow. Meanwhile Eurymachus and Peisander have approached Antinous)

ANTINOUS *(to himself)*:
>Only Ulysses could bend it ...

EURYMACHUS and PEISANDER:
>Only Ulysses ...

CHOIR:
>Dance, beautiful Melantho! Dance, dance!

(Antinous approaches Melantho: with a decisive gesture he hands her the bow. Melantho lowers her head).
(Melantho's dance begins. At first she seems to be looking for inspiration; then the dance develops in a languid and lascivious manner. Eventually, it becomes wild. At its climax the cord of the bow becomes twisted around Melantho's neck, and she utters a terrible cry. At exactly the same time, Telemachus appears on stage with his sword at his side. There is a moment of general amazement. Melantho unwinds the cord that was twisted around her throat, and she throws away the bow which falls beside Ulysses)

CHOIR:
>Telemachus!

ANTINOUS:
>Telemachus! Welcome ...
>We were expecting you this very evening ...

TELEMACHUS:
>A pirate ship
>was expecting me out at sea ...

ANTINOUS:
>Ah, those ships ...

PISANDRO (interrompendo Antinoo):
>Son la vergogna dell'isola nostra ...

EURIMACO:
>Sono la dannazion dei naviganti ...

TELEMACO:
>... ma il mio cuor mi diceva
>di scendere da solo al promontorio
>per sfuggire alla rete

ANTINOO:
>Astuto sei
>come tuo padre. Siedi.
>E deponi la spada. Come vedi,
>noi non siamo armati.

(Telemaco non reagisce. Eurimaco e Pisandro, tentano di ristabilire l'atmosfera di festa)

EURIMACO:
>Splendido viaggio il tuo dev'esser stato!

PISANDRO:
>... Splendido viaggio!
>Tanto, tanto da te saper vogliamo!

EURIMACO:
>Com'è la reggia del biondo Menelao?

PISANDRO:
>Hai veduto di Sparta la Regina?

EURIMACO:
>Elena è sempre bella?

(Telemamaco non risponde)

ANTINOO (intervenendo in modo deciso):
>È appena giunto e voi già lo schiacciate
>con insulse domande. Vada intanto
>dalla Regina a dirle ch'è tornato.

(Ulisse, al riparo della colonna, si è tolto il mantello di mendicante e tutto ciò che gli dava l'aspetto di un vecchio. Prende l'arco ed entra nella sala dove si stava banchettando)

ULISSE (prorompendo):
>Anch'io son ritornato!

TELEMACO (guarda Ulisse con stupore):
>Tu? Tu?

ANTINOO (con ira contenuta):
>C'è qualcuno

PEISANDER (*interrupting Antinous*):
>> They are the shame of our island ...

EURYMACHUS:
>> They are the curse of our sailors ...

TELEMACHUS:
>> ... but something told me
>> to disembark alone at the headland
>> to escape their trap

ANTINOUS:
>> You are shrewd
>> like your father. Sit down.
>> And take off your sword-belt. As you can see,
>> we are not armed.

(Telemachus does not react. Eurymachus and Peisander try to re-establish the festive atmosphere)

EURYMACHUS:
>> You must have had a splendid journey!

PEISANDER:
>> ... A splendid journey!
>> Come on, we want to know all about it!

EURYMACHUS:
>> How is fair Menelaus's kindgom?

PEISANDER:
>> Did you see the Queen of Sparta?

EURYMACHUS:
>> Is Helen as beautiful as ever?

(Telemachus does not answer)

ANTINOUS (*interrupting in a decisive manner*):
>> He has only just arrived, and you are already bombarding him
>> with stupid questions. Leave him alone, and let him go
>> to the Queen to tell her of his return.

(Ulysses, behind a pillar, has taken off his beggar's cloak and the rest of his disguise as an old man. He takes the bow and enters the banqueting hall)

ULYSSES (*bursting in*):
>> I too have returned!

TELEMACHUS (*looking at Ulysses with astonishment*):
>> You? You?

ANTINOUS (*containing his anger*):
>> Someone

che il vino ha reso gaio, questa sera ...
(volgendosi ai Servi, con irosa violenza)
Voi ..., poltroni! Portate altre faci!

(I Servi non si muovono)

ULISSE (calmissimo):
C'è abbastanza luce
per l'occhio mio. Per voi, la luce e l'ombra
non differiscon più.
Melanto sola, la cagna, ha compreso.
Si cominci da lei.
Melanto! Le tue chiome
sembreran fiamme, mentre il tuo bel corpo
appeso a un ramo
s'agiterà l'ultima volta!
Prendetela!

(A un gesto di Ulisse, Eumeo e alcuni servi si precipitano su Melanto e la trascinano fuori)

ANTINOO:
Aiuto! Aiuto!
ULISSE:
Ma chi potrà aiutarti?
Chi ascolta la tua voce?
Antinoo: guardami!

(Flette l'arco e allaccia intorno alla punta l'occhiello della corda. Grido di terrore di tutti gli astanti. Antinoo, colpito da una freccia, stramazza sotto il tavolo. Eurimaco e Pisandro cadono pure. Il Coro cerca di raggiungere le uscite. Ulisse continua a scagliare frecce)

PENELOPE (appare improvvisamente in scena):
Ulisse!

(Ulisse si volge verso di lei)

Ulisse!
(alza le braccia)

(Ulisse alza pure le braccia ... Ulisse e Penelope si guardano intensamente)

Cambiamento di scena

INTERMEZZO SINFONICO

has had too much to drink this evening ...
(*turning to the servants, with angry violence*)
You ..., you sluggards! Bring some more torches here!

(*The servants do not move*)

ULYSSES (*very calmly*):
    There is enough light
    for my eyes. For you, light and darkness
    are now one and the same thing.
    Only the bitch Melantho, understood.
    Let's deal with her first, then.
    Melantho! Your tresses
    will shine like flames, and your beautiful body,
    hanging from the branch of a tree,
    will twist and dance for the last time!
    Seize her!

(*At a gesture from Ulysses, Eumaeus and a few servants seize Melantho and drag her off*)

ANTINOUS:
    Help! Help!
ULYSSES:
    But who can help you?
    Who is listening to you?
    Antinous: look at me!

(*He bends the bow and strings it. All the bystanders utter a cry of terror. Antinous, struck by an arrow, collapses beneath the table. Eurymachus and Peisander also fall. The Chorus makes for the exits. Ulysses continues to shoot arrows*)

PENELOPE (*suddenly appears on stage*):
    Ulysses!

(*Ulysses turns toward her.*)

    Ulysses!
    (*stretches out her arms*)

(*Ulysses also stretches out his arms ... Ulysses and Penelope gaze intensely at each other.*)

Scene change

SYMPHONIC INTERMEZZO

Epilogo

Mare aperto. Ulisse, solo, su una piccola imbarcazione. Notte stellata.

ULISSE:
>No, non sono le Furie ad avventarsi
>su me per vendicare quei che uccisi,
>per rinfacciarmi i compagni perduti:
>sono i mostri (in me Circe li scoperse)
>che rodon questo cuore mai placato.
>Un uomo sono, un uomo che ha guardato
>il mondo nelle foggie più diverse
>e che intorno si vede sorger, muti,
>con occhi interroganti, mille visi,
>mentre nell'alma le memorie farsi
>sembran più dense e dolorose. Quanto
>e cosa appresi? Fole.
>Dopo fatiche inani,
>briciole di sapere, vani
>balbettamenti, sillabe soltanto
>mi son rimaste invece di parole.
>(Guarda in alto)
>Stelle!: quante mai volte contemplai
>sotto cieli diversi
>la vostra pura trepida bellezza!
>Stelle!: quante mai volte interrogai
>i vostri sguardi tersi,
>luce sperando aver da voi, saggezza!
>Perchè tanto diverse m'apparite
>in questa notte? Quando
>fu stabilito il vostro corso, e come?
>V'ho mirate: soffrii pene infinite
>intorno a me cercando
>quanto mi manca: la Parola, il Nome.
>(Sempre piú tomentato)
>Trovar potessi il Nome,   pronunciar la Parola
>che chiarisca a me stesso   così ansioso cercare;
>che giustifichi questa   mia vita, il lungo errare,
>che rasereni l'ora   che rapida s'invola.

Epilogue

The open sea. Ulysses, alone, on a little boat. A starry night.

ULYSSES:
        No, it is not the Furies who hurl themselves
        at me to take revenge for those I have murdered,
        to reproach me for the death of my comrades:
        monsters (which Circe discovered in me)
        gnaw at this heart that can never be placated.
        I am only mortal; a man who has gazed
        at the world in all of its myriad forms,
        and around me there rise up a thousand faces,
        silent, and with questioning eyes,
        while in my soul memories
        seem to accumulate and grow more painful. How much
        and what did I learn? Fairy-tales.
        After vain efforts,
        all I have been left with are
        scraps of knowledge, futile
        stammerings, and syllables
        instead of words.
        (*He looks up*)
        Stars!: how many times
        under different skies
        did I contemplate your pure and tremulous beauty!
        Stars!: how many times did I question
        your limpid gaze,
        hoping to gain light and knowledge from you!
        Why do you appear so different
        tonight? When
        and how was your course established?
        I have watched you: I suffered endless torments,
        searching all around me
        for the thing I need most: the Word, the Name.
        (*Becoming more and more tormented*)
        If only I could find the Name,
        pronounce the Word
        that would clarify for me
        my anxious searching;
        that would justify
        the life I have lived and my long years of wandering;
        that would calm the swiftly
        fleeting passage of time.

Guardare, meravigliarsi   *e tornar a guardare.*
Ancora: tormentarmi   per comprendere il vero.

(Una lunga pausa)

Se una voce rompesse   il silenzio, il mistero ...

(altra lunga pausa: poi, come per improvvisa illuminazione)
Signore!
(calmato)
                    Non più soli sono   il mio cuore e il mare.

FINE DELL'OPERA

Fecisti nos ad te
et inquietum est cor nostrum,
donec requiescat in te.
(Sancti Aurelii Augustini, *Confessionum*, Liber I, Caput I)

To look, to marvel,
and look again.
Here I am, tormenting myself again
in an effort to discover the truth.

(A long pause)

If only a voice would break
the silence, the mystery ...

(another long pause; as if by sudden revelation)
Almighty one!
(now calm)
My heart and the sea
are no longer alone.

THE END

You made us in your image,
and our hearts are restless,
until they find their peace in thee.
(Saint Augustine, *Confessions*, Book I, Chapter I)

Libretto of
Berio's *Laborintus II* (1965)

Part 1:

    a civitate Enoch in Naid

Part 2:

In quella parte; in quella parte della mia memoria; in quella parte del libro; in quella parte del libro della mia memoria incipit vita nova: e apparve vestita di nobilissimo colore, umile e onesto, sanguigno: ecce Deus, ecce Deus fortior me: dominabitur mihi

Part 3:

    Sion speculatio
    a Babylone urbe
    vocata vocata est Hierusalem
    ab urbe Salem in Syria
    et Iebus et Salem vocata est Hierusalem
    Solyma noncupata est
    Aelia vocitata est
    Hierusalem pacifica
    a Babylone urbe ab urbe

Part 4:

    e nel mezzo
    e in una selva
    selvaggia selva e aspra
    ed una lupa
    una lupa
    ma questa bestia uccide
    uccide

Courtesy of Universal Editions. The original libretto is not divided into parts; the divisions here match those used in the commentary provided in Chapter 3.

Libretto of
Berio's *Laborintus II* (1965)

Part 1:

from the city of Enoch in Naid

Part 2:

In that part; in that part of my memory; in that part of the book; in that part of the book of my memory the new life begins: and she appeared clothed in a most noble, humble and sanguine colour: behold God, behold God stronger than me: ruling over me.

Part 3:

Sion observation point
from the city of Babylon
is called is called Hierusalem
from the city of Salem in Syria
and Iebus and Salem is called Hierusalem
it is not called Solyma
it is called Aelia
peaceful Hierusalem
from the city of Babylon from the city

Part 4:

and in the middle
and in a wood
savage and harsh wood
and a wolf
a wolf
but this beast kills
kills

not only in the middle of the way
in the middle
but all the way in the dark wood
in the bramble
the years of *l'entre deux guerres*

Part 5:

una dolorosa infermitade: per nove dí amarissima pena; e ne lo nono giorno, sentendome dolere quasi intollerabilmente, a me giunse uno pensero: e cominciai a piangere: e cominciai a travagliare ed a imaginare in questo modo: Dolcissima Morte vieni a me vieni a me Or vieni a me, io porto già lo tuo colore. Io piangea con li occhi, bagnandoli di vere lagrime, io chiamava la Morte e dicea: Dolcissima Morte, Dolcissima Morte, vieni a me, io porto già lo tuo colore

Part 6:

io vidi cose: che mi fecero proporre di non dire, io vidi cose: io spero di dicer quello che mai non fue detto: mi fecero proporre di non dire di lei: io spero di dicer di lei quello che mai non fue detto d'alcuna

Part 7:

mi dà orrore (uno soave sonno); ma allegro; ma con tanta letizia; ma una maravigliosa visione: e di pauroso aspetto; (amore), piangendo, mangiando dubitosamente; (una nebula di colore di fuoco): ego dominus, ego dominus tuus; (una figura); (uno segnore, amore); e la donna, in amarissimo pianto in grande angoscia, piangendo vide cor tuum

Part 8:

Adam genuit Seth, a quo filii Dei. Seth genuit Enos, qui coepit invocare nomen Domini. Enos genuit Cainan. Cainan genuit Malalehel. Malalehel genuit Iareth. Iareth genuit Enoc, qui translatus est. Enoc genuit Matusalam. Matusalam genuit Lamech. Lamech genuit Noe. Arca aedificatur. Noe genuit Sem, Cham et Iaphet. Factum est diluvium. Cataclismum. Sem post diluvium genuit Arfaxat, a quo Chaldaei. Arfaxat genuit Sala, a quo Samaritae et Indi. Sala genuit Heber, a quo Hebraei. Heber genuit Falec. Turris aedificatur. Divisae sunt linguae et per orbem terrae facta est dispersio in aedificatione turris. Falec genuit Ragau. Dii primum adorantur. Ragau genuit Seruc. Regnum inchoat Scytharum. Seruc genuit Nachor. Regnum Aegyptiorum nascitur. Nachor genuit Thara. Regnum Assyriorum et Siciniorum exoritur. Thara genuit Abraham. Zoroastres magicam repperit

not only in the middle of the way
in the middle
but all the way in the dark wood
in the bramble
the years of *l'entre deux guerres*

Part 5:

A grievous infirmity: for nine days most bitter pain; and on the ninth day, feeling an almost intolerable pain within me, a thought came to me: and I began to cry: and I began to suffer deeply and to imagine in this way: Sweet death come to me come to me now come to me, I already wear your colour. My eyes cried, and became moist with tears, and I called upon Death and said: Sweet, Sweet Death, come to me, I already wear your colour

Part 6:

I saw things: which made me vow not to speak, I saw things: I hope to say what has never been said: they made me vow not to speak of her: I hope to say of her what has never been said of any woman

Part 7:

he horrifies me (a gentle sleep); but happy; but with a great joy; but a marvellous vision: and frightening to behold; (love), crying, eating doubtfully; (a fiery coloured cloud): I am lord, I am your lord; (a figure); (a lord, love); and the woman, weeping bitterly in great anguish, crying behold your heart

Part 8:

Adam begat Seth, from whom descended the sons of God. Seth begat Enos, who began to call on the name of the Lord. Enos begat Cainan. Cainan begat Mahalaleel. Mahalaleel begat Jared. Jared begat Enoch, who was taken by God. Enoch begat Methuselah. Methuselah begat Lamech. Lamech begat Noah. The ark was built. Noah begat Shem, Ham, and Japheth. There was the flood. Cataclysm. Shem after the flood begat Arphaxad, from whom descended the Chaldees. Arphaxad begat Salah, from whom descended the inhabitants of Samaria and India. Salah begat Eber from whom descended the Hebrews. Eber begat Peleg. The tower was built. Tongues were divided and they who built the tower were scattered upon the face of the earth. Peleg begat Reu. The Gods were worshipped for the first time. Reu begat Serug. The kingdom of the Scythians began. Serug begat Nahor. The kingdom of the Egyptians was born. Nahor begat Terah. The kingdom of the Assyrians and the Scythians began. Terah begat Abraham. Zoroastres discovered magic

Part 9:

tutto tutto tutto dalla biblioteca al babbuino: dal 1265 al 1321: dal cianuro di potassio alla cronaca cittadina: dalla cresima alla corte dei conti: dalla oscurità in cui è sempre immersa la nostra vita alla rendita del 4%: dalla carotide alla tibia: dall'elefante di mare, grande foca del Pacifico, fornita di due lunghe zanne al 1965: dal fegato al frigorifero: dal francobollo al formaggio: dalla prova del 9 al cavallo di Troia: dal lapsus linguae alla rivoluzione russa: dall'endecasillabo al tabacco da fiuto: dal piedestallo che sa sostenere tutte le colonne alla folgorazione: atto e effetto del folgorare: alla pietra focaia: alla luna: al rame: alla polvere

ah per te ho inventato il rame e la polvere: ho liberato la lettera 'erre' e la lettera 'ci' da un penitenziario di tabacco: ho trascinato lepri e chiodi in Paradise Valley: di te ho anche detto perfectiones intellegibiles: ho detto: novimus enim tenebras aquas ventos ignem fumum: vediamo insieme il passato, il futuro: ho detto: quoi qu'elle fasse elle est désir improportionabiliter excedens

ho detto ho detto ho detto ho detto ho detto ho detto ho detto

Part 10:

Natura lo suo corso prende da divino intelletto e da sua arte: l'arte vostra quella segue come 'l maestro fa il discente: da queste due convene prender sua vita ed avanzar la gente: l'usuriere altra via tene: per sè natura e per la sua seguace dispregia

with usura hath no man a house of good stone, with usura hath no man a painted paradise on his church wall *harpes et luthes*: with usura no music is made to endure nor to live with but is made to sell and to sell quickly: with usura, sin against nature: with usura the line grows thick

Part 11:

PER ME NELLA CITTA DOLENTE,
PER ME NELL'ETTERNO DOLORE,
PER ME TRA LA PERDUTA GENTE

tutto l'oro ch'è sotto la luna
e che già fu, di quest'anime stanche
non potrebbe farne posare una.
Si percotean non pur con mano,
ma con la testa e col petto e coi piedi,
trocandosi co' denti a brano a brano

Part 9:

all all all from the library to the baboon: from 1265 to 1321: from potassium cyanide to the local news: from confirmation to the Treasury Department: from the darkness in which our lives are constantly immersed to the 4% profit: from the carotid to the tibia: from the sea-elephant, great seal of the Pacific, with its two long tusks to 1965: from the liver to the fridge: from the stamp to the cheese: from casting out nines to the Trojan horse: from the slip of the tongue to the Russian revolution: from the hendecasyllable to the snuff: from the pedestal that can hold up all the columns to the flash of lightning: the act and effect of flashing: to the flint: to the moon: to copper: to the dust

ah for you I invented copper and dust: I freed the letter 'r' and the letter 'c' from a tabacco-prison: I dragged hares and nails into Paradise valley: I also said of you intelligible perfections: I said: we also renew darkness water winds fire smoke: we can see together the past, the future: I said: whatever she does she is desire exceeding out of proportion

I said I said I said I said I said I said I said

Part 10:

Nature takes its course from divine intellect and its art: your art follows nature as the pupil follows the master: by these two mankind should gain its livelihood and advancement: the usurer takes a different route: he despises nature both in herself and in her follower

with usura hath no man a house of good stone, with usura hath no man a painted paradise on his church wall *harpes et luthes*: with usura no music is made to endure nor to live with but is made to sell and to sell quickly: with usura, sin against nature: with usura the line grows thick

Part 11:

THROUGH ME THE WAY TO THE MOURNFUL CITY,
THROUGH ME THE WAY TO ETERNAL PAIN,
THROUGH ME THE WAY TO THE LOST PEOPLE

all the gold that is beneath the moon
and ever was, could never give rest
to one of these weary souls.
They were hitting each other not only with their hands,
but also with their heads, chest, and feet,
tearing each other apart piece by piece with their teeth

che parlano sognando
ma così inquieti
sognando i bambini adesso
adesso sognando i bambini
dormendo adesso sognando
adesso dormendo dormendo
adesso adesso adesso

chattering as they dream
but so restless
dreaming babies now
now dreaming babies
sleeping now dreaming
now sleeping sleeping
now now now

Libretto of
Gentilucci's *Strofe di Ungaretti* (1967)

L'angelo del povero
>   Ora che invade le oscurate menti
>   Più aspra pietà del sangue e della terra,
>   Ora che ci misura ad ogni palpito
>   Il silenzio di tante ingiuste morti,
>
>   Ora si svegli l'angelo del povero,
>   Gentilezza superstite dell'anima ...
>   . . . .
>   (da *I ricordi* di Giuseppe Ungaretti, 1942–46)

Silenzio stellato (1932)
>   E gli alberi e la notte
>   Non si muovono più
>   Se non da nidi
>   (da *L'amore* di Giuseppe Ungaretti)

Non gridate più
>   Cessate d'uccidere i morti,
>   Non gridate più, non gridate
>   Se li volete ancora udire,
>   Se sperate di non perire.
>
>   Hanno l'impercettibile sussurro,
>   Non fanno più rumore
>   Del crescere dell'erba.
>   Lieta dove non passa l'uomo.
>   (da *I ricordi* di Giuseppe Ungaretti, 1942–46)

Courtesy of G. Ricordi & C. SpA Milano

Libretto of
Gentilucci's *Strofe di Ungaretti* (1967)

The poor man's angel
> Now that darkened minds are invaded by
> A most bitter compassion for blood and land,
> Now that the silence of so many unjustly dead people
> Measures us with every heartbeat,
> Now may the poor man's angel
> — The surviving kindness of the soul — awaken ...
>> (from *Memories* by Giuseppe Ungaretti, 1942–46)

Starry silence (1932)
> And the trees and the night
> Do not move anymore
> Except for the movement in nests
>> (from *Love* by Giuseppe Ungaretti)

Do not shout any more
> Stop killing the dead,
> Do not shout anymore, do not shout
> If you still want to hear them,
> If you hope not to perish.

> They whisper imperceptibly,
> They make no more sound
> Than the growing of the grass,
> The happy grass where man does not tread.
>> (from *Memories* by Giuseppe Ungaretti, 1942–46)

Libretto of
Manzoni's *Parole da Beckett* (1970)

Sono indicate tra parentesi quadre le parti del testo che vengono pronunciate dai cori in maniera non intelligibile (bisbigliato, sussurrato, parlato rapido e simili.)

che farei senza questo silenzio dove si spengono i bisbigli

stanco di morire

[farei come ieri come oggi guardando dal mio oblò se non sono solo a errare a girare lontano da ogni vita in uno spazio spasmodico senza voce tra le voci chiuse con me

non voler dire non sapere quel che si vuol dire non poter dire quel che si crede di voler dire e sempre dire o quasi ecco quel che bisogna non perdere di vista nell'ardore della stesura

vivas puellas mortui incurrrrrsant boves

niente emozione tutto è perduto il fondo è scoppiato l'umidità il trascinio l'abrasione gli amplessi le generazioni un vecchio sacco da carbone cinquanta chili, benissimo, tutto andato le scatole l'apriscatole un apriscatole senza scatole mi è stato risparmiato, scatole senza apriscatole stavolta nella vita questo non mi sarebbe capitato]

puis les pas vers les vieilles lumières

un altro giorno divino

Mio figlio dorme. Che dorma pure. Verrà la notte in cui anch'egli, non riuscendo a dormire, si metterà al suo tavolo di lavoro. Io sarò dimenticato

a meno che ti amino

Courtesy of G. Ricordi & C. SpA Milano. The texts in italics were originally written in English; those in Roman type were translated by Beckett from his own French original. Manzoni's libretto contains the English translations given here.

Libretto of
Manzoni's *Parole da Beckett* (1970)

The bracketed texts are those pronounced by the chorus in an unintelligible manner (murmured, whispered, spoken rapidly etc.)

what would I do without this world faceless incurious

tired of dying

[would I do what I did yesterday and the day before peering out of my deadlight looking for another wandering like me eddying far from all the living in a convulsive space among the voices voiceless

not to want to say, not to know what you want to say, not to be able to say what you think you want to say, and never to stop saying, or hardly ever, that is the thing to keep in mind, even in the heat of composition

vivas puellas mortui incurrrrsant boves

no emotion all is lost the bottom burst the wet the dragging the rubbing the hugging the ages old coal-sack five stone six stone that hangs together all gone the tins the opener an opener and no tins I'm spared that this time tins and no opener I won't have had that in my life this time]

then the steps toward the lighted town

another happy day

My son is sleeping. Let him sleep. The night will come when he too, unable to sleep, will get up and go to his desk. I shall be forgotten

unless they love you

stanco di morire stanco di poliziotti

il viso nel fango la bocca aperta il fango nella bocca la sete che si perde l'umanità
riconquisata

morire

questa terra clonica
periodicamente offuscata dal sonno
è grassa mezzo morta il resto gira a vuoto

[esco dal sonno e ci ritorno tra le due cose c'è tutto da fare da sopportare da perdere
da sbrigare da condurre a buon fine prima che la melma si riapra]

Un cane andò in cucina
e si accostò al fornello.
Allora col coltello
il cuoco lo sgozzò.
Ciò visto gli altri cani
scavarono una fossa
e sulla terra smossa scrissero con la coda:
Un cane andò in cucina ...

[Dovrebbe già essere qui.
Non ha detto che verrà di sicuro.
E se non viene?
Torneremo domani.
E magari dopodomani.
Forse.
E così di seguito.
Insomma ...
Fino a quando non verrà.
Sei spietato.
Siamo già venuti ieri.
Ah no! Non esagerare, adesso!
Cosa abbiamo fatto ieri?
...Ha detto sabato. Mi pare.
...Ma quale sabato? E poi, è sabato oggi? Non sarà poi domenica? O lunedì?
O venerdì?]

e la mente annullata
naufraga nel vento

piangendo quella che ha creduto di amarmi

tired of dying tired of policemen

the face in the mud the mouth open the mud in the mouth thirst abating humanity regained

dying

this clonic earth
see-saw she is blurred in sleep
she is fat half dead the rest is free wheeling

[from sleep I come to sleep return between the two there is all all the doing suffering failing bungling achieving until the mud yawns again]

A dog came in the kitchen
And stole a crust of bread.
The cook up with a ladle
And beat him till he was dead.
Then all the dogs came running
And dug the dog a tomb
And wrote upon the tombstone
For the eyes of dogs to come:
A dog came in the kitchen ...

[He should be here.
He didn't say for sure he'd come.
And if he doesn't come?
We'll come back tomorrow.
Possibly.
And so on.
The point is...
Until he comes.
You're merciless.
We came here yesterday.
Ah no, there you're mistaken.
What did we do yesterday?
... He said Saturday. I think.
... But what Saturday? And is it Saturday? Is it not rather Sunday? Or Monday? Or Friday?]

and the mind annulled
wrecked in wind

mourning the first and last to love me

adesso cose talmente vecchie le sento le mormoro tali e quali pianissimo al fango

e può darsi che non sia ancora alla fine del mio viaggio

se potessi diventare sordo e muto credo che riuscirei a tirare avanti fino ai cent'anni

[bisbigli
non passa quasi giorno
sempre la mia storia
questo sarà stato
mi si chieda qualcosa
...sapere cosa sia
stasi da straccio
nascono...
si estinguono...spazzature di santi
si aprisse sotto di me]

allora può cambiare, finire, potrei soffocare, inabissarmi, non insozzare più, il fango, il buio, non turbare più, il silenzio, crepare, CREPARE, IO POTREI CREPARE, IO CREPERÒ

anche questo è stato un altro giorno felice

in the present things so ancient hear them murmur them as they come barely audible to the mud

and perhaps my course is not yet fully run

if I could go deaf and dumb I think I might pant on to be a hundred

[the murmurs
not a day goes by
my story of course
this will have been
when I am asked something
to know what
my raglimp stasis
then flaming and extinguished
as fire by filth and martyrs
to open under me]

so things may change end I may choke sink the dark trouble the peace no more the silence die DIE I MAY DIE I SHALL DIE

this will have been another happy day

Libretto of
Maderna's *Ausstrahlung* (1971)

Nastro magnetico:

> All these worlds
> would have been a dense darkness,
> if the light,
> called Word,
> had not shone
> from the beginning of the world

Soprano:

> Sur le champ les hommes se sont assemblés
> brûlants de combattre.
> Debout sur leurs grands chars de guerre,
> attelés à des coursiers blancs,
> les puissants archers sont des héros,
> prêts à donner leur vie,
> tous maîtres dans l'art du combat.
> Aussitôt résonnèrent les conques et les tambours,
> les cors et les trompettes
> et ce fut un tumulte immense,
> qui retentit comme rugissement du lion.
> Profondément ému par la pitié
> et plein du douleur, Arjuna dit:
> En voyant dans les rangs mes parents
> brûlants de combattre,
> mes jambes fléchissent, et ma bouche
> se dessèche; je n'ai pas la force
> de me ténir debout, et ma raison
> se trouble.
> Je ne voudrais pas les tuer, même si cela
> devait me rendre souverain des trois mondes.
> Les précepteurs, les pères, les fils
> et les grands-pères, les oncles, les beaux-pères,

Libretto of
Maderna's *Ausstrahlung* (1971)

Tape recording:

> All these worlds
> would have been a dense darkness,
> if the light,
> called Word,
> had not shone
> from the beginning of the world

Soprano:

> The men have assembled on the battle field,
> burning with a desire to fight.
> Standing up on their huge war chariots
> harnessed to white chargers,
> the powerful archers are heroes,
> ready to give up their lives;
> all masters in the art of battle.
> As soon as the conch-shells, drums,
> horns, and trumpets rang out,
> there was an immense commotion
> which resounded like the roaring of a lion.
> Deeply moved by pity
> and full of grief, Arjuna said:
> Seeing, among the ranks, my relatives,
> burning with a desire to fight,
> my legs begin to quiver, and my mouth
> dries up; I do not have the strength
> to stand up, and my reasoning
> is confused.
> I would not like to kill them, even if that
> should make me king of the three worlds.
> Teachers, fathers, sons
> and grand-parents, uncles, father-in-laws,

les gendres et tous les parents
si, les armes à la main,
ils allaient me tuer dans la bataille,
moi, je ne veux pas résister.
Ayant ainsi parlé sur le champ de la bataille, Arjuna,
le coeur percé de douleur,
retomba sur le siège de son char
et jeta loin de soi l'arc et la flèche.
Alors le Seigneur dit:
D'où te vient, Arjuna, en cette heure de danger
ce honteux découragement
indigne d'un Aryen?
Celui qui croit qu'il peut tuer et
celui qui croit qu'il peut être tué,
tous les deux sont ignorants.
Il ne peut ni tuer, ni être tué,
il ne naît, ni ne meurt.
Ayant été, il ne peut plus cesser d'être.
Non-né, permanent, éternel, ancien,
il n'est pas détruit
quand le corps est tué.
Les armes ne peuvent le percer,
ni le feu le brûler,
ni les eaux le mouiller,
ni le vent le sécher!
Celui qui habite le corps
est toujours invulnérable.
Tu ne dois donc t'affliger pour aucune créature,
tu ne dois pas trembler, Arjuna.
En vérité, pour un Aryen il n'y a rien
de plus désiderable qu'un juste combat

Power art thou, give me power!
Might art thou, give me might!
Strength art thou, give me strength!
Life art thou, give me life!
Ear art thou, give me hearing!
Eye art thou, give me eyes!
Shield art thou, shield me well!
May I have voice in my mouth,
breath in my nostrils,
sight in my eyes,
hearing in my ears,
hair always shining young,
and much strength in my arms!

son-in-laws, and all my relations,
if, armed with weapons,
they were going to kill me in battle,
I would not resist.
Having spoken thus on the battle field, Arjuna,
his heart pierced with sorrow,
fell down on the seat of his chariot,
and threw his bow and arrow far away from him.
Then the Lord spoke:
Where does this shameful lack of courage,
unworthy of an Aryan,
come from, Arjuna, in this hour of danger?
He who thinks he can kill,
and he who thinks he can be killed,
both are wrong.
He cannot either kill nor be killed,
he is not born, and he does not die.
Having been, he cannot cease to be.
Unborn, permanent, eternal, ancient,
he is not destroyed
when the body is killed.
Weapons cannot pierce him,
nor fire burn him,
nor water soak him,
nor wind dry him up!
He who lives in the body
is always invulnerable.
You must not therefore grieve for any human being,
you should not tremble, Arjuna.
In truth, for an Aryan there is nothing
more desirable than a just war.

Power art thou, give me power!
Might art thou, give me might!
Strength art thou, give me strength!
Life art thou, give me life!
Ear art thou, give me hearing!
Eye art thou, give me eyes!
Shield art thou, shield me well!
May I have voice in my mouth,
breath in my nostrils,
sight in my eyes,
hearing in my ears,
hair always shining young,
and much strength in my arms!

O cuore, fingi d'avere tutte le cose del mondo,
fingi che tutto ti sia giardino delizioso di verde.
E tu, anima mia, su quell'erba verde
fingi d'esser rugiada gocciata là nella notte
e al sorgere dell'alba svanita...

May I have power in my thighs,
swiftness in my legs,
may all my limbs be uninjured
and my soul unimpaired!
Let's walk together, speak together,
may the purpose be common, common the assembly,
common the mind.
So be our thoughts united
may our decision be unanimous

Sulla mia tomba ad ogni primavera
il vento del nord farà piovere fiori

May we see a hundred years!

Sono tutti verdi i rami

May we live a hundred years!
May we know a hundred years!
i peri e gli albicocchi
avevan ricoperto la tomba di fiori

May we progress a hundred years!
May we assert our existence a hundred years!

È fiorito il giardino
Yes, even more than a hundred years!

Nastro magnetico:
Glances to the side,
loving by nature,
announce intense love,
when thrown by loving maidens,
as messengers to
attract lovers

Nastro magnetico:
The mango tree's bud
fills my heart with strong

Oh heart, you pretend to have everything in the world,
you pretend that everything for you is a delightful, green garden.
And you, my soul, you pretend to be a dewdrop
which has fallen there in the night on that green grass,
and disappeared at the rising of dawn ...

May I have power in my thighs,
swiftness in my legs,
may all my limbs be uninjured
and my soul unimpaired!
Let's walk together, speak together,
may the purpose be common, common the assembly,
common the mind.
So be our thoughts united
may our decision be unanimous

The north wind will rain down flowers
on my tomb at every spring.

May we see a hundred years!

The branches are all green.

May we live a hundred years!
May we know a hundred years!
the pear and apricot trees
had covered the tomb with flowers.

May we progress a hundred years!
May we assert our existence a hundred years!

The garden has flowered.
Yes, even more than a hundred years!

Tape recording:
    Glances to the side,
    loving by nature,
    announce intense love,
    when thrown by loving maidens,
    as messengers to
    attract lovers

Tape recording:
    The mango tree's bud
    fills my heart with strong

desire for my lover,
as does the cry of the cuckoos
drunken with love

Soprano:

Il monte, un altro monte
d'argento, d'oro è il prato
l'acqua ora è lucente
ma tenebrosa s'è fatta l'aria.
Tace la colomba,
vuoto è il verziere
muto è l'usignolo
spoglio è il giardino.
Un vento freddo
come sospiro d'amanti all'alba

Nastro magnetico:

They say that the spring
must not cause the lovely
movement of your eyes
and the illusion that they
might be two bees ....

Nastro magnetico:

Ich frage Dich mein Gott
gib Du mir Antwort und Verstehen.
Wie kommt es, daß aller Wahrheit eigen
diese zeugende Kraft,
daß die Sonne dort steht
und die Sterne der Nacht,
entsprungenes Licht,
doch gehalten und wandeln in
stiller Bahn?
Und der Mond in der Kammer
der Schlummernden
so wunderbar ruhe?
Eine Hand legt sich um uns.
Nun weicht sie
so wunderbar
zurück und sein Licht winkt uns zu.
Wie geschieht uns so wunderbar.

Ich frage Dich mein Gott,
wie ruht uns die Erde
so staunend sicher?

desire for my lover,
as does the cry of the cuckoos
drunken with love

Soprano:

The mountain, another silver
mountain, the meadow is golden,
the water is now shining,
but the air has become shadowy.
The dove sings no more,
the orchard is empty,
the lark is silent,
and the garden is bare.
A cold wind blows,
like the sighing of lovers at dawn

Tape recording:

They say that the spring
must not cause the lovely
movement of your eyes
and the illusion that they
might be two bees ....

Tape recording:

I question you, my God,
give me an answer and understanding of these things.
How does it happen that all truth comes
from this generating force;
that the sun is there,
and the night-stars,
liberated light,
preserve themselves and wander on
a silent path?
And the moon in the chamber
of the drowsy
rests so wonderfully?
A hand surrounds us.
Now it draws back
so wonderfully,
and its light winks to us.
And all of that happens to us so wonderfully.

I question you, my God,
how is it that the earth is
so surprisingly still and secure for us?

Und darüber die Wolken
gehoben, gehalten, unsichtbar getragen
und schwebend wohin?
Und es perlen und blinken die Wasser
und Blumen erblühen.
Die Rosse des Windes durchbrausen die Bahn
und der Wagen der Wolken rollt in den Lüften
und wir dürfen das sehen:
Unser Geist hat die Augen.
Wie geschiet uns so wunderbar ...

And how is it that up above the clouds are
high, immobile, invisibly suspended,
and to where do they float?
And the waters sparkle and shine,
and the flowers blossom.
The steeds of the wind blow on their way,
and the chariot of the clouds crosses the breezes,
and we can see all of that:
our spirit has eyes.
And all of that happens to us so wonderfully.

BIBLIOGRAPHY OF WORKS

Select bibliography of Luigi Dallapiccola

Musical compositions by Dallapiccola

Partita. For orchestra and soprano (1930–32); *Tre studi.* For soprano and chamber orchestra. Text by Kalevala, trans. by P. E. Pavolini (1932); *Sei cori di Michelangelo Buonarroti il Giovane* (1933–36); *Divertimento in quattro esercizi.* For soprano, flute, oboe, clarinet, viola, and cello. Poems from the 13th century (1934); *Musica per tre pianoforti (Inni)* (1934); *Tre laudi.* For high voice and chamber orchestra (13 instruments). Texts taken from the *Laudario dei Battuti di Modena,* 1266 (1936–37); *Volo di notte.* One act opera based on *Vol de nuit* by Antoine de Saint-Exupéry. Libretto by Dallapiccola (1937–38); *Canti di prigionia: Preghiera di Maria Stuarda.* For mixed voices and instruments; *Invocazione di Boezio.* For female voices and instruments; *Congedo di Girolamo Savonarola.* For mixed voices and instruments (1938–41); *Piccolo concerto per Muriel Couvreux.* For piano and chamber orchestra (1939–41); *Studio sul Capriccio n. 1 di Niccolò Paganini.* For piano. Later used as the 'finale' of the *Sonatina canonica* (1942); *Marsia.* One act ballet on a theme by Aurel M. Milloss (1942–43); *Frammenti sinfonici dal balletto 'Marsia'.* For orchestra (1942–43); *Sonatina canonica su Capricci di Niccolò Paganini.* For piano (1943); *Liriche greche: Cinque frammenti di Saffo.* For voice and chamber orchestra; *Due liriche di Anacreonte.* For voice, 2 clarinets, piccolo, viola, and piano; *Sex Carmina Alcaei.* For voice (1942–45); *Ciaccona Intermezzo e Adagio.* For solo cello (1945); *Rencesvals.* Three fragments from the *Chanson de Roland.* For baritone and piano (1946); *Due studi.* For violin and piano (1946–47); *Due pezzi per orchestra.* Orchestral version of *Due studi* (1947); *Il prigioniero.* One act opera with prologue, from *La Torture par l'espérance* by Philippe Auguste Villiers de l'Isle-Adam and *La Légende d'Ulenspiegel et de Lamme Goedzak* by Charles de Coster (1944–48); *Quattro liriche di Antonio Machado.* For soprano and piano (1948); *Tre episodi dal balletto 'Marsia'.* For piano (1949); *Job (una sacra rappresentazione).* Text by Dallapiccola, taken from *The Book of Job* (1950); *Tartiniana.* For violin and chamber orchestra on themes by G. Tartini (1951); *Quaderno musicale di Annalibera.* For piano (1952); *Goethe-Lieder.* For mezzo soprano and three clarinets. Text from the *West-östlicher Divan* by Goethe (1953); *Variazioni per orchestra.* Orchestral version of *Quaderno di Annalibera* (1954); *Piccola musica notturna.* For orchestra (1954); *Canti di liberazione.* For choir and orchestra. On texts by Sebastiano Castellio and Saint Augustine (1951–55); *An Mathilde.* Cantata for soprano and orchestra. On poems by Heinrich Heine (1955); *Tartiniana seconda.* *Divertimento* in two versions: for violin and piano; for violin and chamber orchestra (1956); *Cinque canti.* For baritone and 8 instruments. Greek texts trans. by S. Quasimodo (1956); *Concerto per la notte di Natale dell'anno 1956.* For chamber orchestra and soprano. Texts by Jacopone da Todi (1957); *Requiescant.* For mixed choir and orchestra. Texts by Saint Matthew, Oscar Wilde, and James Joyce (1957–58); *Dialoghi.* For cello and orchestra (1960); *Preghiere.* For baritone and chamber orchestra (1962); *Three questions with two answers.* For orchestra (1963); *Parole di San Paolo.* For voice and instruments. Text from the First Letter from St.Paul to the Corinthians (1964); *Quattro liriche di Antonio Machado.* For soprano and chamber orchestra (1964); *Ulisse* (1960–68). Two act opera with prologue. Text by Dallapiccola (1968);

Piccola musica notturna. For chamber ensemble (1968); *Sicut umbra ...* For mezzo soprano and four groups of instruments. Texts by Juan Ramón Jiménez (1970); *Tempus destruendi — Tempus aedificandi*. For mixed chapel choir (1971); *Commiato*. For soprano and chamber ensemble (third movement on a text attributed to Brunetto Latini, 'O fratel nostro, che se' morto e sepolto...' (1972)). Principal publishers: Suvini Zerboni, Universal Edition, Carisch, Schott.

Writings by Dallapiccola

Collected writings. *Appunti, Incontri, Meditazioni* (Milan: Suvini Zerboni, 1970); *Luigi Dallapiccola. Saggi, testimonianze, carteggio, biografia e bibliografia*, ed. by F. Nicolodi (Milan: Suvini Zerboni, 1975); *Parole e musica*, ed. by F. Nicolodi (Milan: Il Saggiatore, 1980), selected writings from *Parole e musica* as *Dallapiccola on Opera*, trans. and ed. by R. Shackelford (London: Toccata, 1987).

Articles (not included in the collections above). 'Opinions sur l'orientation technique, esthétique et spirituelle de la Musique Contemporaine', in *La Revue internationale de musique*, Brussels, 1.4 (October — November 1938), 640–44 (in Italian and in French); 'In margine al recente Congresso internazionale di musica di Firenze', in *La Rassegna Musicale*, 12.6 (June 1939), 288–91; 'Credo nel teatro moderno', in *Il Resto del Carlino* (2 February, 1941), 3; 'Prefazione' in *Il ritorno di Ulisse in patria di Claudio Monteverdi (trascrizione e riduzione per le scene moderne)* (Milan: Suvini Zerboni, 1942); 'La musica fra le due guerre', in *Radiocorriere*, 23..16 (21–27 April, 1946), 3–4; 'Panorama musicale 1939–46', in *Musica*, 1.3–4 (June 1946), 145–46; 'Listening Post: Italy', in *Listen*, 8.2 (June 1946), 17–19; 'Canti di prigionia', in the Programme Notes for the 'IX Festival internazionale di musica contemporanea', Venice, 15–22 September, 1946, pp. 29–30; 'In attesa del nono Festival internazionale di musica cotemporanea', *Il Mondo*, no. 36 (21 September 1946), 10–11; 'Schoenberg et son école', *Le Tre Venezie*, Padova, 21.7-8-9, (July-August-September 1947), 287–90; 'L'artista creatore e il pubblico', *Prospetti*, no. 9 (Autumn 1954), 124–28; 'The Birth-Pangs of a *Job*', *Musical Events*, 15.5 (May 1960), 26–27; 'Livrets et paroles dans l'opéra' in *AA. VV. Zeitgenössisches Musiktheater* (Hamburg: Deutscher Musikrat, 1966), pp. 52–56; 'Musique et humanité', *Journal of the International Folk Music Council*, 16 (1964), 8–10; 'Quattro liriche di Antonio Machado — Parole di San Paolo' in the Programme Notes for the 'XXXIX Festival internazionale di musica contemporanea della Biennale di Venezia', 4–14 September, 1966, pp. 61–62; 'Schoenberg and the Viennese School: three points of view' (round table discussion with R. Kolisch, L. D. R. Sherman, and D. Harris), *The New England Conservatory Bulletin*, I.2 (1968), 24–29; 'Schema di una trasmissione televisiva su Luigi Dallapiccola', ed. by L. Pinzauti, *Nuova rivista musicale italiana*, 9.2 (April-June, 1975), 249–56; 'Saluto a Malipiero', in *Omaggio a Malipiero (Atti del Convegno si Studi Malipieriani)* (Florence: Olschki, 1977), pp. 11–13; 'Dichiarazione sul mio *Job*' in the Programme Notes at the Teatro Comunale di Bologna, 13 October, 1984.

Critical works on Dallapiccola

Books. D. Kämper, *Luigi Dallapiccola* (Florence: Sansoni, 1985); M. Venuti, *Il teatro di Dallapiccola* (Milan: Suvini Zerboni, 1985); *Studi su Luigi Dallapiccola*, ed. by A. Quattrocchi (Lucca: Libreria Musicale Italiana, 1993); P. Michel, *Luigi Dallapiccola* (Geneva: Contrechamps, 1996); M. Ruffini, *L'Opera di Luigi Dallapiccola. Catalogo Ragionato* (Milan: Suvini Zerboni, 2002); R. Fearn, *The Music of Luigi Dallapiccola* (Rochester: University of Rochester Press, 2003).

Articles. F. Ballo, 'Le musiche corali di Dallapiccola', *La Rassegna musicale*, 10.4 (April, 1937), 136–39; F. Goldbeck, 'Luigi Dallapiccola: Musique pour trois pianos (*Hymnes*)',

For flute, clarinet and harp (1971); *Ora*. For soprano, mezzo-soprano, flute, cor anglais, small choir and orchestra (1971); *Bewegung*. For orchestra (1971); *Agnus*. For two sopranos and three clarinettists (1971); *E vo*. For soprano and instruments (1972); *Chemins IIC: Chemins IIB* plus solo bass clarinet (1972); *Après visage*. For tape and orchestra (1972); *Recital*. For mezzo-soprano and eighteen instruments (1972); *Concerto*. For two pianos and orchestra (1971–73); *Still*. For orchestra (1973); *Cries of London*. For six voices (1973); *Eindrücke*. For orchestra (1973–74); *Calmo (in memoriam Bruno Maderna)*. For soprano and instruments. Text by Homer (1974); *Points on the curve to find ....* For piano and twenty-two instruments (1974); *Per la dolce memoria de quel giorno*. Ballet based on Petrarch's *I Trionfi* with cheoreography by Béart. For tape (1974); *Musica leggera*. For flute, viola and cello (1974); *A-Ronne*, radio documentary for five actors. Text by Sanguineti (1974–75); *Chants parallèles*. For tape (1974–75); *Diario immaginario*. Radio-piece. Text compiled by Sermonti after Molière's *Le malade imaginaire* (1975); *Sequenza VIII*. For violin (1975); *Fa-Si*. For organ (1975); *Coro*. For forty voices and instruments (1975–76); *Il ritorno degli Snovidenia*. For cello and thirty instruments (1977); *Les mots sont allés*. For cello (1978); *Chemins V*. For clarinet and digital system (1980); *Sequenza IX*. For clarinet (1980), transcribed for saxophone as *Sequenza IX B* (1981); *La Vera Storia*. Opera in two acts for soprano, mezzo-soprano, tenor, baritone, bass, vocal ensemble and orchestra. Libretto by Calvino (1977–81); *Accord*. For four groups of wind isntruments (1980–81*); Duo, 'teatro immaginario'*. For baritone, two violins, choir and orchestra (1982); *Lied*. For clarinet (1983); *34 duetti*. For two violins (1979–83); *Un re in ascolto, 'azione musicale'* in two acts. Libretto by Calvino and Berio (1979–84); *Requies*. For orchestra (1984); *Voci.* For viola and instrumental ensemble (1984); *Sequenza X*. For trumpet (1984); *Call — St. Louis Fanfare*. For brass quintet (1985); *Luftklavier*. For piano (1985); *Naturale*. For viola, tam-tam, and recorded voice (1985–86); *Ricorrenze*. For wind quintet (1985–87); *Formazioni*. For orchestra (1985–87); *Sequenza XI*. For guitar (1987–88); *Canticum novissimi testamenti*. Ballata for choir. Libretto compiled by Sanguineti (1988); *Ofanim*. For female voice, two children's choirs, two instrumental groups, and Trails Sound Location System. Texts from bible: Ezekiel and *Song of Songs* (1988); *Concerto II (Echoing Curves)*. For piano and two instrumental groups (1988–89); *Rendering, 'Restoration of Fragments from a Symphony by Franz Schubert'*. For orchestra (1988–89); *Calmo*. For mezzo-soprano and small orchestra. Texts from *Song of Songs*, Sanguineti, Sadi and Homer (1989); *Canticum Novissimi Testamenti II*. For eight voices, clarinet quartet, saxophone quartet. Libretto by Sanguineti (1989); *Festum*. For orchestra 91989); *Feuerklavier*. For piano (1989); *Continuo*. For orchestra (1989–90); *Leaf*. For piano (1990); *Brin*. For piano (1990); *Chemins V* on *Sequenza XI*. For guitar and chamber orchestra (1992); *There is no tune*. For chorus (1994); *Twice upon ... .* For six instrumental groups (1994); *Compass*. For ballet-recital, piano and orchestra (1994); *Vor, während, nach Zaide*. With projections of texts by Arruga (1995); *Notturno*. String quartet (1995); *Sequenza XII*. For bassoon (1995); *Shofar*. For soprano, alto, tenor, bass and orchestra. Text by Celan (1995); *Re-call*. For twenty-three instruments (1995); *Sequenza XIII*. For accordian (1995–96); *Outis, 'azione musicale'* (1995–96); *Kol-Od (Chemins VI* on *Sequenza X)*. For trumpet and chamber orchestra (1995–96); *Ekphrasis (Continuo II)*. For orchestra (1996); *Récit (Chemins VII* on *Sequenza IXb)*. For saxophone and orchestra (1996); *Alternatim*. For clarinet, viola, and orchestra (1996–97); *Glosse*. String quartet (1997); *Cronaca del luogo, 'azione musicale'* (1998–99).   Principal publishers: Belwin-Mills, Schott, Suvini Zerboni, Universal.

Writings by Berio

'Prospettive nella musica', *Elettronica*, 3 (1956), 108–15 (French translation in *Musique en jeu*, no. 15 (1974), 60–63); 'Studio di fonologia musicale', *The Score*, no. 15 (1956), 83; 'Aspetti di artigianato formale', *Incontri musicali*, no. 1 (1956), 55–69 (French translation in *Contrechamps,* no. 1 (1983), 10–23); 'Poesia e musica: un'esperienza', *Incontri musicali,* no. 3 (1959), 98–111 (English translation in *Words/Music,* ed. by M. Edwards, Prospice x (Portree 1979), 9–20; French translation in *Contrechamps,* no. 1 (1983), 24–35); 'Du geste et de Piazza Carità' in *La musique et ses problèmes* contemporains, Cahiers Renaud-Barrault, i (Paris 1963), pp. 216–23 (Reproduced in *Contrechamps,* no. 1 (1983), 41–45); 'Commenti al Rock', *Nuova Rivista della Musica Italiana,* 1 (1967), 125–35; 'Eco in ascolto' in *Komponisten des 20. Jahrhunderts in der Paul Sacher Stifung* (Basel, 1986), pp. 329–34 (Reproduced in *Contemporary Music Review,* 5 (1989), 1–8).

Critical Works on Berio

Books. P. Altmann, *'Sinfonia' von Luciano Berio: eine analytische Studie* (Vienna: Univeral edition, 1977); R. Dalmonte and others, *Il gesto della forma: musica, poesia e teatro nell'opera di Luciano Berio* (Milan, 1981); N. Dressen, *Sprache und Musik bei Luciano Berio: Untersuchungen zu seinen Vokalkompositionen* (Regensburg: Gustav Bosse, 1982); D. Osmond-Smith, *Playing on Words: a Guide to Luciano Berio's 'Sinfonia'* (London: 1985); *Two Interviews with R. Dalmonte and B. András Varga,* trans. and ed. by D. Osmond-Smith (London: Marion Boyars, 1985). (Dalmonte's interviews originally published as *Intervista sulla musica* (Rome-Bari: Laterza, 1981); Varga's interviews originally published as *Beszélgetések Luciano Berióval* (Budapest: Editio Musica, 1981)); R. Karlen, *Inventare der Paul Sacher Stiftung: Musikmanuscripte,* ii: *Luciano Berio* (Oxford: Oxford University Press, 1988); D. Osmond-Smith, *Berio* (Oxford: Oxford University Press, 1991); P. F. Stacey, *Contemporary Tendencies in the Relationship of Music and text, with Special Reference to 'Pli selon pli' (Boulez) and 'Laborintus II' (Berio)* (New York: Garland Publishing, 1989); F. Menezes, *Luciano Berio et la phonologie: une approche jakobsonienne de son oeuvre* (Bern: 1993); *Berio,* ed. by E. Restagno (Turin: 1995); T. Gartmann, *'... dass nichts an sich jemals vollendet ist: Untersuchungen zum Instrumentalschaffen von Luciano Berio* (Bern: 1994; 2/1997); G. Ferrari, *Les débuts du théâtre musical d'avant-garde en Italie: Berio, Evangelisti, Maderna* (Paris: L'Harmattan, 2001).

Articles and interviews. R. Smith Brindle, 'Current Chronicle: Italy', *Music Quarterly,* 64 (1958), 95–101; P. Santi, 'Luciano Berio', *Die Reihe,* 4 (1960), 98–102; U. Eco, 'Apertura e "informazione" nella struttura musicale: uno strumento d'indagine', *Incontri musicali,* no. 4 (1960), 57–88; M. Bortolotto, 'The New Music in Italy', in *Contemporary Music in Europe,* ed. by P. H. Lang and N. Broder (New York: 1965), pp. 61–77 (also in *Music Quarterly,* 51 (1965), 61–77); M. Bortolotto, 'Luciano Berio ed dei piaceri', in *Fase seconda* (Turin: 1969), pp. 128–48; P. Castaldi, 'Luciano Berio ed Henri Pousseur: l'aspirazione a una libertà integrale', *Musica moderna,* iii/101 (1969), 65–77; U. Eco, 'Pensée structurale et pensée sérielle', *Musique en jeu,* no. 5 (1971), 45–56; D. Avron and J. F. Lyotard, ' "A few words to sing": *Sequenza III', Musique en jeu,* no.2 (1971), 28–44; F. Delalande: L'*Omaggio a Joyce* de Luciano Berio', *Musique en jeu,* no. 15 (1974), 45–54; W. Gruhn, 'Luciano Berio (1925): *Sequenza III* (1965)', in *Perspektiven neuer Musik,* ed. by E. Zimmerschied (Mainz: 1974), pp. 234–47; D. Osmond-Smith, 'Berio in London', *Music and Musicians* (March 1975), 16–19; D. Osmond-Smith, 'Berio and the Art of Commentary', *Musical Times,* 116 (1975), 871–72; G. W. Flynn, 'Listening to Berio's Music', *Music Quarterly,* 61 (1975), 388–421; J. Thibaudeau, 'Une question à Luciano Berio', in *La musique en projet,* ed. by S. Benmussa and B. Marger (Paris, 1975), pp. 169–72 (interview); P. Schnaus, 'Anmerkungen zu Luciano Berios *Circles*', *Musik und Bildung,* x (1978), 489–97; B. Trumpy, 'Pensées sur la musique de Luciano Berio', *Musique en jeu,* 33 (1978), 128–30; C. Annibaldi, 'Berio' in *The New Grove Dictionary of Music and Musicians* (London: Macmillan, 1980), pp. 554–59; D. Osmond-Smith, 'From Myth to Music: Lévi-Strauss's *Mythologiques* and Berio's *Sinfonia*', *Music Quarterly,* 67 (1981), 230–60; M. Hicks, 'Text, Music, and Meaning in

Berio's Sinfonia, 3rd movement', *Perspectives of New Music*, 20 (1981–82), 199–224; J. Jarvelepp, 'Compositional Aspects of *Tempi Concertati* by Luciano Berio', *Interface,* 11 (1982), 179–93; P. Albéra, 'Introduction aux neuf sequenzas', *Contrechamps*, no. 1 (1983), 91–122; P. Albéra, 'Matériaux et composition: sur trois oeuvres vocales de Luciano Berio', *Canadian University Music Review,* iv (1983), 66–91; J. Demierre, '*Circles*: e. e. Cummings lu par Luciano Berio', *Contrechamps*, no. 1 (1983), 123–80; D. Osmond-Smith, 'Joyce, Berio, et l'art de l'exposition', *Contrechamps*, no. 1 (1983), 83–89; I. Anhalt: 'Berio's *Sequenza III*: A Portrait', in *Alternative Voices* (Toronto: University of Toronto Press, 1984), pp. 25–40; D. Osmond-Smith, 'Intimate Rapport: *Coro* and *Requies*', *Listener*, 114 (1985), 38; I. Calvino, 'Un re in ascolto' in *Sotto il sole giaguaro* (Milan: Garzanti, 1986), pp. 59–92 (English translation by W. Weaver in *Under the Jaguar Sun* (New York: Harcourt Brace Jovanovitch, 1988); D. Osmond-Smith, 'Reinventing the Orchestra: *Concerto for two Pianos* and *Formazioni*', *Listener*, 121 (1987), 40–41; J. Mackay, 'Aspects of Post-Serial Structuralism in Berio's *Sequenza IV* and *VI*', *Interface*, 17 (1988), 223–29; M. Harry, 'Un re in ascolto', *Music and Musicians*, 37.6 (1988–89), 18–22; D. Osmond-Smith, 'Prospero's Peace: The Making of Berio's Opera *Un re in ascolto*', *Listener*, 121 (1989), 34–35; D. Osmond-Smith, 'La mesure de la distance: *Rendering* de Berio', *In Harmoniques*, no. 7 (1991), 147–52; L. Cosso, '*Un re in ascolto*: Berio, Calvino e altri', *Nuova Rivista della Musica Italiana*, 27 (1994), 557–74; J. Noller, 'Sulla forma in musica: Eco, Berio, gli altri e noi', *Sonus*, 6.2–3 (1994), 14–24; J. R. Piano and T. Regge, 'Della creazione', *Micromega*, no. 3 (1995), 29–45; 'Luciano Berio' (anonymous), *The Times*, 28 May 2003, p. 30.

Select bibliography of Armando Gentilucci

Musical Compositions by Gentilucci

Episodio. For 2 pianos (1961). *Fantasia (no. 1)*. For flute, stringed instruments, piano, and percussion (1963); *Tre movimenti sinfonici* (1963); *Recitativo e furioso*. For violin and piano (1965); *Concerto per 5 strumenti* (1965); *Diario*. String ensemble (1965); *Canti da Estravagario di Neruda*. For baritone, oboe, an quintet (1965); *Figure*. For 32 instrumentalists (1966); *Momenti*. For string quartet (1966); *Contrasti per 7 strumenti* (1966); *Elegie*. For piano trio (1966); *Figurazioni*. For flute and piano (1966). *Strofe di Ungaretti*. Mixed vocal sextet (1967); *Epitaffio per C. Pavese*. For clarinet, violin, and cello (1967); *Siamo prossimi al risveglio*. For baritone, double bass, piano and percussion. Text by Novalis (1968); *Sequenze*. For chamber orchestra (1968); *Fantasia (no. 2)*. For flute, stringed instruments, and percussion (1968); *Iter*. For piano (1969); *Frammenti*. For harp and harpsichord (1969). *Phonomimésis*. For chamber orchestra (1969); *Rifrazioni*. For string ensemble (1969); *Canti di Majakovski*. For a speaker, soprano, and 23 instruments (1970); *Diagramma*. For clarinet, violin, and piano (1970); *Diacronie*. For violin and 9 stringed instruments (1970); *Diario II*. For wind quintet (1971); *Crescendo*. For violin, cello, and piano (1971); *Studi per un 'Dies Irae'*. For orchestra (1971–72); *...e ho alzato gli occhi...*. For 2 violins and viola (1973); *Cile*. For wind quintet (1973); *Come qualcosa palpita nel fondo*. For violin and tape (1973); *Coinvolgimento*. For 2 violins, viola, and 19 instruments (1974);*Che voi pensiate*. Ballet with tape music (1975); *Musica Elettroacustica* (1975); *Scontri*. For violin and chamber orchestra (1975); *Tensioni*. For viola and piano (1975–76); *In divenire*. For viola and orchestra (1976); *Tensioni*. For viola and piano (1976); *Contrasto*. For percussionist (1976). *Molteplice*. For violin, cello, piano, and tape (1976–77); *Mensurale*. For 11 stringed instruments (or complete stringed orchestra) (1977); *Tempo-spazio*. For flute and harp (1977); *Trama*. For ten wind instruments (1977); *Dal suono al suono*. For piano (1977); *Musica riservata*. For piano (1977). *Il tempo sullo sfondo*. Ballet for percussion and stringed instruments (1978); *Lied senza parole*. For soprano and piano (1978); *Lieve suonò la notte*. For violin and piano

(1979); *Nel suono I e II*. For piano (1979); *Attraverso il suono*. For oboe, clarinet, and bassoon (1979); *Cantus*. For cello (1979); *Gesti e risonanze*. For clarinet and percussion (1980); *Haleine*. For 2 trumpets, 2 trombones, and bass tuba (1980); *Sei brevi canti*. For flute (1980); *Le secrete vie*. For choir and orchestra. Text by Ugo Foscolo (1980–81); *Voci dal silenzio ('Stimmen aus der Stille')*. For orchestra (1981); *Una traccia, sommessamente*. For violin and piano (1981); *Oh, voce che mi sfuggi*. For flute (1981); *Polifonie per Andrea Centazzo*. For instruments and percussion (1981); *In alto le stelle*. For nine instruments (1981); *Intervalli del tempo*. For string quartet (1981); *Pour un rag-time englouti*. For piano (1982); *Memoria di un gondellied*. For piano (1982); *Ramo di foglia verde*. For bass, 'white' voice, and orchestra. Text from Dante's *Rime* (1982); *Nei quieti silenzi*. For 11 instruments (1983); *In Lebensfluten*. For solo oboe (1983); *Nei labirinti del suono*. For piano duet (1983). *Frammenti di un diario d'autunno*. For piano (1983); *Canto notturno*. For soprano and chamber orchestra (1983); *Al telaio del tempo*. For solo clarinet (1983); *Un mutevole intreccio*. For 2 wind quintets (1983); *Ritorno di un canto dimenticato*. For oboe and small orchestra (1984); *Frammento senza titolo*. For guitar (1984). *Specchi della memoria*. Sextet for wind instruments and piano (1984); *Un mutevole intreccio*. For double wind quintet (1984); *Metafore del tempo*. For piano (1984); *Dal fondo di uno specchio*. For ensemble (1984); *Echi del suono*. For piano duet (1985); *Dove non sono confini*. For solo cello (1985); *Sparì la luna*. For soprano and guitar (1985); *Le clessidre di Dürer*. For violin, cello, and piano (1985); *Il chiarore dell'utopia*. For soprano and orchestra (1985); *Il rinfrangersi di un'ombra*. For piano (1985); *Ai confini dell'aurora*. For trombone and piano (1985); *Fibre di una tela all'orizzonte*. For double bass (1985); *Azzurri abissi*. For clarinet and orchestra (1985–86); *Metamorfosi su un alleluja*. Solo bassoon (1986); *In acque solitarie*. For flute (1986); *Le trame di un labirinto*. For alto saxophone (1986); *Moby Dick*. Opera (1986–88); *Dolce fanciullezza dell'aria e del cielo*. For light soprano, piccolo, clarinet, bass clarinet, and cello (1987); *In acque solitarie* (a marginal note for *Moby Dick*). For solo flute (1987); *Frammenti sinfonici da Moby Dick* (1988); *Due arie cameristiche e coro da Moby Dick*. For soprano, chorus, and instruments (1988); *Una trasfigurata rievocazione cubana*. For 8 instruments (1988); *Nel flusso del tempo, recitativo per chitarra* (1988); *L'aria improvvisa vibrante*. For three trumpets and timpani (1988); *Nell'ombra della tua notte*. For chorus (1988); *Selva di pensieri sonanti*. For clarinet and piano (1988); *Frammenti poetici di Marina Cvetaeva*. For soprano and instruments (1989); *Melodia. 15 ottobre, 1989*. For one stringed or wind instrument; *Oltre il mare aperto*. For soprano and renaissance instruments (1989); *Rien de plus*. For soprano and instruments (1989); *Lo scrigno dei suoni*. For piano (1989). Principal publishers: Ricordi, Sonzogno, Suvini Zerboni.

Writings by Gentilucci

Books. *Guida all'ascolto della musica contemporanea* (Milan: Feltrinelli, 1969); *Introduzione alla musica elettronica* (Milan: Feltrinelli, 1972); *Oltre l'avanguardia: un invito al molteplice* (Fiesole: Discanto Edizioni, 1980).

Articles. 'Il futurismo e lo sperimentalismo musicale d'oggi', *Convegno musicale,1* (1964), 275–303; 'La tecnica corale di Luigi Nono', *Rivista Musicale Italiana*, 2 (1967), 111–29; 'L'alea oggi', *Discoteca*, 77 (1968), 24–25; 'Giacomo Manzoni', *Nuova Rivista Musicale Italiana*, 2 (1968), 1147–61; 'Šostakovič anno 1925', *Nuova Rivista Musicale Italiana*, 4 (1970), 445–62; '"L'action ne doit pas être une réaction mais une creation": appunti su una recente opera di Luigi Nono', *Quaderni della RaM*, no. 5 (1972), 67–74; 'Vittorio Fellegara: una presenza', *Nuova Rivista Musicale Italiana*, 8 (1974), 579–91; 'Gestualità drammatica nel teatro musicale italiano del dopoguerra', *Musica/Realtà*, 1 (1980), 81–93; 'György Ligeti', in *Ligeti*, ed. by E. Restagno (Turin, 1985), pp. 58–64; 'La figura musicale e la terza dimensione', *Quaderni della Civica Scuola di Musica*, 13 (1986), 83–85; 'La musica contemporanea a cavallo tra due decenni: 1970/80', *Musica/Realtà*, 7 (1986),

59–74; 'Attorno a Moby Dick: appunti sulla composizione di un'opera di teatro musicale', *il verri*, 5–6 (1987), 34–45; 'Gli anni sessanta', in *Nono*, ed. by E. Restagno (Turin, 1987), pp. 157–68.

Critical works on Gentilucci

H. W. Heister, 'Kantabilität und Klangkonstruktion: ein Werkporträt des italienischen Komponisten Armando Gentilucci', *Musiktexte*, 12 (1985), 7–10; H. W. Heister, 'Scrigno dei suoni e chiarore dell'utopia: aspetti dell'opera di Armando Gentilucci', *Musica/Realtà*, 11 (1990), 117–32; 'Saggi su Armando Gentilucci', *Musica/Realtà*, 11 (1990), 29–54 (Contributions by Goffredo Petrassi, Mario Baroni, Giordano Gasparini, Giacomo Manzoni, Luigi Pestalozza, and others); G. Ferrari, *Armando Gentilucci. Il suono, il sogno e il chiarore dell'utopia* (Milan: BMG Ricordi Publications, 1999); G. Ferrari, 'Gentilucci, Armando', in *The New Grove Dictionary of Music* (London, Macmillan, 2001), pp. 660–61.

Select bibliography of Giacomo Manzoni

Musical compositions by Manzoni

Piccola Suite. For violin and piano (1952–55); *Klavieralbum: Preludio — "Grave" di W. Cuney — Finale*. For female voice, clarinet, violin, viola, and cello; *Seconda Piccola Suite* (1956); *Cinque Vicariote*. For mixed choir and orchestra (1958); *Improvvisazione*. For viola and piano (1958); *Tre liriche di Paul Éluard*. For soprano, flute, trumpet, violin, and cello (1958); *La sentenza*. One-act theatre piece by Emilio Jona (1960); *Don Chisciotte*. For soprano, small chorus, and chamber orchestra, on a poem by NazimHikmet (1961); *Due sonetti italiani*. For mixed choir. Texts by Cecco Angiolieri and Giacomo Leopardi (1961); *Quattro poesie spagnole*. For baritone, clarinet, viola, and guitar (1962); *Studio per 24*. For chamber orchestra (1962); *Studio no. 2*. For orchestra (1962–63); *Atomtod*. Two-part opera by Emilio Jona (1964); *Studio Tre*. Electronic music (1965); *Musica notturna*. For 5 wind instruments, piano, and percussion (1966); *Insiemi*. For orchestra (1967); *Il ballo delle ingrate di Claudio Monteverdi*. Transcription for modern orchestra (1968); *Ombre (alla memoria di Che Guevara)*. For orchestra and choral voices (1968); *Quadruplum*. For 2 trumpets and 2 trombones (1968); *Parafrasi con finale*. For 10 instruments (1969); *Spiel*. For 11 stringed instruments (1969); *Parole da Beckett*. For 2 choirs, 3 groups of instruments, and a tape (1970–71); *Quartetto*. For strings (1971); *Hölderlin (frammento)*. For chorus and orchestra (1972); *Multipli*. For chamber orchestra (1973); *Variabili*. For orchestra (1973); *Per Massimiliano Robespierre*. Theatre work in 2 parts based on texts by Robespierre, Virginio Puecher, and others (1974); *Percorso a otto*. For double woodwind quartet (1975); *Percorso C*. For bassoon and tape (1975); *Epodo*. For wind quintet (1976); *Percorso C2*. For bassoon and 11 stringed instruments (1976); *Percorso F*. For doublebass (1976); *Sigla*. For 2 trumpets and 2 trombones (1976); *Suite Robespierre*. For soloists, 2 reciters, mixed choir, and orchestra (1976); *Masse: Omaggio a Edgar Varèse*. For piano and orchestra (1977); *Lessico*. For double stringed orchestra of 24 or 52 players (1978); *Modulor*. For 4 orchestras (1979); *Percorso GG*. For clarinet and CD (1979); *Hölderlin: epilogo*. For 10 instruments (1980); *D'improvviso*. For 6 or 12 percussionists (1981); *Echi*. For guitar (1981); *Ode*. For orchestra (1982); *Estremità* For voice. Text by Francesco Leonetti (1983); *Incipit*. For piano (1983); *Incontro*. For violin and string quartet (1983); *Nuovo incontro*. For violin and strings (1984); *Opus 50 (Daunium)*. For 10 instruments and percussion (1984); *Scene sinfoniche per il Doktor Faustus*. With off-stage chorus. Text by Giacomo Manzoni on ideas by Thomas Mann (1984); *Die Strahlen der Sonne...* . For 9 instruments (1985); *Omaggio a Josquin: trascrizione di 'Nymphes des bois ...'* (*Déploration d'Ockeghem*). For soprano, horn, violin, 2 violas, and cello. Text by Jean Molinet (1985); *Studio per il finale del Doktor Faustus*. For chorus and orchestra. Text by Giacomo Manzoni on ideas by Thomas Mann (1985); *Dedica*. On texts by Bruno Maderna for flute, bass, and symphonic orchestra (with instrumental group and off-stage chorus ad libitum) (1985–86); *Percorso H*. For flute (1987); *Uéi preà la biele stele*. For male voice choir in unison, and one or two sound boxes. Text by an anonymous Friulan writer (1987); *Dieci versi di Emily Dickinson*. For light soprano, string quartet, two harps, and ten stringed instruments (1988); *Doktor Faustus*. Scenes from the novel by Thomas Mann. Text by Thomas Mann arranged by Giacomo Manzoni in 3 acts (1988); *Frase*. For clarinet and piano (1988); *Weheklag Doctor Fausti*. Interlude from *Doktor Faustus*, for chorus and orchestra. Text by Histotia von D. Johann Fausten, 1587 (1988); *An die Musik*. For soprano and flute. Text by Rainer Maria Rilke (1989); *To planets and to flowers*. For saxophone quartet (1989); *Adagio e solenne*. For orchestra (1990); *Malinamusik*. For orchestra (1990); *Poesie dell'assenza*. For male reciter and orchestra. Text by Giorgio Caproni (1990); *4 versi di Marina Cvetaeva* (In memory of Armando Gentilucci). For soprano and violin (1990); *Duplum*. For bassoon and trombone (1991); *Essai*. For flute, bass clarinet, and piano (1991); *Finale e aria* (on a poem by Ingeborg Bachmann). For soprano, orchestra, and string quartet (1991); *Hermano aterrado*. For soprano and suspended cymbal. Text by Pablo Neruda (1992); *Il deserto cresce. Tre metafore da Friedrich Nietzsche*. For voice, chorus, and orchestra (1992); *4 Epigrammi*. For baritone, bass clarinet, and instrumental group. Text by Emilio Jona (1993); *Frase 2*. For flute and violin (1993); *Frase 2b*. For 3 violins, suspended cymbal, and 3 crotales (1993); *Musiche per l'Oreste di Vittorio Alfieri*. For tape (1993); *Opus 75*. For seven instruments and percussion (1993); *Ed io non prendo posa*. For bass and 8 instruments. Text by Matteo Maria Boiardo arranged by Luigi Pestalozza (1994); *Una ... voce ...chiama*. For female voice, viola, electronic processors, and tape. Text by Franco Fortini (1994); *Furioso*. For violin and piano (1995); *Les hommes, la terre, les pierres*. For six players and tape. On texts by A. Artaud (1995); *Musica per Inferno di Dante*. For trombone, live electronics, and chorus on tape. Text by Dante Alighieri (1995); *Musica per Pontormo*. For string quartet (1995); *Quanto oscura selva trovai*. On texts by Dante Alighieri (1995); *Allen*. For reader and chamber orchestra. Text taken from *Diario Indiano* by Allen Ginsberg, in the Italian translation by F. Pivano (1996); *Aria della gioia*. For soprano, trumpet, 2 suspended cymbals. Text by William Blake, taken from the volume *L'incarico e il fine* by Luigi Pestalozza (1997); *Moi, Antonin A*. On texts by A. Artaud requested by Giacomo Manzoni for light soprano, reader, and orchestra (1997); *MTRC 1998*. For clarinet in B flat, cello, and piano (1998); *Trame d'ombra*. For soprano, tenor, chorus, and instrumental group (1998); *Transitori d'estinzione*. For 5 instruments (1998); *Du Dunkelheit*. For female voice and piano (1998); *Motto: AMM*. For flute (1999); *Stomp (It Don't Mean ... Breakdown)* (Dedicated to Duke Ellington). For wind quintet (1999); *Videomusik*. For bass clarinet, percussion, viola, cello, and counter bassoon (1999); *Il sorriso svanito*. For flute, bass clarinet, percussion, violin, and viola (1999); *O Europa!* For soprano and orchestra. On texts by Attila József (1999); *Il clamoroso non incominciar neppure*. For orchestra (2000); *Oltre la soglia — alla memoria di Franco Donatoni*. For female voice and string quartet. On texts by Caterina da Siena, Marina Cvetaeva, Karoline Günderrode, Goethe, Margherita, Sylvia Plath, Antonia Pozzi, Amelia Rosselli, and Anne Sexton (2000); *Pensiero XX di Giacomo Leopardi*. For reader, string quartet, and piano (2001); *Largo*. For flute / piccolo, harpsichord, and string quartet (2001); *Freedom*. (Tribute to Jimi Hendrix). For cello and sounds on tape (2001); *Sul passaggio del tempo*. For female voice (or male or female reader, and female voice) and chamber orchestra. Texts by R. Sanesi (2002); *Entrata*. For trombone (2002); *Studio*. For piano (2002). Principal publishers: Ricordi, Suvini Zerboni.

Writings by Manzoni

Books. *Guida all'ascolto della musica sinfonica* (Milan: Feltrinelli, 1967); With L. Pestalozza and V. Puecher, *Per Massimiliano Robespierre* (Bari, 1975); A. *Schönberg. L'uomo, l'opera, i testi musicati* (Milan: Feltrinelli, 1975; "Le Sfere", Ricordi/LIM, 1997); *Scritti*, ed. by Claudio Tempo (Florence: La Nuova Italia, 1991) (a selection of writings from 1955 to 1989); *Tradizione e utopia*, ed. by Antonio De Lisa (Milan: Feltrinelli, 1994) (a selection of writings from 1956 to 1992).

Prefaces to the following volumes. T. W. Adorno, *Dissonanze* (Milan: Feltrinelli, 1959); A. Schoenberg, *Elementi di composizione musicale* (Milan: Suvini Zerboni, 1969); T. W. Adorno, *Il fido maestro sostituito* (Turin: Einaudi, 1969); T. Mann, *Doktor Faustus* (Milan: Mondadori, 1980); E. Varèse, *Il suono organizzato* (Milan: Ricordi/Unicoepli, 1985); E. Girardi, *Guida all'ascolto dell'opera* (Milan: Feltrinelli, 1992).

Articles. 'A *Survivor from Warsaw* di A. Schoenberg', *Il diapason*, 2 (1955), 13; 'Bruno Maderna', *Die Reihe*, 4 (1958), 113–18 (English translation in *Die Reihe*, 4 (1960), 114–20); 'Omaggio a Varèse', *Discoteca*, no. 57 (1966), 22; 'Monteverdi', *I protagonisti della storia universale. Gli stati nazionali*, 6 (Milan: 1966, 2/1972), 281.

Translations. *T.W. Adorno: Dissonanze* (Milan: 1959); *T.W. Adorno: Filosofia della musica moderna* (Turin: 1959); *A. Schoenberg: Manuale di armonia* (Milan: 1963); *T.W. Adorno: Wagner-Mahler* (Turin: 1966); *A. Schoenberg: Funzioni strutturali dell'armonia* (Milan: 1967); *T.W. Adorno: Il fido maestro sostituito: studi sulla comunicazione della musica* (Turin: 1969); *A. Schoenberg: Elementi di composizione musicale* (Milan: 1969); *A. Schoenberg: Esercizi preliminari di contrappunto* (Milan: 1970); *T.W. Adorno: Introduzione alla sociologia della musica* (Turin: 1971, 2/1974); *A. Schoenberg: Analisi e pratica musicale: scritti 1909–50* (Turin: 1974).

Interviews and critical works on Manzoni

F. Degrada, '5 domande a Giacomo Manzoni', *Discoteca*, no. 77 (Milan: 1968), 33–36; A. Gentilucci, 'Giacomo Manzoni', *Nuova Rivista della Musica Italiana*, 2 (1968), 1147–61; A. Gentilucci, 'Luigi Nono e Giacomo Manzoni: avanguardia e impegno: rapporto dialettico', *Musica moderna*, no. 100 (Milan: 1968), 49; A. Gentilucci, *Guida all'ascolto della musica contemporanea* (Milan: Feltrinelli, 1969); A. Gentilucci, *Introduzione alla musica elettronica* (Milan: Feltrinelli, 1972); J. Noller, *Engagement und Form: Giacomo Manzonis Werk in kulturtheoretischen und musikhistorischen Zusammenhängen* (Frankfurt, 1987); H.W. Heister, 'Experiment v. Engagement: zu einigen Werken von Giacomo Manzoni', *Musiktexte*, 23 (February 1988), 6–9; F. Dorsi, *Giacomo Manzoni* (Milan: 1989); J. Noller, 'Musica e grammaturgia del *Doktor Faustus*', *Sonus*, 1.1 (1989), 49–52; G.C. Taccani, 'Scena, musica, società', *Sonus*, 2.1 (1990), 69–89; L. Pestalozza, *L'opposizione musicale* (Milan: 1991), 185–92; P. Santi, 'Musica del diavolo per Dottor Faust dei nostri tempi', Civiltà musicale (Feb 1991), 23–46; *Omaggio a Giacomo Manzoni* (Milan: 1992); *Sonus Contemporary Music Materials*, ed. by A. De Lisa (Potenza: 1993) (includes P. Petazzi, 'Remarks on New Music for the Theatre in Italy', 3–24; A. De Lisa, 'Scenic and Symphonic in the Works of G. Manzoni', 25–30; A. De Lisa, 'About *Faustus* and other things, interview, 31–38); *Per Giacomo Manzoni*, ed. by C. Di Gennaro and L. Pestalozza (Lucca: Libreria Musicale Italiana, 2002).

Select bibliography of Bruno Maderna

Musical compositions by Maderna

Introduzione e passacaglia 'Lauda sion salvatorem'. For orchestra (1942); *Concerto*. For piano (before 1946); *Serenata*. For instrumental group (1946); *Sangue a Ca' Foscari*. Score for film directed by M. Calandri (1946); *Liriche su Verlaine*. For soprano and piano (1946–47); *Concerto*. For two pianos and instrumental group (1948); *Composizione no. 1*. For orchestra (1949); *Liriche greche*. For soprano, chamber chorus, and instruments (1949); *Fantasia*. For two pianos (1949); *Il mistero di Venezia*. Score for film directed by I. Ferronetti (1950); *Studi per il processo di Kafka*. For soprano, reciter, and orchestra (1950); *Il mio cuore è nel sud*. Radio play by G. Patroni Griffi. For instrumental group (RAI, 1950); *Composizione no. 2*. For orchestra (1950); *Le due verità*. Score for film directed by A. Leonviola (1951); *Improvvisazione no. 1*. For orchestra (1951); *Musica su due dimensioni*. For flute, cymbals, and tape (1952); *Il moschettiere fantasma*. Score for film directed by Calandri and W. French (1952); *Das eiserne Zeitalten*. Ballet (1952–53); *Divertimento in 2 tempi*. For flute and piano (1953); *Cantata da camera '4 lettere' per Kranichstein*. For soprano, bass, 2 pianos, and chamber orchestra (1953); *Improvvisazione no. 2*. For orchestra (1953); *Il fabbro del convento*. Score for film directed by A. Leonviola (1953); *Noi cannibali*. Score for film directed by A. Leonviola (1953); *Concerto*. For flute (1954); *Ritratto di città*. Electronic music (in collaboration with L. Berio and R. Leydi) (1954); *Sequenze e strutture*. Electronic music, for tape (1954); *Composizione in tre tempi*. For orchestra (1954); *Opinione pubblica*. Score for film directed by M. Corgnati (1954); *Notturno*. Electronic music, for tape (1955); *Quartetto*. For strings (1955); *Serenata no. 2*. For 11 instruments (1957); *Musica su 2 dimensioni*. For flute and tape (1957); *Syntaxis*. Electronic music, for tape (1957); *Continuo*. Electronic music, for tape (1958); *L'augellin Belverde* . Radio play, after C. Gozzi (1958); 'Dark rapture crawl' in *Divertimento* by Berio and Maderna. For orchestra (1959); *Concerto*. For piano (1959); *L'altro mondo, ovvero Gli stati e imperi della luna*. Radio play by A. Brissoni after J. Swift, *Gulliver's Travels* (1959); *Amor di violino*.Radio play by E. Carsana (1959–60); *Dimensioni no. 2*. ('Invenzione su una voce'). Electronic music and female voice; phonemes by H. G. Helms (1960); *Il cavallo di Troia*. Radio musical, by G. Da Venezia and U. Liberatore (1960); *Il puff*. Radio play by E. Scribe (1960); *Honeyrêves*. For flute and piano (1961); *Don Perlimplin*. Radio opera in 1 act based on the play by F. García Lorca, trans. by Vittorio Bodini (1961); *Serenata no. 3*. Electronic music (1962); *Macbeth*. Ballet by A. A. Milloss, after Shakespeare (1962); *Konzert für Oboe und Kammerorchester* (1962); *Dimensioni III*. For solo flute and orchestra (1962); *Entropia I, II*. For orchestra (included in Hyperion) (1963); *Per Caterina*. For violin and piano (1963); *Aria da Hyperion*. For soprano, solo flute, and orchestra.Text by F. Hölderlin (1964); *Hyperion: Lirica in forma di spettacolo* by Maderna and V. Puecher. After F. Hölderlin; phonemes by H. G. Helms (1964). (Revised as *Hyperion en het geweld*. Texts by W. H. Auden, García Lorca, Hölderlin (1968), and again as *Hyperion-Orfeo dolente* (1968). Concert excerpts: *Hyperion* = *Dimensioni III* + *Aria da Hyperion*; *Hyperion II* = *Dimensioni III* + *Cadenze* (for solo flute) + *Aria da Hyperion*; *Hyperion III* = *Hyperion* + *Stele per Diotima*); *Le rire*. Electronic music (1964); *Stele per Diotima*. For orchestra and soloists (1965); *Dimensioni IV*. For orchestra (includes *Dimensioni III* + *Stele per Diotima*) (1964); *Aulodia per Lothar*. For oboe d'amore and guitar *ad libitum* (1965); *Amanda*. For chamber orchestra (1966); *Widmung*. For solo violin (1967); *Concerto no. 2*. For oboe (1967); *La morte ha fatto l'uovo*. Score for film directed by G. Questi (1968); *Entropia III*. For orchestra (from *Hyperion*) (1968–69); *Ritratto di Erasmo*. Radio play for reciters, chorus, and orchestra (1969/70); *Musica di scena per l'opera televisiva From A to Z di R. Rass*. Electronic music (1969); *Quadrivium*. For 4 percussionists and 4 orchestral groups (1969); *Concerto*. For violin and orchestra (1969); *Serenata per un satellite*. For chamber ensemble (1969); *Suite: Klage, Message, Psalm, Schicksalslied*. For flute, oboe /

oboe d'amore, soprano, chorus, orchestra (from *Hyperion*). Texts by W. H. Auden, García Lorca, Hölderlin) (1969); *Grande aulodia*. For flute, oboe, and orchestra (1970); *Von A bis Z*. Incidental music on tape (1970); *Julliard Serenade*. For small orchestra and tape (1971); *Tempo libero I*. Electronic music (1971); *Tempo libero II = Julliard Serenade + Tempo libero I* (1971); *Viola*. For viola or viola d'amore (1971); *Solo*. For oboe, oboe d'amore,English horn, and musette (1971); *Pièce pour Ivry*. For solo violin (1971); *Ausstrahlung*. For female voice, flute, oboe, orchestra, and tape (1971); *Dialodia*. For 2 flutes or two oboes or other instruments (1972); *Y después*. For guitar (1972); *Aura*. For orchestra (1972); *Venetian Journal*. For tenor, 22 instruments, and tape. Text by J. Levy after J. Boswell (1972); *Biogramma*. For large orchestra (1972); *Giardino religioso*. For small orchestra (1972); *Ages*. Radio play by Maderna and Giorgio Pressburger. For voices, chorus, and orchestra. Text from *As you like it* by Shakespeare (1972); *All the World's a Stage* (included in *Ages*). For chorus (1972); *Ständchen für Tini*. For violin and viola (1972); *Satyricon*. One act opera. Text by Petronius (1973); *Terzo Concerto*. For oboe (1973). Principal publishers: Ricordi, Salabert, Schott, Suvini Zerboni.

Critical works on Maderna

G. Manzoni, 'Bruno Maderna', *Die Reihe*, 4 (1958), 113–19; English translation in *Die Reihe*, iv (1960), 114–20; R. Smith Brindle, Current Chronicle', *Music Quarterly,* 45 (1959), 388–92; V. Puecher, 'Diario di un'esperienza', *Sipario*, 19.224 (1964), 46; P. Steinitz, 'Bruno Maderna's *Greek Lyrics*, *Musical Times*, 106 (1965), 186; R. Smith Brindle, 'Maderna and Berio', *The Listener* (10 June 1971), 761; L. Pinzauti, 'A colloquio con Bruno Maderna', *Nuova Rivista della Musica Italiana*, 6 (1972), 545–52; L. Nono, 'Ricordo di due musicisti', *Cronache musicali Ricordi,* no. 3 (1973), 1–3; F. Donatoni, 'La Grande *Aulodia* di Bruno Maderna' *Chigiana*, n.s., 11 (1974), 375; *La Biennale di Venezia: annuario 1975 / eventi 1974* (Venice, 1975), 829–40 (includes articles by L. Berio, A. Clementi, F. Donatoni, L. Nono, H. Pousseur, K. Stockhausen); M. Mila, *Maderna musicista europeo* (Turin, 1976); H. Weber, 'Form und Satztechnik in Bruno Madernas *Streichquartett*', *Miscellanea del Cinquantenario Edizioni Suvini Zerboni* (Milan, 1978), 206–15; L. Pinzauti, 'La lezione di Maderna', *Nuova Rivista Musicale Italiana*, xix (1980), 393–403; A. Giubertoni, 'Le fonti poetiche dell'*Hyperion* di Bruno Maderna', *Nuova Rivista Musicale Italiana*, 15 (1981), 197–205; F. Magnani, 'Considerazioni sul rapporto fra musica e testo nell'opera di Bruno Maderna', *Ricerche musicali*, 5 (1981), 6–25; M. Baroni and R. Dalmonte, 'Inediti maderniani', *Musica/Realtà*, no. 10 (1983), 41–47; G. Montecchi, 'Bruno Maderna e la musica leggera', *Musica/Realtà*, no. 10 (1983), 55–61; H. Weber, 'Maderna compositore veneziano', *Musica/Realtà*, no. 12 (1983), 31–40; M. Baroni, 'Bruno Maderna dieci anni dopo', *Croniche Musicali Ricordi*, no. 17 (1984), 2; M. Baroni and R. Dalmonte (editors), *Bruno Maderna: Documenti* (Milan, 1985); R. Fearn, 'Bruno Maderna: from the Cafe Pedrocchi to Darmstadt', *Tempo*, no. 155 (1985), 8–14; R. Dalmonte, 'Il caso Maderna: questioni critiche attorno all'edizione di musiche contemporanee', *Per la tutela del lavoro musicologio* (Milan, 1986), 86–90; H. Weber, 'Dallapiccola, Maderna, Nono: Tradition in der italienischen Moderne', *Die Wiener Schule in der Musikgeschichte des 20. Jahrhunderts* (Vienna, 1984), 93–98; C. Bitter, 'Bruno Maderna', *Komponisten des 20 Jahrhunderts in der Paul Sacher Stiftung* (Basel, 1986), 299–302; M. Mila,'Per un ritratto di Maderna', *Komponisten des 20 Jahrhunderts,* 303–13; R. Fearn, 'At the doors of Kranichstein: Maderna's *Fantasia* for 2 pianos', *Tempo*, no. 163 (1987), 14–20; J. Noller, 'Von Marinetti zu Maderna: musikalisches Hörspiel und Radiophonie in Italien', *Zibaldone: Zeitschrift für italienische Kultur der Gegenwart*, no. 8 (1989), 61–74; M. Baroni and R. Dalmonte (editors) *Studi su Bruno Maderna* (Milan, 1989) (includes writings by R. Dalmonte, M. J. Böhlen, M. Romito, M. Garda, J. Noller, G. Montecchi, P. Petrazzi, G. Colombo Taccani,

F. Magnani, A. Vidolin, G. Riva, A. Solbiati, M. Baroni, M. Armellini); G. Borio, 'Der Musik Madernas als Problem der Gegenwart: Konzentration auf die Dimension einer neuen Melodik', *Wienmodern: ein internationales Festival mit Musik* (Vienna, 1989); R. Fearn, *Bruno Maderna* (London, 1990); G. Borio, 'La tecnica seriale in *Studi per 'Il Processo' di Franz Kafka'*, *Musica / Realtà*, no. 32 (1990), 27–39; L. Pestalozza, 'L'interdipendenza di Bruno', *I quaderni della civica scuola di musica*, nos. 21–22 (Milan, 1992), 17–22; G. Montecchi, '*Continuo* di Bruno Maderna', *I quaderni della civica scuola*, 43–57; J. Noller, '*Musica su due Dimensioni* e l'unidimensionalità della musica nuova', *I quaderni della civica scuola*, 65–69; C. Ambrosini, 'Il satellite sereno', *I quaderni della civica scuola*, 81–98; G. Borio and V. Rizzardi,'Die musikalische Einheit von B. Madernas *Hyperion*', *Quellenstudien II: Zwölf componisten des 20. Jahrhunderts* (Winrwethur, 1992), 117–48; V. Rizzardi, L'ultima serie: In margine alla genesi dell'*Hyperion* di Bruno Maderna', *Mitteilungen der paul Sacher Stiftung*, 6 (1993), 26–29; N. Sani, 'Musica elettronica, poetica, scrittura: un colloquio inedito con Bruno Maderna', *Musica/Realtà*, no. 47 (1995), 65–77; N. Verzina, 'Concezione poetica e pensiero formale nel Maderna post-seriale: il *Könzert für Oboe und Kammerensemble* (19622–69), *Studi musicali*, 14 (1995), 131–59; R. Dalmonte, 'Prioritätsrechte nie beansprucht: Madernas Praxis und Poetik', *Von Kranichstein zur Gegenwart* (Darmstaadt, 1996), 199–205; N. Verzina, 'La dernière composition de Bruno Maderna: le *Troisième Concerto pour hautbois et orchestre* (1973)', *Dissonanz/Dissonance*, no. 49 (1996), 16–22; M. Mila, *Maderna. Musicista Europeo* (Turin: Einaudi, 1976); G. Ferrari, *Les débuts du théâtre musical d'avant-garde en Italie: Berio, Evangelisti, Maderna* (Paris: L'Harmattan, 2001).

CRITICAL BIBLIOGRAPHY

ABRAHAM, G., *The Concise Oxford History of Music* (Oxford: Oxford University Press, 1990)

ALVAREZ, A., *Beckett* (Glasgow: Fontana Modern Masters, 1973)

ARCHER, W. G., in *Love Songs of Vidyapati*, trans. by D. Bhattacharya, ed. with notes and intro. by W. G. Archer (London: 1963)

ARMOUR, P., 'Gold, Silver, and True Treasure: Economic Imagery in Dante', *Romance Studies*, 23 (spring 1994), 7–30

BARBERI SQUAROTTI, G., *Astrazione e realtà* (Milan: Rusconi e Paolazzi, 1960)

BAUSANI, A., 'Prefazione' in *Omar Khayyám. Quartine (Robâ'iyyât)* (Turin: Einaudi, 1956)

BHAKTIVEDANTA SWAMI PRABHUPĀDA, A. C. (translation and commentary), *Bhagavad-gītā [As it is]* (New York, Los Angeles, London, Bombay: The Bhaktivedanta Book Trust, 1972)

BOITANI, P., *The Shadow of Ulysses. Figures of a Myth* (Oxford: Clarendon Press, 1994)

BONAVENTURA, A., *Dante e la musica* (Livorno: Raffaellol Giusti, 1904)

BORONI, C., *Giuseppe Ungaretti, dall'Innocenza alla Memoria* (Venice: Corbo e Fiore Editori, 1992)

BROUGH, J., in *Poems from the Sanskrit*. Trans. and intro. by J. Brough (Baltimore: Penguin Books, 1968)

BUSH, R., *The Genesis of Ezra Pound's Cantos* (Princeton: Princeton University Press, 1976)

BROWN, R., 'Dallapiccola's use of symbolic self-quotation', *Studi musicali*, no. 4 (1975), 277–304

CAMBON, G., *Giuseppe Ungaretti* (Columbia: Columbia University Press, 1967)

CARY, J., *Three Modern Italian Poets* (New York: New York University Press, 1969)

CHIASSON, E. J., 'Tennyson's "Ulysses" — A Re-interpretation', in *Critical Essays on the Poetry of Tennyson*, ed. by J. Killham (London: Routledge, 1960), pp. 164–73

CAESAR, M., and P. HAINSWORTH, EDS, *Writers and Society in Contemporary Italy* (Leamington Spa: Berg, 1984)

COE, R., N., *Samuel Beckett* (Edinburgh, London: Oliver and Boyd, 1968)

COLLINS, J., *The Mind of Kierkegaard* (Princeton: Princeton University Press, 1953)

CONTINI, G., 'Dallapiccola and Dante', in *Luigi Dallapiccola: Saggi, testimonianze, carteggio, biografia e bibliografia* (Milan: Suvini Zerboni, 1975), pp. 55–56

DEGRADA, F., and others, *Omaggio a Giacomo Manzoni* (Milan: Ricordi, 1992)

DUCHESNE-GUILLEMIN, J., in *The Hymns of Zarathustra* (Connecticut: Hyperion Press, Inc: 1952)

COOKSON, W., *A Guide to the Cantos of Ezra Pound* (London, Sydney: Croom Helm, 1985)

ELLIS, S., *Dante and English Poetry: Shelley to T. S. Eliot* (Cambridge: Cambridge University Press, 1983)

FERRARI, G., 'Gentilucci, Armando', in *The New Grove Dictionary of Music* (London, Macmillan, 2001), pp. 660–61

—— 'Armando Gentilucci', in *Armando Gentilucci* (Milan: Ricordi, Suvini Zerboni, 2002), pp. 3–12

FITZGERALD, E., 'Introduction' in *Rubáiyát of Omar Khayyám* (London: Bernard Quaritch, 1859), pp. iv-vii

FLORA, F., *La poesia ermetica* (Bari: Laterza & Figli, 1936)

FOX, C., 'Darmstadt School', in *The New Grove Dictionary of Music*, pp. 24–25

GARDINER, P., *Kierkegaard* (Oxford: Oxford University Press, 1988)

GENTILUCCI, A., *Guida all'ascolti della musica contemporanea* (Milan: Feltrinelli, 1969)

—— *Introduzione alla musica elettronica* (Milan: Feltrinelli, 1972)

—— *Oltre l'avanguardia: un invito al molteplice* (Fiesole: Discanto Edizioni, 1980)

GRIFFITH, R. T. H., in *The Hymns of the Atharva-veda*, trans. with a popular commentary by R. T. H. Griffith (Benares: E. J. Lazarus and Co, 1916)

GRIFFITHS, P. *Modern Music* (London: Thames and Hudson, 1978)

GUPTA, D. K., *A Critical Study of Dandin and his Works* (Delki: Meharch and Lachhmandas, 1970)

HANNAY, A., *Kierkegaard* (London: Routledge and Kegan Paul, 1982)

HEISTER, H. W., 'Scrigno dei suoni e chiarore dell'utopia: aspetti dell'opera di Armando Gentilucci', *Musica/Realtà*, 11 (1990), 117–32

HELM, E., 'Luigi Dallapiccola in einem unveröffentlichten Gespräch', *Melos NZ*, 2.6 (November-December 1976), 469

HOLLINGDALE, R. J., *Thomas Mann: A Critical Study* (London: Rupert Hart-Davis, 1971)

HUXLEY, A., 'Introduction' in *Bhagavad-gita [The Song of God]*, trans. by S. Prabhavananda and C. Isherwood (Madras: Sri Ramakrishna Math, 1945), pp. 1–10

JONES, F., *Giuseppe Ungaretti* (Edinburgh: Edinburgh University Press, 1977)

—— *The Modern Italian Lyric* (Cardiff: University of Wales Press, 1986)

KÄMPER, D., *Luigi Dallapiccola* (Florence: Sansoni, 1985)

KILLHAM, J., *Critical Essays on the Poetry of Tennyson* (London: Routledge and Kegan Paul, 1960)

KINCAID, J. R., *Tennyson's Major Poems* (New Haven and London: Yale University Press, 1975)

MACHLIS, J., *Introduction to Contemporary Music* (London: J. M. Dent & Son Ltd., 1961)

MACKEY, L., *Kierkegaard: A Kind of Poet* (Philadelphia: University of Pennsylvania Press, 1971)

MAGNANI, G., '*Ulisse*: per un'analisi antropologico-musicale', in *Studi su Luigi Dallapiccola*, ed. by A. Quattrocchi (Lucca: Libreria Musicale Italiana Editrice, 1993), pp. 103–28

MANGANIELLO, D., *T. S. Eliot and Dante* (London: Macmillan, 1989)

MANZONI, G., *Scritti*, ed. by C. Tempo (Florence: La Nuova Italia, 1991)

MC DOUGAL, S. Y., 'Dreaming a Renaissance: Pound's Dantean Inheritance', in *Ezra Pound among the Poets*, ed. by G. Bornstein (Chicago, London: University of Chicago Press, 1985), pp. 63–81

MERCIER, V., *Beckett/Beckett* (Oxford, New York: Oxford University Press, 1977)

MERWIN, W. S., and J. MOUSSAIEFF MASSON IN *Sanskrit Love Poetry*, trans. by Merwin and Moussaieff Masson (New York: Columbia University Press, 1977)

MILA, M., 'L'*Ulisse*: opera a due dimensioni', in *Luigi Dallapiccola. Saggi, testimonianze, carteggio, biografia e bibliografia* (Milan: Suvini Zerboni, 1975), pp. 31–43

—— *Maderna, Musicista Europeo* (Turin: Einaudi, 1976)

MONTEFOSCHI, P., *Le eclissi della memoria* (Naples, Rome: Edizioni Scientifiche Italiane, 1988)

MONTEROSSO, R., 'Problemi musicali danteschi', *Cultura e Scuola*, 13–14 (1965), 207–12

MOULTON, J. H., in *Early Religious Poetry of Persia* (Cambridge: Cambridge University Press, 1911), pp. 14–16

MURDOCH, J., in *The Vedas and Brahmanas, Hindu Sacred Books*, ed. by J. Murdoch (London and Madras: The Christian Literature Society for India, 1898), I

MURNAGHAN, S., *Disguise and Recognition in the Odyssey* (Princeton: Princeton University Press, 1987)

NATHAN, H., 'Luigi Dallapiccola: Fragments from Conversations', *The Music Review,* 27.4 November (1966), 294–312

NICOLODI, F., ed., *Saggi, testimonianze, carteggio, biografia e bibliografia* (Milan: Suvini Zerboni, 1975)

—— ed., *Parole e musica* (Milan: Il Saggiatore, 1980)

OSMOND-SMITH, D., *Berio* (Oxford: Oxford University Press, 1992)

OSSOLA, C., *Giuseppe Ungaretti* (Milan: Mursia, 1975)

PETRASSI, G., and others, 'Saggi su Armando Gentilucci', *Musica/Realtà,* 11 (1990), 29–54

PORTINARI, F., *Giuseppe Ungaretti* (Turin: Borla, 1967)

POUND, E., *Antheil and the Treatise on Harmony* (Paris: Three Mountains Press, 1924)

PETROBELLI, P., 'Dallapiccola and Ulisse', *Cambridge Opera Journal,* 1–2 (1989–90), 239–49

QUATTROCCHI, A., *Studi su Luigi Dallapiccola* (Lucca: Libreria Musicale Italiana Editrice, 1993)

RAIMONDO, M., ed., *Dialogo con Maderna* (Milan: Rai, 1989)

REBAY, L., *Le origini della poesia di Giuseppe Ungaretti* (Rome: Edizioni di Storia e Letteratura, 1962)

ROUTH, F., *Contemporary Music* (London: The English Universities Press Ltd., 1968)

SADIE, S., *The New Grove Dictionary of Music* (London: Macmillan Publisher Ltd, 2001)

SALZMAN, E., *Twentieth-Century Music* (New Jersey: Prentice-Hall, 1967)

SANGUINETI, E., 'Per una lettura della *Vita nuova*', in *Vita nuova* (Milan: Lerici, 1965)

SAYERS, D., 'The Eighth Bolgia', in *Further Papers on Dante* (London: Methuen, 1957), pp. 114–20

SCHAFER, M., 'Ezra Pound and Music', in *Ezra Pound. A Collection of Critical Essays*, ed. by W. Sutton (New Jersey: Prentice-Hall, 1963), pp. 129–42

SHACKELFORD, R., ED. and TRANS., *Dallapiccola on Opera* (London: Toccata, 1987)

SHAH, I., *The Way of the Sufi* (Harmondsworth: Penguin Books Ltd., 1968)

SINGH, G., 'Inferno XXVI: A Personal Appreciation', in *Dante Commentaries. Eight Studies of the Divine Comedy*, ed. by D. Nolan (Dublin: Irish Academic Press, 1977), pp. 43–62

SMITH, E. E., *The Two Voices. A Tennyson Study* (Lincoln: University of Nebraska Press, 1964)

SPEZZANI, R., 'Per una storia del linguaggio di Ungaretti fino al *Sentimento del tempo*', in *Ricerche sulla lingua poetica contemporanea* (Padua: Liviana Editrice, 1966), pp. 126–57

STACEY, P., *Contemporary Tendencies in the Relationship of Music and Text, with Special reference to 'Pli selon Pli' (Boulez) and 'Laborintus II' (Berio)* (New York, London: Garland, 1989)

STANFORD, W. B., *The Ulysses Theme. A Study in the Adaptability of a Traditional Hero* (Oxford: Blackwell, 1954)

SUVINI-HAND, V., 'Tradition and the avant-garde', in *Mirage and Camouflage: Hiding behind Hermeticism in Ungaretti's L'Allegria* (Troubador: Leicester, 2000), pp. 43–65

TERRY, A., *Antonio Machado. Campos de Castilla* (London: Grant and Cutler Ltd., 1973)

UNGARETTI, G., 'L'estetica di Bergson (1924)', 'Lo stile di Bergson (1924)', in *Vita d'un uomo. Saggi e interventi*, ed. by M. Diacono and L. Rebay (Milan: Mondadori, 1974), pp. 79–86 and 87–89

—— 'Una filosofia dell'effimero e Bergson umorista' in P. Montefoschi, *Le eclissi della memoria*, pp. 183–87

VENUTI, M., *Il teatro di Dallapiccola* (Milan: Suvini Zerboni, 1985)

VON LEWINSKI, W. E., 'Luigi Dallapiccola e la sua opera *Ulisse*. Riflessioni dopo una conversazione con il compositore', in *Saggi*, pp. 27–30

WATKINS, G., *Soundings. Music in the Twentieth Century* (New York: Schirmer Books, Glenn Watkins, 1988)

WILHELM, J., *Il miglior fabbro: The Cult of the Difficult in Daniel, Dante, and Pound* (Maine: National Poetry Foundation, University of Maine, 1982)

INDEX